PHILOSOPHY
AND
SCIENCE

FREDERICK E. MOSEDALE
Millikin University

PHILOSOPHY AND SCIENCE

the wide range of interaction

PRENTICE-HALL, INC., *Englewood Cliffs, New Jersey 07632*

Library of Congress Cataloging in Publication Data

Main entry under title:

Philosophy and Science.

    Bibliography: p.
    1. Science—Philosophy. I. Mosedale, Frederick
E. (date)
Q175.P512   501   78-27517
ISBN 0-13-662577-0

Printed in the United States of America

10 9 8 7 6 5

Editorial/production supervision by Jean Behr and Ruth Anderson
Interior design by Jean Behr
Cover design by Edsal Enterprises
Manufacturing buyer: John Hall

PRENTICE-HALL INTERNATIONAL, INC., *London*
PRENTICE-HALL OF AUSTRALIA PTY. LIMITED, *Sydney*
PRENTICE-HALL OF CANADA, LTD., *Toronto*
PRENTICE-HALL OF INDIA PRIVATE LIMITED, *New Delhi*
PRENTICE-HALL OF JAPAN, INC., *Tokyo*
PRENTICE-HALL OF SOUTHEAST ASIA PTE. LTD., *Singapore*
WHITEHALL BOOKS LIMITED, *Wellington, New Zealand*

To the Ideal of a Liberal Arts Education

Contents

---

section 3
Possible Limitations of Science   **124**

section 7
Science and Society   382

Preface

Here in one volume are readings covering a wide range of issues that involve both philosophy and science. There are a large number of selections on traditional topics in the philosophy of science, and there are many on the implications of scientific findings for God's nature and existence, life after death, body-mind issues, human nature, freedom of the will, limitations of human knowledge, ethics, and social policy.

For scientists and science students with little opportunity to explore ideas outside of science, this book can open a path to the humanities— and for nonscientists who recognize the important role of science and technology in the world today, the readings may provide an especially interesting route to an understanding of these aspects of the world. If the book is used as a text for an introductory philosophy of science course, the instructor can broaden the course's scope and thereby increase its appeal among science students, who have only a limited opportunity to take courses in the humanities.

Many of those who are interested in thinking about the nature of science, and its implications, are not very knowledgeable about the history of science, the traditions of philosophy, or the concepts and findings of a wide range of sciences. Thus they cannot read with enjoyment and profit carefully and complexly reasoned materials on science by philosophers. For this reason the book includes some selections from novels and plays. After a reader confronts an issue in a somewhat simplified form, reflection can lead to a desire to read more fully developed material on the issue. Selections of a more advanced nature are thus included to support this next step in the reader's developing thought.

Space limitations have not made possible the inclusion of simpler selections before each of the more demanding selections. The more demanding ones are so described in the selection summaries, which precede each selection. Teachers may wish to prepare lecture-discussions for presentation before the assignment of these more demanding readings to help the sudents gain a clear understanding of the issues.

Several features of this anthology help make the readings less formidable and more accessible. Most footnotes have been eliminated. Unfamiliar, foreign, and technical vocabulary items are explained either in the text or in the glossary at the end of the book. Most persons mentioned in the various selections are set in historical perspective by inclusion of their birth (and death) dates. Each selection is preceded by a short summary together with information about the authors. Selections are followed by questions—some to help the reader understand the selection and others to encourage further research and reflection. Guides are given for further reading. In addition there are introductions at the beginning of each section of the book.

When using the book as a text, I recommend that early in the course students be required to read selection #1 by Russell and selection #20 by Schroeer covering, respectively, the early history of astronomy and the recent history of physics. I also ask my students to buy and read the lively and pregnant account of the recent revolution in biology, *The Double Helix*, by James D. Watson. This ensures that students share some background knowledge of scientific achievements, which they can use when reflecting on and discussing other readings.

Teachers should also examine for possible classroom use videotapes of Bronowski's series *The Ascent of Man* and some of the programs in the *Nova* series. Both are or have been seen on National Educational Television. In addition videotapes or movies of the following plays can easily be tied into the course: *Galileo*, by Bertolt Brecht; *In The Matter of J. Robert Oppenheimer*, by Heinar Kipphardt; and *R.U.R.*, by Karel Capek. (Request that your theatre department produce one or more of these.)

Although the book has a sufficient number and range of readings to serve as a single text for a complete course, those who favor further development of traditional issues in the philosophy of science might consider using a supplementary text such as Carl Hempel's *Philosophy of Natural Science* (Englewood Cliffs, NJ.: Prentice-Hall, Inc., 1966). Those who would like to further explore issues involving science and ethics will find many new materials published in the field of biomedical ethics that might serve as interesting supplements to this book. The various bibliographies in this book suggest other possible supplements.

I wish to thank my students for their guidance in helping me select the most penetrating and meaningful readings, my friends and relatives for encouraging me when I needed it, the Millikin University library staff for research aid, many of my colleagues for bibliographic aid and suggestions for selections, the Millikin University Research Council for early financial support of the project, Beverly Hayes for expeditious typing of the manuscript, and Mary and Doug Wiersema for helping me put the manuscript together. In addition Helen Nelson was of great help with correspondence necessary to gain permissions to reprint material. The anonymous manuscript readers for Prentice-Hall have saved me from many errors and suggested many thoughtful modifications.

My son, Daniel, has been patient with his father when he was asked to be. My wife, Susan, has been a source of strength, ideas, and perspective.

F.E.M.

PHILOSOPHY
AND
SCIENCE

Introduction

This book is intended for all kinds of students—students majoring in philosophy, students majoring in science, students with fine arts majors, business majors, and so on. It is intended for anyone who realizes the pervasive influence of science in our culture and who wants to come to some understanding of this significant aspect of our lives.

Since this book is said to be about science, one might immediately wonder what its editor understands by the word *science*. Such a question would be a reasonable one, for the kinds of human activities that people have called sciences vary considerably and increase in number each year. It is an interesting exercise to attempt to list all the sciences. Such a list might begin as follows: physics, chemistry, biology, psychology, sociology, anthropology, geology, archeology, linguistics, meteorology, geography. What about medicine, dentistry, oceanography, or engineering fields—are they sciences? Is astronomy a science separate from physics? Is mathematics a science? Are secretarial science and fire science really sciences? Is astrology a science? The editor is not going to take a position on any of these questions, because one of the problems addressed in this book is: What is the nature of science?

A book about philosophy and science might prompt another initial question from a prospective reader: How can philosophy and science have anything to do with each other? To ask such a question is to suppose there is a large gap between philosophy and science.

Is there such a gap? If you have taken courses on the college level in one or more of the sciences, some of your teachers probably have had doctor's degrees in their fields. The degrees in most cases are Ph.D. degrees, that is, doctor of philosophy degrees. Teachers of philosophy obtain doctor of philosophy degrees in philosophy, while physicists, biologists, and sociologists have doctor of philosophy degrees in their respective fields. This would seem to indicate very little gap between philosophy and the sciences.

The explanation of why scientists hold philosophy degrees lies in history. At one time the word *philosophy* meant the careful study of gen-

1

eral principles in almost any field. Thus, in the seventeenth and eighteenth centuries those who carefully studied nature were called natural philosophers. Benjamin Franklin (1706–1790) referred to his laboratory equipment for conducting electrical experiments as his philosophical instruments. The Ph.D. degree preserves this older meaning of the word *philosophy*.

The words *science* and *art* also have a long history. At various times the words *philosophy*, *science*, and *art* have been regarded as almost synonymous. For example, the phrase *liberal arts* has often been used to mean any field of study that helps one understand the world and life better. At one time physics, biology, philosophy, and literature were all regarded as arts—and this explains why a B.A. (Bachelor of Arts) or M.A. (Master of Arts) degree can be obtained at some colleges in scientific fields.

In the twentieth century the words *philosophy, science,* and *art* tend to be given more restricted meanings. In many colleges and universities, philosophy, literature, religion, and the fine arts are classified as the humanities and contrasted with the physical and social sciences and with professional and technological fields (e.g., law and engineering). Although this twentieth-century academic arrangement suggests a gap between philosophy and the sciences, the two areas actually are important to each other. One aim of this collection of readings is to convince the reader that any gap that is thought to separate the two areas of study should be bridged.

Until this century those active in science were often interested and active in philosophy. Some thinkers who are remembered primarily as philosophers took great interest in and contributed to the sciences [e.g., Aristotle (384–322 B.C.), René Descartes (1596–1650), George Berkeley (1685–1753), and Immanuel Kant (1724–1804)]. Others who are remembered primarily as scientists were greatly interested in and sought answers to philosophical problems [e.g., Isaac Newton (1642–1727), Galileo Galilei (1564–1642), Ernst Mach (1838–1916), Thomas Huxley (1825–1895)]. A few thinkers in this century, such as A. N. Whitehead (1861–1947) and Henri Bergson (1859–1941), have attempted to bring science and philosophy together in a philosophical system.

Unfortunately it has become more and more difficult for those interested in either philosophy or science to follow the paths of these past thinkers. Both these fields have become quite specialized, and colleges now offer sufficient courses in each field to keep those students majoring in each field quite busy. Further, as fewer teachers are trained with broad perspectives in both science and philosophy, fewer will understand the value of seeking such perspectives and may fail to encourage efforts in this direction by their students. It is hoped that those who use this book will be convinced, no matter what their fields, that such narrowness must be avoided.

How are science and philosophy important to each other? Three different but related kinds of interactions are possible between science and philosophy: (1) Findings in science can be relevant outside science for the resolution of traditional philosophical problems or they can raise new philosophical questions. (2) The methods and status of the various sciences can be the object of philosophical inquiry. And (3) philosophical issues can arise for the scientists, which until resolved may impede scientific inquiry. Each of these three possibilities is explained further below.

1. Science Gives Rise to or Aids in the Resolution of Philosophical Problems

When Nicolaus Copernicus (1473–1543), Johannes Kepler (1571–1630), Galileo, Newton, and others denied that the earth was at the center of the universe, their astronomical conclusions had repercussions outside of astronomy. When Charles Darwin (1809–1882) and Alfred Wallace (1823–1913) advanced the view that species evolved, their findings had repercussions outside of biology.

Some of the repercussions of these and other scientific findings have seemed relevant to the resolution of traditional philosophical issues. The heliocentric (sun-centered) account of planetary motion and the biological theory of evolution are held by some people to have relevance to the philosophical problems of whether it is possible to prove or disprove God's existence. Some findings and theories in physics, dating back to the times of ancient Greece, seem to have a bearing on the philosophical problems of whether humans have free choice or are merely creatures very analogous to complex machines. Other scientific findings have seemed to some philosophers to have a bearing on whether there are absolute moral values; whether there is life after death; and whether there is a fixed human nature. The relevance of science to each of these issues in philosophy is explored in the readings in this book.

Scientific findings have also given rise to some new philosophical questions. For example, in linguistics some researchers have claimed studies of non-European languages reveal that languages control the way we perceive the world. This, if true, raises the question of whether it is ever possible to escape the biases of one's language and perceive the world as it really is. Twentieth-century physics has been invoked by some to prove that human knowledge may be incomplete and/or relative. Einstein's theory of relativity and Heisenberg's uncertainty principle are the concepts in physics that some people claim raise these questions about the limits of knowledge. Findings in modern physics have also led some to question whether our ordinary descriptions of the world are correct. For example, should a table be described as solid if it is really made up of very small particles separated by empty space?

One of the most obvious ways science has presented us with new philosophical problems is in the life sciences and health fields. New scientific and medical discoveries make us face such ethical issues as how to select patients who will receive a limited supply of a new lifesaving medicine or therapy; when, if ever, to allow a patient to die; and what kinds of birth control techniques are ethical. Many of these issues are also discussed in the readings.

2. Science as a Phenomenon Worthy of Philosophical Scrutiny

Scientific activity (as opposed to specific scientific findings) has itself given rise to a number of issues about science that are not resolvable within science. Many of these issues belong to the philosophy of science as traditionally conceived.

The progress of science (beginning with advances in astronomy and mechanics, and later in biology, electricity, and chemistry) cannot fail to impress one who studies the history of science and the history of mankind. It seems natural to ask whether the sciences have uncovered some special method to unlock the mysteries of nature. If we could clearly identify the method, and deliberately employ it, it would seem that we could progress more quickly in the sciences, and perhaps, armed with this method, found new sciences to study new aspects of nature. A philosophical question, then, is: Is there a scientific method? If so, what is it?

Central to many versions of the scientific method is the idea that observations are crucial to science. But what role does observation play? If a scientist seeks to establish a theory, how do the scientist's observations lend support to the theory? Is there any way of computing how strongly some given evidence supports the theory? Questions about how observations help confirm a theory and other questions about the scientific method have been central to the traditional field of the philosophy of science.

There is another philosophical problem connected with the search for a scientific method. Is there any way to clearly distinguish legitimate sciences from imposters ("pseudo-sciences")? For example, can astrology be shown to be a pseudo-science? Can history, psychology, or anthropology be proven to be sciences?

Other philosophical issues that have been raised about science include the following: Can science answer all questions people raise? If not, why not? What is a cause? What is an explanation? Are scientific explanations superior to other kinds? Does science assume any principles that cannot be proven scientifically? When chemistry, biology, economics, psychology, sociology, political science, and other sciences examine human beings, are the findings of the various sciences in competition or to be added together? Are some sciences more basic than others? For instance, is sociology really a subfield of psychology, or chemistry of physics? Is technology necessarily tied to science? Are science and technology doing more harm than good? Do the social and behavioral sciences reveal any sexist, racist, or "speciesist" assumptions? Can any science study what is inherently private: conciousness? A final question of particular importance is whether there is any real gap between the sciences and the humanities.

These questions and others raised by the existence of the sciences and technology are ones that scientists as scientists are not trained to answer. If at some point in their training the scientists are asked to memorize something alleged to be the scientific method, they usually are not asked to reflect on whether the method is actually employed in their sciences. Psychologists focus their attention on psychological phenomena and not on the scientific method. Linguistics focuses on linguistic phenomena, and so on. Questions about the scientific method, although important to scientific disciplines, are not ones that scientists' training especially equips them to explore.

The point here is that important questions about science are often not taken up fully in science courses. Some scientists and some philosophers have taken them up, and readings in this book provide some of their reflections.

3. Philosophical Problems Within Science

Scientists can perform as scientists and, if they are narrow in their concerns, can be quite ignorant that some of their findings might be directly relevant to traditional philosophical problems. Further, they may carry on with their research oblivious to the existence of philosophical problems about the scientific method and the interrelationships of the sciences. But some philosophical problems come closer to home.

Some kinds of scientific activity have a philosophic component. Philosophers have always concerned themselves with the meaning and applicability of concepts, such as justice, freedom, God, knowledge, beauty, right.

Conceptual studies occur in science too. Scientists not infrequently introduce concepts that seem promising but also seem suspicious. Freud's concept of the unconscious, the concept of instinct in biology, and concepts of space and time in modern physics have perplexing aspects to them. Further, in the past, scrutiny of concepts such as phlogiston in chemistry, spontaneous generation in biology, and aether in physics led eventually to their rejection by scientists. Thus, scientists must sometimes, as part of science, try to clarify and justify fundamental concepts employed in their scientific areas. If the clarification of concepts in science is not regarded by some people as a philosophical activity, it is very like one. In addition, it is well to note that some philosophers have advocated procedures for scientists to use when attempting to define concepts within science, e.g., the method of operational definitions.

Consider another way in which science may depend on philosophical reflections. Scientists often cannot proceed with research unless they get the proper equipment and research aids. This, of course, requires money. And disbursements of large sums will not usually occur these days without groups to allocate and oversee their use. Philosophy enters when these groups ask general questions about how money should be

spent on science. Which kinds of research are most valuable? Should restrictions be placed on how the scientists spend the money once
awarded? What sorts of accountability can be asked of scientists without
hindering scientific creativity?

These questions involve general moral and social policy issues.
Moral issues of other kinds may also confront scientists. For example,
should a scientist work on research likely to produce destructive or horrifying weapons? Should scientists keep their findings secret from their
scientific colleagues in other countries? If a scientific group has found
part of the answer to a scientific question that many scientists are working on, should the group immediately make known its partial answer, or
may the group keep it secret until it has solved the whole problem?
Should scientists feel obligated to publicly volunteer their expert knowledge when it is relevant to the resolution of social and moral problems?
Is there any reason to limit (or control with careful restrictions) experimentation on animals—as antivivisectionists claim? What restrictions
should be placed on experiments on humans? Are there any topics that
scientists should regard as improper ones to study? For instance, is it acceptable to study the affects of marijuana use on sexual responsiveness
by paying subjects to smoke marijuana and then testing their sexual responsiveness using pornographic movies?

All of these philosophical issues of direct relevance to the conduct
of science are discussed in readings in this book. Unfortunately, scientists are seldom trained to consider them. They may be impatient when
the issues intrude in some way in their research. These readings, it is
hoped, will encourage potential scientists to commit themselves to a continuing program of self-education in such issues—so that in the future
they will be able to contribute insightfully when called upon by circumstances to aid in resolving similar issues.

PHILOSOPHICAL TRADITIONS

It should be clear now that science and philosophy are important to
each other. Scientific findings help within philosophy. Philosophers find
some aspects of scientific activity worthy of reflection. And within science
philosophical problems can be found. In sum, sometimes science contributes to philosophy, is studied by philosophy, and becomes involved in
philosophy.

It should be noted that if you go on to read widely in this book, you
will likely find an interest developing in philosophical traditions that are
not so directly related to science. For instance, the book has a number of
readings on ethical issues, some that scientific advances raise and some
that scientists may face within science. Those who read these selections
will probably become interested in the philosophical field of ethics. In
ethics one studies about the foundations of ethical judgments and about
various approaches to ethical judgments.

Similarly, those who examine other issues in this book will probably become interested in the philosophical fields of metaphysics, epistemology, and logic. A brief account of the nature of these fields and how they bear on the topics in this book may be helpful at this point—and for future reference.

(a) *Metaphysics:* Metaphysics is regarded by some philosophers as involving questions about the basic kinds of things that exist. On this view the following would be metaphysical questions: Does God exist? Do nonmaterial souls or minds exist? Does space exist? Does time exist? Does matter exist? Do mathematical objects exist? Another conception of metaphysics is that it involves a study of the most basic categories or concepts that humans use to understand the world. On this view, metaphysics should ask, not "Does God exist?" but rather, "What is the nature of our concept of God (or space, or matter, or whatever)?" To complicate matters, some philosophers regard metaphysics as primarily involving reflections on a reality that is thought to lie behind (and somehow make possible) what we as humans perceive. Finally, some philosophers regard metaphysics as an effort to evolve concepts capable of tying together all aspects of human experience.

The study of traditions in metaphysics may enrich one's understanding of issues encountered in this book. Metaphysical questions are discussed in this book primarily as they relate to science. But not all attempts to resolve metaphysical questions have involved science. Thus, the study of nonscientific aspects of traditional metaphysical areas—such as the existence of God, freedom of the will, or the nature of minds—will serve to broaden the student's understanding.

(b) *Epistemology:* Epistemology is the study of the nature and limits of human knowledge. Philosophers who have been interested in the study of knowledge have often been involved in attempts to respond to epistemological skeptics. Epistemological skeptics deny the possibility of various kinds of knowledge. In this collection are readings illustrating why skeptics might claim that science cannot provide us with knowledge.

Because scientific findings are an outstanding example of human knowledge (assuming the skeptics are wrong), many questions in the traditional field of philosophy of science can be classified as epistemological. This intimate connection with the philosophy of science should make epistemology interesting to the reader in its own right.

(c) *Logic:* Both logic and various portions of mathematics have been developed in axiomatic systems—systems which begin with a small number of basic statements (axioms) and definitions, and which are used to develop theorems and laws. Both logic and mathematics have been called formal sciences to distinguish them from empirical sciences (those based on observation). Studying logic, thus, can lead to reflections on whether and to what extent knowledge gained in logic is different from that gained in the empirical sciences.

Logic and science have another area of interrelationship. Because logicians are interested in identifying principles of correct reasoning, they are interested in the scientific method (if there is such a method) and in the kinds of reasoning employed in science. Thus, philosophy of science students should feel at home in the study of logic. Further, they will be better equipped to understand more advanced writing in the philosophy of science, which sometimes employs the symbolism and techniques developed by logicians.

(d) *Other Areas:* Readings in this book may awaken an interest in still other philosophical areas, such as political philosophy, philosophy of language, philosophy of education, and philosophy of mathematics.

You cannot read all the selections in this book and also learn about all of the philosophical fields mentioned above. However, your teacher and/or supplementary texts can help you occasionally set some of the issues in wider philosophical contexts. Further, you may develop a lasting desire to broaden your knowledge in the areas of philosophy that do not have a direct relevance to science.

We have discussed the ways in which philosophy and science are important to each other. You should now have some idea of the extensive and complex interrelations of philosophy and science—and should recognize the importance of becoming more fully acquainted with many of the philosophical issues in the areas of interrelationship. Enjoy the readings. May they serve to permanently interest you in the issues they raise.

TIPS FOR USING THIS BOOK

You will profit most from this book if you are aware of the following features:

1. The book is divided according to general topic areas into a number of sections, each including a number of readings.
2. Each section begins with a general introduction to the readings and a short list of suggestions for further reading.
3. Each reading selection is preceded by brief statements about its author and the main points of the selection.
4. In most cases footnotes from the original selections have been omitted. In some cases they have been inserted parenthetically in the text. Should you wish more information on a topic area in

a reading, you might seek out the original source of the reading and check the footnotes.

5. Following each selection are two sets of questions. The first set is to guide the student to the main issues in the selection. The second set includes questions for further reflection; these might be used as topics for research papers or projects.

6. Limitations of space prevent the inclusion of selections advocating all the best-known alternatives to every philosophical issue. The book is intended to *introduce* the readers to philosophical questions. For a fuller understanding of alternatives the suggested readings should be consulted.

7. Because the selections in this book were not written specifically for inclusion in a collection such as this, many of them touch on a variety of topics—not just those immediately relevant. For this reason the table of contents includes a column indicating the main topics covered in each selection. Check there to find selections that touch on a topic of interest to you.

8. Efforts have been made to help you with possibly unfamiliar vocabulary items. Explanations of uncommon words or phrases have been inserted in the reading material in brackets. Unfamiliar words and phrases that occur frequently (especially those which form the technical vocabulary of philosophy) are explained in a glossary at the end of the book.

9. Philosophical problems focusing on individual sciences have been, for the most part, omitted. A short bibliography at the end of the book lists works that discuss philosophical problems specific to the various sciences.

Philosophy, Science, and Religion

GENERAL INTRODUCTION

The sciences have aided religions in a number of ways. Findings by those in archaeology, history, and anthropology have helped illuminate some religiously important events and peoples alluded to in sacred writings. Computer analyses of the styles of scriptural writings offer another example of the collaboration of science with religion.

Science and religion, however, have often seemed at odds with each other. Their seeming conflicts are one of the main focuses of this section. The issues raised here are all concerned with the relevance of scientific findings to the appraisal of the truth of religious views. Because these issues involve two different realms of human experience, they do not quite belong to either realm. For this reason they can be regarded as philosophical issues, located within the philosophy of religion or on the border between the philosophy of religion and the philosophy of science.

In many religions views are given about the nature of the world and its origins. In this sense religions have provided the earliest attempts to account for nature. In the West, Christianity has been the focus of a number of conflicts, because the Bible seems to give explanations of some aspects of nature. The book of Genesis, and God's concern for mankind as depicted in both the Old and New Testaments, led some Christian thinkers to two conclusions: that the earth is at the center of the universe, and that the first human beings were specially created by God at a particular instant of time in the past (many accepted 4004 B.C. as the year of creation). Selection #1 by Bertrand Russell recounts some of the conflicts between the findings of modern astronomy and the earth-centered (geocentric) view of the universe. Selection #3 from the Bible and #4 from the play *Inherit the Wind* raise the issue of whether humans were specially created at some instant in the past. Does the biological theory of evolution conflict with the description of creation in the Bible?

These two examples (the status of the earth in the universe, and the origin of human beings) also lead to questions about how to understand Biblical passages. Fundamentalists suggest a literal reading of the Bible and reject any scientific findings that conflict with such a reading. In recent centuries, a variety of more sophisticated ideas about how to understand the Bible have been advanced. The selection by Galileo (selection #2), a scientist persecuted by the church for his defense of modern astronomical theories, presents one kind of suggestion: God gave us reason and the senses to use in learning about the world. The Bible, on this view, is primarily intended by God for spiritual guidance and not as a physics textbook. Other views about how we should understand Biblical passages are given in the informative essay (selection #7) on twentieth-century religion, science, and philosophy by Barbour.

Can God's existence be proven? Philosophers through the centuries have attempted to provide various kinds of rational proofs of God's existence. Scientific findings, however, have not played an important part in most of the proofs. One exception is the argument from design (also known as the teleological argument). Physicist Albert Einstein (in selection #5) and philosopher John Hick (in selection #6) mention how scientific findings can be regarded as evidence for the existence of an intelligent designer of nature, i.e., God. Scientific findings, however, have also been invoked to challenge the argument from design, as noted by Hick. Other attempts to use scientific findings as evidence for God's existence are summarized by Barbour (in selection #7).

Scientific findings about nature have thus been used to challenge literal interpretations of the Bible and to support and challenge the argument from design. But science has not only studied nature apart from mankind; it has also studied religions, and such studies have sometimes been thought to present challenges to religion. Psychology, a relatively new science (some still dispute its title to be called a science), has provided studies of religious experience and attitudes. Sigmund Freud, the founder of one approach to psychology, concluded that religion is an illusion developed by humans to satisfy certain psychological needs. (See selection #8.)

Anthropology, another relatively young science (some also dispute its title to be called a science), has provided us with accounts of an extraordinarily wide range of religious beliefs accepted by various human groups. H. L. Mencken (in selection #9) reminds us in dramatic fashion of the number of gods people have worshipped. Further, he intimates that the findings of anthropology and comparative religion imply that none of the religions is correct. It will be for the reader to ponder how thoughtful religious people might respond to Freud and Mencken.

No discussion of science and religion would be complete without mention of logical positivism. The selection by Barbour (#7) describes the view of logical positivists that science and logic (including mathematics) provide the proper and only roads to truth. Roughly speaking, positivists contended that observation is crucial for ascertaining any truths (except those of logic and mathematics). Since, they claim, no observations are relevant to the truth of religious assertions about God, such religious assertions are to be regarded not as false but as meaningless. Barbour goes on to give responses of religious thinkers to the positivist challenge.

The topics covered in this section are not the only philosophical issues arising from the interaction of science and religion. Many other philosophical issues covered in this book touch on matters relevant to religion. The next section, for example, includes readings on life after death, a doctrine accepted by many (but not all) religions. Other religiously relevant topics discussed in the book include: whether there is a soul, whether human beings have free will, and whether science itself involves an essentially religious commitment to some difficult-to-prove assumptions. (Because philosophical issues are complexly interrelated, it should be clear that subdivisions in a book such as this are somewhat artificial.)

The readings in this section (with the exception of the one by Barbour, #7) are intended to introduce the reader to some philosophical issues. The Barbour selection is more advanced and gives an idea of more sophisticated thinking on some of the issues. Should readers desire to deepen and strengthen their grasp of the problems and possible solutions to them, they should consult the sources below.

Further Reading: Philosophy, Science, and Religion

1. *The Encyclopedia of Philosophy*, ed. PAUL EDWARDS, 8 vols. (New York: Macmillan Publishing Co., 1967). See especially the following entries: "Agnosticism" by RONALD W. HEPBURN; "Atheism" by PAUL EDWARDS; "Creation, Religious Doctrine of" by HEPBURN; "Life Origin of" by T. A. GOUDGE; "Miracles" by ANTONY FLEW; "Mysticism, Nature and Assessment of" by HEPBURN; "Physicotheology" by MEYRICK H. CARRÉ; "Popular Arguments for the Existence of God" by G. C. NERLICH; "Religion, Naturalistic Reconstructions of" by WILLIAM P. ALSTON; "Religion, Psychological Explanations of" by ALSTON; "Religion and Science" by J. J. C. SMART; "Religious Experience, Argument for the Existence of God" by HEPBURN; and "Teleological Argument for the Existence of God" by ALSTON. Also see the *Encyclopedia* index for related topics.

2. *Issues in Science and Religion* by IAN BARBOUR (Englewood Cliffs, N.J.: Prentice-Hall, Inc., 1966). Selection #7 is an excerpt from this book, which contains a wealth of references to further sources on religion, science, and philosophy—as well as thoughtful discussions of many areas of science/religion interaction.

3. *The Logic of God: Theology and Verification*, ed. MALCOLM L. DIAMOND and THOMAS V. LITZENBURG, Jr. (Indianapolis: The Bobbs-Merrill Co., 1975). This anthology focuses on the responses of religious thinkers to the chal-

lenges presented by logical positivism. It has a good bibliography and helpful introductory essays.
4. *A History of the Warfare of Science with Theology in Christendom* by ANDREW
   DICKSON WHITE (New York: D. Appleton & Co., 1896; reprint ed., New
   York: Dover Publications, 1960). This is a classic history of the variety of
   challenges science has presented to Christianity.

selection 1.

Astronomy and Religion

The Author: Bertrand Russell (1872–1970) is one of this century's most influential philosophers. He always manifested a great interest in science. In philosophy he is known especially for his contributions to logic, the philosophy of mathematics, and epistemology. He was an outspoken critic of political and social tyranny. In 1950 he was awarded the Nobel Prize for literature. Russell was not sympathetic to religion.

The Selection: The excerpt traces the replacement by modern astronomy of the earth-centered (geocentric) view of the universe with the sun-centered (heliocentric) view. It focuses on the contributions of Copernicus, Kepler, and Galileo. It also describes the opposition of the church to the new view of the earth's place in the universe.

The first pitched battle between theology and science, and in some ways the most notable, was the astronomical dispute as to whether the earth or the sun was the centre of what we now call the solar system. The orthodox theory was the Ptolemaic [named for the second-century astronomer, Ptolemy], according to which the earth is at rest in the centre of the universe, while the sun, moon, planets, and system of fixed stars revolve round it, each in its own sphere. According to the new theory, the Copernican, the earth, so far from being at rest, has a twofold motion: it rotates on its axis once a day, and it revolves round the sun once a year. . . .

The theory of Copernicus [1473–1543], though important as a fruitful effort of imagination which made further progress possible, was itself still very imperfect. The planets, as we now know, re-

From *Religion and Science* by Bertrand Russell (New York: Oxford University Press, 1935). Reprinted by permission of the publisher.

volve about the sun, not in circles, but in ellipses, of which the sun occupies, not the centre, but one of the foci. Copernicus adhered to the view that their orbits must be circular, and accounted for irregularities by supposing that the sun was not quite in the centre of any one of the orbits. This partially deprived his system of the simplicity which was its greatest advantage over that of Ptolemy, and would have made Newton's generalization impossible if it had not been corrected by Kepler. . . . [Copernicus] long delayed publication because he feared ecclesiastical [= church] censure. . . .

At first, the Protestants were almost more bitter against him than the Catholics. [Martin] Luther [1483–1546] said that "People give ear to an upstart astrologer who strove to show that the earth revolves, not the heavens or the firmament, the sun and the moon. Whoever wishes to appear clever must devise some new system, which of all systems is of course the very best. This fool wishes to reverse the entire science of astronomy; but sacred Scripture tells us that Joshua commanded the sun to stand still, and not the earth.". . . Even [John] Wesley [1703–1791], so late as the eighteenth century, while not daring to be quite so emphatic, nevertheless stated that the new doctrines in astronomy "tend toward infidelity."

In this, I think, Wesley was, in a certain sense, in the right. The importance of Man is an essential part of the teaching of both the Old and New Testaments; indeed God's purposes in creating the universe appear to be mainly concerned with human beings. The doctrines of the Incarnation [= the embodiment of God in Jesus] and the Atonement [= the view that Jesus' death atones for mankind's sins] could not appear probable if Man were not the most important of created beings. Now there is nothing in the Copernican astronomy to *prove* that we are less important than we naturally suppose ourselves to be, but the dethronement of our planet from its central position suggests to the imagination a similar dethronement of its inhabitants. While it was thought that the sun and moon, the planets and the fixed stars, revolved once a day about the earth, it was easy to suppose that they existed for our benefit, and that we were of special interest to the Creator. But when Copernicus and his successors persuaded the world that it is we who rotate while the stars take no notice of our earth; when it appeared further that our earth is small compared to several of the planets, and that they are small compared to the sun; when calculation and the telescope revealed the vastness of the solar system, of our galaxy, and finally of the universe of innumerable galaxies—it became increasingly difficult to believe that such a remote and parochial retreat could have the importance to be expected of the home of Man, if Man had the cosmic significance assigned to him in traditional theology. Mere considerations of scale suggested that perhaps we were not the purpose of the universe; lingering self-esteem whispered that, if *we* were not the purpose of the universe, it probably had no purpose at all. I do not mean to say that such reflections have any logical cogency, still less that they were widely aroused at once by the Copernican system. I mean only that they were such as the system was likely to stimulate in those to whose minds it was vividly present. It is therefore not surprising that the Christian Churches, Protestant and Catholic alike, felt hostility to the new astronomy, and sought out grounds for branding it as heretical.

The next great step in astronomy was taken by Kepler (1571-1630), who, though his opinions were the same as Galileo's, never came into conflict with the Church. On the contrary, Catholic authorities forgave his Protestantism because of his scientific eminence. (Or rather, perhaps, because the Emperor valued his astrological services.) . . . He succeeded Tycho Brahe as "imperial mathematician" under the Emperor Rudolph II, and inherited Tycho's invaluable astronomical records. . . .

The character of Kepler's intellect was very singular. He was originally led to favour the Copernican hypothesis almost as much by Sun worship as by more rational motives. In the labours which led to the discovery of his three Laws, he was guided by the fantastic hypothesis that there must be some connection between the five regular solids and the five planets, Mercury, Venus, Mars, Jupiter and Saturn. [In solid geometry there are five solid figures which can be constructed with all sides the same: the tetrahedron, the cube, the octahedron, the icosahedron, and the dodecahedron.] This is an extreme example of a not infrequent occurrence in the history of science, namely, that theories which turn out to be true and important are first suggested to the minds of their discoverers by considerations which are utterly wild and absurd. The fact is that it is difficult to think of the right hypothesis, and no technique exists to facilitate this most essential step in scientific progress. Consequently, any methodical plan by which new hypotheses are suggested is apt to be useful; and if it is firmly believed in, it gives the investigator patience to go on testing continually fresh possibilities, however many may have previously had to be discarded. So it was with Kepler. His final success, especially in the case of his third Law, was due to incredible patience; but his patience was due to his mystical beliefs that something to do with the regular solids must provide a clue, and that the planets, by their revolutions, produced a "music of the spheres" which was audible only to the soul of the sun—for he was firmly persuaded that the sun is the body of a more or less divine spirit.

The first two of Kepler's laws were published in 1609, the third in 1619. The most important of the three, from the point of view of our general picture of the solar system, was the first, which stated that the planets revolve about the sun in ellipses of which the sun occupies one focus. (To draw an ellipse, stick two pins into a piece of paper, say an inch apart, then take a string, say two inches long, and fasten its two ends to the two pins. All the points that can be reached by drawing the string taut are on an ellipse of which the two pins are the foci. That is to say, an ellipse consists of all the points such that, if you add the distance from one focus to the distance from the other focus, you always get the same amount.) The Greeks had supposed, at first, that all the heavenly bodies must move in circles, because the circle is the most perfect curve. When they found that this hypothesis would not work, they adopted the view that the planets move in "epicycles," which are circles about a point that is itself moving in a circle. (To make an epicycle, take a large wheel and put it [on its side] on the ground, then take a smaller wheel with a nail in the rim, and let the small wheel roll round [inside the rim of] the big wheel while the nail scratches the ground. The mark traced by the nail on the ground is an epicycle. If the earth moved in a circle round the sun, and the moon moved in a circle round the earth, the moon would move in an epicycle round the sun.) Although the Greeks knew a great deal about ellipses, and had carefully studied their mathematical properties, it never occurred to them as possible that the heavenly bodies could move in anything but circles or complications of circles, because their aesthetic sense dominated their speculations and made them reject all but the most symmetrical hypotheses. The scholastics [= medieval philosophers] had inherited the prejudices of the Greeks, and Kepler was the first who ventured to go against them in this respect. Preconceptions that have an aesthetic origin are just as misleading as those that are moral or theological, and on this ground alone Kepler would be an innovator of first-rate importance. His three laws, however, have another and a greater place in the history of science, since they afforded the proof of Newton's law of gravitation.

Kepler's laws, unlike the law of gravitation, were purely descriptive. They did not suggest any general cause of the movements of the planets, but gave the simplest formulae by which to sum up the results of observation. Simplicity of description was, so far, the only advantage of the theory that the planets revolved about the sun rather than the earth, and that the apparent diural [= daily] revolution of the heavens was really due to the earth's rotation. . . .

Galileo Galilei (1564-1642) was the most notable scientific figure of his time, both on account of his discoveries and through his conflict with the Inquisition. . . .

The great merit of Galileo was the combination of experimental and mechanical skill with the power of embodying his results in mathematical formulae. . . .

Galileo discovered that, apart from the resistance of the air, when bodies fall freely they fall with a uniform acceleration, which, in a vacuum, is the same for all, no matter what their bulk or the material of which they are composed. In every second during which a body is falling freely in a vacuum, its speed increases by about 32 feet per second. He also proved that when a body is thrown horizontally, like a bullet, it moves in a parabola [= a curved line of a certain shape], whereas it had previously been supposed to move horizontally for a while and then to fall vertically. These results may not now seem very sensational, but they were the beginning of exact mathematical knowledge as to how bodies move. Before his time, there was pure mathematics, which was deductive and did not depend upon observation, and there was a certain amount of wholly empirical experimenting, especially in connection with alchemy. But it was he who did most to inaugurate the practice of experiment with a view to arriving at a mathematical law. . . .

Experiments on falling bodies, though they might vex pedants, could not be condemned by the Inquisition. It was the telescope that led Galileo on to more dangerous ground. Hearing that a Dutchman had invented such an instrument, Galileo reinvented it, and almost immediately discovered many new astronomical facts, the most important of which, for him, was the existence of Jupiter's satellites. They were important as a miniature copy of the solar system according to the theory of Copernicus, while they were difficult to fit into the Ptolemaic scheme. Moreover, there had been all kinds of reasons why, apart from the fixed stars, there should be just seven heavenly bodies (the sun, the moon, and the five planets), and the discovery of four more was most upsetting. Were there not the seven golden candlesticks of the Apocalypse, and the seven churches of Asia? Aristotelians refused altogether to look through the telescope, and stubbornly maintained that Jupiter's moons were an illusion. . . .

Besides Jupiter's moons, the telescope revealed other things horrifying to theologians. It showed that Venus has phases like the moon; Copernicus had recognized that his theory demanded this, and Galileo's instrument transformed an argument against him into an argument in his favour. The moon was found to have mountains, which for some reason was thought shocking. More dreadful still, the sun had spots! This was considered as tending to show that the Creator's work had blemishes; teachers in Catholic universities were therefore forbidden to mention sun-spots, and in some of them this prohibition endured for centuries. . . .

The result of all this was that the Inquisition took up astronomy, and arrived, by deduction from certain texts of Scripture, at two important truths:

"The first proposition, that the sun is the centre and does not revolve about the earth, is foolish, absurd, false in theology, and heretical, because expressly contrary to Holy Scripture. . . . The second proposition, that the earth is not the centre, but revolves about the sun, is absurd, false in philosophy, and, from a theological point of view at least, opposed to the true faith."

Galileo, hereupon, was ordered by the Pope to appear before the Inquisition, which commanded him to abjure his errors, which he did on February 26, 1616. He solemnly promised that he would no longer hold the Copernican opinion, or teach it whether in writing or by word of mouth. . . .

At the instance of the Pope, all books teaching that the earth moves were thereupon placed upon the Index [of Forbidden Books]; and now for the first time the work of Copernicus himself was condemned. Galileo retired to Florence, where, for a while, he lived quietly and avoided giving offence to his victorious enemies.

Galileo, however, was of an optimistic temperament, and at all times prone to direct his wit against fools. In 1623 his friend Cardinal Barberini became Popè, with the title of Urban VIII, and this gave Galileo a sense of security which, as the event showed, was ill founded. He set to work to write his *Dialogues on the Two Greatest Systems of the World,* which were completed in 1630 and published in 1632. In this book there is a flimsy pretence of leaving the issue open between the two "greatest systems," that of Ptolemy and that of Copernicus, but in fact the whole is a powerful argument in favour of the latter. It was a brilliant book, and was read with avidity throughout Europe.

But while the scientific world applauded, the ecclesiastics were furious. During the time of Galileo's enforced silence, his enemies had taken the opportunity to increase prejudice by arguments to which it would have been imprudent to reply. . . .The Jesuit Father Melchior Inchofer maintained that "the opinion of the earth's motion is of all heresies the most abominable, the most pernicious, the most scandalous; the immovability of the earth is thrice sacred; argument against the immortality of the soul, the existence of God, and the incarnation, should be tolerated sooner than an argument to prove that the earth moves." By such cries of "tally-ho" the theologians had stirred each other's blood, and they were now all ready for the hunt after one old man, enfeebled by illness and in process of going blind.

Galileo was once more summoned to Rome to appear before the Inquisition, which, feeling itself flouted, was in a sterner mood than in 1616. At first he pleaded that he was too ill to endure the journey from Florence; thereupon the Pope threatened to send his own physician to examine the culprit, who should be brought in chains if his illness proved not to be desperate. This induced Galileo to undertake the journey without waiting for the verdict of his enemy's medical emissary—for Urban VIII was now his bitter adversary. When he reached Rome he was thrown into the prisons of the Inquisition, and threatened with torture if he did not recant. The Inquisition, "invoking the most holy name of our Lord Jesus Christ and of His most glorious Virgin Mother Mary," decreed that Galileo should not incur the penalties provided for heresy, "provided that with a sincere heart and unfeigned faith, in Our presence, you abjure, curse, and detest the said errors and heresies." Nevertheless, in spite of recantation and penitence, "We condemn you to the formal prison of this Holy Office for a period determinable at Our pleasure; and by way of salutary penance, we order you during the next three years to recite, once a week, the seven penitential psalms."

The comparative mildness of this sentence was conditional upon recantation. Galileo, accordingly, publicly and on his knees, recited a long formula drawn up by the Inquisition, in the course of which he stated: "I abjure, curse, and detest the said errors and heresies. . . . and I swear that I will never more in future say or assert anything, verbally or in writing, which may give rise to a similar suspicion of me." He went on to promise that he would denounce to the Inquisition any heretics whom he might hereafter find still maintaining that the earth moved, and to swear, with his hands on the Gospels, that he himself had abjured this doctrine. Satisfied that the interests of religion and morals had been served by causing the greatest man of the age to commit perjury, the Inquisition allowed him to spend the rest of his days in retirement and silence, not in prison, it is true, but controlled in all his movements, and forbidden to see his family or his friends. He became blind in 1637, and died in 1642—the year in which Newton was born.

The Church forbade the teaching of the Copernican system as true in all learned and educational institutions that it could control. Works teaching that the earth moves remained on the Index till 1835.

Reading Questions

1. Why did astronomers prefer to think that planets, moons, and stars must move in circles?
2. How did the Copernican doctrine tend to conflict with then current Christine doctrines?
3. Explain why Russell thinks nonscientific factors often play a significant role in new scientific discoveries.
4. What part did each of the following play in advancing the new astronomical theory: Copernicus, Brahe, Kepler, and Galileo?

Questions for Reflection and Research

1. In what ways might one be able to reconcile Biblical accounts of the heavens with modern astronomy? (See selection #7 by Barbour.)
2. What are the present views of various religions and religious sects about modern astronomical findings?
3. Does the earth go round the sun, the sun go round the earth, or is motion relative to the point of observation? (See selection #20 by Schroeer.)

The Bible Is Not an Astronomy Text

The Author: Galileo Galilei (1564–1642) was an Italian mathematician, astronomer, and physicist. He was condemned by the Catholic church because of his advocacy of the view that the earth travels round the sun. He once wrote that "the Book of Nature is written in mathematical characters." For more about his life see selection #1 by Russell.

The Selection: Galileo sets forth the view that the Bible is primarily intended by God for spiritual instruction and should not be regarded as the last word on the nature of the physical world.

The reason produced [by some people] for condemning the opinion that the earth moves and the sun stands still is that in many places in the Bible one may read that the sun moves and the earth stands still. Since the Bible cannot err, it follows as a necessary consequence that anyone takes an erroneous and heretical position who maintains that the sun is inherently motionless and the earth movable.

With regard to this argument, I think in the first place that it is very pious to say and prudent to affirm that the holy Bible can never speak untruth—whenever its true meaning is understood. But I believe nobody will deny that it is often very abstruse, and may say things which are quite different from what its bare words

Adapted excerpt from Stillman Drake's translation of "Letter to the Grand Duchess Christina" in *Discoveries and Opinions of Galileo.* (New York: Doubleday & Company, Inc., 1957). Copyright © 1957 by Stillman Drake. Adapted by permission of Doubleday & Company, Inc.

signify. Hence in expounding the Bible if one were always to
confine oneself to the unadorned grammatical meaning, one might
fall into error. Not only contradictions and propositions far from
true might thus be made to appear in the Bible, but even grave
heresies and follies. Thus it would be necessary to assign to God
feet, hands, and eyes, as well as corporeal [= bodily] and human
affections, such as anger, repentance, hatred, and sometimes even
the forgetting of things past and ignorance of those to come. These
propositions uttered by the Holy Ghost were set down in that manner by the sacred scribes in order to accommodate them to the
capacities of the common people, who are rude and unlearned. For
the sake of those who deserve to be separated from the herd, it is
necessary that wise expositors should produce the true senses of
such passages, together with the special reasons for which they
were set down in these words. This doctrine is so widespread and so
definite with all theologians that it would be superfluous to adduce
evidence for it.

   Hence I think that I may reasonably conclude that whenever the
Bible has occasion to speak of any physical conclusion (especially
those which are very abstruse and hard to understand), the rule has
been observed of avoiding confusion in the minds of the common
people which would render them contumacious [= rebellious] toward the higher mysteries. Now the Bible, merely to condescend to
popular capacity, has not hesitated to obscure some very important
pronouncements, attributing to God himself some qualities extremely remote from (and even contrary to) His essence. Who,
then, would positively declare that this principle has been set aside,
and the Bible has confined itself rigorously to the bare and restricted sense of its words, when speaking but casually of the earth,
of water, of the sun, or of any other created thing? Especially in
view of the fact that these things in no way concern the primary
purpose of the sacred writings, which is the service of God and the
salvation of souls—matters infinitely beyond the comprehension of
the common people.

   This being granted, I think that in discussions of physical problems we ought to begin not from the authority of scriptural passages, but from sense-experiences and necessary demonstrations;
for the holy Bible and the phenomena of nature proceed alike
from the divine Word, the former as the dictate of the Holy Ghost
and the latter as the observant executrix of God's commands. It is
necessary for the Bible, in order to be accommodated to the understanding of every man, to speak many things which appear to differ
from the absolute truth so far as the bare meaning of the words is
concerned. But Nature, on the other hand, is inexorable and immutable; she never transgresses the laws imposed upon her, or
cares a whit whether her abstruse reasons and methods of operation are understandable to men. For that reason it appears that

nothing physical which sense-experience sets before our eyes, or which necessary demonstrations prove to us, ought to be called in question (much less condemned) upon the testimony of biblical passages which may have some different meaning beneath their words. For the Bible is not chained in every expression to conditions as strict as those which govern all physical effects; nor is God any less excellently revealed in Nature's actions than in the sacred statements of the Bible. . . .

From this I do not mean to infer that we need not have an extraordinary esteem for the passages of holy Scripture. On the contrary, having arrived at any certainties in physics, we ought to utilize these as the most appropriate aids in the true exposition of the Bible and in the investigation of those meanings which are necessarily contained therein, for these must be concordant with demonstrated truths. I should judge that the authority of the Bible was designed to persuade men of those articles and propositions which, surpassing all human reasoning, could not be made credible by science, or by any other means than through the very mouth of the Holy Spirit.

Yet even in those propositions which are not matters of faith, this authority ought to be preferred over that of all human writings which are supported only by bare assertions or probable arguments, and not set forth in a demonstrative way. This I hold to be necessary and proper to the same extent that divine wisdom surpasses all human judgment and conjecture.

But I do not feel obliged to believe that that same God who has endowed us with senses, reason, and intellect has intended to forgo their use and by some other means to give us knowledge which we can attain by them. He would not require us to deny sense and reason in physical matters which are set before our eyes and minds by direct experience or necessary demonstrations. This must be especially true in those sciences of which but the faintest trace (and that consisting of conclusions) is to be found in the Bible. Of astronomy, for instance, so little is found that none of the planets except Venus are so much as mentioned, and this only once or twice under the name of "Lucifer." If the sacred scribes had had any intention of teaching people certain arrangements and motions of the heavenly bodies, or had they wished us to derive such knowledge from the Bible, then in my opinion they would not have spoken of these matters so sparingly in comparison with the infinite number of admirable conclusions which are demonstrated in that science. Far from pretending to teach us the constitution and motions of the heavens and the stars, with their shapes, magnitudes, and distances, the authors of the Bible intentionally forbore to speak of these things, though all were quite well known to them. . . .

Reading Questions

1. How does Galileo defend the view that the Bible is not fully trustworthy on astronomical matters?
2. What class of people did God intend the Bible for?

Questions for Reflection and Research

1. Which twentieth-century theological reaction to science most closely parallels Galileo's? (See selection #7 by Barbour.)
2. What does Galileo mean by the words *demonstrated truths*?

The Creation

The Author: Tradition holds Moses (thirteenth century B.C.) to be the author of the book of Genesis. However, present biblical scholarship indicates it was compiled from a number of older sources. Some would add that whoever wrote the book, God inspired the writer(s) and is to be regarded as the real author.

The Selection: The first chapter and the first 25 verses of the second chapter of the first book of the Bible describe the creation of the earth and of Adam and Eve.

CHAPTER 1

In the beginning God created the heaven and the earth.

2 And the earth was without form, and void; and darkness was upon the face of the deep. And the Spirit of God moved upon the face of the waters.

3 And God said, Let there be light: and there was light.

4 And God saw the light, that it was good: and God divided the light from the darkness.

5 And God called the light Day, and the darkness he called Night. And the evening and the morning were the first day.

6 ¶ And God said, Let there be a firmament in the midst of the waters, and let it divide the waters from the waters.

7 And God made the firmament, and divided the waters which were under the firmament from the waters which were above the firmament: and it was so.

The excerpt is from the 1611 translation known as the King James Bible.

8 And God called the firmament Heaven. And the evening and the morning were the second day.

9 ¶ And God said, Let the waters under the heaven be gathered together unto one place, and let the dry land appear: and it was so.

10 And God called the dry land Earth; and the gathering together of the waters called he Seas: and God saw that it was good.

11 And God said, Let the earth bring forth grass, the herb yielding seed, and the fruit tree yielding fruit after his kind, whose seed is in itself, upon the earth: and it was so.

12 And the earth brought forth grass, and herb yielding seed after his kind, and the tree yielding fruit, whose seed was in itself, after his kind: and God saw that it was good.

13 And the evening and the morning were the third day.

14 ¶ And God said, Let there be lights in the firmament of the heaven to divide the day from the night; and let them be for signs, and for seasons, and for days, and years:

15 And let them be for lights in the firmament of the heaven to give light upon the earth: and it was so.

16 And God made two great lights; the greater light to rule the day, and the lesser light to rule the night: he made the stars also.

17 And God set them in the firmament of the heaven to give light upon the earth,

18 And to rule over the day and over the night, and to divide the light from the darkness: and God saw that it was good.

19 And the evening and the morning were the fourth day.

20 And God said, Let the waters bring forth abundantly the moving creature that hath life, and fowl that may fly above the earth in the open firmament of heaven.

21 And God created great whales, and every living creature that moveth, which the waters brought forth abundantly, after their kind, and every winged fowl after his kind: and God saw that it was good.

22 And God blessed them, saying, Be fruitful, and multiply, and fill the waters in the seas, and let fowl multiply in the earth.

23 And the evening and the morning were the fifth day.

24 ¶ And God said, Let the earth bring forth the living creature after his kind, cattle, and creeping thing, and beast of the earth after his kind: and it was so.

25 And God made the beast of the earth after his kind, and cattle after their kind, and every thing that creepeth upon the earth after his kind: and God saw that it was good.

26 ¶ And God said, Let us make man in our image, after our likeness: and let them have dominion over the fish of the sea, and over the fowl of the air, and over the cattle, and over all the earth, and over every creeping thing that creepeth upon the earth.

27 So God created man in his own image, in the image of God created he him; male and female created he them.

28 And God blessed them, and God said unto them, Be fruitful, and multiply, and replenish the earth, and subdue it: and have dominion over the fish of the sea, and over the fowl of the air, and over every living thing that moveth upon the earth.

29 ¶ And God said, Behold, I have given you every herb bearing seed, which is upon the face of all the earth, and every tree, in the which is the fruit of a tree yielding seed; to you it shall be for meat.

30 And to every beast of the earth, and to every fowl of the air, and to every thing that creepeth upon the earth, wherein there is life, I have given every green herb for meat: and it was so.

31 And God saw every thing that he had made, and, behold, it was very good. And the evening and the morning were the sixth day.

CHAPTER 2

Thus the heavens and the earth were finished, and all the host of them.

2 And on the seventh day God ended his work which he had made; and he rested on the seventh day from all his work which he had made.

3 And God blessed the seventh day, and sanctified it: because that in it he had rested from all his work which God created and made.

4 ¶ These are the generations of the heavens and of the earth when they were created, in the day that the LORD God made the earth and the heavens,

5 And every plant of the field before it was in the earth, and every herb of the field before it grew: for the LORD God had not caused it to rain upon the earth, and there was not a man to till the ground.

6 But there went up a mist from the earth, and watered the whole face of the ground.

7 And the LORD God formed man of the dust of the ground, and breathed into his nostrils the breath of life; and man became a living soul.

8 ¶ And the LORD God planted a garden eastward in Eden; and there he put the man whom he had formed.

9 And out of the ground made the LORD God to grow every tree that is pleasant to the sight, and good for food; the tree of life also in the midst of the garden, and the tree of knowledge of good and evil. . . .

15 And the LORD God took the man, and put him into the garden of Eden to dress it and to keep it.

16 And the LORD God commanded the man, saying, Of every tree of the garden thou mayest freely eat:

17 But of the tree of the knowledge of good and evil, thou shall not eat of it: for in the day that thou eatest thereof thou shalt surely die.

18 ¶ And the LORD God said, It is not good that the man should be alone; I will make him an help meet for him.

19 And out of the ground the LORD God formed every beast of the field, and every fowl of the air; and brought them unto Adam to see what he would call them: and whatsoever Adam called every living creature, that was the name thereof.

20 And Adam gave names to all cattle, and to the fowl of the air, and to every beast of the field; but for Adam there was not found an help meet for him.

21 And the LORD God caused a deep sleep to fall upon Adam, and he slept: and he took one of his ribs, and closed up the flesh instead thereof;

22 And the rib, which the Lord God had taken from man, made he a woman, and brought her unto the man.

23 And Adam said, This is now bone of my bones, and flesh of my flesh: she shall be called Woman, because she was taken out of Man.

24 Therefore shall a man leave his father and his mother, and shall cleave unto his wife: and they shall be one flesh.

25 And they were both naked, the man and his wife, and were not ashamed.

Reading Questions

1. Are the creation accounts in the two chapters consistent?
2. How did God create? What existed prior to creation?

Questions for Reflection and Research

1. How do other translations of the Bible compare with the King James translation?
2. How does one know how literally to interpret this account of creation?
3. If interpreted literally, how do these verses conflict with scientific findings?
4. How can those who accept the Bible as a religious guide explain the seeming conflict between science and these passages from the book of Genesis?
5. Bishop James Ussher in 1658 in his book *The Annals of the World* calculated that God began his creation of the world on Sunday, October 23, 4004 B.C. How could Ussher determine the date with such precision?

selection 4.

Evolution vs. Fundamentalism: A Trial in Tennessee

The Authors: Jerōme Lawrence (b. 1915) and Robert E. Lee (b. 1918) are both American playwrights. They have collaborated on many plays, including *The Night Thoreau Spent in Jail* and *Auntie Mame*.

ı **The Selection:** The selection dramatically portrays the conflict between the theory of evolution (as developed by Charles Darwin and Alfred Wallace) and fundamentalist interpreters of the Bible. The following is from a condensed version of the play *Inherit the Wind*—a play loosely based on a trial that took place in July 1925 in Dayton, Tennessee. In the original trial John Scopes, a high school science teacher, was charged with breaking the law by teaching the theory of evolution. He was defended by the famous lawyer Clarence Darrow. The prosecution was led by William Jennings Bryan, who had lost three different elections for president of the United States. In the play Cates represents Scopes, Drummond is Darrow, and Brady is Bryan.

SCENE II

Two days later, Brady [the prosecuting attorney] has Howard, an uncomfortable thirteen-year-old pupil of Cates', on the stand. Establishing the fact that Cates [the defendent] made no reference to Genesis in his teaching the world's beginnings, "Ladies and gentlemen," says Brady with an oversized gesture. . . , "I am sure that

From *The Best Plays of 1954–1955*, ed. Louis Kronenberger (New York: Dodd, Mead & Company, 1955), act 2, scene 2. Originally published by Random House, Inc. (New York, 1955). Reprinted by permission of Dodd, Mead & Company; Random House, Inc.; and Brandt & Brandt. *Inherit the Wind*: Copyright as an unpublished work 1951 by Jerome Lawrence and Robert E. Lee. Copyright © 1955 by Jerome Lawrence and Robert E. Lee.

everyone on the jury, everyone within the sound of this boy's voice, is moved by his tragic confusion. He has been taught that he wriggled up like an animal from the filth and the muck below! (*Continuing fervently, the spirit is upon him.*) I say that these Bible-haters, these 'Evil-utionists,' are brewers of poison. And the legislature of this sovereign state has had the wisdom to demand that the peddlers of poison—in bottles or in books—clearly label the products they attempt to sell! (*There is applause.* HOWARD *gulps.* BRADY *points at the boy.*) I tell you, if this law is not upheld, this boy will become one of a generation shorn of its faith by the teachings of Godless science! But if the full penalty of the law is meted out to Bertram Cates, the faithful the whole world over, who are watching us here and listening to our every word, will call this courtroom blessed! (*Applause. Dramatically,* BRADY *moves to his chair. Condescendingly, he mutters:*) Your witness, sir. . . ."

Drummond [the defense attorney] . . . continues in a relaxed and amiable fashion to talk to Howard, wishing to establish over the objections of Prosecutor Davenport that Howard has a right to *think,* that the teachings of Cates didn't hurt Howard in any way, physically or morally. Brady cries: "Ask him if his Holy Faith in the scriptures has been shattered." "When I need your valuable help, Colonel," replies Drummond, "you may rest assured I shall humbly ask for it." Then he asks Howard: "Do you believe everything Mr. Cates told you?" Howard isn't sure. "I gotta think it over," he says. "Good for you," says Drummond.

Noting that Howard's father is a farmer with a new tractor, Drummond now asks Howard if he figures the tractor's "sinful" because it's not mentioned in the Bible; or if the telephone's an instrument of the Devil? "I never thought of it that way," replies the boy. "Neither did anybody else," booms Brady. "Your Honor, the defense makes the same old error of all Godless men! They confuse material things with the great spiritual realities of the Revealed Word! Why do you bewilder this child?" he asks Drummond. . . . Howard . . . is benevolently excused by Drummond.

Davenport calls the next witness for the prosecution, Rachel Brown. Looking to neither right nor left, wanting to get it over with as quickly as possible, Rachel hurries to the stand. Brady, now with exaggerated gentleness, takes her on. First, he wishes to know if Bert Cates and Rachel still attend the same church, and if Cates dropped out, why? Rachel tells Cates' reason for no longer attending: One of his favorite pupils drowned. At the child's funeral, Reverend Brown [Rachel's father] said that this fine eleven-year-old, being unbaptized, had not died in a state of grace. Cates leaps to his feet, shouting: "Tell 'em what your father really said! That Tommy's soul was damned, writhing in hell-fire!" A juror yells: "Cates, you sinner!" Cates cries out: "Religion's supposed to comfort people, isn't it? Not frighten them to death!" Drummond pushes

Cates back into his seat, requesting that his remarks be stricken from the record. "But how," says Brady, "can we strike this young man's bigoted opinions from the memory of this community?" Then turning, all set to play his trump card, Brady says: "Now, my dear. Will you tell the jury some more of Mr. Cates' opinions on the subject of religion?"

Over Drummond's objections to this hearsay testimony, Rachel is told to continue. This she finds nearly impossible to do. The Judge reminds her she is testifying under oath. Brady prompts her to describe her innermost feelings when Bert Cates said to her: "God did not create man! Man created God!" Hemmed in by the crowd's loud reactions and by Drummond's loud objections, Rachel blurts out: "Bert didn't say that. He was just joking. What he said was: 'God created man in his own image—and man, being a gentleman, returned the compliment.' ". . .

Brady. . . is pleased; and goes on to question Rachel about Bert's comments on the holy state of matrimony, and whether he had compared it with the breeding of animals. Close to collapse, Rachel is unable to say another word. Brady excuses her from the stand over the loud objections of Drummond, who wants to cross-examine her. Cates, distressed at Rachel's condition, tells Drummond to let her go, which he reluctantly does. After Rachel steps down, the prosecution intends calling no further witnesses; the Judge instructs the defense to proceed with its case.

But the defense has nowhere to go. Drummond calls one after another of the experts he has brought to testify in Bert Cates' behalf, but Brady objects to each and every one of them. He turns down the head of the Department of Zoology at the University of Chicago; he won't let agnostic scientists use this courtroom for their heresies. But he also turns down a deacon of the Congregationalist Church, who happens to be professor of geology and archaeology at Oberlin. Drummond next calls one of the most brilliant minds in the world, a famous anthropologist and author. Brady smugly objects.

Drummond tells the bench that these noted scientists' testimony is basic to the prisoner's defense—that, far from being a crime, what Bert Cates quietly told his class is accepted in enlightened communities everywhere. "In this community," states the Judge, "the opposite is true. Therefore, no experts are needed to question the validity of a law already on the books." "In other words," scowls Drummond, "the court rules out any expert testimony on Charles Darwin's 'Origin of Species' or 'Descent of Man'?" The court so rules.

Flabbergasted, Drummond for a single moment is helpless; but the next minute he has a gleam in his eye—and the possibility of an acceptable witness who can give expert testimony on the Holy Bible. This time Brady handsomely makes no objection to such a

Contents

man. "Good," says Drummond, and with relish announces, "I call to the stand one of the world's foremost experts on the Bible and its teachings—Matthew Harrison Brady."

The spectators break loose; the prosecutor objects; the Judge is confused. Over the prosecutor's worried protests, Brady grandly says he will take the stand. Whereupon the Judge, rapping for order, says: "The court will support you if you wish to decline to testify—as a witness against your own case. . . ." Brady, with magnificent conviction, retorts: "Your Honor, I shall not testify *against* anything. I shall speak out, as I have all my life—on behalf of the Living Truth of the Holy Scriptures!"

The giant of a man is sworn in, and on preliminary questioning modestly admits to being an expert on the Bible. . . .

Now playing in Brady's "ball park," [Drummond] thumbs through the Bible while play-acting and lightly wisecracking. He feels his way from Jonah to Joshua—from "the big fish" of the Bible to the sun's standing still. Brady lets "faith" and God take care of his answers on the solar system and all questions of natural law: "Natural law," answers Brady calmly and patiently, "was born in the mind of the Heavenly Father. He can change it, cancel it, use it as He pleases. It constantly amazes me that you apostles of science, for all your supposed wisdom, fail to grasp this simple fact."

Still thumbing through the Bible, Drummond stops to inquire about Cain's wife—where in the world did she come from?

DRUMMOND. Mrs. Cain. Cain's wife. If, "In the beginning" there was only Adam and Eve, and Cain and Abel, where'd this extra woman spring from? Ever figure that out?
BRADY (*cool*). No, sir. I will leave the agnostics to hunt for her. (*Laughter.*) . .

Drummond [passes] on to all the "begats" at the beginning of the Bible. ". . . and Arphaxad begat Salah; and Salah begat Eber—" These, says Brady, are the generations of holy men and women of the Bible. How, wonders Drummond, did they go about all this begatting? About the same way as today? Brady gets a fine laugh with: "The process is about the same. I don't think your scientists have improved it any." Drummond then calls begatting the biological function known as *sex*, and asks Brady what he, not as a father, or as a husband, or as a Presidential candidate thinks of it, but as a Biblical expert. Brady names it "Original Sin"; Drummond narrowly asks him if this made the holy men and women then less holy, and for answer gets a scowl from Brady; an interruption from the prosecutor, who would like to know how this bears on the case; and a request from the court to justify this line of questioning. Drummond gives a fiery answer: "You've ruled out all my witnesses. I must be allowed to examine the one witness you've left me in my own way!" With great dignity, Brady tells the court that he is willing

to endure Mr. Drummond's contempt for all that is holy, because
he is simultaneously pleading the case of the prosecution. Drummond shouts his objections: something *is* holy to Drummond. The
individual human mind is what he holds most sacred. And he pas-
sionately sings the praise of reason, and the advance of man's
knowledge. He also acknowledges the lovely things one loses with
every step of progress: when Darwin moved us forward to a hilltop,
from where we could see the way we had come, we had to abandon
our faith in the pleasant poetry of Genesis. Brady shouts: "We must
not abandon faith. Faith is the important thing!"

   But then why did God plague us with the power to think?
Drummond asks Brady. "Why do you deny the *one* faculty which
lifts man above all other creatures on the earth: the power of his
brain to reason? What other merit have we? The elephant is larger,
the horse is stronger and swifter, the butterfly more beautiful, the
mosquito more prolific, even the simple sponge is more durable!
(*Wheeling on* BRADY.) Or does a *sponge* think?"

BRADY. I don't know. I'm a man, not a sponge. (*There are a few snickers at
this; but the crowd seems to be slipping away from* BRADY *and aligning itself more
and more with* DRUMMOND.). . .

   Introducing a rock covered with fossils of prehistoric marine
creatures, Drummond says that his uncalled witness, Dr. Page of
Oberlin, believes this rock is at least ten million years old, that these
creatures were in this county when the mountains were submerged
in water. Brady regains his confidence, and immediately feels very
much at home when the "Flood" is brought into the picture. Only,
he corrects Drummond's professor's date: the rock cannot be more
than six thousand years old. He has his own authority, a Biblical
scholar, a Bishop, who has determined the exact time of the Creation: the twenty-third of October, 4004 B.C., at nine A.M. Drummond
lightly takes hold of this hour of Creation, and mildly wonders
whether it was *Eastern Standard* or *Rocky Mountain* Time. He draws
laughter from the spectators: "It wasn't Daylight Saving Time, was
it? Because the Lord didn't make the sun until the fourth day!"

BRADY (*fidgeting*). That is correct.
DRUMMOND (*sharply*). That first day. Was it a twenty-four-hour day?
BRADY. The Bible says it was a day.
DRUMMOND. There wasn't any sun. How do you know how long it was?
BRADY (*determined*). The Bible says it was a day.
DRUMMOND. A normal day, a literal day, a twenty-four-hour day?
(*Pause.* BRADY *is unsure.*)
BRADY. I do not know.
DRUMMOND. What do you think?
BRADY (*floundering*). I do not think about things that. . . I do not think
about!
DRUMMOND. Do you ever think about things that you *do* think about?
(*There is some laughter. But it is damped by the knowledge and awareness through-*

out the courtroom that the trap is about to be sprung.) Isn't it possible that first day was twenty-five hours long? There was no way to measure it, no way to tell! Could it have been twenty-five hours? (*Pause. The entire courtroom seems to lean forward.*)

BRADY (*hesitates—then*): It is possible....(DRUMMOND's *got him. And he knows it! This is the turning point. From here on,* DRUMMOND *is fully in the driver's seat. He pounds his questions faster and faster.*)

DRUMMOND. Oh. You interpret that the first day recorded in the Book of Genesis could be of indeterminate length.

BRADY (*wriggling*). I mean to state that the day referred to is not necessarily a twenty-four-hour day.

DRUMMOND. It could have been thirty hours! Or a month! Or a year! Or a hundred years! (*He brandishes the rock underneath* BRADY's *nose.*) Or *ten million years*!

The prosecutor leaps up in protest. By this time there is so much tension, so much excited reaction in the court, that the Judge pounds for order. Davenport demands to know what Drummond is trying to do; Brady knows what he's trying to do: he's trying to destroy universal belief in the Bible. Drummond now shouts that he's trying to stop these bigots and ignoramuses from controlling education in the United States. No one can hear Davenport's plea as the Judge hammers for order.

Drummond answers Brady's blast by saying that the Bible is a good book but not the only book. . . .

Reading Questions

1. Why does the judge deny Drummond the use of scientific experts as witnesses?
2. How do the theory of evolution and the evidence used to support it seem to conflict with the Bible? (See the previous selection from the Bible.)

Questions for Reflection and Research

1. Should students be required to learn scientific findings if their religion rejects the findings?
2. How can the Bible be interpreted so that it need not be held to be inconsistent with evolutionary theory? (See selection #7 by Barbour.)
3. How can a fundamentalist interpreter of the Bible account for fossils and the remains of long-extinct animals?
4. Does the play fairly represent all sides? Should it?
5. How does the play differ from the trial?
6. What other conflicts have there been between science and religion?

Einstein Reflects on God's Nature and Existence

The Author: Albert Einstein (1879–1955), the German physicist, became the most widely known figure in twentieth-century science because of his revolutionary ideas about Brownian motion, electromagnetic radiation, and his general and special theories of relativity. For an account of these see selection #20 by Schroeer. Einstein was also interested in social justice and issues in the philosophy of science.

The Selection: Einstein seems to offer reasons to believe in God. He also criticizes some traditional religious ideas.

The most beautiful thing we can experience is the mysterious. It is the source of all true art and science. He to whom this emotion is a stranger, who can no longer pause to wonder and stand rapt in awe, is as good as dead: his eyes are closed. This insight into the mystery of life, coupled though it be with fear, has also given rise to religion. To know that what is impenetrable to us really exists, manifesting itself as the highest wisdom and the most radiant beauty which our dull faculties can comprehend only in their most primitive forms—this knowledge, this feeling, is at the center of true religiousness. In this sense, and in this sense only, I belong in the ranks of devoutly religious men.

I cannot imagine a God who rewards and punishes the objects of his creation, whose purposes are modeled after our own—a God,

From *Living Philosophies* (New York: Simon and Schuster, 1931), pp. 6–7. Reprinted by permission of the Estate of Albert Einstein.

in short, who is but a reflection of human frailty. Neither can I believe that the individual survives the death of his body, although feeble souls harbor such thoughts through fear or ridiculous egotism. It is enough for me to contemplate the mystery of conscious life perpetuating itself through all eternity, to reflect upon the marvelous structure of the universe which we can dimly perceive, and to try humbly to comprehend even an infinitesimal part of the intelligence manifested in nature.

Reading Questions

1. Does Einstein believe God exists? What is God's nature?
2. Why does he reject belief in life after death?
3. Why does he reject the idea that God rewards and punishes humans?
4. What is the foundation of true religiousness according to Einstein?

Questions for Reflection and Research

1. Is there any evidence that suggests an intelligence is not at work in the universe? (See selection #6 by Hick.)
2. Are his objections to the idea that there is life after death good ones? (See selection #13 by Ducasse.)
3. What scientific findings seem to suggest that no God exists?
4. What scientific findings seem to suggest there is a God?
5. Can God's existence be proven or disproven?
6. Can science help us know what God's nature is (if God exists)?

Does Science Reveal That the World Was Designed?

The Author: John H. Hick (b. 1922) began his career as a Presbyterian minister in England. He was educated at the University of Edinburgh and at Cambridge and Oxford Universities. He has taught at universities in both England and the United States. His writings on topics in the philosophy of religion have been influential.

The Selection: The classical version of the argument from design (the teleological argument) for God's existence is described. Hume's criticisms of the argument are explained and updated to include the theory of evolution.

[The design (or teleological) argument] has always been the most popular of the theistic arguments, tending to evoke spontaneous assent in simple and sophisticated alike. The argument occurs in philosophical literature from [the] *Timaeus* [of Plato (428-347 B.C.] onward. (It appears again as the last of [the] five Ways [of St. Thomas Aquinas (1224–1274)].) In modern times one of the most famous expositions of the argument from, or to, design is that of William Paley (1743–1805) in his *Natural Theology: or Evidences of the Existence and Attributes of the Deity Collected from the Appearances of Nature* (1802). The argument is still in active commission, especially in more conservative theological circles.

Paley's analogy of the watch conveys the essence of the argument. Suppose that while walking in a desert place I see a rock lying on the ground and ask myself how this object came to exist. I can properly attribute its presence to chance, meaning in this case the

From John Hick, *Philosophy of Religion*, 2nd ed., © 1973, pp. 23–26. Reprinted and adapted by permission of Prentice-Hall, Inc.

operation of such natural forces as wind, rain, heat, frost and volcanic action. However, if I see a watch lying on the ground, I cannot reasonably account for it in a similar way. A watch consists of a complex arrangement of wheels, cogs, axles, springs, and balances, all operating accurately together to provide a regular measurement of the lapse of time. It would be utterly implausible to attribute the formation and assembling of these metal parts into a functioning machine to the chance operation of such factors as wind and rain. We are obliged to postulate an intelligent mind which is responsible for the phenomenon.

Paley adds certain comments that are important for his analogy between the watch and the world. First, it would not weaken our inference if we had never seen a watch before (as we have never seen a world other than this one) and therefore did not know from direct observation that watches are products of human intelligence. Second, it would not invalidate our inference from the watch to the watchmaker if we found that the mechanism did not always work perfectly (as may appear to be the case with the mechanism of the world). We would still be obliged to postulate a watchmaker. And third, our inference would not be undermined if there were parts of the machine (as there are of nature) whose function we are not able to discover.

Paley argues that the natural world is as complex a mechanism, and as manifestly designed, as any watch. The rotation of the planets in the solar system, and on earth the regular procession of the seasons and the complex structure and mutual adaptation of the parts of a living organism, all suggest design. In a human brain, for example, thousands of millions of cells function together in a co-ordinated system. The eye is a superb movie camera, with self-adjusting lenses, a high degree of accuracy, color-sensitivity, and the capacity to operate continuously for many hours at a time. Can such complex and efficient mechanisms have come about by chance, as a stone might be formed by the random operation of natural forces?

Paley (in this respect typical of a great deal of religious apologetics in the eighteenth century) develops a long cumulative argument drawing upon virtually all the sciences of his day. As examples of divine arrangement he points to the characteristics and instincts of animals, which enable them to survive (for example, the suitability of a bird's wings to the air and of a fish's fins to the water). He is impressed by the way the alternation of day and night conveniently enables animals to sleep after a period of activity. We may conclude with an example offered by a more recent writer, who refers to the ozone layer in the atmosphere, which filters out enough of the burning ultraviolet rays of the sun to make life as we know it possible on the earth's surface. He writes:

The Ozone gas layer is a mighty proof of the Creator's forethought. Could anyone possibly attribute this device to a chance evolutionary process? A wall which prevents death to every living thing, just the right thickness, and exactly the correct defense, gives every evidence of plan.

The classic critique of the design argument occurs in . . . *Dialogues Concerning Natural Religion* [by David Hume (1711–1776)]. Hume's book was published in 1779, twenty-three years earlier than Paley's; but Paley took no account of Hume's criticisms—by no means the only example of lack of communication between theologians and their philosophical critics! Three of Hume's main criticisms are as follows.

1. He points out that any universe is bound to have the appearance of being designed. For there could not be a universe at all in which the parts were not adapted to one another to a considerable degree. There could not, for example, be birds that grew wings but, like fish, were unable to live in the air. The persistence of any kind of life in a relatively fixed environment presupposes order and adaptation, and this can always be thought of as a deliberate product of design. The question, however, whether this order could have come about otherwise than by conscious planning remains to be answered. As an alternative, Hume suggests the Epicurean hypothesis: the universe consists of a finite number of particles in random motion. In unlimited time these go through every combination that is possible to them. If one of these combinations constitutes a stable order (whether temporary or permanent), this order will in due course be realized and may be the orderly cosmos in which we now find ourselves.

   This hypothesis provides a simple model for a naturalistic explanation of the orderly character of the world. The model can be revised and extended in the light of the special sciences. The Darwinian theory of natural selection, for example, presents a more concrete account of the internal coherence of animal bodies and of their external adaptation to environment. According to Darwin's theory, animals are relatively efficient organisms in relation to their environment for the simple reason that the less well adapted individuals have perished in the continual competition to survive and so have not perpetuated their kind. The "struggle for survival," operating as a constant pressure toward more perfect adaptation, lies behind the evolution of life into increasingly complex forms, culminating in *homo-sapiens*. To refer back to the ozone layer, the reason animal life on earth is so marvelously sheltered by this filtering arrangement is not that God first created the animals and then put the ozone layer in place to protect them, but rather that the ozone layer was there first, and only those forms of life capable of existing in the precise level of ultraviolet radiation that penetrates this layer have developed on earth.

2. The analogy between the world and a human artifact, such as a watch or a house, is rather weak. The universe is not particularly like a vast machine. One could equally plausibly liken it to a great inert animal

such as a crustacean, or to a vegetable. But in this case the design argument fails, for whether crustaceans and vegetables are or are not consciously designed is precisely the question at issue. Only if the world is shown to be rather strikingly analogous to a human artifact, is there any proper basis for the inference to an intelligent Designer.

3. Even if we could validly infer a divine Designer of the world, we would still not be entitled to postulate the infinitely wise, good, and powerful God of Christian tradition. From a given effect we can only infer a cause sufficient to produce that effect; and therefore, from a finite world we can never infer an infinite creator. To use an illustration of Hume's, if I can see one side of a pair of scales, and can observe that ten ounces is outweighed by something on the other side, I have good evidence that the unseen object weighs more than ten ounces; but I cannot infer from this that it weighs a hundred ounces, still less that it is infinitely heavy. On the same principle, the appearances of nature do not entitle us to affirm the existence of *one* God rather than many, since the world is full of diversity; or of a wholly *good* God, since there is evil as well as good in the world; nor, for the same reason, of a perfectly *wise* God or an unlimitedly *powerful* one.

It has, therefore, seemed to most philosophers that the design argument, considered as a proof of the existence of God, is fatally weakened by Hume's criticisms.

Reading Questions

1. What aspects of the world seem analogous to a watch?
2. What criticisms are there of the design argument?

Questions for Reflection or Research

1. Compare the treatment of the argument from design in this selection with that in the selection by Barbour (#7).
2. Can you think of any further facts about the world that would support either side?
3. What other proofs of God's existence have been offered by religious thinkers? Can science be used to support or attack any of these proofs?
4. What defense of their beliefs is given by present-day scientists who are also religious believers? (For some possibilities see selection #7 by Barbour.)

Science, Religion, and Philosophy in the Twentieth Century

The Author: Ian Barbour (b. 1923) has a degree in theology from Yale University as well as a Ph.D. in physics from the University of Chicago. He has written extensively on the interaction of religion and science and has taught in both fields at Carleton College in Minnesota.

The Selection: Barbour explains how some recent philosophical schools (positivism, linguistic philosophy, existentialism, and process philosophy) and theological schools (neo-orthodoxy and liberalism) have responded to advances in science. He also touches on the thought of those who believe science gives support to theism. Barbour explores these issues in greater depth than preceding selections, and the reading is more demanding.

[This chapter] is intended for the reader unfamiliar with recent developments in *philosophy* (positivism, linguistic analysis, existentialism, process philosophy) and in *theology* (neo-orthodoxy, liberalism). Each of these viewpoints leads to a distinctive way of looking at the relations of science and religion, which we will simply describe briefly here. . . . Any scheme for classifying these contemporary viewpoints is somewhat arbitrary, but for convenience we group them in three sections: "Contrasts of Theology and Science," "Parallels of Theology and Science," and "Derivations of Theology from Science."

From Ian G. Barbour, *Issues in Science and Religion,* © 1966, pp. 115–33. Adapted and reprinted by permission of Prentice-Hall, Inc.

I. CONTRASTS OF THEOLOGY AND SCIENCE

We present first some variations on the theme that *the methods of science and religion are radically different.* The two enterprises, according to these authors, should be completely separate and independent. Not only do their content and subject matter have nothing in common, but their ways of knowing are so dissimilar that there are no points of fruitful comparison or analogy. The defense of religion from attack by science is accomplished by totally separating them; no conflicts are possible because any issue is assigned to one field or the other, but never both, on jurisdictional grounds. But by the same token neither can contribute positively to the other. What is of interest to theology is not of interest to science nor accessible to it, and vice versa. They occupy, as it were, watertight compartments in human thought. Past "conflicts" are attributed to failures in recognizing these distinctions.

Varying accounts are given of the reasons for the discontinuity between theological and scientific understanding. In *neo-orthodoxy*, it is the uniqueness of revelation that distinguishes theology from all human discovery. In *existentialism*, the dichotomy between personal existence and impersonal objects is the ground of the contrast. For *linguistic analysis*, the difference in the functions of religious and scientific language is the basis of the distinction. But the three interpretations unite, not only in contrasting theology and science, but in expressing reservations about the competency of reason in reaching religious understanding. They also agree on *the absence of metaphysical implications* in scientific theories. They join in asserting that science yields only technical knowledge of predictable regularities in nature and should not be expected to provide the basis for a philosophy of life or a set of ethical norms. These authors all decline the services of metaphysics as a bridge between science and religion, and they attack attempts by theists and atheists alike to use science in the support of theological and philosophical positions. Scientist and theologian, it is said, should each tend to his own business and not meddle in the affairs of the other.

1. God's Self-Revelation versus Man's Discovery (Neo-Orthodoxy)

No single man has had greater influence on twentieth-century Protestant thought than Karl Barth [1886–1968]. . . . He reacted sharply *against the nineteenth-century liberalism* in which he had been trained. Barth claimed that in the hands of the liberals Christianity had lost its distinctive message: God had become an immanent [=indwelling] force within the cosmic process, Christ was reduced to an example of human goodness, man's sinfulness was ignored in the assumption of inevitable progress and—most important of all—divine revelation had been replaced by human attempts to discover God through philosophical reflection, moral conscience, or religious experience.

Against such views, Barth insisted that God is always the "wholly other," the transcendent Lord, who can be known only *when he chooses to reveal himself,* as he did preeminently in Jesus Christ. This sovereign and holy God is radically distinct from the world, separated from sinful man by a gulf which could be crossed only from the divine, not the human side. God's self-disclosure to man, not man's search for God, must be the starting point of theology. . . .

Barth maintains that the primary revelation was *the person of Christ,* the Word made flesh. Scripture is a purely human record witnessing to this revelatory event. God acted in Christ, not in the dictation of an infallible book; hence we can accept everything that historical criticism and documentary analysis discover about the human limitations of the writers of the Bible and the cultural influences on their thought. . . .

Barthian theology received widespread response in Europe between the wars. It had recovered the Reformation conviction of the sovereignty of God, the centrality of Christ, the power of sin and grace, and the distinctiveness of revelation, all of which had been lost by modernists and by many liberals; yet Barthians did not reject the historical analysis of biblical documents, as fundamentalists and many conservatives had done. Here was a reformulation of the concept of revelation that could take biblical criticism into account. This new orthodoxy, or "neo-orthodoxy" as it came to be called, influenced religious thought throughout the West, and appeared in modified form in the writings of Emil Brunner [1899–1966], Reinhold Niebuhr [1892–1971], and others. It is still common among Protestant theologians on the Continent and is strongly represented in America (though since World War II many of its adherents have moved closer to the more sober liberalism of recent decades). . . .

The distinction between the methods of theology and science, according to neo-orthodoxy, derives from the difference between their objects of knowledge. Theology deals with the transcendent and mysterious God, who is so radically unlike the world which science studies that the same methods cannot be expected to be used in both disciplines. God is known only because he has revealed himself in Christ; science advances by human discovery and contributes nothing to a religious faith which depends entirely on divine initiative. Neo-orthodox authors are very critical of any natural theology which argues from evidences of design in nature. God is not known through his creation apart from Christ, for sin blinds human reason to the vision of the world as God's handiwork. The gap between man and God cannot be bridged from the human side. There are no points of contact between the ideas of science and those of theology.

Science can thus *neither contribute to nor conflict with* theology. . . . According to neo-orthodoxy, scripture tells us nothing authoritative about scientific questions; the "scientific" ideas of the biblical authors were the erroneous speculations of ancient times. As Niebuhr puts it, we should take the Bible "seriously but not literally.". . . For example, . . . most contemporary biblical scholars represent the Genesis story as a symbolic portrayal of the basic relation of man and the world to God; its message concerns man's creatureliness and dependence on God, and the goodness of the natural order. These religious meanings can be separated from the ancient cosmology in which they were expressed. Adam is taken not as a historical individual but as a symbol of Everyman in his movement from innocence to responsibility, sin and guilt. Such insights have nothing to do with scientific accounts of origins. Thus the scientist is free to carry out his work without interference from the theologian, and vice versa, for their methods and their subject matter are totally dissimilar.

2. Subjective Involvement versus Objective Detachment (Existentialism)

In existentialism the divergence between methods in theology and science arises primarily from the contrast between the sphere of *personal selfhood* and the sphere of *impersonal objects*. Existentialism is not a system of ideas but an attitude or orientation finding very diverse expression among theistic and atheistic authors. [Sören] Kierkegaard [1813–1855], the intense Danish theologian . . . , was the seminal influence, though his writings went almost unnoticed until the present century. Many existentialist themes were powerfully set forth in the literature of postwar Europe, especially in the plays and novels of [Jean Paul] Sartre [b. 1905] and [Albert] Camus [1913–1960]. In [Martin] Heidegger [1889–1976] and [Karl] Jaspers [1883–1969] these themes appeared in philosophical form, and theologians as different as [Martin] Buber [1878–1965] and [Rudolph] Bultmann [1884–1976] have given them expression within particular religious traditions.

Existentialism in all its forms asserts that we can know authentic human existence *only by being personally involved* as concrete individuals making free decisions—not by formulating abstract general concepts or universal laws about man. Each of us is a unique creative subject who must resist being treated as an object in a system of ideas or in the machinations of a mass society. A few existentialists have criticized scientists for treating man deterministically as an object to be manipulated and controlled, or for contributing to the depersonalization which technology has inflicted on human culture. But most existentialist authors have granted the usefulness of scientific knowledge, claiming only that the central events in the life of personal selfhood are beyond its scope. They have maintained that the most significant facets of *human existence* are understood only by decision, commitment, and involvement in life, and never in the detached, rationalistic attitude of the scientist. Of the many themes of existentialism—anxiety, despair, guilt, death, freedom, creativity, decision—our concern here is only its epistemology, namely a subject-centered approach to knowledge. Here the basic antithesis is between *personal subjectivity* and *impersonal objectivity*.

The Jewish philosopher Martin Buber has given a widely quoted account (in *I and Thou*, 1937) of the difference between the way a person is related to an object and the way he is related to another person. The first, which Buber calls *I-It*, is the detached analysis and manipulative control of impersonal things. *I-Thou* relationships, by contrast, are characterized by total involvement and participation of the whole self, directness and immediacy of apprehension, and concern for the other person as an end in himself. Such encounter occurs in the reciprocal interaction and openness of true dialogue, and in the awareness, sensitivity, and availability of genuine love. The I-Thou encounter can be entered into, but it cannot be reduced to concepts from the world of "It," the realm of space and time and causality. For Buber, man's confrontation with God always has the immediacy and involvement of an I-Thou relationship, whereas scientific inquiry occurs in the domain of the I-It.

Rudolph Bultmann has developed a distinctive and influential form of *Christian existentialism*. One of his central theses is that the Bible erroneously speaks of God's activity as though it could be described in the language of space and time. Any such "objective" terminology, used to represent the divine which transcends space and time, Bultmann calls *"mythical."* Today, he insists, we know from science that spatiotemporal events are governed by rigorous causal laws, and we know from theological reflection that the transcendent God and his acts cannot be "objectified" as if they were on the same plane as natural occurrences. But instead of dismissing mythical language as simply false (as nineteenth-century liberalism did), Bultmann wants to preserve what he takes to be its original existential meaning in human experience, translating it into the language of man's self-understanding, his hopes and fears, decisions and actions. The key question is always: what does the mythical imagery say about *my personal existence* and about *my relationship to God*? The Christian message always refers to new possibilities for my life—decision, rebirth, the realization of my true being—and not to observable occurrences in the external world apart from my involvement. For example, he holds that the Resurrection was not a physical event of the sort that might have been photographed, but rather an occurrence in the experience of the early church, the return of faith in Christ—which is repeated in the life of the believer today when the salvation-event transforms his own existence. Similarly, the doctrine of creation is not a statement about cosmological origins, but a confession that I am totally dependent on God. Thus the Christian message refers not to objective happenings in the world, but to *the new understanding of ourselves* that is given by God amid the anxieties and hopes of our personal life histories. Theology, dealing with the realms of selfhood and transcendence, has no points of contact with science, which investigates impersonal objects in the external world without the personal involvement of the subject.

3. The Variety of Uses of Language (Linguistic Analysis)

In addition to the neo-orthodox emphasis on revelation, and the existentialist insistence on personal involvement, a third development in twentieth-century thought has contributed to the sharp differentiation of science from religion: the rise of linguistic analysis, which is today the dominant viewpoint among British and American philosophers. We must start by describing its precursor, the *logical positivist* movement of the 1930's. Logical positivism was in part a revival of *the empiricist tradition*. It returned to [the] argument [of David Hume (1711-1776)] that all one can know of reality are fleeting fragments of separate sense-data. We recall Hume's contention that what we call causality is simply a habit of associating certain items of sense-data because of their past conjunction. According to the positivist, a scientific theory is not a representation of the world, but a shorthand calculational device for summarizing sense-data; it provides for economy of thought in organizing observations and making predictions. . . .

Another influence in the formation of logical positivism was *the revolution in physics* in the early twentieth century. In relativity theory, the length of an object and the time between two events are not absolute properties of objects in themselves; they are the results of particular measuring processes and vary according to the frame of reference of the observer. Length and time are not attributes of things in the world, but relationships defined by specifying experimental procedures. The positivists concluded that the scientist should use only concepts for which he can give "operational definitions" in terms of observations. Moreover, in quantum physics an electron does not have position and velocity; its wave function is an abstract symbolism from which certain correlations among observable quantities can be derived. These somewhat technical developments, which need not detain us now, cast doubt on the commonsense "realist" view that a scientific theory is a picture or replica of the real world as it exists apart from the observer, and gave some support to the view that a theory is simply a scheme for correlating experimental data.

A third aspect of logical positivism was the new interest in *the logical structure of language*. In the writings of the "Vienna Circle" in the 1930's, and in A. J. Ayer's popularization (*Language, Truth, and Logic,* 1936), the logic of scientific discourse was taken as the norm, for all propositions. In the notorious *"verification principle"* it was asserted that only empirical statements verifiable by sense-experience have meaning (formal definitions or tautologies are also meaning-ful but convey no factual information). Most traditional sentences in philosophy, and all those in metaphysics, ethics, and theology, were said to be neither true nor false, but meaningless (that is, "vacuous pseudostatements" devoid of any literal significance); hav-ing no factual content, they state nothing and merely express the speaker's emotions or feelings. Logical positivism held that the task of the philosopher is not to assert anything about the world (which only the scientist can do) but to clarify the language and the con-cepts used in the various sciences.

The difficulties in the logical positivist position and its develop-ment into *linguistic analysis*. . . . will not be recounted here. Suffice it to say that where the logical positivists saw sentences as doing only one legitimate job (reporting empirical facts), the linguistic analysts are impressed by the variety of functions which language serves. The viewpoint now prevalent in British philosophy is indicated by the slogan: "Don't ask about the meaning of a statement; ask about its use." What are people doing in using it? Since various types of sentences reflect differing interests—artistic, moral, scientific, re-ligious, and so forth—each area of discourse must use the categories and the logic it finds most appropriate for its purposes. In the case of science, analysts often adopt an "instrumental" view in which theories are said to be "useful" rather than true; the main function of scientific language is said to be prediction and control.

A variety of *functions of religious language* have been delineated. The broadest function is the provision of a total life orientation in terms of an object of ultimate concern and devotion. Some authors emphasize the ethical aspects and take religious language to be a recommendation of a way of life and an acknowledgment of al-legiance to a set of moral principles. Again, religious statements are said to propose a distinctive self-understanding, engendering characteristic attitudes toward human existence. Other statements serve primarily to express and evoke commitment and worship; religious language, it is urged, must always be examined in the con-text of its use, that is, in the worshiping community. These func-tions, which are very different from those served by scientific lan-guage, were excluded from meaningful discourse by the logical positivists but are now topics extensively discussed by philosophers.

Linguistic analysts agree with logical positivists, however, in in-sisting that scientific language itself has a limited and essentially technical function which is always closely tied to its own distinctive type of observations. We will call this a *"positivistic" view of science,* the view that scientific inquiry does not yield any metaphysical generalizations about the nature of reality. . . .

It is not uncommon today for *neo-orthodox* or *existentialist theology* to be combined with *a positivistic view of science.* In such a combina-tion, the separation of the spheres of science and religion is en-forced from both sides. The metaphysical disclaimers of many scientists and philosophers today are welcomed by these men, for they help to "clear the field" for religion by undermining rival naturalistic faiths which once claimed the support of science. Neo-orthodox writers even welcome positivistic attacks on natural theology. Moreover, if science leads only to technical knowledge of regularities in phenomena, and if in addition philosophy is confined to the analysis of language, then religious faith is outside the scope of possible scientific or philosophical attack. The independence of the two fields is guaranteed from both sides if each is restricted to its own domain. Such total isolation of science and religion represents the dominant attitude in recent decades, but [there are] a number of reasons for calling it into question. [These are discussed in Part II of Barbour's book.—ED.]

II. THE PARALLELS OF THEOLOGY AND SCIENCE

The authors in the first group—advocates of neo-orthodoxy, existentalism, and linguistic analysis—conceive of theology as contrasting strongly with science. They interpret science positivistically as an undertaking that yields useful technical knowledge but not wider philosophical or theological conclusions. They view theology, on the other hand, as an autonomous enterprise with its own starting point in revelation, its own relevance for human existence, and its own distinctive use of language. The group we now consider finds *methodological parallels* between the two fields; the word "parallel" is taken to imply considerable independence of content with significant similarities in structure. These authors do not attempt (as do those in the third group below) to derive theological conclusions directly from scientific discoveries. But they do find points of comparison among methods of inquiry, and they hold that many of the rational and empirical attitudes of the scientist can be shared by the theologian. These men try to see both science and religion within a unified view of the world. *Liberal theology* is interested in attitudes of inquiry; it claims that a man's religious beliefs should be a reasonable interpretation of all areas of human experience, employing critical reflection not unlike that which the scientist applies in his work. *Process philosophy* elaborates a metaphysical system applicable to all aspects of reality including God and events in the world. These thinkers are usually critical of the positivistic view of science, and their writings show at least limited interaction between scientific and theological ideas.

1. Similar Attitudes in Science and Religion (Liberal Theology)

We traced the rise of *liberal theology* in the nineteenth century in [Friedrich] Schleiermacher's [1768–1834] view of theology as the interpretation of religious experience and in the concentration on moral experience among the followers of [Immanuel] Kant [1724–1804]. The movement continued in the twentieth century and assumed a wide variety of forms. . . . Common themes of liberal theology have been its stress on the immanence rather than the transcendence of God, the example of Christ's life rather than the effects of his atoning death, and the possibilities of man's moral improvement rather than his sinfulness. In each of the pairs of terms between which neo-orthodoxy emphasizes discontinuity, liberalism finds *continuity:* continuity between revelation and reason, between faith and human experience, between God and the world, between Christ and other men, between Christianity and other religions. There are no radical gaps here—there are differences in degree, but not in kind.

According to most liberals, *attitudes similar to those of the scientist are appropriate in religious inquiry.* Theology, it is said, should be broadly empirical and rational; it should provide a consistent and comprehensive world-view based on the critical interpretation of all human experience. Religious beliefs are pragmatically vindicated by their consequences in human life and their ability to fill man's deepest needs. The spirit of openness and tentativeness which the scientist exemplifies should be adopted by the theologian too; religious and moral experience are among the most significant evidence to be considered. Liberals do not usually eliminate the concept of revelation, but they reinterpret it in two ways. First, they tend to minimize the uniqueness of biblical revelation. God reveals himself through many channels: through the structures of the created order, through man's moral conscience, and through the various religious traditions of the world—and preeminently, but by no means exclusively, in Christ. Second, it is asserted that revelation must always be received and interpreted by men and is distorted by limited human comprehension. Thus liberals talk about man's discovery of God, as well as God's initiative toward man. The Bible is viewed as the record of a people's progressive search for God and response to him.

Charles Raven [1885–1964] has expressed many of the characteristic themes of liberalism. He advocates *a broadly empirical attitude toward religious experience.* Concerning methods of inquiry, he writes that "the main process is the same whether we are investigating the structure of an atom or a problem in animal evolution, a period of history or the religious experience of a saint." The primary data of theology are "the lives and experience of the saints through whom God most fully reveals himself to us." Man responds to the infinite in awe and penitence, but he must then interpret this encounter rationally. The resulting religious beliefs can be tested pragmatically by their fruits, especially in creative human relations of love and service. Raven shares the liberal's distrust of all dichotomies, including the sharp division of the natural from the supernatural. Our account of things must "tell a single tale which shall treat the whole universe as one and indivisible."

To take another example, the Oxford physicist, C. A. Coulson [b. 1910], holds that *the methods of science and religion have much in common*. The scientist's experience as a human being goes beyond his laboratory data and may include a sense of reverence and humility, an awareness of beauty and order, and a reflective contemplation of the world. . . .

In addition to the assertion that enlightened religion uses methods basically similar to those in science, it is claimed that, conversely, *science involves presuppositions and moral commitments* not unlike those in religion. The gulf between science and religion is here narrowed, as it were, from both sides. Thus Coulson argues that science has presuppositions—for example, that the world is lawful and intelligible; the scientist has an unprovable faith in the orderliness of the universe. Moreover the moral attitudes required by science are similar to the religious virtues: humility, cooperation, universality, and integrity. In contrast to the positivist view, prominence is given to the role of human factors in science, such as the scientist's personal judgment, commitment to truth, and participation in a community of inquiry. This interpretation presents many features of science that resemble those of religion, and vice versa.

2. An Inclusive Metaphysical System (Process Philosophy)

An impressive attempt to include science and religion within a unified view of reality is the "process philosophy" of Alfred North Whitehead [1861–1947], which perhaps represents the only new systematic metaphysics developed in the twentieth century. Whitehead made important contributions to mathematics and philosophy of science before he turned (in *Process and Reality*, 1929) to the construction of "a system of ideas which bring aesthetic, moral and religious interests into relation with those concepts of the world which have their origin in natural science." Whitehead defines *metaphysics* as the study of the most general characteristics of events. By imaginative generalization from immediate experience, he seeks the development of an inclusive conceptual scheme whose categories will be sufficiently universal to be exemplified by all entities in the world, a set of ideas in terms of which every element in experience can be interpreted. Metaphysics must be *coherent,* Whitehead maintains; that is, its concepts not only should be logically consistent but should be part of a unified system of interrelated ideas that presuppose each other. But it also should have empirical relevance, for it must be *applicable to experience;* one should be able to interpret all types of events in terms of its fundamental ideas. Whitehead recognizes that the discrimination of elements in experience is itself influenced by one's interpretive categories, which provide a new way of looking at the world. Nevertheless he holds that the justification of any system of thought lies in its ability to organize and elucidate immediate experience.

Among the data that metaphysics must consider, Whitehead suggests, are both religious and scientific experience. He maintains (in *Religion in the Making*, 1926) that *religion* "contributes its own independent evidence, which metaphysics must take account of in framing its description."

Religion claims that its concepts, though derived primarily from special experiences, are yet of universal validity, to be applied by faith to the ordering of all experience. Rational religion appeals to the direct intuition of special occasions, and to the elucidatory power of its concepts for all occasions. . . . The dogmas of religion are the attempts to formulate in precise terms the truths disclosed in the religious experience of mankind. In exactly the same way the dogmas of physical science are the attempts to formulate in precise terms the truths disclosed in the sense perception of mankind.

However, in his systematic writing Whitehead's concept of God is derived less from consideration of religious experience than from the requirements of his total system; God is primarily understood as the ground of order and novelty in the world. . . .

The *science* of the twentieth century, with which Whitehead was thoroughly familiar, had considerable influence on his thinking; he was not, of course, attempting to invent a new scientific theory, but to suggest ways in which our most general concepts about the nature of reality should take the new science into account. Let us summarize some of *the basic ideas of process philosophy:*

1. *The primacy of time.* The world is a process of becoming, a flux of events. Transition and activity are more fundamental than permanence and substance. . . .

2. *The interfusion of events.* The world is a web of interconnected events, a network of mutual influences. Events are interdependent; every event has essential reference to other times and places. An entity is actually constituted by its relationships (for example, a person is who he is precisely in his various interpersonal roles). . . .

3. *Reality as organic process.* The word "process" implies temporal change and interconnected activity. Whitehead also calls his metaphysics "the philosophy of organism"; the basic analogy for interpreting the world is not a machine but an organism, which is a highly integrated and dynamic pattern of interdependent events. The parts contribute to and are also modified by the unified activity of the whole. . . .

4. *The self-creation of each event.* Although Whitehead emphasizes the interdependence of events he does not end with a monism in which the parts are swallowed up in the whole. An event is not just the intersection of lines of interaction; it is an entity in its own right with its own individuality. He maintains a genuine pluralism in which every event is a unique synthesis of the influences on it, a new unity formed from an initial diversity. . . . Whitehead wants us to look at the world from the viewpoint of the entity itself, imagining it as an experiencing subject. Reality thus consists of an interacting plurality of individual acts of experience.

These four ideas indicate merely the general character of process philosophy. Their usefulness can be judged only as the system is further developed and applied to the interpretation of particular areas of experience. . . . For our immediate purposes what is important is the method used, namely, the development of an inclusive metaphysical system that is held to be relevant tó both science and religion. It differs from the metaphysics of atomistic materialism in the eighteenth century and evolutionary naturalism in the nineteenth, both in its more complex and dynamic view of nature and in its attempt to do justice to a wide range of human experience—aesthetic, moral, and religious; Whitehead recognizes the abstractive, partial, and symbolic character of scientific concepts.

III. DERIVATIONS OF THEOLOGY FROM SCIENCE

The group of authors we first considered (Section I) holds that the methods of science and theology are radically different, and that scientific discoveries have no theological implications. The second group finds parallels in the methods of the two fields; liberal theology encourages in religious inquiry attitudes similar to those in scientific inquiry, and process philosophy seeks metaphysical categories applicable to all aspects of reality including God and nature. A third group draws theological conclusions more directly from science, claiming that the existence of God can be inferred either from general features of nature, such as design and order, or from specific findings, such as the directedness of evolution, the increase of entropy [= increase of unavailable energy in the universe], or the mathematical character of modern physics. These are the modern exponents of the tradition we have traced through the centuries as "natural theology" (defined as a theology derived from nature). . . .

1. Arguments from Design and Order

These very general characteristics of nature do not refer to any particular findings of science. They are often invoked in liberal theology and play an important part in process philosophy, and thus could have been included in the previous section. We list them separately only because they are frequently presented as independent arguments, usually with explicit reference to scientific findings. The older form of teleology, based on the "design" of particular organs (the eye, for instance), was of course undermined by Darwin. The *reformulated teleological argument,* however, finds evidence of design built into the structure of a world in which evolution can occur, in the total system of laws and conditions whereby life and intelligence and personality were brought forth, and in the interconnectedness, coordination and harmonization of different levels of existence. Such reasoning yields no irrefutable proof of a

Designer, but it is claimed that there is considerable evidence for which theism is the most plausible assumption.

Among the features cited are the congruence between the human mind and the rational structure of the world, the ubiquity of beauty, and the fitness of the world to produce and sustain moral personality (for example, the presence of both stability and plasticity in the environment). Even at the chemical level, life depends on the intricate dovetailing of many complex properties, and higher levels require the cooperative interaction of many apparently independent features. Again, the presence of conditions for the realization of such human values as love, friendship, and justice seem to point to dimensions of reality beyond chemical and biological laws. A number of scientists see orderliness, in one or another of these forms, as evidence for the existence of an intelligent Designer.

2. Arguments from Physics and Biology

A number of more specific scientific discoveries have been interpreted as evidence for theism. These are not usually "gaps" within the scientific account of the sort exploited for theological purposes in previous centuries; but they are claimed to represent limits to scientific explanation, or clues to the nature of reality, to which science itself witnesses. . . .

1. Astronomical evidence for *the "instantaneous creation" theory,* or physical evidence for *the Second Law of Thermodynamics* (increasing entropy), is said to indicate a finite timespan for the universe, and thus to support the idea of God as Creator.

2. *The Heisenberg Uncertainty Principle,* understood as evidence of indeterminancy at the atomic level, is said to provide a scientific basis for the defense of the idea of human freedom.

3. *The abstract, mathematical character of twentiety-century physics,* in which atoms are the wave patterns of differential equations rather than billiard-ball particles, is taken to support philosophical idealism, the thesis that reality is basically mental.

4. *The directional advance of evolution* is taken as evidence of a creative force in nature, a guidance toward higher forms. In arguments of this kind particular scientific findings are taken to have important theological implications. . . .

Reading Questions

1. What were the theological views of nineteenth-century liberalism?
2. What are the main tenets of neo-orthodoxy, religious existentialism, logical positivism, linguistic analysis, liberal theology, and process philosophy?

3. What are some of the views of those who propose a modern natural theology based on scientific findings?

Questions for Reflection and Research

1. Barbour has, for various reasons, omitted consideration of other major twentieth-century religious responses to science—most notably those of the Catholic church (Thomism), of Eastern religions, and of fundamentalists. What have their responses been?
2. How would Barbour classify Einstein's views? (See selection #5.)
3. Read views of scientists who profess religious beliefs. How do they defend their beliefs? How would Barbour classify each of them?
4. What (if anything) is wrong with the positivists' verification principle?
5. What is Barbour's considered evaluation of the various views he describes? (See Barbour's book.)

Freud Explains Religion Away

The Author: Sigmund Freud (1856–1939) studied medicine at the University of Vienna. He was also a brilliant student of classics, English, and French. His earliest scientific studies involved the nervous system but he gradually became interested in nonneurological methods of treating mental disorders. He became the founder of psychoanalysis. Later in his life he attempted to apply the pyschoanalytic approach to the study of various aspects of culture.

The Selection: Freud in this excerpt written in 1927 declares that religion is an illusion and seeks to explain its prevalence as a matter of wish-fulfillment.

We must ask where the inner force of religious doctrines lies and to what it is that they owe their efficacy. . . .

I think we have prepared the way sufficiently for an answer to both these questions. It will be found if we turn our attention to the psychical origin of religious ideas. These, which are given out as teachings, are not precipitates of experience or end-results of thinking: they are illusions, fulfilments of the oldest, strongest and most urgent wishes of mankind. The secret of their strength lies in the strength of those wishes. As we already know, the terrifying impression of helplessness in childhood aroused the need for protection—for protection through love—which was provided by the father; and the recognition that this helplessness lasts through-

From Sigmund Freud, *The Future of an Illusion,* translated by James Strachey (New York: W. W. Norton & Company, Inc., 1961), pp. 29–33. Also in volume XXI of *The Standard Edition of the Complete Psychological Works of Sigmund Freud,* pp. 29–30, translated and edited by James Strachey. Reprinted by permission of W. W. Norton & Company, Inc., and Hogarth Press Ltd.

out life made it necessary to cling to the existence of a father, but this time a more powerful one. Thus the benevolent rule of a divine Providence allays our fear of the dangers of life; the establishment of a moral world-order ensures the fulfilment of the demands of justice, which have so often remained unfulfilled in human civilization; and the prolongation of earthly existence in a future life provides the local and temporal framework in which these wish-fulfilments shall take place. Answers to the riddles that tempt the curiosity of man, such as how the universe began or what the relation is between body and mind, are developed in conformity with the underlying assumptions of this system. . . .

When I say that these things are all illusions, I must define the meaning of the word. An illusion is not the same thing as an error; nor is it necessarily an error. Aristotle's belief that vermin are developed out of dung (a belief to which ignorant people still cling) was an error; so was the belief of a former generation of doctors that *tabes dorsalis* [= a disorder of the nervous system caused by syphilis] is the result of sexual excess. It would be incorrect to call these errors illusions. On the other hand, it was an illusion of Columbus's that he had discovered a new sea-route to the Indies. The part played by his wish in this error is very clear. One may describe as an illusion the assertion made by certain nationalists that the Indo-Germanic race is the only one capable of civilization; or the belief, which was only destroyed by psycho-analysis, that children are creatures without sexuality. What is characteristic of illusions is that they are derived from human wishes. In this respect they come near to psychiatric delusions. But they differ from them, too, apart from the more complicated structure of delusions. In the case of delusions, we emphasize as essential their being in contradiction with reality. Illusions need not necessarily be false—that is to say, unrealizable or in contradiction to reality. For instance, a middle-class girl may have the illusion that a prince will come and marry her. This is possible; and a few such cases have occurred. That the Messiah will come and found a golden age is much less likely. . . .

Having thus taken our bearings, let us return once more to the question of religious doctrines. We can now repeat that all of them are illusions and insusceptible of proof. No one can be compelled to think them true, to believe in them. Some of them are so improbable, so incompatible with everything we have laboriously discovered about the reality of the world, that we may compare them—if we pay proper regard to the psychological differences—to delusions. Of the reality value of most of them we cannot judge; just as they cannot be proved, so they cannot be refuted. We still know too little to make a critical approach to them. The riddles of the universe reveal themselves only slowly to our investigation; there are many questions to which science to-day can give no answer. But scientific work is the only road which can lead us to a knowledge of reality outside ourselves. . . .

At this point one must expect to meet with an objection. 'Well then, if even obdurate sceptics admit that the assertions of religion cannot be refuted by reason, why should I not believe in them, since they have so much on their side—tradition, the agreement of mankind, and all the consolations they offer?' Why not, indeed? Just as no one can be forced to believe, so no one can be forced to disbelieve. But do not let us be satisfied with deceiving ourselves that arguments like these take us along the road of correct thinking. If ever there was a case of a lame excuse we have it here. Ignorance is ignorance; no right to believe anything can be derived from it. In other matters no sensible person will behave so irresponsibly or rest content with such feeble grounds for his opinions and for the line he takes. It is only in the highest and most sacred things that he allows himself to do so. . . . Where questions of religion are concerned, people are guilty of every possible sort of dishonesty and intellectual misdemeanour. Philosophers stretch the meaning of words until they retain scarcely anything of their original sense. They give the name of 'God' to some vague abstraction which they have created for themselves; having done so they can pose before all the world as deists, as believers in God, and they can even boast that they have recognized a higher, purer concept of God, notwithstanding that their God is now nothing more than an insubstantial shadow and no longer the mighty personality of religious doctrines. Critics persist in describing as 'deeply religious' anyone who admits to a sense of man's insignificance or impotence in the face of the universe, although what constitutes the essence of the religious attitude is not this feeling but only the next step after it, the reaction to it which seeks a remedy for it. The man who goes no further, but humbly acquiesces in the small part which human beings play in the great world—such a man is, on the contrary, irreligious in the truest sense of the world.

To assess the truth-value of religious doctrines does not lie within the scope of the present enquiry. It is enough for us that we have recognized them as being, in their psychological nature, illusions. . . .

Reading Questions

1. Why are religious convictions so strong?
2. What does Freud mean by the word *illusion*?
3. What does science show about the truth of religious claims?
4. What beliefs do deists hold?

Questions for Reflection and Research

1. What are Freud's complete views in *The Future of an Illusion*?
2. How do present-day religious thinkers reply to Freud?
3. How true are Freud's claims about philosophers' conceptions of God?
4. Would Freud retract his claims if one could prove to him that God and life after death exist?
5. Can Freud's views about religion be tested scientifically?
6. Was Freud a scientist?

Anthropology and Religion

The Author: Henry L. Mencken (1880–1956) was an American newspaper reporter, editorial writer, literary critic, dictionary maker, and admirer of the philosopher Nietzsche. He was a controversial critic of American life and ideas.

The Selection: Mencken points to the findings of anthropology and comparative religion that humans have worshipped a great variety of gods, many of which are no longer worshipped. He suggests that these facts cast doubt on the existence of any gods.

Where is the grave-yard of dead gods? What lingering mourner waters their mounds? There was a day when Jupiter was the king of the gods, and any man who doubted his puissance [=power] was *ipso facto* [= by that fact alone] a barbarian and an ignoramus. But where in all the world is there a man who worships Jupiter to-day? And what of Huitzilopochtli? In one year—and it is no more than five hundred years ago—50,000 youths and maidens were slain in sacrifice to him. To-day, if he is remembered at all, it is only by some vagrant savage in the depths of the Mexican forest. Huitzilopochtli, like many other gods, had no human father; his mother was a virtuous widow; he was born of an apparently innocent flirtation that she carried on with the sun. When he frowned, his father, the sun, stood still. When he roared with rage, earthquakes en-

The Selection was originally entitled "Memorial Service" and is from *Prejudices: Third Series*, by H. L. Mencken. Copyright 1922 and renewed 1950 by H. L. Mencken. Reprinted by permission of Alfred A. Knopf, Inc.

gulfed whole cities. When he thirsted he was watered with 10,000 gallons of human blood. But to-day [in 1921] Huitzilopochtli is as magnificently forgotten as Allen G. Thurman. [Allen G. Thurman and the names of people mentioned in the next sentence refer to nineteenth- and early twentieth-century figures well known in their time.—ED.] Once the peer of Allah, Buddha and Wotan, he is now the peer of General Coxey, Richmond P. Hobson, Nan Petterson, Alton B. Parker, Adelina Patti, General Weyler and Tom Sharkey.

Speaking of Huitzilopochtli recalls his brother, Tezcatilpoca. Tezcatilpoca was almost as powerful: he consumed 25,000 virgins a year. Lead me to his tomb: I would weep, and hang a *couronne des perles* [= crown of pearls]. But who knows where it is? Or where the grave of Quitzalcoatl is? Or Tialoc? Or Chalchihuitlicue? Or Xiehtecutli? Or Centeotl, that sweet one? Or Tlazolteotl, the goddess of love? Or Mictlan? Or Ixtlilton? Or Omacatl? Or Yacatecutli? Or Mixcoatl? Or Xipe? Or all the host of Tzitzimitles? Where are their bones? Where is the willow on which they hung their harps? In what forlorn and unheard of hell do they await the resurrection morn? Who enjoys their residuary estates? Or that of Dis, whom Caesar found to be the chief god of the Celts? Or that of Tarves, the bull? Or that of Moccos, the pig? Or that of Epona, the mare? Or that of Mullo, the celestial jack-ass? There was a time when the Irish revered all these gods as violently as they now hate the English. But to-day even the drunkest Irishman laughs at them.

But they have company in oblivion: the hell of dead gods is as crowded as the Presbyterian hell for babies. Damona is there, and Esus, and Drunemeton, and Silvana, and Dervones, and Adsalluta, and Deva, and Belisama, and Axona, and Vintios, and Taranuous, and Sulis, and Cocidius, and Adsmerius, and Dumiatis, and Caletos, and Moccus, and Ollovidius, and Albiorix, and Leucitius, and Vitucadrus, and Ogmios, and Uxellimus, and Borvo, and Grannos, and Mogons. All mighty gods in their day, worshiped by millions, full of demands and impositions, able to bind and loose—all gods of the first class, not dilettanti [= not amateurs]. Men labored for generations to build vast temples to them— temples with stones as large as hay-wagons. The business of interpreting their whims occupied thousands of priests, wizards, archdeacons, evangelists, haruspices [= a special class of priests], bishops, archbishops. To doubt them was to die, usually at the stake. Armies took to the field to defend them against infidels: villages were burned, women and children were butchered, cattle were driven off. Yet in the end they all withered and died, and to-day there is none so poor to do them reverence. Worse, the very tombs in which they lie are lost, and so even a respectful stranger is debarred from paying them the slightest and politest homage.

What has become of Sutekh, once the high god of the whole Nile Valley? What has become of:

Resheph	Ahijah	Shalem
Anath	Isis	Dagon
Ashtoreth	Ptah	Sharrab
El	Anubis	Yau
Nergal	Baal	Amon-Re
Nebo	Astarte	Osiris
Ninib	Hadad	Sebek
Melek	Addu	Molech?

All these were once gods of the highest eminence. Many of them are mentioned with fear and trembling in the Old Testament. They ranked, five or six thousand years ago, with Jahveh himself; the worst of them stood far higher than Thor. Yet they have all gone down the chute, and with them the following:

Bilé	Tammuz	Jupiter
Lêr	Venus	Cunina
Arianrod	Bau	Potina
Morrigu	Mulu-hursang	Statilinus
Govannon	Anu	Diana of Ephesus
Gunfled	Beltis	Robigus
Sokk-mimi	Nusku	Pluto
Memetona	Ni-zu	Ops
Dagda	Sahi	Meditrina
Kerridwen	Aa	Vesta
Pwyll	Allatu	Tilmun
Ogyrvan	Sin	Zer-panitu
Dea Dia	AbilAddu	Merodach
Ceros	Apsu	U-ki
Vaticanus	Dagan	Dauke
Edulia	Elali	Gasan-abzu
Adeona	Isum	Elum
Iuno Lucina	Mami	U-Tin-dir ki
Saturn	Nin-man	Marduk
Furrina	Zaraqu	Nin-lil-la
Vediovis	Suqamunu	Nin
Consus	Zagaga	Persephone
Cronos	Gwydion	Istar
Enki	Manawyddan	Lagas
Engurra	Nuada Argetlam	U-urugal
Belus	Tagd	Sirtumu
Dimmer	Goibniu	Ea
Mu-ul-lil	Odin	Nirig
Ubargisi	Llaw Gyffes	Nebo
Ubilulu	Lleu	Samas
Gasan-lil	Ogma	Ma-banba-anna
U-dimmer-an-kia	Mider	En-Mersi
Enurestu	Rigantona	Amurru
U-sab-sib	Marzin	Assur
U-Mersi	Mars	Aku

Beltu	Kaawanu	Qarradu
Dumu-zi-abzu	Nin-azu	Ura-gala
Kuski-banda	Lugal-Amarada	Ueras

You may think I spoof. That I invent the names. I do not. Ask the rector to lend you any good treatise on comparative religion: you will find them all listed. They were gods of the highest standing and dignity—gods of civilized peoples—worshipped and believed in by millions. All were theoretically omnipotent [=all-powerful], omniscient [= all-knowing] and immortal. And all are dead.

Reading Questions

1. What is the reader supposed to conclude?
2. Make explicit the premises that Mencken thinks support his conclusion.

Questions for Reflection and Research

1. How might a Christian, a Jew, a Hindu, or a follower of any religion respond to Mencken's essay?
2. How would a member of the Baha'i faith respond to the essay?
3. Can science settle which religion (if any) is correct?
4. An equally long list of refuted scientific theories could be compiled. Would this show that there is no true scientific theory or that all theories are false?

Philosophy, Science, and Human Nature

Many questions about human nature are amenable to scientific study and can be answered in a definite way. For example, we can find out how well humans can survive on various diets, how they react to various drugs, how various cultures express anger or embarrassment, how old people have lived to be, and so forth. There are, however, other questions about human nature to which science contributes answers but that nevertheless resist a definitive settlement. Consider four examples:

(1) Are Humans Just Machines?

Are humans merely very complex machines? In recent decades science and technology have developed complex machines that are said to think. It would seem that with further advances in science, a device could be built that would look and move like a human—and perhaps would think like one. Selection #10 from the play *R.U.R.* raises questions about whether robots can think, or feel, or have rights, and (by implication) whether people are really nothing but sophisticated robots.

Often human-machine discussions turn on the issue of whether machines can really think. Are programmed operations thinking? This question, even though it arises as a consequence of scientific and technological progress, does not seem to be a scientific one. It requires reflection on our ideas about the nature of thought and not collection of experimental data.

(2) Can Human Beings Survive Death?

In the selection from *R.U.R.* one of the characters asserts that robots cannot be people because robots do not have souls. Historically souls have been talked of in religious contexts and have been regarded as things that will survive death and be judged in afterlife. But do human beings actually possess souls that survive death? This question provides a second example of a philosophical issue about human nature in which scientific findings are thought to have a bearing.

Can science determine whether souls exit? An Arizona miner, James Kidd, willed $230,000 for "some scientific proof of a soul of the human body which leaves at death." Reputable scientific institutions applied for the money. (See selection #12.)

The philosopher C. J. Ducasse in selection #13 discusses in some detail scientific findings that are thought to show there can be no life after death. He argues that the findings are not conclusive and then goes on to suggest that a new area of research (he is reluctant to call it a science), psychical research, does provide evidence of life after death.

(3) What Is the Mind?

Discussion of the existence of a soul that survives death are intimately connected with a third human-nature issue: the so-called body-mind problem. Actually the body-mind problem is a whole group of questions that have to do with the nature of mental activities and states.

As anatomists and physiologists in recent centuries have come to better understand the workings of the body and brain, the nature of such mental phenomena as thinking, dreaming, sensations, emotions, seeing, and believing have come under discussion. Selection #11 by Paul Edwards (and to some extent #13 by Ducasse) reviews some theories about the nature of mental phenomena. Each theory involves some reference to findings in science, and often objections to the theories also invoke scientific findings.

The theory most in harmony with the ideas of those who think there is a soul that survives death is one that views the soul (or "mind" or "consciousness"—words often used interchangeably in such discussions) as a nonphysical substance, witnessable only by its owner. On this view one's thoughts are nonphysical and known only to oneself unless one chooses to communicate them. One difficulty with this view is claimed to be that it violates conservation-of-energy laws by allowing nonphysical events (such as thoughts) to cause physical events (such as writing a letter). Other philosophers and scientists have advocated a view that is claimed to be more in harmony with science. According to this view mental events should be regarded as changes in the brain. This view is especially approved of by its partisans because it requires no mysterious nonphysical substances to explain human conduct. There are objections to this theory, however—and even more complex theories are offered to escape the objections. It will be seen that the body-mind issue is a particularly complex and frustrating one.

(4) Are Humans Free?

A fourth and related issue involving human nature is that of human freedom. To what extent is our conduct beyond our control?

It has been contended that science by its nature regards what it studies as produced by external causes. If this is true, then the various sciences studying humans must be attempting to show that outside factors produce and control our conduct. Human beings are studied and theorized about in such scientific fields as anthropology, biology, economics, history, political science, psychology, sociology, and linguistics. Included in this section are selections focusing on some of these fields (selections #14, #15, and #16).

In selection #14 the views of E. O. Wilson (a sociobiologist) and Robert Ardrey (a popularizer of paleoanthropology) are discussed. Both thinkers contend that some human behavior patterns are based on hereditary factors. Selection #15 by B. F. Skinner (a psychologist) advocates behaviorism, the view that our conduct is determined by training or conditioning supplied by the environment. In selection #16 a movement in theoretical linguistics (called transformational grammar) is described. Its founder, Noam Chomsky, asserts that it shows humans' linguistic behavior is at least partly based on heredity.

The implications of these findings in these various sciences have all been disputed, sometimes bitterly. All of these theories and findings seem to support the idea that our conduct is not as free as we like to think—that we are to some considerable extent victims of our heredity and environment. (Chomsky denies, however, that transformational grammar has such implications.)

Selection #17 by Arthur J. Minton reviews three classical philosophical theories about human freedom. The theories are all to some extent responses to conceptions of human nature emerging from the sciences. Minton brings out the fact that the issue of the extent of human freedom is one with important consequences. If people's aggressiveness, for instance, is hereditary, then no punishment can eliminate it. Furthermore, if what we do is not controlled by us, praise and blame for our conduct are not justified. Thus answers to the question of whether we are free can affect our ideas about moral, judicial, and educational policies.

In conclusion, it should be evident that these four topics about human nature are complexly interrelated and interwoven with science. Scientific findings in each case have precipitated fuller discussion of the issues. The issues, however, are not purely empirical. They require reflection on what we mean by some of the concepts employed in stating them. Further they often require that one try to reconcile conflicting conclusions arising from different scientific fields.

The selections by Edwards, Ducasse, and Minton (#11, #13, and #17, respectively) are attempts to briefly summarize some of the main philosophical reasoning that has evolved in discussion of the issues. The other selections in this section are intended to encourage the reader to develop his own ideas before reading the summaries.

Each of the four issues has been widely discussed in philosophy, and one can considerably enhance one's understanding of them by referring to some of the following sources.

Further Reading: Philosophy, Science, and Human Nature

1. *The Encyclopedia of Philosophy,* ed. PAUL EDWARDS, 8 vols. (New York: Macmillan Publishing Co., 1967). For a discussion of humans and machines see the entry "Cybernetics" by KEITH GUNDERSON. The entry "Mind-Body Problem" by JEROME SHAFFER explains in more detail than selection #11 the various body-mind theories. For a more complete overview of issues of human freedom see the entry "Determinism" by RICHARD TAYLOR, especially the sections entitled "Physical Determinism" and "Psychological Determinism."

2. *Mentality and Machines* by KEITH GUNDERSON (Garden City, N.Y.: Doubleday and Co., 1971). This is a short but complexly developed discussion of many issues connected with human and machine nature.

3. *A Critical Examination of the Belief in a Life after Death* by C. J. DUCASSE (Springfield, Ill.: Charles C Thomas, 1961). This book by the author of selection #13 contains a detailed discussion of many aspects of the subject of life after death.

4. *Parapsychology: Sources of Information* by RHEA A. WHITE and LAURA A. DALE (Metuchen, N.J.: Scarecrow Press, 1973). A guide to sympathetic and critical writings on psychic research including research on phenomena related to life after death.

5. *A Modern Introduction to Philosophy,* revised ed., PAUL EDWARDS and ARTHUR PAP, eds. (New York: Free Press, 1965). This book has a good annotated bibliography on body-mind topics and on life after death. See pp. 266-78.

6. *The Human Conspiracy* by NIGEL CALDER (New York: Viking Press, 1976). A helpful overview of human nature studies focusing on nature-nurture controversies including the one generated by sociobiology.

7. To follow up on philosophical implications of scientific findings about human nature such as those touched on in selections #14, #15, and #16 one must seek out book reviews and journal articles discussing the new theories. The periodicals *Scientific American, Science,* and *Psychology Today* are good places to begin searching.

Can Robots Be People?

The Author: Karel Čapek (1890–1938) was a Czech playwright, novelist, and essayist. He studied philosophy before he decided to devote himself to writing. His plays and novels often focus on the problems of machine-dominated society and are reminiscent of science fiction.

The Selection: The play *R.U.R.* derives its name from its main setting, Rossum's Universal Robots, a robot factory. Rossum is supposed to have invented the robot. (Incidentally, the English word *robot* came from this play.) The main concern of the play and of the excerpt given here is what, if anything, distinguishes human beings from creatures produced by science and technology—creatures that look and act like human beings.

ACT ONE

Central office of the factory of Rossum's Universal Robots. Entrance on the right. The windows on the front wall look out on the rows of factory chimneys. On the left more managing departments. Domin *is sitting in the revolving chair at a large American writing table. On the left-hand wall large maps showing steamship and railroad routes. On the right-hand wall are fastened printed placards. ("Robot's Cheapest Labor," etc.) In contrast to*

From *R.U.R. (Rossum's Universal Robots)* by Karel Capek, trans. Paul Selver, in *Chief Contemporary Dramatists: Third Series,* Thomas H. Dickinson ed. (Boston: Houghton Mifflin Co., 1930). Copyright, 1923, by Doubleday, Page and Company. Reprinted by permission of Samuel French, Inc. Copies of this play, in individual paper covered acting editions, are available from Samuel French, Inc., 25 W. 45th St., New York, N.Y. 10036 or 7623 Sunset Blvd., Hollywood, Calif. 90046 or in Canada Samuel French, (Canada) Ltd., 80 Richmond Street East, Toronto M5C 1P1, Canada.

these wall fittings, the floor is covered with a splendid Turkish carpet, a sofa, leather armchair, and filing cabinets. . . .

[*Enter* Helena Glory.]

HELENA. How do you do?
DOMIN. How do you do. [*Standing up.*] What can I do for you?
HELENA. You are Mr. Domin, the General Manager.
DOMIN. I am.
HELENA. I have come—
DOMIN. With President Glory's card. That is quite sufficient.
HELENA. President Glory is my father. I am Helena Glory.
DOMIN. Miss Glory, this is such a great honor for us to be allowed to welcome our great President's daughter. . . . First would you like to hear the story of the invention?
HELENA. Yes, indeed.
DOMIN [*observes* Helena *with rapture and reels off rapidly*]. It was in the year 1920 that old Rossum, the great physiologist, who was then quite a young scientist, took himself to this distant island for the purpose of studying the ocean fauna. . . . On this occasion he attempted by chemical synthesis to imitate the living matter known as protoplasm until he suddenly discovered a substance which behaved exactly like living matter although its chemical composition was different. That was in the year of 1932, exactly four hundred and forty years after the discovery of America. Whew!
HELENA. Do you know that by heart?
DOMIN. Yes. You see physiology is not my line. Shall I go on?
HELENA. Yes, please. . . .
DOMIN. First of all he tried making an artificial dog. That took him several years and resulted in a sort of stunted calf which died in a few days. I'll show it to you in the museum. And then old Rossum started on the manufacture of man. . . . Do you know anything about anatomy?
HELENA. Very little.
DOMIN. Neither do I. Well, he then decided to manufacture everything as in the human body. I'll show you in the museum the bungling attempt it took him ten years to produce. It was to have been a man, but it lived for three days only. Then up came young Rossum, an engineer. He was a wonderful fellow, Miss Glory. When he saw what a mess of it the old man was making, he said: "It's absurd to spend years making man. If you can't make him quicker than nature, you might as well shut up shop." Then he set about learning anatomy himself. . . . Anyone who has looked into human anatomy will have seen at once that man is too complicated, and that a good engineer could make him more simply. So young Rossum began to overhaul anatomy and tried to see what could be left out or simplified. In short—but this isn't boring you, Miss Glory?
HELENA. No indeed. You're—it's awfully interesting.
DOMIN. So young Rossum said to himself: "A man is something that feels happy, plays the piano, likes going for a walk, and in fact, wants to do a whole lot of things that are really unnecessary."

HELENA. Oh.

DOMIN. That are unnecessary when he wants, let us say, to weave or count. Do you play the piano?

HELENA. Yes.

DOMIN. That's good. But a working machine must not play the piano, must not feel happy, must not do a whole lot of other things. A gasoline motor must not have tassels or ornaments, Miss Glory. And to manufacture artificial workers is the same thing as to manufacture gasoline motors. The process must be of the simplest, and the product of the best from a practical point of view. What sort of worker do you think is the best from a practical point of view? . . .

HELENA. Perhaps the one who is the most honest and hard-working.

DOMIN. No; the one that is the cheapest. The one whose requirements are the smallest. Young Rossum invented a worker with the minimum amount of requirements. He had to simplify him. He rejected everything that did not contribute directly to the progress of work—everything that makes man more expensive. In fact, he rejected man and made the Robot. My dear Miss Glory, the Robots are not people. Mechanically they are more perfect than we are, they have an enormously developed intelligence, but they have no soul.

HELENA. How do you know they've no soul?

DOMIN. Have you ever seen what a Robot looks like inside?

HELENA. No.

DOMIN. Very neat, very simple. Really, a beautiful piece of work. Not much in it, but everything in flawless order. The product of an engineer is technically at a higher pitch of perfection than a product of nature.

HELENA. But man is supposed to be the product of God.

DOMIN. All the worse. God hasn't the least notion of modern engineering. . . .

HELENA. I saw the first Robots at home. The town counsel bought them for—I mean engaged them for work.

DOMIN. Bought them, dear Miss Glory. Robots are bought and sold.

HELENA. These were employed as street sweepers. I saw them sweeping. They were so strange and quiet.

DOMIN. Rossum's Universal Robot factory doesn't produce a uniform brand of Robots. We have Robots of finer and coarser grades. The best will live about twenty years. [He rings for Marius.]

HELENA. Then they die?

DOMIN. Yes, they get used up.

[Enter Marius.]

DOMIN. Marius, bring in samples of the Manual Labor Robot. [Exit Marius.]

DOMIN. I'll show you specimens of the two extremes. This first grade is comparatively inexpensive and is made in vast quantities.

[Marius reenters with two Manual Labor Robots.]

DOMIN. There you are; as powerful as a small tractor. Guaranteed to have average intelligence. That will do, Marius. [Marius exits with Robots.]

HELENA. They make me feel strange.

DOMIN [*rings*]. Did you see my typist? [*He rings for* Sulla.]

HELENA. I didn't notice her.   [*Enter* Sulla.]

DOMIN. Sulla, let Miss Glory see you.

HELENA. So pleased to meet you. You must find it terribly dull in this out-of-the-way spot, don't you?

SULLA. I don't know, Miss Glory.

HELENA. Where do you come from?

SULLA. From the factory.

HELENA. Oh, you were born there?

SULLA. I was made there.

HELENA. What?

DOMIN [*laughing*]. Sulla is a Robot, best grade.

HELENA. Oh, I beg your pardon.

DOMIN. Sulla isn't angry. See, Miss Glory, the kind of skin we make. [*Feels the skin on* Sulla's *face.*] Feel her face.

HELENA. Oh, no, no.

DOMIN. You wouldn't know that she's made of different material from us, would you? Turn around, Sulla.

HELENA. Oh, stop, stop.

DOMIN. Talk to Miss Glory, Sulla.

SULLA. Please sit down. [Helena *sits.*] Did you have a pleasant crossing?

HELENA. Oh, yes, certainly.

SULLA. Don't go back on the *Amelia,* Miss Glory. The barometer is falling steadily. Wait for the *Pennsylvania.* That's a good, powerful vessel.

DOMIN. What's its speed?

SULLA. Twenty knots. Fifty thousand tons. One of the latest vessels, Miss Glory.

HELENA. Thank you.

SULLA. A crew of fifteen hundred, Captain Harpy, eight boilers—

DOMIN. That'll do, Sulla. Now show us your knowledge of French.

HELENA. You know French?

SULLA. I know four languages. I can write: Dear Sir, Monsieur, Geehrter Herr, Cteny pane.

HELENA. [*jumping up*]. Oh, that's absurd! Sulla isn't a Robot. Sulla is a girl like me. Sulla, this is outrageous! Why do you take part in such a hoax?

SULLA. I am a Robot.

HELENA. No, no, you are not telling the truth. I know they've forced you to do it for an advertisement. Sulla, you are a girl like me, aren't you?

DOMIN. I'm sorry, Miss Glory. Sulla is a Robot.

HELENA. It's a lie!

DOMIN. What? [*Rings.*] Excuse me, Miss Glory, then I must convince you. [*Enter* Marius.]

DOMIN. Marius, take Sulla into the dissecting room, and tell them to open her up at once.

HELENA. Where?

DOMIN. Into the dissecting room. When they've cut her open, you can go and have a look.

HELENA. No, no!

DOMIN. Excuse me, you spoke of lies.

HELENA. You wouldn't have her killed?

DOMIN. You can't kill machines.

HELENA. Don't be afraid, Sulla, I won't let you go. Tell me, my dear, are they always so cruel to you? You mustn't put up with it, Sulla. You mustn't.

SULLA. I am a Robot.

HELENA. That doesn't matter. Robots are just as good as we are. Sulla, you wouldn't let yourself be cut to pieces?

SULLA. Yes.

HELENA. Oh, you're not afraid of death, then?

SULLA. I cannot tell, Miss Glory.

HELENA. Do you know what would happen to you in there?

SULLA. Yes, I should cease to move.

HELENA. How dreadful!

DOMIN. Marius, tell Miss Glory what you are.

MARIUS. Marius, the Robot.

DOMIN. Would you take Sulla into the dissecting room?

MARIUS. Yes.

DOMIN. Would you be sorry for her?

MARIUS. I cannot tell.

DOMIN. What would happen to her?

MARIUS. She would cease to move. They would put her into the stamping-mill.

DOMIN. That is death, Marius. Aren't you afraid of death?

MARIUS. No.

DOMIN. You see, Miss Glory, the Robots have no interest in life. They have no enjoyments. They are less than so much grass.

HELENA. Oh, stop. Send them away.

DOMIN. Marius, Sulla, you may go.

[*Exeunt* Sulla *and* Marius.]

HELENA. How terrible! It's outrageous what you are doing.

DOMIN. Why outrageous?

HELENA. I don't know, but it is. Why do you call her Sulla?

DOMIN. Isn't it a nice name?

HELENA. It's a man's name. Sulla was a Roman general.

DOMIN. Oh, we thought that Marius and Sulla were lovers.

HELENA. Marius and Sulla were generals and fought against each other in the year—I've forgotten now.

DOMIN. Come here to the window.

HELENA. What?

DOMIN. Come here. What do you see?

HELENA. Bricklayers.

DOMIN. Robots. All our work people are Robots. And down there, can you see anything?

HELENA. Some sort of office.

DOMIN. A counting house. And in it—

HELENA. A lot of officials.

DOMIN. Robots. All our officials are Robots. And when you see the factory— [*Factory whistle blows.*]

DOMIN. Noon. We have to blow the whistle because the Robots don't know when to stop work. In two hours I will show you the kneading trough.

HELENA. Kneading trough?

DOMIN. The pestle for beating up the paste. In each one we mix the ingredients for a thousand Robots at one operation. Then there are the vats for the preparation of liver, brains, and so on. Then you will see the bone factory. After that I'll show you the spinning-mill.

HELENA. Spinning-mill?

DOMIN. Yes. For weaving nerves and veins. Miles and miles of digestive tubes pass through it at a time.

HELENA. Mayn't we talk about something else?

DOMIN. Perhaps it would be better. There's only a handful of us among a hundred thousand Robots, and not one woman. We talk about nothing but the factory all day, every day. It's just as if we were under a curse, Miss Glory.

HELENA. I'm sorry I said that you were lying. [*A knock at the door.*]

DOMIN. Come in.

[*From the right enter* Mr. Fabry, Dr. Gall, Dr. Hallemeier, Mr. Alquist.]

DR. GALL. I beg your pardon, I hope we don't intrude.

DOMIN. Come in. Miss Glory, here are Alquist, Fabry, Gall, Hallemeier. This is President Glory's daughter.

HELENA. How do you do.

FABRY. We had no idea—

DR. GALL. Highly honored, I'm sure—

ALQUIST. Welcome, Miss Glory.

[Busman *rushes in from the right.*]

BUSMAN. Hello, what's up?

DOMIN. Come in, Busman. This is Busman, Miss Glory. This is President Glory's daughter.

BUSMAN. By jove, that's fine! . . .

HELENA. . . . I've come to disturb your Robots for you.

DOMIN. My dear Miss Glory, we've had close upon a hundred saviours and prophets here. Every ship brings us some. Missionaries, anarchists, Salvation Army, all sorts . . . .

HELENA. And you let them speak to the Robots?

DOMIN. So far we've let them all, why not? The Robots remember everything, but that's all. They don't even laugh at what the people say. Really, it is quite incredible. If it would amuse you, Miss Glory, I'll take you over to the Robot warehouse. It holds about three hundred thousand of them.

BUSMAN. Three hundred and forty-seven thousand.

DOMIN. Good! And you can say whatever you like to them. You can read the Bible, recite the multiplication table, whatever you please. You can even preach to them about human rights.

HELENA. Oh, I think that if you were to show them a little love—

FABRY. Impossible, Miss Glory. Nothing is harder to like than a Robot.

HELENA. What do you make them for, then?

BUSMAN. Ha, ha, ha, that's good! What are Robots made for?

FABRY. For work, Miss Glory! One Robot can replace two and a half workmen. The human machine, Miss Glory, was terribly imperfect. It had to be removed sooner or later.

BUSMAN. It was too expensive.

FABRY. It was not effective. It no longer answers the requirements of modern engineering. Nature has no idea of keeping pace with modern labor. For example: from a technical point of view, the whole of childhood is a sheer absurdity. So much time lost. And then again—

HELENA. Oh, no! No!

FABRY. Pardon me. But kindly tell me what is the real aim of your League—the . . . the Humanity League.

HELENA. Its real purpose is to—to protect the Robots—and—and ensure good treatment for them. . . . What we really want is to—to liberate the Robots.

HALLEMEIER. How do you propose to do that?

HELENA. They are to be—to be dealt with like human beings.

HALLEMEIER. Aha. I suppose they're to vote? To drink beer? to order us about?

HELENA. Why shouldn't they drink beer?

HALLEMEIER. Perhaps they're even to receive wages?

HELENA. Of course they are.

HALLEMEIER. Fancy that, now! And what would they do with their wages, pray?

HELENA. They would buy—what they need . . . what pleases them.

HALLEMEIER. That would be very nice, Miss Glory, only there's nothing that does please the Robots. Good heavens, what are they to buy? You can feed them on pineapples, straw, whatever you like. It's all the same to them, they've no appetite at all. They've no interest in anything, Miss Glory. Why, hang it all, nobody's ever yet seen a Robot smile.

HELENA. Why . . . why don't you make them happier?

HALLEMEIER. That wouldn't do, Miss Glory. They are only workmen.

HELENA. Oh, but they're so intelligent.

HALLEMEIER. Confoundedly so, but they're nothing else. They've no will of their own. No passion. No soul.

HELENA. No love?

HALLEMEIER. Love? Rather not. Robots don't love. Not even themselves. . . .

DR. GALL. . . . At present I am making pain-nerves.

HELENA. Pain-nerves?

DR. GALL. Yes the Robots feel practically no bodily pain. You see, young Rossum provided them with too limited a nervous system. We must introduce suffering.

HELENA. Why do you want to cause them pain?

DR. GALL. For industrial reasons, Miss Glory. Sometimes a Robot does damage to himself because it doesn't hurt him. He puts his hand into the machine, breaks his finger, smashes his head, it's all the same to him. We must provide them with pain. That's an automatic protection against damage.

HELENA. Will they be happier when they feel pain?

DR. GALL. On the contrary; but they will be more perfect from a technical point of view.

HELENA. Why don't you create a soul for them?

DR. GALL. That's not in our power.

FABRY. That's not in our interest.

BUSMAN. That would increase the cost of production. . . .

Reading Questions

1. Why are robots regarded as superior to people and why are they thought inferior?
2. What do the characters seem to think a soul adds to those who possess one?
3. Why does Helena want to liberate the robots?

Questions for Reflection and Research

1. Could science and technology produce a soul?
2. Assume that science could make artificial human organs and tissues. Assume also that technology could produce from these parts a device that looked and moved like a human. Would this device be a human being? Why or why not?
3. Are nonhuman animals essentially complex machines? Do animals have souls? (See selection #46 for some relevant considerations.)
4. Do machines think? How can we find out?
5. Is the soul, if it exists, physical? If not, how can it interact with the body? (See selection #11.)

Some Theories about the Mind

The Author: Paul Edwards (b. 1925) was educated at the University of Melbourne and at Columbia University and has taught at a number of American universities including the City College of New York, Brooklyn. He was editor for (and contributed to) the monumental *Encyclopedia of Philosophy*. He has also contributed to philosophical journals and written a book on ethics.

The Selection: The dualist position that humans have both material bodies and immaterial minds that interact with each other is first explained and found problematic. Materialist doctrines are also explained and criticized. The view that an immaterial mind is the by-product of and fully controlled by the brain is similarly rejected, leaving the reader with no satisfactory account of mental events and states. The selection is moderately demanding.

Some philosophers have maintained that a human being is simply his body and nothing else besides. Thus [Friedrich] Nietzsche [1844–1900] once remarked: "Body am I entirely, and nothing more; and soul is only the name of something in the body." The same view is also expressed in an epigram coined by the German philosopher [Ludwig] Feuerbach [1804–1872]. "A man," he said, "is what he eats." However, the great majority of philosophers, and especially those with a religious background, have agreed that human beings are something more than their bodies; and this something more has variously been referred to as the mind, the

Reprinted with permission of Macmillan Publishing Co., Inc., from *A Modern Introduction to Philosophy*, edited by Paul Edwards and Arthur Pap. Copyright © 1957, 1965 by The Free Press, a Division of The Macmillan Company.

self, or the soul. Is a human being really a mind in addition to his body? If he is, what exactly is this mind and how is it related to the body? . . .

At least at first sight, it seems exceedingly plausible to contend that a human being is something over and above his body. Things like houses and mountains and also of course human and animal bodies are publicly observable. All these "physical" objects have extension and occupy positions in space. By contrast, only a person himself can experience his feelings, sensations, dreams, or thoughts. A dentist can observe the cavity which causes his patient's pain, but only the patient himself can feel the pain. If I am angry and shake my fist, an outsider can see this manifestation of my anger but not the anger itself. Assuming that a person's dreams or thoughts can be correlated with certain specific movements of brain molecules, it is theoretically feasible that scientists might one day perceive these molecular motions. But they would not even then be experiencing the dreams or thoughts of the person whose brain they were observing. Feelings, sensations, dreams, and thoughts are the sort of phenomena which are usually classified as "mental." In calling them mental, philosophers usually mean that, unlike physical objects, they are "private" or directly knowable by one person only. Some philosophers also include having no extension and no spatial location in the meaning of "mental." This, however, might prove a confusing definition since certain sensations and feelings do seem to have extension and a location in space.

It is plausible, then, to maintain that a human being possesses a mind as well as a body. It seems just as reasonable to hold, in the absence of special considerations to the contrary, that there are causal connections between body and mind. To give a few simple illustrations: cavities in teeth cause pain, the impact of light-waves on the retina leads to visual sensations, contact of the tongue with food causes taste sensations, indigestion gives rise to morbid feelings, consumption of large quantities of alcohol produces hallucinations, some drugs make us calm, others more excited. All these are instances of causal influence by the body on the mind, but there seems just as ample evidence of causal relations in the opposite direction: a person who is ill and has nothing to live for is far less likely to recover than one who has many interests and is filled with hope. Expectations of pleasant encounters affect our body in one way, expectations of unpleasant encounters in quite another. Embarrassment causes [some races] to blush, fear [causes us] to tremble, happiness to smile and sometimes to cry. Perhaps the plainest cases of mind-body causation are "voluntary movements." A man intends to see the tennis matches at Forest Hills, and, other things being equal, he really gets there. It would seem very odd indeed to maintain that in this and similar situations the intention or volition was not part of the cause of the person's action.

Philosophers who first make a distinction between the body and the mind and who then proceed to assert that there are causal influences in both directions are known as "Dualistic interactionists." . . .

To many philosophers it has seemed that interactionism is open to a number of fatal objections. . . . It is easy enough, the critics have declared, to speak of interaction between body and mind in general terms. As soon, however, as we try to visualize concretely the manner in which the supposed interaction takes place, we are utterly baffled. How exactly, for example, is the last member in the physiological series following the impact of light-rays on the retina transformed into a visual sensation? What exactly does a volition do to the brain-molecules to set in motion the train of events culminating in the person's overt reaction? It is evident that the brain-molecules must somehow be moved for this purpose, but how can something which does not occupy space and which has no extension move a material particle? In the words of W. K. Clifford, a 19th-century mathematician and philosopher:

> . . . if anybody says that the will influences matter, the statement is not untrue, but it is nonsense. The will is not a material thing, it is not a mode of material motion. . . . The only thing which influences matter is the position of surrounding matter or the motion of surrounding matter.

[Another thinker has asserted that] there is an "enormous gulf," an "impassable chasm," "a gap which cannot be bridged" between phenomena as radically different as brain events on the one hand and psychological events like sensations or volitions on the other. . . .

Moreover, interactionism seems to these philosophers inconsistent with the continuity of physiological processes and also with certain well-established principles of physics. From the point of view of physiology and physics, it is argued, mental events which cause or are caused by bodily events are disturbing and unwanted interlopers for which there is no room. If the causal story were what the interactionist believes it to be, then we should expect a break in the physiological sequences in the body at certain times. The last brain event, for instance, would be followed not by another brain event but by a non-physical event—the sensation; this by another non-physical event—the volition; and this then by the outgoing physiological sequence. In actual fact, however, the critics claim, no such interruption or discontinuity in the physiological processes is ever found.

Even worse, perhaps, interaction appears to be in conflict with the law of the Conservation of Energy. This principle, in one of its most familiar formulations, maintains that the amount of energy in the universe is always constant. This means that energy can be neither created nor destroyed. Yet, if interaction occurs, then energy would be lost when the body affects the mind and energy would be gained when the mind affects the body. We should in all such cases have exceptions to the Conservation of Energy. There is, however, no evidence that such violations of the principle take place. The occurrence of sensations, for example, is not, as far as we know, accompanied by decreases of energy in the body. Nor are volitions followed by increases of energy.

In the light of these and similar considerations numerous philosophers regard interactionism as untenable. They have put forward several alternative theories which would avoid the difficulties we mentioned. Perhaps the simplest of these is the theory known as "monistic" or "reductive" materialism. On this view all psychological terms really refer to some kind of physiological events or processes. It maintains, to use another formulation, that matter alone is real, that a human being is simply his body. This is the position to which we briefly referred at the beginning of this introduction.

Reductive materialism has been held in many different forms. The 18th-century physiologist [Pierre] Cabanis asserted that "thought is a secretion of the brain," a view echoed by the German biologist [Karl] Vogt [1817–1895], who wrote that "the relation between thought and the brain is roughly of the same order as that between bile and the liver or urine and the bladder." [Thomas] Hobbes [1588–1679] and some German materialists of the 19th century believed that thought is nothing more than the movement of particles in the brain and the Danish physiologist [Carl] Lange [1834–1900] claimed that emotions are really nothing but functional disturbances of the body. However, most of these writers also expressed more moderate views not compatible with reductive materialism. Early in the 20th century the German chemist [Wilhelm] Ostwald [1853–1932] and his followers claimed that mental processes are a form of physical energy. In our own day the favorite type of reductive materialism is behaviorism, or at any rate, certain specially radical forms of it. Some behaviorists, it is true, do not maintain that consciousness is identical with any bodily processes. But others, or the same behaviorists on other occasions, maintain that all psychological terms really refer to nothing more than bodily reactions of some kind—to actual bodily responses or to dispositions to respond in certain ways.

Reductive or monistic materialism is in many ways a highly attractive theory. Like other "monistic" theories it would satisfy the widespread intellectual craving to reduce everything to one ultimate reality. It presents the universe as all "of one piece." It also appeals to those who wish to do away with mystery and who fear that once something immaterial is allowed to exist anywhere in the world, the door has been opened to let in such unwelcome guests as the immortal soul or even God. But most important of all, the theory undoubtedly avoids all the supposed difficulties of interactionism. We now no longer have the problem of bridging the "chasm" between body and mind or of visualizing the causal influence of volitions on brain molecules; we no longer need to postulate a gap in the physiological processes of the organism and of course we no longer have any violations of the Conservation of Energy.

In spite of these attractive features the great majority of philosophers reject reductive materialism. They maintain that it is simply not a true account of our experience. To talk of thought as a "secretion" is absurd. Bile and urine are substances which can be publicly observed, which occupy space, which can be weighed and even bottled. None of this is true of our thoughts. If for example I think of Freud's theory of the death instinct or of the assassination of Abraham Lincoln, my thoughts are not publicly observable; they do not occupy space; they cannot be weighed or bottled. It seems no less absurd to identify thought with movement of brain molecules or emotions with contractions and dilations of blood vessels. It may well be the case that thoughts are always accompanied by certain molecular motions and that emotions always occur along with certain contractions and dilations of blood vessels, but this does not mean that the mental events *are* the bodily processes. To say that thought is really nothing but a certain movement, as the German philosopher Friedrich Paulsen [1846–1908] put it in his celebrated critique of reductive materialism, is about as sensible as to say that iron is really made of wood:

> Turn it which way you will, you will never find thought in movement. The common man knows nothing whatever of the motion in the brain or of the vasomotor process, but he knows what anger is, and what thought is, and he means these, when he speaks of them, and not something else of which the physiologist alone knows or thinks he knows.

It is also not the case that sensations are identical with any kind of bodily process or reaction. A person's awareness of red, for example, cannot be the same thing as a molecular movement. It makes sense to ask about the molecular movement such questions as "Is it swift or slow, straight or circular?" But . . . it would make no sense at all to raise these questions about the awareness of red. Conversely, it makes perfectly good sense to ask about the awareness whether it is clear or confused, but such a question could not sensibly be asked about a molecular movement. If a person touches a piece of red-hot iron . . . the throb of pain he feels is not at all like the act of withdrawing his hand nor "like anything described in textbooks of physiology as happening in the nervous system or the brain." The difference between sensations and bodily events . . . is not a question of *a priori* speculative metaphysics, but "as much an empirical matter as that between sight and sound."

Another rival to interactionism is the theory known as "epiphenomenalism." On this view mental events are distinct from any kind of physical substances or movements. They are, however, powerless to interfere with anything in the physical world. Mental states are caused by brain processes, but do not in turn exert any causal influence. They are mere by-products ("epiphenomenon" is the Greek for "by-product"), mere accompanying echoes or shadows of bodily events. Only material structures, including of course human bodies and their parts, are causally active. In the words of [George] Santayana [1863–1952], one of the most famous advocates of this theory:

There are not two parallel streams, but one stream which, in slipping over certain rocks or dropping into certain pools, begins to babble a wanton music; not thereby losing any part of its substance or changing its course, but unawares enriching the world with a new beauty.

. . . Consciousness is a lyric cry in the midst of business. . . .

Epiphenomenalism is usually considered a form of "materialism" and perhaps a few words of explanation are needed about the meanings of this term in philosophical discussion. We may distinguish a narrower and a broader sense. In the narrower sense materialism asserts that whatever exists is material or physical. In the view "mental" events, in so far as they really exist, are a sub-class of physical occurrences. In the broader sense, materialism merely asserts that matter is in some way the "primary" or "most fundamental" reality. In the latter sense, somebody could be a materialist and at the same time allow that there are mental processes which are not a sub-class of physical occurrences. In this sense, dualism and materialism are not contradictory theories. Epiphenomenalism is not a form of materialism in the narrower sense, but it clearly is a form of materialism in the broader sense. In the broader sense, even quite a number of dualistic interactionists could be regarded as materialists. There are many interactionists who, after conceding that mind is distinct from body and that there is causal influence both ways, proceed to maintain that matter can exist without mind but that mind cannot exist without matter, or at least that this is highly probable on the basis of a great deal of empirical evidence. Bertrand Russell [1872–1970]. . . likens the relation between mental events and the brain to that between a river and a river-bed. When the brain is dissolved at death there is no more reason to suppose that mental events will continue than that a river "will persist in its old course after an earthquake has raised a mountain where a valley used to be." Moreover, a river-bed can exist without a river but a river cannot exist without a river-bed; and the same holds for the mind and the body. Writers like Russell may be considered materialists in the broader sense, since they do assert that matter is more "basic" in the way just explained. . . .

However, to return to epiphenomenalism. It does not identify mental events with any kind of physiological processes and therefore circumvents the main difficulty of reductive materialism. But in the opinion of many philosophers, it, too, is open to a number of serious objections. In the first place, since it allows causal influence in the direction from body to mind, epiphenomenalism escapes only half of whatever difficulties beset interactionism. Secondly, it has been charged that epiphenomenalism is a "self-stultifying" theory: if it were true we could never be justified in believing that it is true. For if it were true then all our beliefs are entertained not because of any prior awareness of good grounds or adequate evidence, but solely because of physical changes in the brain and nervous system. None of our conclusions, including epiphenomenalism itself, would be based on logic. We would always think, in [the] words [of J. B. Pratt (1875–1944)] "the way our mechanical brains constrain us to think"; and if in any given case our thought is true, this is so because the brain molecules happened to shake down in a lucky fashion."

Perhaps the most momentous objection to epiphenomenalism consists in the enormous quantity of *prima facie* [= apparent] evidence that the mental processes of human beings do make a difference to their lives and indirectly to inanimate nature as well. It is said that epiphenomenalism implies a truly staggering paradox in this connection. Father Maher [1860–1918], a scholastic [= Roman Catholic] critic, has stated this objection very forcefully:

But reflection discovers consequences still more surprising. The whole past history of the world, the building of cities, the invention of machinery, the commerce of nations, the emigrations of peoples, the rise and fall of civilizations, all that has been done on this planet by human beings, might have happened in precisely the same way if there had never awoke to consciousness a single human mind! All the pain and sorrow, all the joy and gladness, all the love and anger that we suppose have governed the world's history might never have been, and that history *might have run exactly the same course!* The neural groupings, the cerebral movements, which were the true, ultimate, and *only* causes of the various actions of human beings, have never once been interrupted, modified, or interfered with by those "aspects" or "phases" which constitute the "parallel" series of conscious states, since the first man appeared on the earth. Given the original collocation of the material atoms from which the present cosmos has evolved, and every event, down to the least incident of our daily life, was therein rigidly and sufficiently determined, even though no single act of intelligence or volition had ever wakened into life!

Interactionism may have its problems; but according to a number of philosophers they are small when compared with this paradox of epiphenomenalism. . . .

Those philosophers today who are opposed to materialism in all its more radical varieties incline . . . to interactionism in spite of the difficulties with which this theory appears to be confronted. Some of them . . . may be termed "agnostic interactionists." Their position is roughly that while interaction in both directions is a plain and undeniable fact, the "how" of interaction is still a mystery. The "meeting place" between mind and brain, and exactly "what the mind takes over" at the meeting place . . . has not yet been discovered. . . . This belief . . . is supported by many eminent scientists. Thus Sir Charles Sherrington [1857–1952], who was probably the greatest physiologist of this century, declared that "we have to regard the relation of mind to brain as still not merely unsolved, but still devoid of a basis for the very beginning [of a solution]. . . ." Professor [William] Le Gros Clark [b. 1895], a distinguished Oxford anatomist, writes that physiology and anatomy are unable "even to suggest how the physico-chemical phenomena associated with the passage of nervous impulses from one part of the brain to another can be translated into a mental experience." . . .

Reading Questions

1. What considerations seem to support the dualist interactionist position, the reductive materialist position, and epiphenomenalism?
2. What objections are there to the three positions?

Questions for Reflection and Research

1. What other theories of mind are there besides those mentioned in the selection?
2. What positions do various schools of psychology (behaviorism, psychoanalysis, gestalt psychology, and so on) take with regard to the nature of the mind?
3. What view do present-day brain physiologists take about the relation of the brain to mental activities (thinking, perceiving, and so on)?
4. What are the implications of the various mind theories for issues about freedom of the will and life after death? (See selections #17 and #13, respectively.)
5. Can science settle the questions about the nature and existence of the mind? Why or why not? (See selection #24.)
6. What is the difference between souls, minds, and spirits?

Science and Life after Death:
The Will of Mr. James Kidd

The Author: James Kidd (1879–1949) was a mine worker in Arizona and a prospector. He lived by himself and invested what little money he earned in stocks. He never married and left no survivors. His estate was estimated to be worth $230,000.

The Selection: When Mr. Kidd died, he left behind a handwritten will in his rooming house. The selection is the complete will. The will led to a thirteen-week hearing to determine which of the 130 claimants (including universities) could most satisfactorily comply with the will. The court decided to award the estate to the American Society for Psychical Research, which in turn gave a portion to the Psychical Research Foundation associated with Duke University. The will and Mr. Kidd's life are described in *Life*, March 3, 1967, pp. 76–85.

> Phoenix Arizona
> Jan 2nd 1946
> this is my first and only will and is dated the second day in January 1946. I have no heires (have not been married in my life) after all my funeral expenses have been paid and $100, one hundred dollars, to some preacher of the gospital to say farewell at my grave sell all property which is in cash and stocks with E F Hutton Co Phoenix some in safety box, and have this balance money to go in a research or some scientific proof of a soul of the human body which leaves at death I think in time their can be a Photograph of soul leaving the human at death.
> James Kidd

Reading Question

1. What exactly does Mr. Kidd want his money used for?

Questions for Reflection and Research

1. What evidence is there of life after death? (See selection #13.)
2. Can science determine whether there is life after death? Why or why not? (See selection #13 for some suggestions.)
3. If there is a soul that leaves the body at death, is it physical? If not, how does it interact with the body during life? (See selection #13.)
4. Obtain copies of the Psychical Research Foundation's publication *Theta*. Report on and evaluate reports contained therein on research pertaining to life after death.

Are There Rational Grounds to Believe in Life after Death?

The Author: Curt John Ducasse (1881–1969) was born in France and educated in the United States at the University of Washington and Harvard University. He taught at Brown University and was affiliated with the Association of Symbolic Logic and the American Society for Psychical Research. He published extensively in many fields of philosophy.

The Selection: First described and examined are considerations that support the view that mind or consciousness is dependent on the body. These considerations are rejected as insufficiently supported, and their initial persuasiveness is attributed to our unconscious acceptance of physical sciences as the only source of empirical data. Paranormal phenomena are described that are alleged to give strong support to the view that life can survive death.

Are there rational or empirical grounds for believing that man's personality survives the death of his body? Or, on the contrary, is the belief in survival purely gratuitous, or perhaps even demonstrably false? This is the question which will now occupy us. It is commonly termed the question as to the immortality of the human soul. But immortality means incapacity to die—everlastingness of life—and it is perfectly conceivable that whatever, if anything, is left of a man's personality when his body dies might continue to exist not forever but only for a finite time, whether long or short. Hence we shall not concern ourselves here with immortality in the

Portions of this selection are moderately demanding. From C. J. Ducasse, *A Philosophical Scrutiny of Religion* (New York: Copyright 1953, The Ronald Press Company), pp. 380–412. Reprinted by permission of The Ronald Press Company.

above strict sense, but only with the more modest and in any case prior question of survival. . . .

THE CONTENTION THAT NO LIFE AFTER DEATH IS POSSIBLE

There are, first of all, a number of facts which definitely suggest that both the existence and the nature of consciousness wholly depend on the presence of a functioning nervous system. It is pointed out, for example, that wherever consciousness is observed, it is found associated with a living and functioning body. Further, when the body dies, or the head is struck a heavy blow, or some anesthetic is administered, the familiar outward evidences of consciousness terminate, permanently or temporarily. Again, we know well that drugs of various kinds—alcohol, caffein, opium, heroin, and many others—cause specific changes at the time in the nature of a person's mental states. Also, by stimulating in appropriate ways the body's sense organs, corresponding states of consciousness— namely, the various kinds of sensations—can be caused at will. On the other hand, cutting a sensory nerve immediately eliminates a whole range of sensations. Again, the contents of consciousness, the mental powers, or even the personality, are modified in characteristic ways when certain regions of the brain are destroyed by disease or injury or are disconnected from the rest by such an operation as prefrontal lobotomy. And that the nervous system is the indispensable basis of mind is further suggested by the fact that, in the evolutionary scale, the degree of intelligence of various species of animals keeps pace closely with the degree of development of their brain.

That continued existence of mind after death is impossible has been argued also on the basis of theoretical considerations. It has been contended, for instance, that what we call states of consciousness—or more particularly ideas, sensations, volitions, feelings, and the like—are really nothing but the minute physical or chemical events which take place in the tissues of the brain. For, it is urged, it would be absurd to suppose that an idea or a volition, if it is not itself a material thing or process, could cause material effects such as contractions of muscles. Moreover, it is maintained that the possibility of causation of a material event by an immaterial mental cause is ruled out *a priori* by the principle of the conservation of energy; for such causation would mean that an additional quantity of energy suddenly pops into the nervous system out of nowhere.

Another conception of consciousness, which is more often met with today than the one just mentioned, but which also implies that consciousness cannot survive death, is that "consciousness" is only the name we give to certain types of behavior, which differentiate the higher animals from all other things in nature. According to this view, to say, for example, that an animal is conscious of a difference between two stimuli means nothing more than that it responds to each by different behavior. That is, the difference of *behavior* is what consciousness of difference between the stimuli *consists in;* and is not, as is commonly assumed, only the behavioral *sign* of something mental and not public, called "consciousness that the stimuli are different." . . .

THE IMPOSSIBILITY OF SURVIVAL NOT PROVED

Such, in brief, are [some of] the chief reasons commonly offered for holding that the mind or personality of a man cannot possibly survive the death of his body. Let us now ask whether those arguments do indeed prove this, or if not, whether they at least show survival to be improbable.

To be considered first is the assertion that "thought," or "consciousness," is but another name for . . . some . . . form of behavior, or for molecular processes in the tissues of the brain. As [Friedrich] Paulsen [1846–1908] and others have pointed out, no evidence ever is or can be offered to support that assertion, because it is in fact but a disguised proposal to make the words "thought," "feeling," "sensation," "desire." and so on, denote facts quite different from those which these words are commonly employed to denote. To say that those words are but other names for certain chemical, neural, or behavioral events is as grossly arbitrary and as futile as it would be to say that "wood" is but another name for glass, or "potato" but another name for cabbage. What thought, desire, sensation, and other mental states are like, each of us can observe directly by introspection; and what introspection reveals is that they do not in the least resemble muscular contraction, or glandular secretion, or any other known bodily events. No tampering with language can alter the observable fact that thinking is one thing and muttering quite another; that the feeling called anger has no resemblance to the bodily behavior which usually goes with it; or that an act of will is not in the least like anything we find when we open the skull and examine the brain. Certain mental events are doubtless connected in some way with certain bodily events, but they are not those bodily events themselves. The connection is not identity.

This being clear, let us next consider the arguments offered to show that mental processes, although not identical with bodily processes, nevertheless totally depend on them. We are told, for instance, that some head injuries, or anesthetics, totally extinguish consciousness for the time being. The strict fact, however, is only that the usual bodily signs of consciousness are then absent. But they are also absent when a person is asleep; and yet, at such a time, dreams, which are states of consciousness, may be occurring.

It is true that when the person concerned awakens, he often remembers his dreams, whereas the person who has been anesthetized or injured has usually no memories relating to the period of apparent blankness. But this could mean that his consciousness was, for the time, dissociated from its ordinary channels of manifestation, as was the case with the co-conscious personalities of some of the patients of Dr. Morton Prince [1854–1929]. Moreover, it sometimes occurs that a person who has been in an accident reports lack of memories not only for the period during which his body was unresponsive but also for a period of several hours *before* the accident, during which he had given to his associates all the ordinary external signs of being conscious as usual.

But, more generally, if absence of memories relating to a given period proved unconsciousness for that period, this would force us to conclude that we were unconscious during the first few years of our lives, and indeed have been unconscious also most of the time since; for the fact is that we have no memories whatever of most of our days. That we were alive and conscious on any long past specific date is, with only a few exceptions, not something we actually remember, but only something which we infer must have been true.

Let us now turn to another of the arguments against survival. That states of consciousness entirely depend on bodily processes, and therefore cannot continue when the latter have ceased, is proved, it is contended, by the fact that various states of consciousness—in particular, the several kinds of sensations—can be caused at will by appropriately stimulating the body.

Now, it is very true that sensations and some other mental states can be so caused; but we have just as good and abundant evidence that mental states can cause various bodily events. [John] Laird [1887–1946] mentions, among others, the fact that merely willing to raise one's arm normally suffices to cause it to rise; that a hungry person's mouth is caused to water by the idea of food; that feelings of rage, fear, or excitement cause digestion to stop; that anxiety causes changes in the quantity and quality of the milk of a nursing mother; that certain thoughts cause tears, pallor, blushing, or fainting; and so on. The evidence we have that the relation is one of cause and effect is exactly the same here as where bodily processes are asserted to cause mental states.

It is said, of course, that to suppose something nonphysical, such as a thought, to be capable of causing motion of a physical object, such as the body, is absurd. But I submit that if the heterogeneity of mind and matter makes this absurd, then it makes equally absurd the causation of mental states by stimulation of the body. Yet no absurdity is commonly found in the assertion that cutting the skin causes a feeling of pain, or that alcohol, caffein, bromides, and other drugs, cause characteristic states of consciousness. As David Hume [1711–1776] made clear long ago, no kind of causal connection is intrinsically absurd. Anything might cause anything; and only observation can tell us what in fact can cause what.

Somewhat similar remarks would apply to the allegation that the principle of the conservation of energy precludes the possibility of causation of a physical event by a mental event. For if it does, then it equally precludes causation in the converse direction, and this, of course, would leave us totally at a loss to explain the occurrence of sensations. But, as [Morris] Keeton [b. 1917] and others have pointed out, that energy is conserved is not something observation has revealed or could reveal, but only a postulate—a defining postulate for the notion of an "isolated physical system." That is, conservation of energy is something one has to have if, but only if, one insists on conceiving the physical world as wholly self-contained, independent, isolated. And just because the metaphysics which the natural sciences tacitly assume does insist on so conceiving the physical world, this metaphysics compels them to save conservation by postulations *ad hoc* [= by arbitrary postulations] whenever dissipation of energy is what observation reveals. It postulates, for instance, that something else, which appears at such times but was not until then regarded as energy, is energy too, but, it is then said, "in a different form." . . .

A word, next, on the parallelism between the degree of development of the nervous systems of various animals and the degree of their intelligence. This is alleged to prove that the latter is the product of the former. But the facts lend themselves equally well to the supposition that, on the contrary, an obscurely felt need for greater intelligence in the circumstances the animal faced was what brought about the variations which eventually resulted in a more adequate nervous organization.

In the development of the individual, at all events, it seems clear that the specific, highly complex nerve connections which become established in the brain and cerebellum of, for instance, a skilled pianist are the results of his will over many years to acquire the skill. . . .

WHY THE ARGUMENTS AGAINST SURVIVAL SEEMED WEIGHTY

We have now examined . . . the . . . reasons cited earlier for judging survival impossible; and we have found that none of them establishes the alleged impossibility or even bears on the probability or improbability of survival.

Yet, at first sight, those reasons appeared weighty; and it may be that even after our criticisms of them, a certain aura of impressiveness still clings to them. If so, this indicates that we have not yet gained the philosophical detachment indispensable for a completely objective view of the question. We gain this detachment only when we have perceived what exactly it is, which makes those reasons seem to have the force they really lack.

The source of their appearance of weight is a certain tacit major premise under which they automatically present themselves to us, namely, that only material things can have substantive, self-dependent existence; or, in other words, that *to exist at all is to be some part of or process in the material world.*

But a moment's reflection is enough to show that this conception of existence is perfectly arbitrary, as being not a hypothesis, capable of being tested and proved true or false, but merely a specification of the particular range of existence to which the sciences called "natural sciences" choose to confine their interest. That conception of existence simply marks off their particular horizon: the "natural" sciences are those which take as their specific and sole task to investigate the constituents and processes of the material world, and their relations to one another.

Hence, to make clear the true import of the statement italicized above, it is necessary to qualify it accordingly, making it read: *For the natural sciences,* to exist is to be some part of or process in the material world.

But in our days the natural sciences have made enormous progress. It is to them that we owe the marvellous modern achievements in transportation, communication, engineering, manufacture, sanitation, medicine, agriculture, and so on, which have revolutionized the life of man wherever they have spread. Because of this the natural sciences now have immense prestige—so much prestige that not only the average man in our cities, but also the majority of natural scientists, and indeed even some philosophers, who should know better, today take these particular sciences to be all that the word "science" really denotes; and hence tacitly assume that the material world, which in fact is the subject matter of only these sciences, is all there is to be explored.

It follows from this psychological state of affairs that when natural scientific considerations of the kinds we mentioned are presented, which seem to preclude the possibility of man's mind surviving death, the mere fact of their belonging to the domain of the natural sciences tacitly carries with it, *and induces us unawares to assume,* the materialistic premise pointed out above. But although, as we have seen, that premise correctly defines the horizon of the natural sciences and is therefore absolutely valid *within* those sciences, yet it is valid *only within them.* . . .

It is only when one has achieved a quite definite conception of what the material sciences undertake, that one is in position to discern with equal definiteness what else there is, which is foreign to *their* undertaking and which therefore *they* rightly ignore; but which exists nonetheless and is just as capable as is the material world of being scientifically observed and investigated—namely, the facts of mind. These, however, are not accessible to external perception but only to introspective observation, for the latter alone exhibits mental states and activities *themselves,* instead of—as does perceptual observation of the body—only the *bodily signs* of certain mental states and activities. . . .

THE EMPIRICAL FACTS ALLEGED TO PROVE SURVIVAL

When one has familiarized himself with the abundant well-established facts, of various kinds, which are held by some to constitute empirical proof of survival, but are regarded by others as insufficient to prove it, he realizes that the truly crucial question on the subject is as to just what evidence, if it could be had, would establish survival beyond possibility of rational doubt; for the facts available in evidence are of the very kinds which would naturally suggest themselves to most of us as appropriate to establish it. . . .

The account which follows borrows to some extent from a fuller discussion of the same subject by [Gardner] Murphy [b. 1895] in two excellent articles, "An Outline of Survival Evidence" and "Difficulties Confronting the Survival Hypothesis," which interested persons should not fail to read.

The *prima facie* evidences of survival that are psychologically most impressive probably are those consisting of apparitions [= ghosts]. The apparition may be that of a person who is dying or has just died, to others unaware that he was ill or in danger; or it may be [an] apparition of a person known to have died but revealing facts unknown to the percipient. . . .

Once such case is that of a traveling salesman who was busy writing up his orders in his room at the hotel in St. Joseph, Missouri. "I suddenly became conscious," his report reads, "that someone was sitting on my left, with one arm resting on the table. Quick as a flash I turned and distinctly saw the form of my dead sister," who had died nine years before. Whereupon the apparition vanished. So impressed was he that, instead of continuing his trip, he took the next train to St. Louis, his home, and there related to his parents what had occurred, mentioning among other details of the apparition "a bright red line or scratch on the right-hand side of [his] sister's face." When he mentioned this, his mother rose tremblingly to her feet and declared that she herself had made that scratch accidentally after the sister's death, and that, pained at the disfiguration, she had immediately obliterated all trace of it with powder and had never mentioned it to anyone.

Another famous case is that of a father whose apparition in several dreams to one of his sons some time after death revealed to him the existence and location of an unsuspected second will, benefiting him, which, upon being then looked for, was found as indicated. . . .

Other striking instances are those of an apparition seen simultaneously by several persons. It is on record that an apparition of a child who, it turned out, had just died, was perceived first by a dog, that the animal's rushing at it, loudly barking, interrupted the conversation of the seven persons present in the room, thus drawing their attention to the apparition, and that the latter then moved through the room for some fifteen seconds, followed by the barking dog. . . .

Another class of occurrences asserted to constitute empirical evidence of survival consists of the communications given by the persons called automatists [= mediums]. These are men or women, whose organs of expression—their hand, holding a pencil, or their vocal organs—function at times automatically; that is, write or speak words that are not the expression of thoughts present to their consciousness at the time or of knowledge they possess, but appear to be as independent of these as, for instance, my words at this moment are independent of the thoughts of, and of the stock of knowledge possessed by, another person who happens to read them. The automatist is usually in trance at such times, but there are many cases where he is not, and where, for example, he will be engaged in conversation with someone present, and yet his hand will at the same time be writing, on some totally different subject, a lengthy communication of whose content he knows nothing until he reads it afterward.

The communications so obtained generally purport to come— either directly or through some invisible intermediary referred to as the automatist's "control"—from a person who has died and whose spirit has survived death. Such communications are far less spectacular than apparitions, and are therefore perhaps less impressive to most of the persons who receive them; but in many cases they have contained numerous items of evidence, of the very kinds which, for instance, would satisfy one of the identity of a person claiming to be his brother, with whom he could communciate at the time only through the intermediary of some third person or by telephone.

Some of the most evidential communications of this kind on record were given by the celebrated automatist, Mrs. Leonora Piper, who was investigated by men of science perhaps for more years, and more systematically and minutely, than any other automatist. In giving here a sample of the evidential sort of material contained in some of her communications, there is no need to go into details as to the manner of their reception, except to say that she was in trance at such times. The instance I shall cite is that of communications which had been received, and were published in 1901, by James H. Hyslop, Professor of Logic and Ethics at Columbia University. They purported to come from several of his dead relatives, and in particular from his father. Their content included a statement of Professor Hyslop's name, James; of his father's name, and of the names of three others of his father's children. Also, references to a number of particular conversations the father had had with Professor Hyslop, to many special incidents and facts, and to family matters. Examples would be that the father had trouble with his left eye, that he had a mark behind the ear, that he used to wear a thin coat or dressing gown mornings and that he once wore a black skull cap at night, that he used to have one round and one square bottle on his desk and carried a brown-handled penknife with which he used to pare his nails, that he had a horse called Tom, that he used to write with quill pens which he trimmed himself; and so on. A number of these facts were unknown to Professor Hyslop, but were found to be true after inquiry. The communications also contained favorite pieces of advice, which the father had been in the habit of uttering, and these worded in ways characteristic of his modes of speech.

The communications which purported to come from other dead relatives, and indeed those given by Mrs. Piper to scores and scores of other sitters over the years, were often similarly of facts or incidents too trivial to have become matters of public knowledge, or indeed to have been ascertainable by a stranger without elaborate inquiries, if at all. Facts of this kind are therefore all the more significant as *prima facie* [= apparent] evidences of identity.

The question immediately arises, of course, whether the giving out of such facts by an automatist may not be explicable on some other hypothesis than that of communication with the dead. The first to suggest itself is that she obtained antecedently in some perfectly normal manner the information communicated. In Mrs. Piper's case, however, this explanation is completely ruled out by the elaborate precautions which were taken. For example, both Mrs. Piper and her husband were watched for weeks by detectives, to find out whether they went about making inquiries concerning the relatives and family history of persons they might have expected to come for sittings. Nothing in the slightest degree suspicious was ever found. . . .

A place is reached in such cases, where . . . one has to ask himself what, if he could get it, he would regard as definite proof of survival; and he then has to answer for himself the question whether such facts as just referred to furnish it. All that can be said here is that, when one reads, not as above mere summaries or samples of the communications, but the original full reports of the sittings, with all the detail of the conversation between the sitter and the communicators and between one communicator and another, one realizes why the impersonation hypothesis has in some cases seemed so implausible in the concrete to the sitters and to many close students of the records. Some of the keenest-minded and best informed persons, who studied the evidence over many years in a highly critical spirit, eventually came to the conclusion that, in some cases at least, only the survival hypothesis remained plausible. . . .

Reading Questions

1. What reasons favor the view that consciousness depends on the body? What is Ducasse's appraisal of each of these reasons?
2. If science cannot prove the existence of surviving consciousnesses, is this proof that they do not exist?
3. What kinds of paranormal phenomena tend to be most persuasive of life after death?

Questions for Reflection and Research

1. Compare and contrast the treatments of materialism and dualism in this selection and in selection #11 by Edwards.
2. What reasons do people currently give for belief in life after death? Are these reasons rationally defensible?
3. Since 1953, when Ducasse wrote this selection, what have subsequent controlled studies of the paranormal concluded about survival after death?
4. Is psychic research a science? If not, does this mean the research is not rationally acceptable?

Sociobiology and Human Nature

The Author: Maitland A. Edey (b. 1910) has been a writer and editor for Time-Life Books. As editor of the Life Nature Library he conceived and produced 25 volumes.

Edward O. Wilson (b. 1929) is the main focus of this selection. He was educated at the University of Alabama and Harvard University. He has published extensively on a number of topics in biology, including the behavior of the social insects. In addition, he is a faculty member at Harvard and curator of entomology at the Museum of Comparative Zoology.

The Selection: An abbreviated account is offered of Edward O. Wilson's book *Sociobiology, the New Synthesis.* Sociobiology's conception of human beings is contrasted with that of Robert Ardrey and that of B. F. Skinner. Sociobiology attempts to isolate animal behavior patterns that are evolutionarily advantageous and, perhaps, thus, genetically controlled. It is thought possible that some or much human conduct is not chosen, but is solely a product of heredity.

"Rarely has the world been offered such a splendid stepping stone to the exciting future of a new science." With these words, a leading scientific magazine greeted the appearance last year [1976] of a book that, in many respects, deserves to be compared with Charles Darwin's *Origin of Species,* published more than a century ago.

Unlike Darwin's epochal proclamation of the theory of evolution, this new work by Edward O. Wilson of Harvard does not break new

"Momentous New Science" by Maitland Edey from *1977 Nature/Science Annual* published by Time-Life Books Inc.

scientific ground. Its title—*Sociobiology, the New Synthesis*—is an open acknowledgment of a heavy debt to others, notably Darwin himself. Nonetheless, the accomplishment is stunning. Wilson has clarified some chronic trouble spots in evolutionary theory; at the same time, he has offered an instrument for bridging a gap that has long existed in the study of man—the gap between social scientists, who tend to ignore evolution theory in their investigations, and biologists, who accept it as the cornerstone of everything they do. . . .

Wilson is a formidably erudite man who seems to be as much at home talking about the digestive peculiarities of termites as he is talking about herding among dinosaurs, the schooling of herrings, cooperative nest-building by South American parrots, child-rearing among baboons, conversation among dolphins and the evolutionary future of man.

The link that holds these diverse subjects together is social behavior. Termite, parrot, dolphin and man are all social creatures. They live together in mutually supportive groups. Togetherness has affected their behavior.

The purpose of Wilson's book is to examine as great a diversity of social behavior as he can in an effort to find its biological base: i.e., how much of it is hereditary. In the case of humankind, this subject is a veritable mine field of strongly held—and, in some cases, diametrically opposed—views. At one extreme are men like Robert Ardrey [b. 1908], a persuasive popularizer of paleoanthropology [= the study of early forms of human beings]. He has termed man the killer ape, suggesting that there is a human genetic streak that explains man's long history as a hunter, a murderer, a fierce defender of his territory, and that his climb up from apehood and his development of a culture can be explained in terms of that genetic killer instinct. Boiling Ardrey's thesis down and swallowing it whole, one can argue that man is the cruel creature he is because his genes have made him that way for millions of years. From this it follows that he will not change his killer ways unless he changes his genes.

At the opposite pole stand men like the behavioral psychologist B. F. Skinner [b. 1904] of Harvard. Skinner argues that any creature capable of learning can have that learning shaped by rewarding "good" responses. According to this argument—and again, simplifying it—if a monkey gets a banana every time it pats its brother, brotherhood among monkeys can be encouraged, regardless of genes.

The implications of these two positions, as far as the future evolution of man and his culture are concerned, are, obviously, very strong. Developments in genetics, along with the discovery of DNA and its role as the master blueprint of the individual, suggest that before too long man will begin to have the capability to shape himself and his destiny by deliberately controlling his genes—*if* his genes do indeed play a significant role in his behavior. According to Ardrey's extreme view of evolution, the genetic component of behavior could be overwhelming. According to the Skinnerian view, it could be negligible.

Is social behavior genetic? Yes, says Wilson, some of it is—but the reasons that this is so are not always obvious. If one is willing to think like a sociobiologist, he points out, one must begin by discarding a basic human prejudice that the individual is important.

A SUITCASE FOR GENES

In genetics the individual counts for nothing. What matters is the preservation and change of the genes in response to environmental change and challenge—the process Darwin called natural selection. From the point of view of the gene, a body is simply a convenient suitcase for protecting the gene until it can produce more genes; as Samuel Butler [1835–1902] once put it: "A hen is only an egg's way of making another egg." Looked at in this way, a population of human beings or a colony of ants becomes not so much a group of individuals as a collection of genes, most of them alike, but with enough variability in them to enable the selection process to work. Such a collection is known as a gene pool.

Wilson's book examines sociality throughout the animal kingdom and shows that, on balance, it proves to be uncontestably adaptive—that is, designed to improve the survival chances of genes within the gene pools. Social behavior is just another device serving the ends of survival and reproduction, basically no different from limbs, hearts and digestive enzymes. This is true for extremely primitive marine creatures like corals, whose colonies exist in a togetherness so tight that they are physically attached to one another. It is also true for a great number of higher animals including antelopes, dogs, lions and apes—and men.

To nail this down, it is necessary to tick off only a few examples of the advantages conferred by sociality. Mutual defense is an obvious one; a troop of baboons is a formidable adversary to a prowling leopard, whereas a single baboon would provide an easy meal. . . .

Cooperative hunting also turns out to be more productive than solo efforts. A lioness hunting alone enjoys not much more than half the success that two or three enjoy when acting together. For one thing, the familiar tactic of driving prey in the direction of a hidden partner is impossible for a single lion. Another example: wild dogs, although weighing only about 50 pounds each, are able, in packs, to hunt down and kill antelopes that weigh up to 10 times as much as they do. This would be far beyond the capability of a single dog.

Breeding success is also improved through sociality. Studies of gull colonies show that not only does sexual activity increase under the mutual stimulation of hundreds or thousands of like-minded gulls in close proximity with one another, but also that the continuous presence of numerous adult gulls, either sitting on their nests or flying over the rookery [= breeding grounds], tends to discourage cruising . . . egg- and chick-eaters, such as skuas [= a species of large sea birds]. Among wildebeests, mating takes place during a period of great activity over a short time. The result is that the calves are all dropped within a few days of one another. And although all the lions and leopards and hyenas and wild dogs in the region feast on young wildebeests for a few days, the mass of births simply overwhelms the predators, and most of the calves survive their first critical hour of helplessness.

The survival value of certain kinds of behavior was apparent to Charles Darwin when he formulated his theory of evolution in 1859. But the significance of other sorts of behavior remained utterly baffling to evolutionists until sociobiology came to the rescue. Ant society is a prime example, and it receives a long, careful examination in Wilson's book—partly to illustrate the insights attainable by the new science, and partly because social insects are Wilson's specialty. He knows as much about them as any man alive.

Ants—along with other social insects such as termites and certain bees and wasps—have developed togetherness to an extraordinary degree. An ant colony does not consist of one kind of ant, but usually three: queen, worker and male. Some species of ants have a fourth form called a soldier. Each of the forms is physically different from the others, and each performs specialized tasks that the others do not. A worker ant can never become a queen, nor can a queen ever become a worker.

Queens are nothing but oversized egg-laying machines, pouring out eggs around the clock to maintain the population of the colony. Other ants in the community are usually incapable of reproduction: the males exist solely for the purpose of fertilizing the queen; the workers and soldiers are sterile females, only rarely laying eggs. The workers take care of all the chores but one—defense. That is the responsibility of the soldiers, which have larger heads and stronger jaws than workers. Soldiers are designed to fight, and they rush to repel any threat to the colony, either taking defensive positions in a breach of the fortifications, or actively attacking an invader.

What stumped Darwin was the existence of sterile workers and soldiers. For in thinking about them in terms of natural-selection theory, he ran headlong into a paradox: how could these castes of insect societies have evolved if they leave no offspring?

Wilson takes a hard look at that paradox, and also at a second and related one: the evolution of altruistic behavior. Wilson defines altruism as an act that occurs "when a person (or animal) increases the fitness of another at the expense of his own fitness." By the terms of that definition, a soldier ant that gives up its life for the benefit of its fellows is acting altruistically. And by the same logic that makes the evolution of insect castes a mystery, equally mysterious is the development of such self-sacrifice among ants. How can the trait ever manage to concentrate itself in the genes in significant amounts if the behavior itself frequently leads to the death of the ant? In short, is not altruism self-destroying? . . .

The twin problems of caste and altruism continued to plague evolutionary biologists until 1963, when a solution was proposed by a young British entomologist and geneticist, William D. Hamilton.

Hamilton pointed out that ants—like most other social insects—determine sex in an unusual way. They use the so-called haplodiploid mode, which simply means that unfertilized eggs produce males and fertilized eggs produce females. Since the queen is the only producer of eggs in the colony, it follows that all the other females (the sterile workers and soldiers that are the daughters of the queen) will be sisters. These sisters have about 75 percent of their genes in common. In other words, one soldier ant is very close genetically to another soldier ant. So, when the soldier sacrifices its life to save the lives of all the others in the colony, it is acutally saving a great many of its own genes—more, in fact, than it would save if it were not sterile, but mated and had offspring of its own. In that case the offspring would have only half of the soldier-mother's genes, the other half having been donated by a male with a set of quite different genes.

The apparent elimination of certain genes by the suicidal behavior of an altruistic ant therefore turns out to be the preservation of the same genes in all the other ants. A fine thing all around; for not only does it help protect the ants from present danger, but it also helps perpetuate altruism, and thus the future of the colony, by helping to ensure that future generations of equally altruistic soldiers will be on hand to make their own sacrifices for the colony when the appropriate time comes.

The success of any sort of social behavior can be measured by the ability of a species to survive, to increase its numbers, to spread out in its environment, or, by evolution, to occupy more and more niches in an environment. By these definitions of success, the ant version of sociality is an unparalleled triumph. At the present moment about 8,000 different species of ants are known. At the rate new ones are being discovered, it is estimated that the total number of known species will ultimately rise to 12,000. "There are more species of ants," says Wilson, "in one square kilometer of Brazilian forest than all the species of primates in the world, more workers in a single colony of driver ants than all the lions and elephants in Africa." The backyard of any suburbanite in temperate North America may have a hundred or a thousand times as many ants in it as his town has people.

THE EVOLUTION OF ALTRUISM

For all its usefulness to ants, altruism is not an evolutionary panacea. In a survey of social traits from the lowest creatures on up, Wilson finds that altruism generally decreases the higher one looks on the evolutionary scale. . . .

In a sense, man appears to have rediscovered altruism—or at least reversed the downward trend displayed by other vertebrates. Unlike other mammals, he is an inveterate sharer. He is constantly giving things away, not so much out of the goodness of his heart as because he is the only animal intelligent enough to look ahead and see the validity of the proposition: I'll help you now, you help me later. All barter, all commerce is built on that proposition. So is the invention of money. So, ultimately, is culture, and finally the post-industrial technological behemoth that we have forged for our current dwelling place. Altruism, however one cares to look at it philosophically (that is to say, morally), turns out to be an indispensable component for the survival of intelligent beings who are designed to live in groups—as men are.

Wilson goes much further than simply looking at humans in terms of their altruism. However, he proceeds cautiously, well aware that sociologists and many psychologists are uncomfortable with ideas that base the complexities of human behavior on genes. There is every reason for such discomfort.

Soon after Darwin's theory of natural selection was enunciated, it began to be distorted by people who did not fully understand it but who, at the same time, were not above using it to bolster their own social or political ideas. Social Darwinism emerged. This was the belief that the survival of the fittest was not the survival of populations but the survival of individuals, of *rugged* individuals who survived at the expense of others. "Nature red in fang and claw"—as the poet Alfred Lord Tennyson [1809–1892] phrased it—became the byword of Social Darwinism, and it was used to justify the heartless inequities of the class system in England, accentuated by the onset of the Industrial Revolution. The poor were poor because they deserved to be; they were genetically unfit and demonstrated their unfitness by their poverty—a neatly circular argument. The same argument was used to justify the subjugation of other peoples throughout the world by the British during the build-up of their empire.

Modern sociobiology is in many ways the opposite of the old Social Darwinism. It sees competition as only one of the processes at work within societies, and stresses the roles of cooperation and altruism. Sociobiologists also acknowledge the overriding importance of experience and culture in shaping the fine details of human behavior. Nevertheless, Wilson would still search for human behavioral attributes that are universal. These, properly understood, should provide a steady base for analyzing the more changeful and enigmatic behavior that results.

The problem, then, is to identify traits so ingrained in human behavior that we may not even recognize them for what they are: evolved patterns of action critical to our survival. Since man is a primate, he shares some of these traits with apes and monkeys. Others, which explain why he is a man and not an ape, he has to himself. In the first category, Wilson lists the following:

- Aggressive dominance systems, with males dominant over females.
- Scaling of responses, especially in aggressive reactions. This simply means that facial and other behavioral signals change and become more emphatic as the tension rises. When the boss raises his eyebrow, he does not mean the same thing as when his face gets purple and he bangs his desk with his fist. Woe to the clerk who does not understand this.
- Prolonged maternal care, accompanied by pronounced socialization among the young. Care is widespread in the animal world. Even ants are solicitous of their eggs and larvae, but they have no adolescence as we understand it. An ant never plays; it does not need to. Only the higher animals with larger brains do that. Among these higher species, socialization is a critical tool for teaching youngsters how to get along in the complicated society they are about to join—how to interpret the boss's frown, for example.
- Matrilineal organizations. Despite the dominance hierarchies that males work out among themselves, the real glue that holds many primate societies together, including many human ones, is the ties between females—sisters and their offspring.

Wilson then lists four traits peculiar to humans:

- True language and elaborate culture.
- Sexual activity continuous throughout the menstrual cycle. Among other mammals, females are sexually attractive to males only when in heat.
- Formalized incest taboos and rules for marriage exchange . . . . In a small population . . . what traits there are in [the gene pool] will double up and become increasingly concentrated through inbreeding of close relatives. Some of those traits are potentially harmful. If carried singly in the recessive state by an individual, they do not express themselves, and he goes happily through life without ever realizing he has them. But if he marries someone with a bad trait like his own, it could double up and appear damagingly in his children.

  A strong case can be made for man's instinctive loathing of incest as an evolved behavioral device for avoiding too close inbreeding. The trait would have developed early in man's evolutionary history, long before he had any understanding of what he was doing—any more than gibbons have when they throw adolescents out of the family to seek mates elsewhere in the forest, or a female mouse has when, confronted with a choice of mates, she selects the one that smells the least like her father.

- Cooperative division of labor between adult males and females. The degree and complexity to which this developed in humans has no parallel among animals. Ants, bees and wasps divide labor, but they do not do it along sexual lines, since both workers and soldiers are females.

MAN'S HUNTER-GATHERER HERITAGE

In considering the deep-set characteristics of human behavior, it should be emphasized that they have evolved over a tremendously long period of time during which man's way of life did not really change much. He remained a scavenger and a hunter-gatherer, living in small bands, aggressive, fiercely loyal, suspicious of strangers but aware of distant relationships, able to devise ways of outbreeding for his young. So he has continued through thousands of generations, his instincts shaped to serve his way of life.

Now he finds himself suddenly confronted with a way of life that the old traits may not be suited to. No matter that he created that new way himself, no matter that he has shown a good deal of flexibility in adapting to it. He still has to live in it with an old set of instincts, which appear to be increasingly anachronistic [= out of date] in dealing with the new problems of overpopulation, habitat destruction, exhaustion of natural resources, greater and greater imbalances in standards of living throughout the world—and a technology now so potent that he can wipe himself out overnight if the old angers and suspicions prove so strong in a crisis that they affect his decisions.

Sociobiology carries with it the clear implication that somewhere in its future lies the necessity for some intelligent social engineering in humans. This will not be accomplished, says Wilson, by designing the kind of perfect cultural environments that Skinner would have. For all the conditioning Skinner would give us, some of our genes may not accept that environment. Under sufficient stress, they may react by burning it down or blowing it up.

Nor is man simply a killer ape, the victim of his genes. In fact, and despite Robert Ardrey, he is not really much of a killer at all compared to many other animals. Hyenas, for example, habitually practice cannibalism: cubs feeding on an animal carcass must be guarded by their mothers lest they be eaten by other members of the hyena clan. Lions and monkeys sometimes fight to the death. Says Wilson: "We are among the more pacific mammals as measured by serious assaults or murders per individual per unit time, even when our episodic wars are averaged in."

What makes man appear so bloodthirsty is that he is so good at killing. When he decides to do it, he kills more efficiently and more intelligently and on a larger scale than any other creature known, just as he does nearly everything else more efficiently and more intelligently. Therein lies his greatest power and his greatest peril.

As possessors of a culture, we have learned how to do many things superlatively well. We are also unique in the animal world in being able to think about the consequences of what we do, and to make elaborate plans for the future. In that planning, sociobiology seems to be telling us, let us not forget our genes. They just may be fatally ill-designed for the new world we are creating. As Wilson puts it: "Social evolution has locked us onto a particular course which the early hominids still within us may not welcome."

If so, we had better get on with the job of thinking more like sociobiologists in order to find out more about our deep-set behaviors, how to analyze them, how to control them, how to change them. That will take time, and time is running out. Technologically we are moving at breakneck speed; biologically we are moving at an imperceptible crawl. If we are to survive as a species, we had better do something about ourselves before the gap created by those different speeds becomes too great. According to Wilson, we have about a hundred years.

Reading Questions

1. What is the goal of sociobiology?
2. Compare and contrast theories of human nature offered by Wilson, Ardrey, and Skinner.
3. What is altruism as defined by Wilson?
4. If some of our behavior is genetically inherited, how could this be detrimental to people who live in a rapidly developing technological society?

Questions for Reflection and Research

1. See *The New York Review of Books* and *Science* for accounts of the strong reaction against Wilson's book among some Harvard faculty. What were the objections? Were the objections good ones?
2. Is sociobiology committed to the view that human beings have no free will?
3. Is Wilson's conception of altruism different from the ordinary one? If so, is he or are his critics guilty of carelessly moving from one conception to another?
4. When we help others, do we choose to do so—or are we compelled by hereditary forces?
5. How do Ardrey and other advocates (e.g., Tiger, Morris, and Lorenz) of strong genetic control of behavior defend their conclusions? What objections are there to their conclusions?
6. There are a number of sciences that examine human beings and their

conduct (psychology, sociology, sociobiology, linguistics, and so on). Can any science really explain why we act as we do? Which one? (See selections #36, #38, and #39.)

7. Is sociobiology a pseudo-science? (See selection #50 by M. Gardner.)

Human Freedom, Human Nature, and the Science of Behavior

The Author: B. F. Skinner (b. 1904) has been one of the most articulate advocates of behaviorist psychology. Educated at Hamilton College and Harvard University, he became known in his field for the innovative animal learning experiments he devised. He has been a professor of psychology at Harvard since 1948.

The Selection: In the novel *Walden II,* from which this selection is taken, Skinner portrays a utopia run on principles of behaviorist psychology. Frazier is the leader of the utopia, which has been named Walden II. Castle, a visitor, is hostile both to Walden II and to the principles on which it is based. In this selection Frazier tries to convince Castle that we are never free in our actions.

"Isn't it time we talked about freedom?" I said. "We parted a day or so ago on an agreement to let the question of freedom ring. It's time to answer, don't you think?"

"My answer is simple enough," said Frazier. "I deny that freedom exists at all. I must deny it—or my program would be absurd. You can't have a science about a subject matter which hops capriciously about. Perhaps we can never *prove* that man isn't free; it's an assumption. But the increasing success of a science of behavior makes it more and more plausible."

"On the contrary, a simple personal experience makes it untenable," said Castle. "The experience of freedom. I *know* that I'm free."

"It must be quite consoling," said Frazier.

"And what's more—you do, too," said Castle hotly. "When you

Reprinted with permission of Macmillan Publishing Co., Inc., from *Walden II* by B. F. Skinner. Copyright 1948 by B. F. Skinner, renewed 1976 by B. F. Skinner.

deny your own freedom for the sake of playing with a science of behavior, you're acting in plain bad faith. That's the only way I can explain it." He tried to recover himself and shrugged his shoulders. "At least you'll grant that you *feel* free."

"The 'feeling of freedom' should deceive no one," said Frazier. "Give me a concrete case."

"Well, right now," Castle said. He picked up a book of matches. "I'm free to hold or drop these matches."

"You will, of course, do one or the other," said Frazier. "Linguistically or logically there seem to be two possibilities, but I submit that there's only one in fact. The determining forces may be subtle but they are inexorable. I suggest that as an orderly person you will probably hold—ah! you drop them! Well, you see, that's all part of your behavior with respect to me. You couldn't resist the temptation to prove me wrong. It was all lawful. You had no choice. The deciding factor entered rather late, and naturally you couldn't foresee the result when you first held them up. There was no strong likelihood that you would act in either direction, and so you said you were free."

"That's entirely too glib," said Castle. "It's easy to argue lawfulness after the fact. But let's see you predict what I will do in advance. Then I'll agree there's law."

"I didn't say that behavior is always predictable, any more than the weather is always predictable. There are often too many factors to be taken into account. We can't measure them all accurately, and we couldn't perform the mathematical operations needed to make a prediction if we had the measurements. The legality is usually an assumption—but none the less important in judging the issue at hand."

"Take a case where there's no choice, then," said Castle. "Certainly a man in jail isn't free in the sense in which I am free now."

"Good! That's an excellent start. Let us classify the kinds of determiners of human behavior. One class, as you suggest, is physical restraint—handcuffs, iron bars, forcible coercion. These are ways in which we shape human behavior according to our wishes. They're crude, and they sacrifice the affection of the controllee, but they often work. Now, what other ways are there of limiting freedom?" . . .

"Force or the threat of force—I see no other possibility," said Castle after a moment.

"Precisely," said Frazier.

"But certainly a large part of my behavior has no connection with force at all. There's my freedom!" said Castle.

"I wasn't agreeing that there was no other possibility—merely that *you* could see no other. Not being a good behaviorist—or a good Christian, for that matter—you have no feeling for a tremendous power of a different sort."

"What's that?"

"I shall have to be technical," said Frazier. "But only for a moment. It's what the science of behavior calls 'reinforcement theory.' The things that can happen to us fall into three classes. To some things we are indifferent. Other things we like—we want them to happen, and we take steps to make them happen again. Still other things we don't like—we don't want them to happen and we take steps to get rid of them or keep them from happening again.

"*Now*," Frazier continued earnestly, "if it's in our power to create any of the situations which a person likes or to remove any situation he doesn't like, we can control his behavior. When he behaves as we want him to behave, we simply create a situation he likes, or remove one he doesn't like. As a result, the probability that he will behave that way again goes up, which is what we want. Technically it's called 'positive reinforcement.'

"The old school made the amazing mistake of supposing that the reverse was true, that by removing a situation a person likes or setting up one he doesn't like—in other words by punishing him—it was possible to *reduce* the probability that he would behave in a given way again. That simply doesn't hold. It has been established beyond question. What is emerging at this critical stage in the evolution of society is a behavioral and cultural technology based on positive reinforcement alone. We are gradually discovering—at an untold cost in human suffering—that in the long run punishment doesn't reduce the probability that an act will occur. We have been so preoccupied with the contrary that we always take 'force' to mean punishment. We don't say we're using force when we send shiploads of food into a starving country, though we're displaying quite as much *power* as if we were sending troops and guns."

"I'm certainly not an advocate of force," said Castle. "But I can't agree that it's not effective."

"It's *temporarily* effective, that's the worst of it. That explains several thousand years of bloodshed. Even nature has been fooled. We 'instinctively' punish a person who doesn't behave as we like—we spank him if he's a child or strike him if he's a man. A nice distinction! The immediate effect of the blow teaches us to strike again. Retribution and revenge are the most natural things on earth. But in the long run the man we strike is no less likely to repeat his act."

"But he won't repeat it if we hit him hard enough," said Castle.

"He'll still *tend* to repeat it. He'll *want* to repeat it. We haven't really altered his potential behavior at all. That's the pity of it. If he doesn't repeat it in our presence, he will in the presence of someone else. Or it will be repeated in the disguise of a neurotic symptom. If we hit hard enough, we clear a little place for ourselves in the wilderness of civilization, but we make the rest of the wilderness still more terrible.

"Now, early forms of government are naturally based on punishment. It's the obvious technique when the physically strong control the weak. But we're in the throes of a great change to positive reinforcement—from a competitive society in which one man's reward is another man's punishment, to a cooperative society in which no one gains at the expense of anyone else.

"The change is slow and painful because the immediate, temporary effect of punishment overshadows the eventual advantage of positive reinforcement. We've all seen countless instances of the temporary effect of force, but clear evidence of the effect of not using force is rare. That's why I insist that Jesus, who was apparently the first to discover the power of refusing to punish, must have hit upon the principle by accident. He certainly had none of the experimental evidence which is available to us today, and I can't conceive that it was possible, no matter what the man's genius, to have discovered the principle from casual observation."

"A touch of revelation, perhaps?" said Castle.

"No, accident. Jesus discovered one principle because it had immediate consequences, and he got another thrown in for good measure."

I began to see light.

"You mean the principle of 'love your enemies'?" I said.

"Exactly! To 'do good to those who despitefully use you' has two unrelated consequences. You gain the peace of mind we talked about the other day. Let the stronger man push you around—at least you avoid the torture of your own rage. *That's* the immediate consequence. What an astonishing discovery it must have been to find that in the long run you could *control the stronger man* in the same way!" . . .

"Now that we *know* how positive reinforcement works and why negative doesn't," he said at last, "we can be more deliberate, and hence more successful, in our cultural design. We can achieve a sort of control under which the controlled, though they are following a code much more scrupulously than was ever the case under the old system, nevertheless *feel free*. They are doing what they want to do, not what they are forced to do. That's the source of the tremendous power of positive reinforcement—there's no restraint and no revolt. By a careful cultural design, we control not the final behavior, but the *inclination* to behave—the motives, the desires, the wishes.

"The curious thing is that in that case *the question of freedom never arises*. Mr. Castle was free to drop the matchbook in the sense that nothing was preventing him. If it had been securely bound to his hand he wouldn't have been free. Nor would he have been quite free if I'd covered him with a gun and threatened to shoot him if he let it fall. The question of freedom arises when there is restraint—either physical or psychological.

"But restraint is only one sort of control, and absence of restraint isn't freedom. It's not control that's lacking when one feels 'free,' but the objectionable control of force. Mr. Castle felt free to hold or drop the matches in the sense that he felt no restraint—no threat of punishment in taking either course of action. He neglected to examine his positive reasons for holding or letting go, in spite of the fact that these were more compelling in this instance than any threat of force.

"We have no vocabulary of freedom in dealing with what we want to do," Frazier went on. "The question never arises. When men strike for freedom, they strike against jails and the police, or the threat of them—against oppression. They never strike against forces which make them want to act the way they do. Yet, it seems to be understood that governments will operate only through force or the threat of force, and that all other principles of control will be left to education, religion, and commerce. If this continues to be the case, we may as well give up. A government can never create a free people with the techniques now allotted to it.

"The question is: Can men live in freedom and peace? And the answer is: Yes, if we can build a social structure which will satisfy the needs of everyone and in which everyone will want to observe the supporting code. But so far this has been achieved only in Walden Two. Your ruthless accusations to the contrary, Mr. Castle, this is the freest place on earth. And it is free precisely because we make no use of force or the threat of force. Every bit of our research, from the nursery through the psychological management of our adult membership, is directed toward that end—to exploit every alternative to forcible control. By skillful planning, by a wise choice of techniques we *increase* the feeling of freedom. . . ."

Reading Questions

1. How does Frazier reconcile his view that we are not free with his view that he cannot predict behavior?
2. Why, according to Frazier, are punishment and force ineffective means of control?
3. In *Walden II* to what extent are the inhabitants free?

Questions for Reflection and Research

1. Is all learning merely a matter of repeating what is reinforced? (See Chomsky's views described in selection #16.)
2. Does science proceed on the assumption that humans are not free?
3. To what extent are behaviorists willing to allow heredity as a controlling factor in behavior? (Compare with selection #14.)

4. If humans are not free, what are the implications for religion? For social policy?
5. Can science determine whether we are free?
6. What reasons are there to think we are free? What reasons are there to think our behavior is determined? (See selection #17.)

selection 16.

The Science of Linguistics and Implications about Human Nature

The Author: John Lyons (b. 1932) is the author of a lucid account of modern linguistics: *Introduction to Theoretical Linguistics*. He has taught in the United States and in Great Britain, where he is affiliated with the University of Edinburgh.

Noam Chomsky (b. 1928) is the main focus of this selection. As an undergraduate at the University of Pennsylvania he studied linguistics, mathematics, and philosophy. His graduate work in linguistics was done at Harvard University and the University of Pennsylvania. In addition to his major contributions to linguistics Chomsky is known for his political writings. He teaches at Massachusetts Institute of Technology.

The Selection: Some of the consequences of an approach to linguistics called transformational grammar are described. Specifically, the views of the founder of transformational grammar, Noam Chomsky, are given. Chomsky claims that linguistics reveals innate and possibly universal structures of the human mind—structures which are passed on genetically. He argues that behaviorism is incorrect in both its account of human nature and its arguments against human freedom.

[Noam] Chomsky believes that linguistics can make an important contribution to the study of the human mind and that, even now, it provides evidence in favor of one position rather than the other in the long-standing philosophical dispute between *rationalists* and *empiricists*. The difference between these two doctrines, at its most extreme, is as follows: the rationalist claims that the mind (or "reason"—hence the term "rationalism") is the sole source of human knowledge, the empiricist that all knowledge derives from experience ("empiricism" comes from the Greek word for "experience"). But there are, of course, less extreme formulations of the difference; and in the long history of Western philosophy the debate between representatives of the two camps has taken a variety of forms.

In the seventeenth and eighteenth centuries, and in a good deal of European and American philosophy since then, one of the main points at issue has been the relationship between the mind (if there is such a thing, as many empiricists would deny) and our perception of the external world. Is this simply a matter of the passive registration of sense-impressions and their subsequent combination in terms of laws of "association," as the British empiricists, [John] Locke [1632–1704], [George] Berkeley [1685–1753], and [David] Hume [1711–1776], claimed was the case? Or should we say, rather, with such philosophers as Descartes, that our perception and understanding of the external world rests upon a number of "ideas" . . . and that these "ideas" are "innate," and not derived from experience? The empiricist doctrine has been very influential in the development of modern psychology; and, combined with *physicalism* and *determinism,* it has been responsible for the view, held by many psychologists, that human knowledge and human behavior are wholly determined by the environment, there being no radical difference in this respect between human beings and other animals, or indeed between animals and machines. (By "physicalism" is meant, in this context, the philosophical system according to which all statements made about a person's thoughts, emotions, and sensations can be reformulated as statements about his bodily condition and observable behavior, and can thus be brought within the scope of "physical" laws; by "determinism" is meant the doctrine that all physical events and phenomena, including those actions and decisions of human beings that we might describe as resulting from "choice" or "free will," are determined by earlier events and phenomena and are subject to the laws of cause-and-effect, so that our impression of freedom of choice is totally illusory. Behaviorism [is] . . . a particular version of physicalism and determinism.) Chomsky's view of man is very different: he believes that we are endowed with a number of specific faculties (to which we give the name "mind") that play a crucial role in our acquisition of knowledge and enable us to act as free agents, undetermined (though not necessarily unaffected) by external stimuli in the environment. These are the issues that Chomsky deals with in many of his most recent publications, most notably in *Cartesian Linguistics* and *Language and Mind.* Before plunging into these deep and turbulent waters, it will be as well to discuss the linguistic evidence to which Chomsky appeals as a support for his rationalist philosophy. . . .

Most American linguists (and many linguists in other parts of the world too, it must be admitted), if they had been asked, ten or fifteen years ago, what was the main purpose of linguistics, would probably have said that it was "to describe languages"; and they might well have referred to the practical advantages of a training in the subject for anthropologists, missionaries, and others whose business it was to communicate with peoples speaking a language for which grammars had not yet been written. They would have left the matter at that. Very few of them, if any, would have given the kind of answer that [Edward] Sapir [1884–1939] had suggested to this question in his book *Language,* published a generation before: that language is worth studying because it is unique to man and indispensable for thought. Indeed, they might well have challenged the propriety of using the word "language" in the singular in the way that I have just done, since this tends to imply that all languages have something in common. . . . [Leonard] Bloomfield [1887–1949] himself had said, in a much-quoted passage, that "the only useful generalizations about language are inductive generalizations," and the "features which we think ought to be universal may be absent from the very next language that becomes accessible."

Chomsky's attitude, as expressed in his most recent publications, is radically opposed to Bloomfield's. He holds that it is the central purpose of linguistics to construct a deductive theory of the structure of human language that is at once sufficiently general to apply to all languages (and not only all known languages, but also all possible languages . . .) and not so general that it would also be applicable to other systems of communication or anything else that we should not wish to call languages. In other words, linguistics should determine the universal and essential properties of human language. . . .

Chomsky believes that there are certain phonological [= sound], syntactic [= gramatical], and semantic [= meaning] units that are *universal,* not in the sense that they are necessarily present in all languages, but in the somewhat different, and perhaps less usual, sense of the term "universal," that they can be defined independently of their occurrence in any particular language and can be identified, when they do occur in particular languages, on the basis of their definition within the general theory. For example, it is held that there is a fixed set of up to twenty *distinctive features* of phonology (e.g., the feature of *voicing* that distinguishes *p* from *b* or *t* from *d* in the pronunciation of the English words *pin* and *bin* or *ten* and *den*, or the feature of *nasality* that distinguishes *b* from *m* or *d* from *n* in *bad* and *mad* or *pad* and *pan*). Not all of these will be found in the phonemes [= sound units] of all languages; but from their various possible combinations every language will, as it were, make its own selection. Similarly at the level of syntax and semantics. Such syntactic categories as Noun or Verb or Past Tense, and such components of the meaning of words as "male" or "physical object," belong to fixed sets of elements, in terms of which it is possible to describe the syntactic and semantic structure of all languages, although no particular language will necessarily manifest all the elements recognized as "universal" in the general theory. These phonological, syntactic, and semantic elements are what Chomsky calls the *substantive universals* of linguistic theory.

Far more characteristic of Chomsky's thought, and more original, is his emphasis on what he refers to as *formal universals;* that is, the general principles that determine the form of the rules and the manner of their operation in the grammars of particular languages. . . .

Chomsky himself has been more cautious than some of his followers in accepting that languages are more similar in their deep structure than they are in their surface structure. He attaches far more importance to the fact (and let us grant, provisionally, that it is a fact) that different languages make use of the same [forms of] operations in the construction of grammatical sentences. And it is upon this kind of similarity between languages . . . that he rests his case for a rationalist philosophy of language. . . .

We now come to the philosophical consequences of Chomsky's notion of universal grammar. If all human languages are strikingly similar in structure, it is natural to ask why this should be so. It is equally natural, or so it might appear to an empiricist philosopher, to answer this question by appealing to such obviously relevant facts as the following: all human languages make reference to the properties and objects of the physical world, which, presumably, is perceived in essentially the same way by all physiologically and psychologically normal human beings; all languages, in whatever culture they might operate, are called upon to fulfill a similar range of functions (making statements, asking questions, issuing commands, etc.); all languages make use of the same physiological and psychological "apparatus," and the very way in which this operates may be held responsible for some of the formal properties of language. Now all these facts are, as I have said, relevant; and they may well have exerted an influence upon the structure of language. But many of the universal features of language . . . are not readily explained in this way. The only conceivable explanation, says Chomsky, in terms of our present knowledge at least, is that human beings are genetically endowed with a highly specific "language faculty" and that it is this "faculty" which determines [the] universal features [of language]. . . . It is at this point that Chomsky makes contact with the rationalist tradition in philosophy.

Chomsky's conclusion is reinforced, he claims, by a consideration of the process by which children learn their native language. All the evidence available suggests that children are not born with a predisposition to learn any one language rather than any other. We may therefore assume that all children, regardless of race and parentage, are born with the same ability for learning languages; and, in normal circumstances, children will grow up as what we call "native speakers" of that language which they hear spoken in the community in which they are born and spend their early years. But how does the child manage to develop that creative command of his native language which enables him to produce and understand sentences he has never heard before? Chomsky maintains that it is only by assuming that the child is born with a knowledge of the highly restrictive principles of universal grammar, and the predisposition to make use of them in analyzing the utterances he hears about him, that we can make any sense of the process of language learning. Empiricist theories of language learning cannot bridge the gap between the relatively small number of utterances (many of them full of errors, distortions, and hesitations) which the child hears about him and his ability to construct for himself on the basis of this scanty and imperfect data, in a relatively short time, the grammatical rules of the language. It is the child's inborn knowledge of the universal principles governing the structure of human language that supplies the deficiency in the empiricist account of language acquisition. These principles are part of what we call the "mind," being represented in some way, no doubt, in the structure or mode of operation of the brain, and may be compared with the "innate ideas" of Descartes and the rationalist tradition going back to Plato [427–347 B.C.]. . . .

Having been trained himself in the predominantly empiricist tradition of modern science, he is well aware that his notion of the genetic transmission of the principles of universal grammar will strike many philosophers and scientists as absurdly fanciful. As he pointed out in [a] radio discussion . . . : "The empiricist view is so deep-seated in our way of looking at the human mind that it almost has the character of superstition." After all, we do not accuse the biologist of unscientific mysticism when he postulates the genetic transmission and subsequent maturation of the quite complex "instinctual" behavior patterns characteristic of various species. Why should we be so ready to believe that human behavior, which is demonstrably more complex and more flexible, *must* be accounted for without the postulation of certain highly specialized abilities and dispositions (to which we give the name "mind") with which we are genetically endowed and which manifest themselves, in the appropriate circumstances, at a certain stage of our development?

It is of course the traditional associations of the word "mind" that are responsible for much of the hostile reaction to Chomsky's rationalism (or "mentalism"). Many philosophers, and most notably, perhaps, Descartes, have drawn a very sharp distinction between "body" and "mind"; and they have claimed that the physiological functions and operations of the "body," unlike the workings of the "mind," are subject to the same "mechanical," or "physical," laws as the rest of the "material" world. Chomsky's position is, however, somewhat different. Like Descartes and other "mentalists," he believes that human behavior is, in part at least, undetermined by external stimuli or internal physiological states: he is thus opposed to "mechanism" (or "physicalism," in the usual sense). On the other hand, he differs from Descartes and most philosophers who would normally be called "mentalist" in that he does not subscribe to the ultimate irreducibility of the distinction between "body" and "mind." In the radio interview to which I have referred, he makes the point that "the whole issue of whether there's a physical basis for mental structures is a rather empty issue," because, in the development of modern science, "the concept 'physical' has been extended step by step to cover anything we understand," so that "when we ultimately begin to understand the properties of mind, we shall simply . . . extend the notion 'physical' to cover these properties as well." He does not even deny that it is possible in principle to account for "mental phenomena" in terms of "the physiological processes and physical processes that we now understand." It will be clear from these quotations that, although Chomsky describes himself as a "mentalist," it is mechanistic determinism, and more particularly behaviorism, to which he is opposed, and that, in contrast with such philosophers as Plato or Descartes, he might equally well be described as a "physicalist."

Reading Questions

1. How do empiricists and rationalists differ in their conception of knowledge and of human nature?
2. How do Chomsky's views on the goals of linguistics differ from those of most of his predecessors?
3. What aspects of human nature does Chomsky regard as universal?
4. How do facts about language learning disprove empiricist theories of language learning (behaviorism)?
5. Is Chomsky a determinist? How does he defend his view?

Questions for Reflection and Research

1. Is Chomsky's account of human nature consistent with that of sociobiology? (See selection #14.)
2. Review Chomsky's writings for his developed objections to behaviorism.

3. Can science decide which science (behavioristic psychology or Chomskian linguistics) is correct?
4. How can Chomsky believe both that we are free and that our mental phenomena can be accounted for physiologically?
5. Is linguistics a science?

_____

selection 17.

_____

Theories about Human Freedom

_____

The Author: Arthur J. Minton (b. 1942) teaches philosophy at the University of Missouri, Kansas City. In the introductory philosophy text from which the following selection is excerpted Professor Minton asserts: "There is no hard and fast distinction between philosophy and science." His summary of the free-will issue is a good example of how philosophy and science can intermingle.

The Selection: Three theories about human freedom are described. The hard determinist position seems to be in harmony with scientific assumptions but conflicts with our feeling of freedom. Libertarianism is in harmony with the latter and not with the former. Soft determinism is in harmony with science but also claims to find a place for moral appraisal of human conduct. Social, moral, and religious consequences of these theories are briefly explained.

_____

THE PARADOX OF FREEDOM

I have quit smoking. The cigarettes lie on the desk before me. I remember the delightful sensation of smoke filling my lungs. My fingers begin to twitch. I force myself to think of the consequences of resuming the habit—the health dangers, the responsibilities I have to others. But I am especially nervous today and smoking would calm me down. Besides, just one couldn't hurt. . . . I pick up the pack. But then I hesitate, gather myself together, and throw them away. I have won against powerful forces within myself. I am not a passive victim, for I have exerted my will.

_____

This sort of struggle is a familiar story to everyone. As we experience it, we feel that we can go one way or another. The future is open, and the outcome is under our control. But there are facts which cloud this assumption. If every event has a cause, as science seems to say, how can we be in control of things? In a burst of scientific enthusiasm, the nineteenth-century mathematician [Pierre] LaPlace [1749–1827] remarked that if a person of great intelligence knew the exact configuration of atoms at any specific time, as well as the laws which govern the movement of matter, that person could predict every future state of the universe with absolute certainty. Every event is conditioned to be just as it is by what immediately precedes it, and those events by what precedes them, and so on. A million years ago God could have predicted that I would throw the cigarettes away. Whatever happens *must* happen—there is no alternative.

The dominant image of life which emerges from this dilemma seems clearly pessimistic. The individual is a passive object, manipulated by hidden forces that are impossible to resist. Try as we might, we cannot alter the future which is laid down at the beginning of time. In our own time, new developments in psychology have added detail to this picture. Many psychologists emphasize the extent to which our choices are governed by unconscious forces created by early childhood experiences. Our lives are depicted as the working out of blind mechanical processes over which we have no control.

Yet the feeling of freedom persists. At least some of the time, we believe that we are in control of our future. Above all, we see ourselves as morally responsible agents, ready to stand accountable for what we do, because we could have done otherwise. Is this feeling of freedom an unscientific illusion, or is the realm of choice somehow exempt from the laws of causality?

Determinism is the view that every event has a cause. At first glance, this seems to be a reasonable assumption, but it is one which has confounded every thinker who has pondered its implications. Modern science assumes that the universe is a deterministic system. To explain, predict, and establish lawful relations between things requires that the past and the future be connected, and this, in turn, seems to mean that the future flows necessarily from the past. If things and events are caused, then it is possible to specify a set of conditions which, when present, produce the effect *without exception*. On the other hand, an indeterministic universe would be one where sometimes events would lead up to what appeared to be an inevitable consequence, and yet something new might occur—something which could not be predicted from the past, not even by God.

How does the issue of determinism affect our belief that we are free agents? The most natural position to adopt is that a deterministic universe rules out free will. If this assumption is correct, then one is forced to choose between free will and determinism. The position known as *hard-determinism* rejects free will, whereas its opposite counterpart, *libertarianism,* asserts that determinism is false.

The hard-determinist claims that the human personality is within the normal course of nature, and so free will cannot exist. If it did exist, it would be possible for a person to choose a course of action against all the forces of heredity and training which have been building in the opposite direction. But the hard-determinist believes that every choice can be completely explained by previous causes, and so the subjective feeling of freedom to choose between alternatives is an illusion. Naturally, this affects the normal view of moral responsibility. Character—that is, habits, beliefs, values, dispositions, and capacities—is a unique product of heredity and environment. Our decisions flow from our character with the same necessity as an unfolding chemical reaction. But we are not responsible for our character, and so we cannot be held responsible for the actions produced by it. . . .

It is not easy, however, to reject the nagging feeling of freedom that most people experience in their daily lives. Libertarianism, like hard-determinism, is based on the assumption that free will cannot exist in a deterministic universe. Because of the experienced quality of freedom, the libertarian denies that the universe is completely deterministic. William James [1842–1910], for example, believed that chance is an ultimate factor in nature. Most libertarians do not go so far as James for fear of denying the obvious successes of science. Rather than regarding the uniformities of nature as a series of happy coincidences, they grant that most events are under the rule of causal necessity. There is, however, a range of events where alternative possibilities are available—namely, the events of human choice. Therefore, libertarians all agree that some decisions cannot be completely explained by prior causes.

Libertarianism is a doctrine which seeks to preserve the sense of self-control which is required for moral responsibility. People do not merely passively respond to the world. The person is a wellspring of creative activity which stands over against the flow of events and controls them. Determinism, consequently, is a view that runs counter to the predominant trend of experience. William James argues that our feelings of regret do not make sense in a determined world. We regret the occurrence of things that are bad. But according to the determinist, they *must* occur. How can we regret something that must be? We might as well regret the falling of a stone when we drop it. As a result, James held that determinism leads to moral complacency, for, without regrets, we must be satisfied with the world as it is.

We seem to be on the horns of a dilemma: give up free will or give up determinism. Either alternative is intellectually discomforting. But there is a middle position. This is the theory called *soft-determinism*. Soft-determinists claim that free will and determinism are compatible. Indeed, soft-determinists believe that determinism is a necessary condition for moral responsibility. William James called this view a "quagmire of evasion."

The soft-determinist maintains that our actual moral practices cannot be squared with indeterminism, and that they make sense only if we suppose that a person's behavior is caused by certain ingredients of the personality. If someone commits a murder while under the influence of a hypnotist, for example, it is absurd to hold that person responsible. The chief cause of the action lay outside the person's character—in this case, in the character of the hypnotist. Similarly, if someone behaves irrationally because of a brain tumor, or as a result of excruciating pain, responsibility is diminished. Once again, these are causes which lie outside the wants and desires that make up the personality. The reason why we do not punish individuals under these conditions is that the punishment would not affect such behavior under similar circumstances. Punishment, like rewards, makes sense only under the assumption that *it will serve as a cause for future behavior*. Libertarianism, therefore, cannot provide an adequate account of moral responsibility because it is a theory in which decisions are not caused by the central mechanisms of the personality. If a person's decisions do not spring from the personality—if they simply "pop" into existence—then they are capricious. In such a world, the person is a victim of chance, not a free agent. Moral freedom is not freedom from all causes, but rather it is freedom from certain *kinds* of causes. When we are prevented by an external constraint from acting as we want to act, or when our actions result from causes foreign to our personality, we are not free. We are free when our actions result from the uncompelled choices of the personality.

According to soft-determinism, both libertarianism and hard-determinism are founded on a shared misconception. Both positions have correctly noted that freedom requires that more than one alternative be available to the agent. They have interpreted this to mean that a free agent must be able to act independently of prior causes. But this is an error. When we say that a person has alternatives available, we simply mean that no matter which course of action is chosen, there are no external constraints which would prevent the person from acting on that choice. A free agent could have done otherwise, in the sense that nothing stood in the way of doing otherwise, *if another choice had been made*.

What are the practical consequences of these theories? Does accepting one of them make a difference? The answer to this is an unqualified "yes." To see the practical effect of a belief in hard-determinism, [consider] Clarence Darrow's moving defense of

Leopold and Loeb, two admitted murderers. Darrow [1867–1938] argues that the death penalty is cruel and senseless because the defendants were not responsible for what they did. Indeed, Darrow would argue that punishment of any kind is unjustified. If people are to be locked up, it is only to protect society—not because they deserve it. A libertarian, on the other hand, believes that wrong doing merits retribution. That is, punishment is justified because the agent *could have done otherwise.* Also, the libertarian position supposes that the human person cannot be fully analyzed by the methods of science, and therefore transcends the normal order of nature. Soft-determinism accepts something from both positions. It counsels mercy, because the sole function of punishment is to reform. Like Darrow, the soft-determinist cannot regard the infliction of punishment as retribution for past wrongs. Therefore, the doctrine of eternal punishment which is a feature in many religions is senseless. But like the libertarian, the soft-determinist believes that people can be held responsible for their actions under certain conditions, because holding them responsible serves as a cause for socially desired behavior.

Reading Questions

1. What is the difference between determinism and indeterminism?
2. What reasons are given in favor of and against each of the three theories?
3. What are the consequences of each theory for morality, punishment, and religion?
4. What assumption is modern science said to make that has a bearing on the issue of free will?

Questions for Reflection and Research

1. Does Heisenberg's uncertainty principle or the probabilistic nature of quantum mechanics show that modern physics is really indeterministic? (These two findings in modern physics are described in selection #20.)
2. Which of the three theories do people in the following selections accept: #10, #14, #15, and #16?
3. Which of the body-mind theories described in selection #11 seems most compatible with libertarianism?
4. Can science prove which of the theories is correct? Why or why not?
5. Are there other ways of responding to the free-will issue?

section 3

Possible Limitations of Science

An epistemological skeptic is a person who claims that we cannot gain knowledge. A number of considerations advanced from various quarters are supposed to convince us that knowledge about the world, or aspects of it, may be inherently out of our reach. Epistemology is conceived by some philosophers as a field of philosophy in which attempts are made to prove that such skeptical claims are wrong.

Consider some of the reasons that might be advanced to show that science itself may not be a trustworthy source of knowledge:

(1) Some Eskimo tribes have many different words for white—and can distinguish many different whites. Benjamin Lee Whorf and Edward Sapir concluded from this and other evidence about differences between languages that one's language influences how one sees the world. The implication for science seems to be that there can be no one correct physics or one correct kind of science. Because of one's language there can be no unbiased view of the world. Each culture's science would be different. (See selection #18 by Whorf.)

(2) Scientists observe aspects of the world, but how can they be sure that what they see originates in a world outside their minds? Perhaps all the data the scientist has (e.g., his or her past records and data recorded by others) are part of a dream. Can a scientist prove his or her life has not been a dream? If not, then it is possible that science may not be about the world but merely about the scientist's dream.

(3) Even if one could be sure there was a world external to oneself, can one trust the scientific data and theories supplied by others? Other people may mean something else by words than the scientist means. Unless one can enter others' minds one cannot be sure what they mean by the words they write or speak. Furthermore, it may be that other people have no

minds. The sounds and marks (writing) they make may mean nothing at all. Unless a scientist can find a way to prove that others mean what one thinks they mean, one cannot be confident how to interpret the marks and sounds they make.

(4) Even if a scientist somehow could be confident that others meant what he or she did by the words they speak and that there is a world external to his or her mind, another problem arises. Can one trust the knowledge one thinks one has about the past? Memories and records are used by scientists to guide present research. In some sciences fossils and ancient human artifacts are regarded as useful evidence for conclusions. But perhaps what we regard as records, traces, and memories of the past were all created, say, five minutes ago. Until we can prove that the world complete with fossils and memories was not created recently, we cannot be confident that we have knowledge of the past.

(5) Even if we could overcome the above difficulties, how can we justify generalizations and predictions in science? When we have seen a sample, how can we be confident that we can extend our results to the entire class under study? Will the class as a whole conform to the patterns found in the sample? For instance, we have a large number of instances of rocks falling when they are released from a height. From the fact that we have observed rocks falling in the past can we correctly infer that rocks will fall in the future? Is there any proof that tomorrow will be like today? See selection #19 by Bertrand Russell for the skeptical challenges mentioned in (2) through (5) above. Also see #21 by Max Black for a fuller account of the problem described here in (5) and for a summary of some attempts to eliminate the problem.

(6) Physics contributes yet another problem for those who wish to regard science as a trustworthy path to knowledge. Werner Heisenberg, a physicist, has argued that our knowledge of submicroscopic events is limited by the fact that our observation of such events disturbs what is observed. Thus even though we may know something about a subatomic particle's previous position or velocity, our observation of the particle makes it impossible to predict with full accuracy its future position and velocity. Hence science is limited in what it can know about submicroscopic events. See selection #20 by Dietrich Schroeer for a more complete account.

(7) Often sciences introduce concepts that seem to refer to substances or events as yet unobserved and perhaps unobservable. For example, no one has seen an electron—only what are regarded as signs of electrons. Can we really be confident such theoretical entities exist? This issue is discussed by Stephen Toulmin in selection #22.

(8) Finally, consider the claim that whenever we study and reflect about the world we make assumptions that cannot themselves be the subject of scientific scrutiny. We assume, for example, that the universe is amenable to rational study. Such metaphysical assumptions, it has been argued, are both unavoidable and difficult to prove true by any method. As a consequence, science stands on, and will always stand on, a not completely secure foundation. For more on this topic see selection #23 by Hugo Thompson.

If these factors are not enough to undermine one's confidence and respect for science, one must consider a challenge set forth by some philosophers in this century, philosophers referred to often as either existentialists or phenomenologists. These philosophers tend to reject the approach to philosophy advocated by analytic philosophers, the dominant present philosophical school in a number of countries including the United States, Canada, and Great Britain. Selection #24 by William A. Earle presents the challenge. He asserts that science and philosophy as advocated by analytical philosophers are relatively trivial and unimportant undertakings. What is important is understanding life as we live it—the conscious, personal, and private aspect of ourselves. We need first to study life's possibilities in order to learn to live in a meaningful way. This learning and reflection cannot be accomplished by science, and what science does accomplish is only remotely connected thereto.

Any future scientist or previous admirer of science will be hard pressed to restore science to its lofty position after reading the selections in this section. Black in selection #21 and Toulmin in selection #22 give some help in overcoming the challenges to scientific knowledge. Can all the challenges be overcome?

Further Reading: Possible Limitations of Science

1. *The Encyclopedia of Philosophy*, ed. Paul Edwards, 8 vols (New York: Macmillan Publishing Co., 1967).
   (a) For topics touched upon by Russell in selection #19, Thompson in selection #23, and Black in selection #21 see especially the following entries: "Certainty" by C. D. Rollins; "Illusions" by R. J. Hirst; "Induction" by Max Black; "Knowledge and Belief" by Anthony Quinton; "Memory" by Sidney Shoemaker—especially the sections entitled "Skepticism" and "Justification of Memory"; "Other Minds" by J. M. Shorter; "Paradigm Case Argument" by Keith S. Donnellan; "Sensationalism" by Peter Alexander; "Skepticism" by Richard A. Popkin; and "Solipsism" by Rollins.
   (b) For one account of the philosophical stance from which Earle (in selection #24) writes see "Phenomenology" by Richard Schmitt. His attitude toward science is somewhat different from Earle's.

(c) For further discussion of the philosophical consequences of twentieth-century physics see "Quantum Physics, Philosophical Implications of" by NORWOOD RUSSELL HANSON.

(d) For a view of language similar to Whorf's (in selection #18) see "Mauthner, Fritz" by GERSHON WEILER.

(e) For further discussion of the existence of theoretical entities (as introduced in selection #22 by Toulmin) see "Laws and Theories" by MARY· HESSE. See especially the section entitled "The Cognitive Status of Theories."

2. *Language, Thought and Reality: Selected Writings of Benjamin Lee Whorf,* ed. JOHN B. CARROLL (Cambridge, Mass.: M.I.T. Press, 1956). In the introduction to this collection (pp. 27–31) there are some criticisms of the Sapir-Whorf hypothesis, as well as references to more fully developed criticisms. For a clarification of Whorf's view and a persuasive criticism see the two-part essay "Whorf's Linguistic Relativism" by JOHN W. COOK in the journal *Philosophical Investigations,* vol. 1, nos. 1 and 2 (Spring and Summer 1978).

selection 18.

The Implications of Some Findings in Linguistics for Our Knowledge of the World

The Author: Benjamin Lee Whorf (1897–1941) obtained an undergraduate degree in chemical engineering from Massachusetts Institute of Technology and was employed by an insurance company to be a fire prevention inspector. His interest in linguistics began when he was 27, at which time he studied Hebrew to help him better understand the Bible. He soon thereafter became interested in and taught himself the American Indian languages of Aztec, Maya, and Hopi, contributing research findings on these languages to journals in the field of linguistics.

The Selection: Whorf explains a view about language that he and another linguist, Edward Sapir, formulated. The Sapir-Whorf hypothesis is a theory about how language influences our thought and our perception of the world. It asserts that the way one sees the world depends on the structure of one's language. One consequence of this view would seem to be that there is no correct way of seeing the world. Or, expressed in another way, different languages will give rise to different scientific concepts. The selection is moderately demanding.

Every normal person in the world, past infancy in years, can and does talk. By virtue of that fact, every person—civilized or uncivilized—carries through life certain naïve but deeply rooted ideas about talking and its relation to thinking. Because of their firm connection with speech habits that have become unconscious and automatic, these notions tend to be rather intolerant of opposi-

From "Science and Linguistics," originally published in *Technology Review* 42: 229–31, 247–48, no. 6. Reprinted from *Language, Thought and Reality: Selected Writings of Benjamin Lee Whorf,* John B. Carroll, by permission of The M.I.T. Press, Cambridge, Massachusetts. Copyright © 1956, by Massachusetts Institute of Technology.

tion. They are by no means entirely personal and haphazard; their basis is definitely systematic, so that we are justified in calling them a system of natural logic—a term that seems to me preferable to the term common sense, often used for the same thing.

According to natural logic, the fact that every person has talked fluently since infancy makes every man his own authority on the process by which he formulates and communicates. He has merely to consult a common substratum of logic or reason which he and everyone else are supposed to possess. Natural logic says that talking is merely an incidental process concerned strictly with communication, not with formulation of ideas. Talking, or the use of language, is supposed only to "express" what is essentially already formulated nonlinguistically. Formulation is an independent process, called thought or thinking, and is supposed to be largely indifferent to the nature of particular languages. Languages have grammars, which are assumed to be merely norms of conventional and social correctness, but the use of language is supposed to be guided not so much by them as by correct, rational, or intelligent THINKING.

Thought, in this view, does not depend on grammar but on laws of logic or reason which are supposed to be the same for all observers of the universe—to represent a rationale in the universe that can be "found" independently by all intelligent observers, whether they speak Chinese or Choctaw. In our own culture, the formulations of mathematics and of formal logic have acquired the reputation of dealing with this order of things: i.e., with the realm and laws of pure thought. Natural logic holds that different languages are essentially parallel methods for expressing this one-and-the-same rationale of thought and, hence, differ really in but minor ways. . . .

If a rule has absolutely no exceptions, it is not recognized as a rule or as anything else; it is then part of the background of experience of which we tend to remain unconscious. . . .

For instance, if a race of people had the physiological defect of being able to see only the color blue, they would hardly be able to formulate the rule that they saw only blue. The term blue would convey no meaning to them, their language would lack color terms, and their words denoting their various sensations of blue would answer to, and translate, our words "light, dark, white, black," and so on, not our word "blue." In order to formulate the rule or norm of seeing only blue, they would need exceptional moments in which they saw other colors. The phenomenon of gravitation forms a rule without exceptions; needless to say, the untutored person is utterly unaware of any law of gravitation, for it would never enter his head to conceive of a universe in which bodies behaved otherwise than they do at the earth's surface. Like the color blue with our hypothetical race, the law of gravitation is a part of the untutored individual's background, not something he isolates from that background. The law could not be formulated until bodies that always fell were seen in terms of a wider astronomical world in which bodies moved in orbits or went this way and that. . . .

Natural logic . . . does not see that the phenomena of a language are to its own speakers largely of a background character and so are outside the critical consciousness and control of the speaker who is expounding natural logic. Hence, when anyone, as a natural logician, is talking about reason, logic, and the laws of correct thinking, he is apt to be simply marching in step with purely grammatical facts that have somewhat of a background character in his own language or family of languages but are by no means universal in all languages and in no sense a common substratum of reason. . . .

These background phenomena are the province of the grammarian—or of the linguist, to give him his more modern name as a scientist. . . . Scientific linguists have long understood that ability to speak a language fluently does not necessarily confer a linguistic knowledge of it, i.e., understanding of its background phenomena and its systematic processes and structure, any more than ability to play a good game of billiards confers or requires any knowledge of the laws of mechanics that operate upon the billiard table.

The situation here is not unlike that in any other field of science. All real scientists have their eyes primarily on background phenomena that cut very little ice, as such, in our daily lives; and yet their studies have a way of bringing out a close relation between these unsuspected realms of fact and such decidedly foreground activities as transporting goods, preparing food, treating the sick, or growing potatoes, which in time may become very much modified, simply because of pure scientific investigation in no way concerned with these brute matters themselves. Linguistics presents a quite similar case; the background phenomena with which it deals are involved in all our foreground activities of talking and of reaching agreement, in all reasoning and arguing of cases, in all law, arbitration, conciliation, contracts, treaties, public opinion, weighing of scientific theories, formulation of scientific results. . . .

When linguists became able to examine critically and scientifically a large number of languages of widely different patterns, their base of reference was expanded; they experienced an interruption of phenomena hitherto held universal, and a whole new order of significances came into their ken. It was found that the background linguistic system (in other words, the grammar) of each language is not merely a reproducing instrument for voicing ideas but rather is itself the shaper of ideas, the program and guide for the individual's mental activity, for his analysis of impressions, for his synthesis of his mental stock in trade. Formulation of ideas is not an independent process, strictly rational in the old sense, but is part of a particular grammar, and differs, from slightly to greatly, between different grammars. We dissect nature along lines laid down by our native languages. The categories and types that we isolate from the world of phenomena we do not find there because they stare every observer in the face; on the contrary, the world is presented in a kaleidoscopic flux of impressions which has to be organized by our minds—and this means largely by the linguistic systems in our minds. We cut nature up, organize it into concepts, and ascribe significances as we do, largely because we are parties to an agreement to organize it in this way—an agreement that holds throughout our speech community and is codified in the patterns of our language. The agreement is, of course, an implicit and unstated one, BUT ITS TERMS ARE ABSOLUTELY OBLIGATORY; we cannot talk at all except by subscribing to the organization and classification of data which the agreement decrees.

This fact is very significant for modern science, for it means that no individual is free to describe nature with absolute impartiality but is constrained to certain modes of interpretation even while he thinks himself most free. The person most nearly free in such respects would be a linguist familiar with very many widely different linguistic systems. As yet no linguist is in any such position. We are thus introduced to a new principle of relativity, which holds that all observers are not led by the same physical evidence to the same picture of the universe, unless their linguistic backgrounds are similar, or can in some way be calibrated.

This rather startling conclusion is not so apparent if we compare only our modern European languages, with perhaps Latin and Greek thrown in for good measure. Among these tongues there is a unanimity of major pattern which at first seems to bear out natural logic. But this unanimity exists only because these tongues are all Indo-European dialects cut to the same basic plan, being historically transmitted from what was long ago one speech community; because the modern dialects have long shared in building up a common culture; and because much of this culture, on the more intellectual side, is derived from the linguistic backgrounds of Latin and Greek. Thus this group of languages satisfies the special case of the clause beginning "unless" in the statement of the linguistic relativity principle at the end of the preceding paragraph. From this condition follows the unanimity of description of the world in the community of modern scientists. But it must be emphasized that "all modern Indo-European-speaking observers" is not the same thing as "all observers." That modern Chinese or Turkish scientists describe the world in the same terms as Western scientists means, of course, only that they have taken over bodily the entire Western system of rationalizations, not that they have corroborated that system from their native posts of observation.

When Semitic, Chinese, Tibetan, or African languages are contrasted with our own, the divergence in analysis of the world becomes more apparent; and, when we bring in the native languages of the Americas, where speech communities for many millenniums have gone their ways independently of each other and of the Old World, the fact that languages dissect nature in many different ways becomes patent. The relativity of all conceptual systems, ours included, and their dependence upon language stand revealed. That American Indians speaking only their native tongues are never called upon to act as scientific observers is in no wise to the point. To exclude the evidence which their languages offer as to what the human mind can do is like expecting botanists to study nothing but food plants and hothouse roses and then tell us what the plant world is like!

Let us consider a few examples. In English we divide most of our words into two classes, which have different grammatical and logical properties. Class 1 we call nouns, e.g., 'house, man', class 2, verbs, e.g., 'hit, run.' Many words of one class can act secondarily as of the other class, e.g., 'a hit, a run,' or 'to man (the boat),' but, on the primary level, the division between the classes is absolute. Our language thus gives us a bipolar division of nature. But nature herself is not thus polarized. If it be said that 'strike, turn, run,' are verbs because they denote temporary or short-lasting events, i.e., actions, why then is 'fist' a noun? It also is a temporary event. Why are 'lightning, spark, wave, eddy, pulsation, flame, storm, phase, cycle, spasm, noise, emotion' nouns? They are temporary events. If 'man' and 'house' are nouns because they are long-lasting and stable events, i.e., things, what then are 'keep, adhere, extend, project, continue, persist, grow, dwell,' and so on doing among the verbs? ... It will be found that an "event" to us means "what our language classes as a verb" or something analogized there from. And it will be found that it is not possible to define 'event, thing, object, relationship,' and so on, from nature, but that to define them always involves a circuitous return to the grammatical categories of the definer's language.

In the Hopi language, 'lightning, wave, flame, meteor, puff of smoke, pulsation' are verbs—events of necessarily brief duration cannot be anything but verbs. 'Cloud' and 'storm' are at about the lower limit of duration for nouns. Hopi, you see, actually has a classification of events (or linguistic isolates) by duration type, something strange to our modes of thought. On the other hand, in Nootka, a language of Vancouver Island, all words seem to us to be verbs, but really there are no classes 1 and 2; we have, as it were, a monistic [= unitary] view of nature that gives us only one class of word for all kinds of events. 'A house occurs' or 'it houses' is the way of saying 'house,' exactly like 'a flame occurs' or 'it burns.' These terms seem to us like verbs because they are inflected for durational and temporal nuances, so that the suffixes of the word for house event make it mean long-lasting house, temporary house, future house, house that used to be, what started out to be a house, and so on.

Hopi has one noun that covers every thing or being that flies, with the exception of birds, which class is denoted by another noun. The former noun may be said to denote the class $(FC-B)$—flying class minus bird. The Hopi actually call insect, airplane, and aviator all by the same word, and feel no difficulty about it. The situation, of course, decides any possible confusion among very disparate members of a broad linguistic class, such as this class $(FC-B)$. This class seems to us too large and inclusive, but so would our class 'snow' to an Eskimo. We have the same word for falling snow, snow on the ground, snow packed hard like ice, slushy snow, wind-driven flying snow—whatever the situation may be. To an Eskimo, this all-inclusive word would be almost unthinkable; he would say that falling snow, slushy snow, and so on, are sensuously and operationally different, different things to contend with; he uses different words for them and for other kinds of snow. The Aztecs go even farther than we in the opposite direction, with 'cold,' 'ice,' and 'snow' all represented by the same basic word with different terminations; 'ice' is the noun form; 'cold,' the adjectival form; and for 'snow,' 'ice mist.'

What surprises most is to find that various grand generalizations of the Western world, such as time, velocity, and matter, are not essential to the construction of a consistent picture of the universe. The psychic experiences that we class under these headings are, of course, not destroyed; rather, categories derived from other kinds of experiences take over the rulership of the cosmology and seem to function just as well. Hopi may be called a timeless language. It recognizes psychological time . . . but this "time" is quite unlike the mathematical time, T, used by our physicists. Among the peculiar properties of Hopi time are that it varies with each observer, does not permit of simultaneity, and has zero dimensions; i.e., it cannot be given a number greater than one. The Hopi do not say, "I stayed five days," but "I left on the fifth day." A word referring to this kind of time, like the word day, can have no plural. . . .

Hopi grammar, by means of its forms called aspects and modes, also makes it easy to distinguish among momentary, continued, and repeated occurrences, and to indicate the actual sequence of reported events. Thus the universe can be described without recourse to a concept of dimensional time. How would a physics constructed along these lines work, with no T (time) in its equations? Perfectly, as far as I can see, though of course it would require different ideology and perhaps different mathematics. Of course V (velocity) would have to go too. The Hopi language has no word really equivalent to our 'speed' or 'rapid.' What translates these terms is usually a word meaning intense or very, accompanying any verb of motion. Here is a clue to the nature of our new physics. We may have to introduce a new term I, intensity. Every thing and event will have an I, whether we regard the thing or event as moving or as just enduring or being. . . .

A scientist from another culture that used time and velocity would have great difficulty in getting us to understand these concepts. We should talk about the intensity of a chemical reaction; he would speak of its velocity or its rate, which words we should at first think were simply words for intensity in his language. Likewise, he at first would think that intensity was simply our own word for velocity. At first we should agree, later we should begin to disagree, and it might dawn upon both sides that different systems of rationalization were being used. He would find it very hard to make us understand what he really meant by velocity of a chemical reaction. We should have no words that would fit. He would try to explain it by likening it to a running horse, to the difference between a good horse and a lazy horse. We should try to show him, with a superior laugh, that his analogy also was a matter of different intensities, aside from which there was little similarity between a horse and a chemical reaction in a beaker. We should point out that a running horse is moving relative to the ground, whereas the material in the beaker is at rest.

One significant contribution to science from the linguistic point of view may be the greater development of our sense of perspective. We shall no longer be able to see a few recent dialects of the Indo-European family, and the rationalizing techniques elaborated from their patterns, as the apex of the evolution of the human mind, nor their present wide spread as due to any survival from fitness or to anything but a few events of history—events that could be called fortunate only from the parochial point of view of the favored parties. They, and our own thought processes with them, can no longer be envisioned as spanning the gamut of reason and knowledge but only as one constellation in a galactic expanse. A fair realization of the incredible degree of diversity of linguistic system that ranges over the globe leaves one with an inescapable feeling that the human spirit is inconceivably old; that the few thousand years of history covered by our written records are no more than the thickness of a pencil mark on the scale that measures our past experience on this planet; that the events of these recent millenniums spell nothing in any evolutionary wise, that the race has taken no sudden spurt, achieved no commanding synthesis during recent millenniums, but has only played a little with a few of the linguistic formulations and views of nature bequeathed from an inexpressibly longer past. Yet neither this feeling nor the sense of precarious dependence of all we know upon linguistic tools which themselves are largely unknown need be discouraging to science but should, rather, foster that humility which accompanies the true scientific spirit, and thus forbid that arrogance of the mind which hinders real scientific curiosity and detachment.

Reading Questions

1. What is meant by "natural logic"?
2. What is the point of the example of the people who see only blue?
3. What is the "new principle of relativity" and how is it supported?
4. What is the world really like according to Whorf? Can anyone actually see it the way it is? Why or why not?
5. Why do scientists in many different cultures agree on scientific concepts and conclusions if they see the world differently?

Questions for Reflection and Research

1. If one's language makes one see the world one way, how then can one learn a quite different language?
2. Compare the views of Noam Chomsky (see selection #16) and Whorf about whether there are elements common to all languages. Would any evidence settle this dispute?
3. If language influences how we think and how we perceive the world, is there any way to overcome such linguistic bias?
4. Is Whorf's claim correct that cultures with different languages would develop quite different sciences? (Do we gain scientific concepts from our culture or do the phenomena of nature force the concepts on us?)
5. Does becoming a scientist involve learning a new language?
6. Are the concepts of the science of linguistics also culture-bound? If so, is Whorf's theory thereby revealed to be self-defeating?

selection 19.

Can Scientists or Anyone Know Anything?

The Author: Bertrand Russell. For biographical information on Russell see selection #1.

The Selection: Russell summarizes a number of considerations that seem to support the view that we can be certain of almost nothing. First he raises questions about the certainty of physical things outside the mind. Memory is shown to lack certainty, as is the testimony of other people. It is even difficult to be certain we know what we mean when we ourselves speak. Finally, questions are raised about the use of induction to make generalizations upon which predictions can be based. As a consequence of Russell's reflections it seems that we cannot be certain of the existence of other minds, of the existence of anything outside our minds, of the meaning of what we ourselves say, of the existence of the self, of the existence of a past, or of the nature of the future. Science cannot give us any certainty unless it can somehow show us how to reject the various reasons for being skeptical about the possibility of knowledge. The selection is moderately demanding.

Philosophy arises from an unusually obstinate attempt to arrive at real knowledge. What passes for knowledge in ordinary life suffers from three defects: it is cocksure, vague, and self-contradictory. The first step towards philosophy consists in becoming aware of these defects, not in order to rest content with a lazy scepticism, but in order to substitute an amended kind of know-

---

From *An Outline of Philosophy* by Bertrand Russell. Published by The World Publishing Company, 1960. The World Publishing Company edition was reprinted by arrangement with George Allen & Unwin Ltd. An earlier American edition was published in 1927 by W. W. Norton & Company, Inc., under the title *Philosophy*. All rights reserved.

ledge which shall be tentative, precise, and self-consistent. There is of course another quality which we wish our knowledge to possess, namely, comprehensiveness: we wish the area of our knowledge to be as wide as possible. But this is the business of science rather than of philosophy. . . .

I mentioned . . . three defects in common beliefs. . . . It is the business of philosophy to correct these defects so far as it can, without throwing over knowledge altogether. . . .

The three defects which I have mentioned are interconnected, and by becoming aware of any one we may be led to recognise the other two. I will illustrate all three by a few examples.

Let us take first the belief in common objects, such as tables and chairs and trees. We all feel quite sure about these in ordinary life, and yet our reasons for confidence are really very inadequate. Naïve common sense supposes that they are what they appear to be, but that is impossible, since they do not appear exactly alike to any two simultaneous observers; at least, it is impossible if the object is a single thing, the same for all observers. If we are going to admit that the object is not what we see, we can no longer feel the same assurance that there is an object; this is the first intrusion of doubt. However, we shall speedily recover from this set-back, and say that of course the object is "really" what physics says it is. Now physics says that a table or a chair is "really" an incredibly vast system of electrons and protons in rapid motion, with empty space in between. This is all very well. But the physicist, like the ordinary man, is dependent upon his senses for the existence of the physical world. If you go up to him solemnly and say, "Would you be so kind as to tell me, as a physicist, what a chair really is?" you will get a learned answer. But if you say, without preamble, "Is there a chair there?" he will say, "Of course there is; can't you see it?" To this you ought to reply in the negative. You ought to say, "No, I see certain patches of colour, but I don't see any electrons or protons, and you tell me that they are what a chair consists of". He may reply: "Yes, but a large number of electrons and protons close together look like a patch of colour". "What do you mean by 'look like'?" you will then ask. He is ready with an answer. He means that light-waves start from the electrons and protons (or, more probably, are reflected by them from a source of light), reach the eye, have a series of effects upon the rods and cones, the optic nerve, and the brain, and finally produce a sensation. But he has never seen an eye or an optic nerve or a brain, any more than he has seen a chair: he has only seen patches of colour which, he says, are what eyes "look like". That is to say, he thinks that the [visual] sensation you have when (as you think) you see a chair, has a series of causes, physical and psychological, but all of them, on his own showing, lie essentially and forever outside experience. Nevertheless, he pretends to base his science upon observation. Obviously there is here a problem for the logician, a problem belonging not to physics, but to quite another kind of study. This is a first example of the way in which the pursuit of precision destroys certainty.

The physicist believes that he infers his electrons and protons from what he perceives. But the inference is never clearly set forth in a logical chain, and, if it were, it might not look sufficiently plausible to warrant much confidence. In actual fact, the whole development from common-sense objects to electrons and protons has been governed by certain beliefs, seldom conscious, but existing in every natural man. These beliefs are not unalterable, but they grow and develop like a tree. We start by thinking that a chair is as it appears to be, and is still there when we are not looking. But we find, by a little reflection, that these two beliefs are incompatible. If the chair is to persist independently of being seen by us, it must be something other than the patch of colour we see, because this is found to depend upon conditions extraneous to the chair, such as how the light falls, whether we are wearing blue spectacles, and so on. This forces the man of science to regard the "real" chair as the cause (or an indispensable part of the cause) of our sensations when we see the chair. Thus we are committed to causation as an *a priori* belief without which we should have no reason for supposing that there is a "real" chair at all. Also, for the sake of permanence we bring in the notion of substance: the "real" chair is a substance, or collection of substances, possessed of permanence and the power to cause sensations. This metaphysical belief has operated, more or less unconsciously, in the inference from sensations to electrons and protons. The philosopher must drag such beliefs into the light of day, and see whether they still survive. Often it will be found that they die on exposure.

Let us now take up another point. The evidence for a physical law, or for any scientific law, always involves both memory and testimony. We have to rely both upon what we remember to have observed on former occasions, and on what others say they have observed. In the very beginnings of science, it may have been possible sometimes to dispense with testimony; but very soon every scientific investigation began to be built upon previously ascertained results, and thus to depend upon what others have recorded. In fact, without the corroboration of testimony we should hardly have had much confidence in the existence of physical objects. Sometimes people suffer from hallucinations, that is to say, they think they perceive physical objects, but are not confirmed in this belief by the testimony of others. In such cases, we decide that they are mistaken. It is the similarity between the perceptions of different people in similar situations that makes us feel confident of the external causation of our perceptions; but for this, whatever naïve beliefs we might have had in physical objects would have been dissipated long ago. Thus memory and testimony are essential to science.

Nevertheless, each of these is open to criticism by the sceptic. Even if we succeed, more or less, in meeting his criticism, we shall, if we are rational, be left with a less complete confidence in our original beliefs than we had before. Once more, we shall become less cocksure as we become more accurate. . . .

Memory is a word which has a variety of meanings. The kind that I am concerned with at the moment is the recollection of past occurrences. This is so notoriously fallible that every experimenter makes a record of the result of his experiment at the earliest possible moment: he considers the inference from written words to past events less likely to be mistaken than the direct beliefs which constitute memory. But some time, though perhaps only a few seconds, must elapse between the observation and the making of the record, unless the record is so fragmentary that memory is needed to interpret it. Thus we do not escape from the need of trusting memory to some degree. Moreover, without memory we should not think of interpreting records as applying to the past, because we should not know that there was any past. Now, apart from arguments as to the proved fallibility of memory, there is one awkward consideration which the sceptic may urge. Remembering, which occurs now, cannot possibly—he may say—prove that what is remembered occurred at some other time, because the world might have sprung into being five minutes ago, exactly as it then was, full of acts of remembering which were entirely misleading. Opponents of Darwin . . . urged a very similar argument against evolution. The world, they said, was created in 4004 B.C., complete with fossils, which were inserted to try our faith. The world was created suddenly, but was made such as it would have been if it had evolved. There is no logical impossibility about this view. And similarly there is no logical impossibility in the view that the world was created five minutes ago, complete with memories and records. This may seem an improbable hypothesis, but it is not logically refutable.

Apart from this argument, which may be thought fantastic, there are reasons of detail for being more or less distrustful of memory. It is obvious that no *direct* confirmation of a belief about a past occurrence is possible, because we cannot make the past recur. We can find confirmation of an indirect kind in the revelations of others and in contemporary records. The latter, as we have seen, involve some degree of memory, but they may involve very little, for instance when a shorthand report of a conversation or speech has been made at the time. But even then, we do not escape wholly from the need of memory extending over a longer stretch of time. Suppose a wholly imaginary conversation were produced for some criminal purpose, we should depend upon the memories of witnesses to establish its fictitious character in a law-court. And all memory which extends over a long period of time is very apt to be mistaken; this is shown by the errors invariably found in autobiographies. Any man who comes across letters which he wrote many years ago can verify the manner in which his memory has falsified past events. For these reasons, the fact that we cannot free ourselves from dependence upon memory in building up knowledge is, *prima facie* [= it seems apparent], a reason for regarding what passes for knowledge as not quite certain. . . .

Testimony raises even more awkward problems. What makes them so awkward is the fact that testimony is involved in building up our knowledge of physics, and that, conversely, physics is required in establishing the trustworthiness of testimony. Moreover, testimony raises all the problems connected with the relation of mind and matter. . . .

For our purposes, we may define testimony as noises heard, or shapes seen, analogous to those which we should make if we wished to convey an assertion, and believed by the hearer or seer to be due to someone else's desire to convey an assertion. Let us take a concrete instance: I ask a policeman the way, and he says, "Fourth to the right, third to the left". That is to say, I hear these sounds, and perhaps I see what I interpret as his lips moving. I assume that he has a mind more or less like my own, and has uttered these sounds with the same intention as I should have had if I had uttered them, namely to convey information. In ordinary life, all this is not, in any proper sense, an inference; it is a belief which arises in us on the appropriate occasion. But if we are challenged, we have to substitute inference for spontaneous belief, and the more the inference is examined the more shaky it looks.

The inference that has to be made has two steps, one physical and one psychological. The physical inference is of the sort we considered a moment ago, in which we pass from a [visual or auditory] sensation to a physical occurrence. We hear noises, and think they proceed from the policeman's body. We see moving shapes, and interpret them as physical motions of his lips. This inference, as we saw earlier, is in part justified by testimony; yet now we find that it has to be made before we can have reason to believe that there is any such thing as testimony. And this inference is certainly sometimes mistaken. Lunatics hear voices which other people do not hear; instead of crediting them with abnormally acute hearing, we lock them up. But if we sometimes hear sentences which have not proceeded from a body, why should this not always be the case? Perhaps our imagination has conjured up all the things that we think others have said to us. But this is part of the general problem of inferring physical objects from sensations, which, difficult as it is, is not the most difficult part of the logical puzzles concerning testimony. The most difficult part is the inference from the policeman's body to his mind. I do not mean any special insult to policemen; I would say the same of politicians and even of philosophers.

The inference to the policeman's mind certainly *may* be wrong. It is clear that a maker of waxworks could make a life-like policeman and put a gramophone inside him, which would cause him periodically to tell visitors the way to the most interesting part of the exhibition at the entrance to which he would stand. They would have just the sort of evidence of his being alive that is found convincing in the case of other policemen. Descartes believed that animals have no minds, but are merely complicated automata. Eighteenth-century materialists extended this doctrine to men. . . . Even a materialist must admit that, when he talks, he means to convey something, that is to say, he uses words as signs, not as mere noises. It may be difficult to decide exactly what is meant by this statement, but it is clear that it means something, and that it is true of one's own remarks. The question is: Are we sure that it is true of the remarks we hear, as well as of those we make? Or are the remarks we hear perhaps just like other noises, merely meaningless disturbances of the air? The chief argument against this is analogy: the remarks we hear are so like those we make that we think they must have similar causes. But although we cannot dispense with analogy as a form of inference, it is by no means demonstrative [= certain], and not infrequently leads us astray. We are therefore left, once more, with a *prima facie* reason for uncertainty and doubt.

This question of what we mean ourselves when we speak brings me to another problem, that of introspection. . . .

The difference between introspection and what we call perception of external objects seems to me to be connected, not with what is primary in our knowledge, but with what is inferred. We think, at one time, that we are seeing a chair; at another, that we are thinking about philosophy. The first we call perception of an external object; the second we call introspection. Now we have already found reason to doubt external perception, in the full-blooded sense in which common sense accepts it. . . . [W]hat is indubitable in "seeing a chair" is the occurrence of a certain pattern of colours. But this occurrence, we shall find, is connected with me just as much as with the chair; no one except myself can see exactly the pattern that I see. There is thus something subjective and private about what we take to be external perception, but this is concealed by precarious extensions into the physical world. I think introspection, on the contrary, involves precarious extensions into the mental world: shorn of these, it is not very different from external perception shorn of its extensions. To make this clear, I shall try to show what we know to be occurring when, as we say, we think about philosophy.

Suppose, as the result of introspection, you arrive at a belief which you express in the words: "I am now believing that mind is different from matter". What do you know, apart from inferences, in such a case? First of all, you must cut out the word "I": the person who believes is an inference, not part of what you know immediately. In the second place, you must be careful about the word "believing". I am not now concerned with what this word should mean in logic or theory of knowledge; I am concerned with what it can mean when used to describe a direct experience. In such a case, it would seem that it can only describe a certain kind of feeling. And as for the proposition you think you are believing, namely, "mind is different from matter", it is very difficult to say what is really occurring when you think you believe it. It may be mere words, pronounced, visualised, or in auditory or motor images. It may be images of what the words "mean", but in that case it will not be at all an accurate representation of the logical content of the proposition. You may have an image of a statue of Newton "voyaging through strange seas of thought alone", and another image of a stone rolling downhill, combined with the words "how different!" Or you may think of the difference between composing a lecture and eating your dinner. It is only when you come to expressing your thought in words that you approach logical precision.

Both in introspection and in external perception, we try to express what we know in WORDS.

We come here, as in the question of testimony, upon the social aspect of knowledge. The purpose of words is to give the same kind of publicity to thought as is claimed for physical objects. A number of people can hear a spoken word or see a written word, because each is a physical occurrence. If I say to you, "mind is different from matter", there may be only a very slight resemblance between the thought that I am trying to express and the thought which is aroused in you, but these two thoughts have just this in common, that they can be expressed by the same words. Similarly, there may be great differences between what you and I see when, as we say, we look at the same chair; nevertheless we can both express our perceptions by the same words.

A thought and a perception are thus not so very different in their own nature. If physics is true, they are different in their correlations: when I see a chair, others have more or less similar perceptions, and it is thought that these are all connected with light-waves coming from the chair, whereas, when I think a thought, others may not be thinking anything similar. But this applies also to feeling a toothache, which would not usually be regarded as a case of introspection. On the whole, therefore, there seems no reason to regard introspection as a different *kind* of knowledge from external perception. . . .

As for the *trustworthiness* of introspection, there is again a complete parallelism with the case of external perception. The actual datum, in each case, is unimpeachable, but the extensions which we make instinctively are questionable. Instead of saying, "I am believing that mind is different from matter", you ought to say, "certain images are occurring in a certain relation to each other, accompanied by a certain feeling". No words exist for describing the actual occurrence in all its particularity; all words, even proper names, are general, with the possible exception of "this", which is ambiguous. When you translate the occurrence into words, you are making generalisations and inferences, just as you are when you say "there is a chair". There is really no vital difference between the two cases. In each case, what is really a datum is unutterable, and what can be put into words involves inferences which may be mistaken.

When I say that "inferences" are involved, I am saying something not quite accurate unless carefully interpreted. In "seeing a chair", for instance, we do not first apprehend a coloured pattern, and then proceed to infer a chair: belief in the chair arises spontaneously when we see the coloured pattern. But this belief has causes not only in the present physical stimulus, but also partly in past experience, partly in reflexes. In animals, reflexes play a very large part; in human beings, experience is more important. The infant learns slowly to correlate touch and sight, and to expect others to see what he sees. The habits which are thus formed are essential to our adult notion of an object such as a chair. The perception of a chair by means of sight has a physical stimulus which affects only sight directly, but stimulates ideas of solidity and so on through early experience. The inference might be called "physiological". An inference of this sort is evidence of past correlations, for instance between touch and sight, but may be mistaken in the present instance; you may, for example, mistake a reflection in a large mirror for another room. Similarly in dreams we make mistaken physiological inferences. We cannot therefore feel certainty in regard to things which are in this sense inferred, because, when we try to accept as many of them as possible, we are nevertheless compelled to reject some for the sake of self-consistency.

We arrived a moment ago at what we called "physiological inference" as an essential ingredient in the common-sense notion of a physical object. Physiological inference, in its simplest form, means this: given a stimulus S, to which, by a reflex, we react by a bodily movement R, and a stimulus S' with a reaction R', if the two stimuli are frequently experienced together, S will in time produce R'. (For example, if you hear a sharp noise and see a bright light simultaneously often, in time the noise without the light will cause your pupils to contract.) That is to say, the body will act as if S' were present. Physiological inference is important in theory of knowledge. . . . I have mentioned it partly to prevent it from being confused with logical inference, and partly in order to introduce the problem of *induction*. . . .

Induction raises perhaps the most difficult problem in the whole theory of knowledge. Every scientific law is established by its means, and yet it is difficult to see why we should believe it to be a valid logical process. Induction, in its bare essence, consists of the argument that, because A and B have been often found together and never found apart, therefore, when A is found again, B will probably also be found. This exists first as a "physiological inference", and as such is practised by animals. When we first begin to reflect, we find ourselves making inductions in the physiological sense, for instance, expecting the food we see to have a certain kind of taste. Often we only become aware of this expectation through having it disappointed, for instance if we take salt thinking it is sugar. When mankind took to science, they tried to formulate logical principles justifying this kind of inference. . . . They seem to me very unsuccessful. I am convinced that induction must have validity of some kind in some degree, but the problem of showing how or why it can be valid remains unsolved. Until it is solved, the rational man will doubt whether his food will nourish him, and whether the sun will rise to-morrow. I am not a rational man in this sense, but for the moment I shall pretend to be. And even if we cannot be completely rational, we should probably all be the better for becoming somewhat more rational than we are. At the lowest estimate, it will be an interesting adventure to see whither reason will lead us.

The problems we have been raising are none of them new, but they suffice to show that our everday views of the world and of our relations to it are unsatisfactory. . . .

Reading Questions

1. Why can't we or the physicist be certain of the existence of chairs or electrons?
2. What considerations make memory always uncertain?
3. What are all the reasons supporting the conclusion that the testimony of others never leads to certainty?
4. What uncertainties does Russell think must be admitted about beliefs based on what he calls introspection?
5. What is meant by physiological inference?
6. Why can we not have full confidence in scientific laws?

Questions for Reflection and Research

1. Can science prove that the physical world exists?
2. Is Russell using the words *certainty* and *doubt* in a peculiar way? That is, are his reasons for doubting (or for being less certain) really reasons for doubting (or being less certain)?

3. Is there any way to justify induction, to prove that the future will be like the past? (See selection #21 by Black.)

4. How did the philosopher G. E. Moore (1873–1958) attempt to reject skepticism of the sort Russell describes?

5. Select what you regard as a well-established scientific finding in a field familiar to you. Explain how Russell's reasoning could be used to undermine the finding.

6. If the skeptical arguments described by Russell are correct, what unproved assumptions prop up science? (Compare selection #23 by Thompson.)

Recent Physics and Limits of Knowledge

The Author: Dietrich Schroeer (b. 1925) was educated in physics at Ohio State University and studied on a postdoctoral fellowship at the Technical University in Munich. He has taught physics at the University of North Carolina at Chapel Hill. As a researcher he specializes in nuclear and solid-state physics.

The Selection: The development of twentieth-century physics is reviewed, beginning with some puzzles about certain aspects of light. The emergence from these puzzles of relativity theory and quantum mechanics is sketched in. The relative and probabilistic nature of the new physics is asserted to be an ineradicable limitation on scientific knowledge.

In 1900 Lord Kelvin [1824–1907] felt he could say that there were only two minor 19th-century "clouds" which dimmed the otherwise brilliant sky of the new scientific century. . . . These two clouds were the controversy over the nature of the ether and the nonexistence of the ultraviolet catastrophe in light emission. As a matter of fact, these two minor clouds were not so minor after all; the first led to the theory of relativity and the second to quantum mechanics. And it is precisely these two theoretical developments which make up the different character of contemporary physics, which provide such a contrast with the preceding views of the physical universe, and which have led to the suspicion that we can never

From Dietrich Schroeer, *Physics and Its Fifth Dimension: Society,* 1972, Addison-Wesley, Reading, Massachusetts, pp. 154–62. Reprinted by permission of Addison-Wesley Publishing Company, Inc.

really know all the complexities of the universe—that there are limits to our observational abilities. . . .

[One] particularly fascinating aspect [of] this 20th-century revolution [was that] the development of the theories . . . displayed an extensively metaphysical character. The founders of relativity and quantum mechanics frequently seemed more like philosophers than scientists in their speculations. Yet in all cases the ultimate test was comparison with reality. . . .

THE NATURE OF LIGHT

The background of the 20th-century revolution in physics lies in the history of the scientific studies of light. The interpretation of the nature of light has been a varied one. [Isaac] Newton [1642–1727], for example, was the chief proponent of one of the two opposing views of light; he believed that light consists of moving particles. He believed this on the basis of the fact that light appears to travel in straight lines and make sharp shadows, and that light can be separated into various colors, suggesting that it is made up of distinct constituent entities. Then in the 18th century, interference phenomena were observed for light—interference similar to that observed in the crossing of the ripples from two stones thrown simultaneously into a pond. One consequent article of faith was then that these waves of light must be transmitted by a medium, just as water waves travel in the water medium and sound waves are transmitted by air. This medium was called the ether, a word used earlier by Aristotle [384–322 B.C.] to describe nonearthly material.

If the ether exists, then it should be possible to measure the motion of the earth in this ether, just as one can measure the position of a boat relative to the water in which it floats. In the period 1882–1887, A. A. Michelson [1852–1931] and E. W. Morley [1838–1923] performed such an experiment in Cleveland at the Case School of Applied Science. With a $10,000 grant, they built an extremely precise device, now known as the Michelson-Morley interferometer, with many mirrors, lights, and lenses mounted on a huge slab floating in a pool of mercury on top of cement poured onto bedrock. In this device, light was sent along two different paths; one path was parallel and the other path was perpendicular to the suspected motion of the earth through the ether. Just as it is harder to swim against a current in a river than at a right angle to it, so the light in the parallel path should be slowed down by the ether flow. Interference effects were then used to try to detect this slowing down. The beautiful thing about the experiment was that *no* motion relative to the ether could be detected. The simplest conclusion which agreed with the Michelson-Morley experiment was that the ether did not exist. . . . Something was clearly wrong with the attempt to explain the behavior of light by classical wave theory.

The other difficulty about the nature of light had to do with its origins. In particular there was the puzzle known as the "ultraviolet catastrophe." This catastrophe has to do with the color distribution of the light emitted by hot bodies such as the tungsten filament in light bulbs. This color distribution can be calculated using classical theory, but the prediction is wrong. Classically, hot bodies should radiate primarily very high-energy photons of light (i.e., ultraviolet), so that if one opened the door of an oven at home one should get bombarded by high-energy x-rays. Since x-rays are rather deadly, it is lucky for us that an actual oven emits mostly red light; the ultraviolet catastrophe is notable for not occurring.

EINSTEIN'S THEORY OF RELATIVITY

The lack of an ether was not the only unexplained problem in 1905. For example, by 1901 it was already known that an electron moving at high speeds behaved anomalously [= contrary to what current theories would predict]. Albert Einstein [1879–1955] provided the answer to these problems with his special theory of relativity.

Einstein was born . . . in Ulm, Germany. . . . After obtaining his Ph.D. in Switzerland with difficulty (because he studied what he, rather than the professors, felt to be important), he worked as a patent examiner. This job left him enough leisure to work in his real avocation, and in 1905 he published three papers, any of which was worthy of the Nobel prize. One of these papers explained Brownian motion (such as dust particles dancing in the air); one showed that in the photoelectric effect, light does at times act like a particle when knocking electrons out of a metal (this won Einstein a Nobel prize); and the third proposed the special theory of relativity.

Let me first illustrate the nature of Einstein's starting assumptions in explaining the relativistic phenomena.

1. He assumed that the speed of light is measured to be the same by all observers who are moving at a constant speed. This assumption goes utterly against common sense. If a ball is thrown at 60 mph due East, parallel to a car going 54 mph due East, the driver of the car will see the ball slowly passing him at 6 mph. If an astronaut passes us in his spaceship at 167,400 mph (90% the speed of light), and we shine light after him (traveling 100% the speed of light), we would by analogy expect the astronaut to measure the speed of the light to be 18,600 mph (10% the speed of light). This, however, is not true; the astronaut would also measure the speed of that light to be exactly 186,000 mph. It seems to make no difference who measures the speed of light; it always comes out to be the same. This explains the Michelson-Morley experiment: there is no ether to slow down the light; it travels at the same speed . . . in both arms of the interferometer.

2. The second Einsteinian assumption was that all laws of nature hold equally well in all nonaccelerating systems; this simply brought out again the fact that no one reference frame is preferred over another.

Einstein's special theory of relativity predicts many puzzling and anti-common-sense phenomena. For example, it shows that, since energy and mass are equivalent, a body has more mass when moving rapidly than when it is at rest, since its kinetic energy appears as an increase in the mass. This explains why no material object can ever reach the speed of light; as it goes faster and faster, and hence becomes heavier and heavier, the same force (as in a rocket motor) will produce less and less acceleration. Since the mass of the body approaches infinity as its speed approaches the speed of light, an infinite force would be required to break the light barrier. . . . There also is the relativistic "twin paradox." The theory of relativity says that time passes more slowly in a moving system than in a stationary one. This can be illustrated by means of identical twins. One of these we send off as an astronaut at a high velocity into space, while the other stays behind. When the twins are finally reunited upon the return of the astronaut, the traveler turns out to be younger than the stay-at-home. . . . (It is the initial acceleration which defines which is the moving twin.) A final puzzle is that of the relativistic contraction of objects at high speed. Note that all these phenomena become noticeable only at speeds close to that of light, i.e., at speeds not on the order of miles per hour but rather of thousands of miles per second. But if you wanted to play basketball with 7'-1" Wilt Chamberlain on more even terms, perhaps this might be the way: if Wilt would go up for a rebound at 90% the speed of light, he would appear only 4'-3" tall, a much more manageable opponent. Of course, it may be somewhat difficult to play any kind of game with an opponent who is moving that fast, but that is a minor detail. (Another minor detail is the fact that at the same time the basket would seem to Wilt to be only six feet high, so that he seemingly wouldn't even have to jump.)

QUANTUM MECHANICS

The other 19th-century cloud was finally resolved by Max Planck [1859–1947] at the end of 1900, when he suggested that light is emitted in a quantized way. As finally made clear by Einstein, the energy carried by each quantum of light (called a photon) is then proportional to its frequency. . . . If a 100-watt light bulb is burnt all day, it will emit about 20 million-billion-billion light quanta; i.e., the energy carried per quantum is quite small by human standards. Note that this relationship between the energy and the frequency incorporates the particle-wave duality in the sense that the energy implies a quantum or particle, while the frequency implies a wave characteristic. This assumption nicely explains away the ultraviolet catastrophe, and ultimately led to all of the developments of quantum mechanics.

One of the more beautiful quantum effects occurs when gases have an ionizing current passed through them; light is then emitted which has certain very distinct frequencies (colors) which are characteristic of the particular gas. This phenomenon is not explainable on any prequantum basis. The Danish physicist Niels Bohr [1885–1962] took the first step toward a satisfactory solution of this problem in 1913 when he suggested that the electrons travel around the atomic nucleus in certain very definite orbits, and that light quanta are emitted when the electrons jump from one orbit to another. This theory predicted frequencies for the light from hydrogen which agreed very well with already existing experimental data, and it put quantum mechanics into a very heady period of development. Much of the subsequent work was inspired by, and performed at, the Institute for Theoretical Physics in Copenhagen, an institute directed by Niels Bohr . . . and funded by the Carlsberg Brewery (an example of the impact of beer on physics?).

The full-fledged quantum theory extended this particle-wave duality of light to all matter. In this formulation all particulate matter is a wave—or has a wave associated with it—whose wavelength is inversely proportional to the particle's mass. This explains why we do not see wave phenomena in our day-to-day living; a car, for example, is simply so massive that its wavelength is vanishingly small. But an electron has such a small mass that the wavelength associated with it can be fairly large, that the electron can actually behave *noticeably* like a wave on an atomic scale. When water waves pass through two openings, interference phenomena occur where the parts of the wave from the two openings overlap. In this case, it makes sense to say that the wave went through both holes. In a similar way, it is possible to make a discrete electron pass simultaneously through several holes on the atomic scale of a crystal lattice— or rather it is possible to set up an experiment in which it is impossible to determine through which of several holes an electron actually passed. . . . In general, quantum mechanics is a method of looking at all matter as waves and then asking the probabilities of certain events, probabilities which one can then proceed to check by repeated experiments. One does not know how to predict exactly what will happen in a given case; only probabilities are predictable. However, for large-scale (nonatomic) phenomena, the uncertainties in the predictions are ordinarily quite small in this wave-distribution sense.

THE HEISENBERG UNCERTAINTY PRINCIPLE

All the implications of the wave-particle duality, and of this statistical uncertainty, are contained in the Heisenberg Uncertainty Principle [named for Werner Heisenberg (1901–1976)]. It states that it is impossible to do any experiment in which all the variables can be measured with unlimited accuracy. If one wants to measure the position of a particle with extreme precision, then one gives up the ability to measure simultaneously the speed of the particle with a similar unlimited precision. In fact, the Uncertainty Principle sets a quantitative lower limit on the product of the precision of these two simultaneous measurements.

THE IMPLICATIONS OF RELATIVITY AND QUANTUM MECHANICS

The physical implications of the theory of relativity run frequently counter to common sense. One might be tempted to say that, since the effects we have described become significant only at high speeds, they do not make the theory very revolutionary. And it is true that the classical Newtonian laws still hold except for objects moving at nearly the speed of light. But in a sense, Newton's laws, or at least some of their implications, have been totally overthrown.

The theory of relativity says that we can no longer give preference to one central coordinate system in space (a central system originally associated with the ether) or to a specific time system. We cannot say how fast we are moving in space; we can only say how fast we are traveling relative to some other object. An element of indefiniteness is introduced. With relativity, the observer once again becomes the center of the universe. Where the whole Galilean astronomy labored to destroy the idea of the uniqueness of the earth, and hence of man, now the Einsteinian mechanics indicated that it is important to talk about phenomena only in terms of observation by a real observer. Only by observation can sense be made of the measures of space and time.

Quantum mechanics raises similar fundamental questions. In classical Newtonian mechanics, man was limited in what he could know, and hence predict, because it required effort to measure with sufficient accuracy the position and speed of many particles. Now quantum mechanics says man does not need to bother to try for a better precision, since it is unattainable in any case due to the Heisenberg Uncertainty Principle. And no one has been able to discover a way to defeat this principle. It seems to be just as the romantics have been claiming for so long: the observer cannot be separated from the experiment. When measurements are carried out on microscopic phenomena, then the observer adds enough disturbance to the system to affect the observed data. In quantum mechanics there are rigorous limits on our capability to know, as opposed to the classical limit on our capacity to know. We are limited in our ability to know all about nature; there are certain questions which we cannot ask because they are unanswerable. This is, in a sense, a very pessimistic new view about the universe and about our role in it; there is no longer a Creator who opens the universe like a book for us to read. If all of science is statistical probabilities, how can we even talk about ultimate consensus on anything?

But there is an even deeper question involved in quantum

mechanics, a question which is answered very differently by the two primary schools of quantum-mechanical thought. One school is represented by the older generation of physicists like Einstein, who are reluctant to believe in a dice-playing God, feel that there is a basic reality to all phenomena, and believe that only the observational interference makes the universe appear nonclockwork. On the other hand, the Copenhagen school, as represented by Bohr and Heisenberg, believes that there is no basic underlying reality except that which we can physically measure; only contact with measurable reality is ultimately significant. In this approach there is no point in discussing something which can never be seen or measured, which is simply not real. . . . [There were] many debates between Einstein and Bohr, in which Einstein tried very hard to invent thought experiments which might circumvent the Uncertainty Principle.

It is such debates, so necessary to the development of both relativity and quantum mechanics, which make the modern physics seem at times very metaphysical . . . . The equations, numbers, and usefulness of the various points of view are not so much under discussion. But considering the influence of the Newtonian mechanical viewpoint of the universe, it is not surprising that these metaphysical problems have wide-ranging implications. Modern physics has added elements of uncertainty and indefiniteness; it has in a sense recombined the quantitative aspects of physics with the organismic reintroduction of the observer into the phenomenon.

Reading Questions

1. What was the ultraviolet-catastrophe puzzle and how was it eliminated?
2. How was the nonexistence of ether shown? What conclusion did Einstein draw from its nonexistence?
3. Does the theory of relativity imply that our knowledge is limited? Explain.
4. What is Heisenberg's uncertainty principle and what limits does it place on human knowledge?
5. What are the two alternative ways of interpreting Heisenberg's principle?

Questions for Reflection and Research

1. Explain and evaluate the dispute between Einstein and Heisenberg and Bohr.

2. Does the earth travel around the sun, the sun around the earth, or is there another alternative?
3. Can Heisenberg's uncertainty principle be confirmed or disconfirmed by using evidence and experimentation?
4. If space and time are dependent on the observer, does this dependence lead to another limitation on human knowledge? Can we always translate information from one observer's viewpoint to another's?

Is Induction an Acceptable Scientific Tool?

The Author: Max Black (b. 1909) was born in Russia, educated in England, and came to the United States in 1940, eventually accepting a permanent teaching position in philosophy at Cornell University. His main philosophical concerns have been in the philosophy of mathematics, philosophy of language, and philosophy of logic. He has been a philosophy journal editor, translator of philosophical works, and prolific author of essays and books in philosophy.

The Selection: This essay on the old and famous problem of induction begins by noting the distinction between induction and deduction. The problem of induction is: How can we justify the transition in inductive reasoning from a number of observations to a generalization involving more cases than those originally observed? Four attempts to resolve the problem are described: (A) Karl Popper's appeal to falsification, (B) the use of inductive procedures, (C) the supplementation of inductive arguments with a uniformity-of-nature principle, and (D) the pragmatic justification. Black rejects the four attempts and argues that the problem arises from an unacceptable assumption. It is (incorrectly) assumed that unless induction is shown to be deduction, induction will be defective. The selection is moderately demanding.

If a dog barks at me each time I pass by, I naturally expect him to bark again the next time he sees me. This is an example of *inductive reasoning* in its most primitive form. From knowledge about a *sample* of cases, those in which the dog has already barked, I draw a conclusion about a case not included in that sample—I anticipate what will happen the next time.

Excerpted from "The Justification of Induction," by Max Black, in *Philosophy of Science Today,* edited by Sidney Morgenbesser, © 1967 by Basic Books, Inc., Publishers, New York.

Let us now take a more sophisticated example: On applying a lighted match to a scrap of cellophane, I find that it catches fire; I conclude that any similar piece of cellophane would also burn in a similar situation. Here we have an inference from what happened in *one case* to what would happen in *any* similar case. One last example: An entomologist [= insect specialist] finds that each examined beetle of a certain species has a green spot on its back and concludes that *all* beetles of that species will have the same marking.

Such familiar examples of inductive reasoning involve a transition from information about a given set of objects or situations to a conclusion about some wider, more inclusive, set. We might say that all of them consist of reasoning from *samples*. Let us therefore agree to understand by an inductive argument one in which the conclusion refers to at least one thing that is not referred to by the premises.

The simplest forms of inductive arguments, on whose correctness the more sophisticated ones ultimately depend, can be represented as follows: "Such and such *A*'s are *B*; therefore another *A* is *B*" or, again, "*Some A's* (selected in such and such a fashion) are *B*; therefore all *A*'s are *B*." We need not consider ways of improving these formulas, since the problem of justifying induction remains essentially the same in all forms of inductive reasoning, whether primitive or sophisticated.

It has been held, very widely though not universally, that the use of inductive reasoning is a distinctive feature of scientific method, integrally connected with the discovery of scientific laws and generalizations. In strict *deductive* reasoning, we are limited to rearranging information about the data referred to in the premises, and never advance to knowledge about the hitherto unobserved; by means of inductive reasoning, however, we make the leap from "some" to "all"; from the known present to the predicted future; from the finite data of observation to laws covering all that will be and could be. The so-called "inductive leap" (from "some" to "any" and "all") seems indispensable in science no less than in ordinary life. . . .

It is altogether reasonable to wonder how the use of this powerful method of reasoning can be justified. Indeed, certain features of inductive argument, as we have defined it, can easily awaken serious disquiet. In [deductive] logic, we [are] taught that the transition from a "some" in the premises to an "all" in the conclusion is a transparent fallacy: if some men are white-skinned, it by no means follows that *all* men are; how, then, can we be justified in wholesale violation of this plain and simple rule? Again, inductions are notoriously fallible; the gambler who expects a sequence of reds on the roulette wheel to continue indefinitely will soon be undeceived. In our dealings with nature, are we in any stronger position than the gambler who has had a lucky sequence of throws? Are we perhaps about to come to the end of our lucky guesses about nature? How can we possibly *know* that the sun will rise tomorrow?

For the sake of clarity, it is essential to distinguish such sweeping skeptical doubts from practical questions about the reliability of inductive procedures. It is one thing to ask whether a given inductive procedure is sufficiently reliable for a given purpose; different and more basic questions are at issue when we ask how *any* inductive argument can be justified. . . .

The question of justification raised by the philosopher is one of the utmost generality. He is perplexed to understand how *any* inductive reasoning, no matter how satisfactory by the standards of common sense or of good statistical practice, can really count as acceptable. He finds it hard to understand how the "inductive leap," which seems to involve a plain logical fallacy, could *ever* be justified. The problem has no immediate bearing upon scientific practice, but is of the first importance for evaluating the claims of science to be a vehicle of truth about the universe. It seems that unless induction can be justified, our claims to have scientific *knowledge* must be rejected as unfounded and science will have to count as no better than any other unsubstantiated *faith*. However appealing such a skeptical conclusion might be to those who welcome any proof of man's impotence, it is one to be accepted only after the most careful investigation.

In the course of the intensive consideration that philosophers of science have given to this problem, almost every conceivable answer has been defended.

[A.] Perhaps the most drastic solution available consists of a denial that induction plays, or ought to play, any part in scientific method. This view has been most eloquently defended in recent times by Professor Karl Popper [b. 1902], who has argued in numerous writings that the proper business of science is the *deductive testing* of empirical hypotheses. According to him, there is no rational way of arriving at generalizations from the examination of sampled cases—no rational way of making the inductive leap—but once such a generalization has been produced, by whatever means, there *is* a rational way of discovering whether it meets the tests of observation and experiment. Such generalizations or hypotheses can be conclusively *falsified*, but never verified, never shown to be true. The task of empirical science is falsification, putting to the trial of experience bold "conjectures" about the world, and not the impossible task of discovering truth.

For all the ingenuity with which this provocative view has been argued (to which I cannot do justice in this brief essay), the "no induction" view, as it might be called, has not received wide acceptance. It seems too paradoxical a conception of science that it should consist only of the elimination of error, rather than the progressive discovery of approximations to the truth. And induction seems to creep in by the back door in Popper's theory of "corroboration," that is, of the criteria by which we discriminate between the relative strengths of hypotheses, none of which are falsified by the known observational facts.

[B.] One might think that common sense can provide a simple and satisfactory answer to the problem of induction. If a layman is asked why he trusts an inductive argument from "some" to "all," the chances are he will say that this kind of argument has "always worked in the past." (One might have some doubts about that "always," but no matter.) How foolish it would be, we can imagine the plain man saying, to abandon techniques that have worked so well and have produced such spectacular successes in technology and in pure science. Well, let it be granted that induction *has* "worked" in the past; what grounds does this give us for expecting it to work in the future? If we conclude that induction *will* work because it *has* worked we are arguing—inductively!

As the philosopher David Hume [1711–1776] pointed out long ago in a famous discussion of the problem, we seem here to be begging the question [= assuming what we are trying to prove]. The best method we have for settling specific empirical questions— arguing from the known character of observed instances—leaves us in the lurch when we try to find a *general* justification of induction. To offer an inductive justification to anybody who doubts that induction is *ever* justified is obviously futile. . . .

[C.] A favorite approach to the problem of justification begins by asserting that inductive arguments, in the form considered in this essay, are basically *incomplete*. Transition from "some" to "all," from a premise about a sample to a conclusion about the population from which that sample was drawn, is held to rely upon unstated *assumptions*. Until such assumptions are made explicit, the inductive inference is unsound—the inductive *leap* is never justified by itself: an inductive argument needs an extra premise in order to become valid. There needs to be supplied some principle that "the future will resemble the past" or some more general principle of "the Uniformity of Nature." Once such a principle has been introduced into the argument, and only then, that argument will become logically respectable. (It will be noticed that this line of attack on the problem tacitly assumes that only *deductive* argument is irreproachable. By implicitly denying the possibility of distinctive inductive arguments, this position resembles the "no induction" view previously mentioned.)

The formulation of general principles that might plausibly play the part of missing premises in inductive arguments is a matter of great difficulty. Since nature obviously exhibits variety as well as uniformity, irregularity as well as order, it is hard to state a principle of uniformity without producing something that is plainly false. For example, the principle that *whenever* some *A*'s are *B*, all *A*'s are

B is a grotesque overstatement. . . . It seems fair to say that nobody has yet produced a suitably qualified candidate for the title of the "Basic Principle of Inductive Inference"—although many have tried.

We need not enter into the technicalities of this attempt to bolster induction by supplying an additional grand premise. There is in my opinion a conclusive objection against this whole line of approach. . . . The search for grand principles of induction . . . merely shifts the problem without solving it: the problem of establishing such principles is just the old one of justifying induction—in another and even less tractable form. . . .

[D.] I turn, finally, to the so-called "pragmatic" justifications of induction, which have seemed to many modern students of the problem to provide a satisfactory answer to this ancient puzzle. The basic ideas underlying this approach were independently formulated by Charles Sanders Peirce [1839–1914] and by Hans Reichenbach [1891–1953], the latter of whom argued the position with great ingenuity and pertinacity.

Consider the following familiar position in ordinary life. A doctor, who is treating a patient suffering from some serious disease, has reason to believe that the only chance of saving the patient's life is to perform a certain operation; suppose also that there is no guarantee of the operation's proving successful: if the doctor is right in thinking that the patient will die in any case if the operation is not performed, he is justified in operating. To put the matter in another way: If a *necessary condition* for saving the patient's life is performing the operation, then that operation is justified, even though the outcome is unknown and the risks are great. This might be called a case of "nothing to lose by trying"—resort to the dangerous operation may be a "forlorn hope," but it is a justifiable one.

Those who apply this idea to the justification of induction argue as follows: Hume was right when he said that it was impossible to argue from the present to the future, from the known to the unknown. The "inductive leap" cannot be justified in the way that philosophers and scientists have hoped. Nevertheless, we badly need knowledge ranging beyond our observations and nothing can prevent us from trying to obtain it. Suppose it could be shown that the *only way* to reach such knowledge is by following inductive procedures. Then we should be in the position of the doctor or the patient in the original example, with nothing to lose by trying. If following inductive procedures is a *necessary condition* for anticipating the unknown, we shall be practically or—as people say, "pragmatically"—justified in following that procedure.

We may agree that the general line of argument is plausible; its contribution to the problem of justifying induction will depend upon how successful its defenders are in showing that some kind of inductive procedure is a necessary condition for making correct generalizations about the unknown or the unobserved.

The model usually employed has approximately the following character: Suppose we are performing a series of observations and are interested in some property P. If in the first 100 trials we find that P has appeared in 65 cases, we assume provisionally that in the *long run* the proportion of favorable cases will be close to 65/100. As we continue our trials, we may find, say, 87 favorable cases in the first 150 observations: we therefore correct our estimate and now expect the proportion of favorable cases to be near 85/150. We proceed in this same way: whenever we find that k out of l trials exhibit the property P, we provisionally assume that the proportion in the long run will be close to k/l.

Since there is no guarantee that the fractions we progressively find in this way will ultimately converge to a limit, our attempt to anticipate the overall character of the entire series of observations may be defeated after all. But *if* there is a limit (which we cannot know) this procedure of successive correction will eventually bring us close to the true value of that limit. We are justified in following the procedure, because we have nothing to lose. If the series of successive fractions is sufficiently irregular, *no* method of forecasting its ultimate character will be possible; while if it has the regularity of a convergent series, our method will bring us close to the desired answer sooner or later.

This idea is too ingenious and too complicated to be criticized in a few words. I have argued at length elsewhere that it fails. . . . The basic objection is that the whole approach concedes too much to the skeptical critics of induction. Those who agree with Hume that *knowledge* of the unobserved is, strictly speaking, impossible, will always find themselves with empty hands at the conclusion of an inductive procedure, no matter how ingeniously they try to wriggle out of their predicament.

We seem now to have arrived at a stalemate. None of the ways of justifying induction that have been explored by a long line of able and acute thinkers seem to offer any prospects of success. Attempts to justify induction by using inductive procedures seem hopelessly circular; attempts to find principles expressing the alleged uniformity of nature simply raise the old questions in a new form . . . and the fashionable "pragmatic" justifications really leave us helpless against skeptical objections to induction. Considering the intensity with which the problem has been studied, there is no hope that we shall do better where so many powerful intellects have labored in vain.

Now when we meet with a situation like this, there is usually reason to suppose that the nature of the problem has been misconceived, and that the apparently insurmountable difficulties arise from misunderstanding. The view is steadily gaining ground that this is the situation with regard to the celebrated problem of justifying induction.

The very notion of justification implies some *standard* of justification: to justify induction must be to show that that kind of reasoning satisfies some relevant criterion of what is regarded as reasonable. Now the long history of the subject shows that nearly everybody who has grappled with the problem has really had before his mind the standards of *deductive* reasoning: however widely the various attempts to justify induction differ, they all assume that the only really reputable mode of reasoning, the only "strict" method, is that in which the conclusion follows by logical necessity from the premises.

But induction, *by definition,* is not deduction: the idea of the so-called "inductive leap" is built into our conception of an inductive argument. To try to convert inductive arguments into deductive ones is as futile an attempt as that of the child who argued that a horse was really a cow—only without horns. The beginning of wisdom in this extremely complicated and controversial domain is therefore the recognition that no *general* justification of induction, of the sort that philosophers of science have hoped to uncover, is either possible or needed. What we *mean* by justifying a specific empirical generalization is an inductive demonstration, using principles that have been found to work in the kind of case in question, that the generalization is true or at least probable. When we try to apply this relatively definite notion of justification to induction itself, the very notion of justification becomes unclear.

It is not so much that we do not know how to justify induction as that we do not know and cannot imagine what we would *accept* as such a justification. Clarity, here—which cannot, of course, be achieved without the hardest intellectual labor—ought to result in the disappearance of the alleged "problem of induction." If this view is correct, as I hold it to be, the problem of induction will eventually be classified with such famous "insoluble" problems as that of squaring the circle or that of inventing perpetual-motion machines. And as in those famous cases, the quest for the impossible does not seem, from the long perspective of history, to have been futile. For the byproducts of serious investigation may be even more important than its ostensible goal. If our knowledge of the character of inductive procedures is as rich and as sophisticated as it is today, no little of the credit must be assigned to those who have labored so long and so unsuccessfully at trying to justify induction.

Reading Questions

1. What is the difference between inductive and deductive reasoning? Give examples of each.

2. Using an example of inductive reasoning, explain what seems to need justifying in the example and for any inductive reasoning.
3. Using an example of inductive reasoning, explain each of the four attempts to justify induction included in this selection.
4. Would Popper think that it is true that the sun will rise tomorrow? If not, how certain would he think we can be of this?
5. Explain Black's objection to the second and third attempts at justification.
6. Why does Black say we will never be able to justify induction?

Questions for Reflection and Research

1. If Black's conclusion is correct that induction cannot be justified, should science not employ it? Why or why not?
2. Is it at all possible that if you were to jump from a high building tomorrow, you might not fall? Why or why not?
3. When we reason by induction, do we really assume that nature is uniform? If so, can we prove this to be true?
4. What role does induction actually play in science? (See selections #26, #27, and #28.)

selection 22.

Can We Know Whether Theoretical Entities Exist?

The Author: Stephen Toulmin (b. 1922) received his training in philosophy at Cambridge University in England. He has been especially interested as a philosopher in epistemology and the history and philosophy of science. He has taught in England, Australia, and in the United States, currently at the University of Chicago. In addition to his publications in the areas mentioned above he has written on the uses of reason and argument.

The Selection: It has sometimes been argued that since we cannot see an electron even with the best microscope, there may be none. Perhaps, then, there are no electrons—electrons being entities introduced in a theory to serve as a convenient explanatory device for some phenomena that we can perceive with our senses (such as changes in voltmeter readings). Toulmin points out that there are various kinds·of existence questions. He does this to clarify just which kind of question about the existence of theoretical entities is being asked. He then contends that whether or not the entities do exist, the concepts can be quite fruitful for the advancement of science. The selection is moderately demanding.

Non-scientists are often puzzled to know whether the electrons, genes and other entities scientists talk about are to be thought of as really existing or not. Scientists themselves also have some difficulty in saying exactly where they stand on this issue. Some are inclined to insist that all these things are just as real, and exist in the same sense as tables and chairs and omnibuses. But others feel a certain

From Stephen Toulmin, *The Philosophy of Science: An Introduction* (New York: Harper & Row, Publishers, Inc., Harper Torchbook, 1960), pp. 134–39. Reprinted by permission of Harper & Row, Publishers, Inc.

embarrassment about them, and hesitate to go so far; they notice the differences between establishing the existence of electrons from a study of electrical phenomena, inferring the existence of savages from depressions in the sand, and inferring the existence of an inflamed appendix from a patient's signs and symptoms; and it may even occur to them that to talk about an electromagnet in terms of 'electrons' is a bit like talking of Pyrexia [= fever] of Unknown Origin when the patient has an unaccountable temperature. Yet the theory of electrons does *explain* electrical phenomena in a way in which no mere translation into jargon, like 'pyrexia', can explain a sick man's temperature; and how, we may ask, could the electron theory work at all if, after all, electrons did not really exist?

Stated in this way, the problem is confused: let us therefore scrutinize the question itself a little more carefully. For when we compare Robinson Crusoe's discovery with the physicist's one, it is not only the sorts of discovery which are different in the two cases. To talk of existence in both cases involves quite as much of a shift, and by passing too swiftly from one use of the word to the other we may make the problem unnecessarily hard for ourselves.

Notice, therefore, what different ideas we may have in mind when we talk about things 'existing'. If we ask whether dodos exist or not, i.e. whether there are any dodos left nowadays, we are asking whether the species has survived or is extinct. But when we ask whether electrons exist or not, we certainly do not have in mind the possibility that they may have become extinct: in whatever sense we ask this question, it is not one in which 'exists' is opposed to 'does not exist any more'. Again, if we ask whether Ruritania exists, i.e. whether there is such a country as Ruritania, we are asking whether there really is such a country as Ruritania or whether it is an imaginary, and so a non-existent country. But we are not interested in asking of electrons whether they are genuine instances of a familiar sort of thing or non-existent ones: the way in which we are using the term 'exist' is not one in which it is opposed to 'are non-existent'. In each case, the word 'exist' is used to make a slightly different point, and to mark a slightly different distinction. As one moves from [Robinson Crusoe's] Man Friday to dodos, and on from them to Ruritania, and again to electrons, the change in the nature of the cases brings other changes with it: notably in the way one has to understand sentences containing the word 'exist'.

What, then, of the question, "Do electrons exist?" How is this to be understood? A more revealing analogy than dodos or Ruritania is to be found in the question, "Do contours exist?" A child who had read that the equator was 'an imaginary line drawn round the centre of the earth' might be struck by the contours, parallels of latitude and the rest, which appear on maps along with the towns, mountains and rivers, and ask of them whether *they* existed. How should we reply? If he asked his question in the bare words, "Do contours exist?", one could hardly answer him immediately: clearly the only answer one can give to this question is "Yes and No." They 'exist' all right, but do they *exist*? It all depends on your manner of speaking. So he might be persuaded to restate his question, asking now, "Is there really a line on the ground whose height is constant?"; and again the answer would have to be "Yes and No", for there is (so to say) a 'line', but then again not what you might call a *line*. . . . And so the cross-purposes would continue until it was made clear that the real question was: "Is there anything to show for contours—anything visible on the terrain, like the white lines on a tennis court? Or are they only cartographical devices, having no geographical counterparts?" Only then would the question be posed in anything like an unambiguous manner. The sense of 'exists' in which a child might naturally ask whether contours existed is accordingly one in which 'exists' is opposed not to 'does not exist any more' or to 'is non-existent', but to 'is only a (cartographical) fiction'.

This is very much the sense in which the term 'exists' is used of atoms, genes, electrons, fields and other theoretical entities in the physical sciences. There, too, the question "Do they exist?" has in practice the force of "Is there anything to show for them, or are they only theoretical fictions?" To a working physicist, the question "Do neutrinos exist?" acts as an invitation to 'produce a neutrino', preferably by making it *visible*. If one could do this one would indeed have something to show for the term 'neutrino', and the difficulty of doing it is what explains the peculiar difficulty of the problem. For the problem arises acutely only when we start asking about the existence of *sub-microscopic* entities, i.e. things which by all normal standards are invisible. In the nature of the case, to produce a neutrino must be a more sophisticated business than producing a dodo or a nine-foot man. Our problem is accordingly complicated by the need to decide what is to count as 'producing' a neutrino, a field or a gene. It is not obvious what sorts of thing ought to count: certain things are, however, generally regarded by scientists as acceptable—for instance, cloud-chamber pictures of [alpha-] ray tracks, electron microscope photographs or, as a second-best, audible clicks from a Geiger counter. They would regard such striking demonstrations as these as sufficiently like being shown a live dodo on the lawn to qualify as evidence of the existence of the entities concerned. And certainly, if we reject these as insufficient, it is hard to see what more we can reasonably ask for: if the term 'exists' is to have any application to such things, must not this be it?

What if no such demonstration were possible? If one could not show, visibly, that neutrinos existed, would that necessarily be the end of them? Not at all; and it is worth noticing what happens when a demonstration of the preferred type is not possible, for then the difference between talking about the existence of electrons or genes, and talking about the existence of dodos, unicorns or nine-foot men becomes all-important. If, for instance, I talk plausibly about unicorns or nine-foot men and have nothing to show for them, so that I am utterly unable to say, when challenged, under what circumstances a specimen might be, or might have been seen, the conclusion may reasonably be drawn that my nine-foot men are imaginary and my unicorns a myth. In either case, the things I am talking about may be presumed to be non-existent, i.e. are discredited and can be written off. But in the case of atoms, genes and the like, things are different: the failure to bring about or describe circumstances in which one might point and say, "There's one!", need not, as with unicorns, be taken as discrediting them.

Not all those theoretical entities which cannot be shown to exist need be held to be non-existent: there is for them a middle way. Certainly we should hesitate to assert that any theoretical entity really existed until a photograph or other demonstration had been given. But, even if we had reason to believe that no such demonstration ever could be given, it would be too much to conclude that the entity was non-existent; for this conclusion would give the impression of discrediting something that, as a fertile explanatory concept, did not necessarily deserve to be discredited. To do so would be like refusing to take any notice of contour lines because there were no visible marks corresponding to them for us to point to on the ground. The conclusion that the notion must be dropped would be justified only if, like 'phlogiston', 'caloric fluid' and the 'ether', it had also lost all explanatory fertility. No doubt scientists would be happy if they could refer in their explanations only to entities which could be shown to exist, but at many stages in the development of science it would have been crippling to have insisted on this condition too rigorously. A scientific theory is often accepted and in circulation for a long time, and may have to advance for quite a long way, before the question of the real existence of the entities appearing in it can even be posed.

The history of science provides one particularly striking example of this. The whole of theoretical physics and chemistry in the nineteenth century was developed round the notions of atoms and molecules: both the kinetic theory of matter, whose contribution to physics was spectacular, and the theory of chemical combinations and reactions, which turned chemistry into an exact science, made use of these notions, and could hardly have been expounded except in terms of them. Yet not until 1905 was it definitively shown by [Albert] Einstein [1879–1955] that the phenomenon of Brownian motion could be regarded as a demonstration that atoms and molecules really existed. Until that time, no such demonstration had ever been recognized, and even a Nobel prize-winner like [Wilhelm] Ostwald [1853–1932], for whose work as a chemist the concepts 'atom' and 'molecule' must have been indispensable, could be sceptical until then about the reality of atoms. Moreover by 1905 the atomic theory had ceased to be the last word in physics: some of its foundations were being severely attacked, and the work of Niels Bohr [1885–1962] and J. J. Thomson [1856–1940] was beginning to alter the physicist's whole picture of the constitution of matter. So, paradoxically, one finds that the major triumphs of the atomic theory were achieved at a time when even the greatest scientists could regard the idea of atoms as hardly more than a useful fiction, and that atoms were definitely shown to exist only at a time when the classical atomic theory was beginning to lose its position as the basic picture of the constitution of matter.

Evidently, then, it is a mistake to put questions about the reality or existence of theoretical entities too much in the centre of the picture. In accepting a theory scientists need not, to begin with, answer these questions either way: certainly they do not . . . commit themselves thereby to a belief in the existence of all the things in terms of which the theory is expressed. . . . When a scientist adopts a new theory, in which novel concepts are introduced (waves, electrons or genes), it may seem natural to suppose that he is committed to a belief in the existence of the things in terms of which his explanations are expressed. But again, the question whether genes, say, really exist takes us beyond the original phenomena explained in terms of 'genes'. To the scientist, the real existence of his theoretical entities is contrasted with their being only useful theoretical fictions: the fact of an initial explanatory success may therefore leave the question of existence open.

Having noticed that a theory may be accepted long before visual demonstrations can be produced of the existence of the entities involved, we may be tempted to conclude that such things as cloud-chamber photographs are rather overrated: in fact, that they only seem to bring us nearer to the things of which the physicist speaks as a result of mere illusion. This is a conclusion which [W. C.] Kneale [b. 1906] has advanced, on the ground that physical theories do not stand or fall by the results obtained from cloud-chambers and the like rather than by the results of any other physical experiments. But this is still to confuse two different questions, which may be totally independent: the question of the acceptability of the theories and the question of the reality of the theoretical entities. To regard cloud-chamber photographs as showing us that electrons and [alpha-] particles really exist need not mean giving the cloud-chamber a preferential status among our grounds for accepting current theories of atomic structure. These theories were developed and accepted before the cloud-chamber was, or indeed could have been invented. Nevertheless, it was the cloud-chamber which first showed in a really striking manner just how far nuclei, electrons, [alpha-] particles and the rest could safely be thought of as real things; that is to say, as more than explanatory fictions.

Reading Questions

1. What does a person want to know when he asks about the existence of Man Friday, dodos, Ruritania, contours, and electrons?

2. What special difficulties are there in attempting to *show* that electrons or genes exist?

3. If it were clear that no way could be devised to show a theoretically inferred entity, should a scientist then stop talking about the entity?

4. Because theories often are accepted before there is any evidence that their theoretical terms all refer to existing entities, does this mean that trying to detect the inferred entities is a waste of time? (What is the point of attempting to detect the entities, if the theory is accepted already?)

Questions for Reflection and Research

1. What proof is there that electrons exist? Is this proof direct or indirect (or is this distinction senseless)?

2. What is the point of Toulmin's explanation of the various ways of using the word *exist*?

3. What would have happened if cloud-chamber photographs showed no trace of electrons? Would electrons have been dropped from atomic theory?

4. In the years since Toulmin's book was written have genes been *shown* to exist?

5. How can theoretical concepts such as "electron" or "gene" be of significant use in science if the existence of entities corresponding to these concepts has not been demonstrated?

6. What might make one conclude that it will never be possible to determine whether a given theoretical entity exists? (See, for example, the discussion of Heisenberg's uncertainty principle in selection #20.)

selection 23.

Science and Metaphysical Assumptions

The Author: Hugo W. Thompson (b. 1900) was educated at the University of Minnesota, Yale University, and United Theological Seminary. He taught philosophy at Macalester College in Minnesota and has been active as a churchman and in social action. Recently he has been instrumental in organizing and evaluating efforts to introduce the teaching of philosophy into high schools.

The Selection: Thompson contends that anything we say about the world, even within science, rests on prior assumptions—metaphysical assumptions. Even though some philosophers have contended that metaphysical questions are unresolvable, we cannot avoid basing our lives on metaphysical views. It is true, however, that we cannot with any great confidence prove a metaphysical standpoint to be correct. Nevertheless, as in other human undertakings, past experience and careful reason should guide us in perfecting our metaphysical standpoints.

Very long ago Aristotle [384–322 B.C.] argued that anything we say about the natural world or about the processes of human thought must rest upon prior assumptions and judgments about "ultimate" questions. These questions and judgments lie at the far border of our ability to put together or imagine ideas about things. Once we have developed some of these ultimate ideas we begin to construct a "standpoint" from which we derive and interpret other ideas. For instance, we may assume, as Aristotle did, that the natural world and its processes are such that human senses can

From *Love-justice* by Hugo W. Thompson (North Quincy, Mass.: Christopher Publishing House, 1970), pp. 140–45. Reprinted by permission of Hugo W. Thompson.

perceive them accurately and human thought can organize these perceptions into a reasonably accurate model or description. Or we might assume, as the Sophists before him did, that our sensory perceptions, and the descriptive models which our thought may devise upon them, are radically unreliable guides to any true and ultimate reality. In either case, these assumptions make a great deal of difference as to how we understand, discuss and use the practical descriptions of ordinary things. For instance, the goals of science (to understand, predict, and control the operations of nature) are valid if Aristotle was right, but meaningless on Sophist assumptions.

The examination of this problem has come to be called "metaphysics," a study of the ultimate grounds of meaning and knowledge in the ultimate character of total reality. In recent times, as at various times earlier in philosophy, there have been thinkers who held that this was a silly pursuit. It is said that there is really no valid way of proving that one answer to "metaphysical questions" is preferable to another. Therefore, it is pointless to ask such questions or debate over the answers.

Clearly, the questions as to the existence or nature of God belong in this classification. Theology, the study of God, is a special type of metaphysical study. . . .

From the very nature of experience and thought it is necessarily true that all human acts and thoughts are possible only because of assumptions and hypotheses that are inseparable from them. Behind our operating assumptions are others concerning the ultimate nature of the universe and its meaning, of "mind," of the natural world and its grounds. We are led inescapably to "First Principles" or metaphysics and/or theology. Some interpretation of the ultimate ground of total reality, some assumptions about process and structure of the whole behind the portions we analyze in detail, some views as to the nature of "Being" and knowledge, which is to say some metaphysics are inescapable for any systematic thought which undertakes to formulate coherent concepts applicable to a wide range of experience.

One is dealing here with matters which begin on the very outer edge of the range of human comprehension and move beyond this range into the literally "unknowable." We cannot reach perfect certainty about matters of everyday experience and prediction, but in metaphysics we have a different kind as well as degree of uncertainty. Whether we can "know" and "prove" or not, we are compelled to make assumptions, to adopt a viewpoint, in order to make meaning out of what we do know. What is possible and required in this situation is to develop a cluster of assumptions, postulates, and propositions, such that each in itself will be defensible on grounds of logic or experience, they will be coherent with one another, and together they will present a total viewpoint which offers a fruitful perspective for explanation and further research.

The statement of such a position can be presented more appropriately around certain "Root Metaphors" rather than in simple direct propositions. Adequate metaphors must be congenial to the general view to which they refer, clear enough to discriminate between one world-view and another, yet flexible and open enough to allow for some adjustment to developing knowledge and outlook. An example would be the metaphor "Father" to refer to God. Obviously the word is not meant literally but as a meaningful picture or image helpful for thought.

Metaphysical statements are incapable of formal proof because their ultimate and final reference leads beyond both experience and reason. A cluster of metaphysical statements constituting a system presumes to speak of the totality of what is real. . . .

We can study bits of the real universe with a high degree of objectivity and with a completeness adequate to our purposes. Hence science is possible. But no man can rise beyond the limitations of his finite knowledge, perspective, and capacity even in thought. Only an infinite mind, i.e., one at a level of existence beyond time and space, could have the possibility of a completely adequate or certain metaphysical theory. Since human minds cannot achieve perfect understanding each human theory has imperfections, and none is ultimate. This applies to theological systems as well as to those more philosophical.

The choice is not "to have or not to have" such assumptions and beliefs. The choice is between (a) using beliefs that have been examined and tested by experience and reason to the limit of our ability and then adopted frankly as chosen among possibles, or (b) using assumptions that are not consciously acknowledged, examined or tested. Views of type (b) might be borrowed from some source that has made the tests carefully. Or they may be happy accidents. That is, type (b) assumptions *may* be very useful and excellently applicable in the world we know, just as a naive victim of gambler salesmanship may win the Irish sweepstakes. But that does not prove validity of the method.

There is a place for imaginative trial and error in scientific research, but the much more reliable normal procedure is to use carefully tested knowledge and logical deduction to reach highly probable hypotheses as guides to further experiment. There is not clear reason to prefer other procedure in social action or ethical thought—or theology.

Reading Questions

1. What is one kind of metaphysical assumption made by Aristotle and science?

2. What is a metaphysical assumption?
3. What should one strive for in devising a metaphysical stance?
4. Why can we not reach a high degree of certainty in metaphysics?
5. What value do metaphors have in metaphysics?
6. Why have some philosophers rejected metaphysics? Why does Thompson regard the rejection as preposterous?

Questions for Reflection and Research

1. Select an example of a scientific finding in a field familiar to you. What assumptions about the world have been made by scientists who were involved in establishing the finding? (See selections #18, #19, #20, #21, #22, and #24 for possible candidates.)
2. What reasons were given by logical positivists for rejecting metaphysics?
3. If science is really based on metaphysical assumptions and these assumptions cannot be made very certain, does this prove that scientific findings are also not very certain?
4. Is Russell in selection #19 making the same point as Thompson but using a somewhat different vocabulary?

Science and the Philosophy of Science Cannot Examine Life as It Is Lived

The Author: William A. Earle (b. 1919) was educated at the University of Chicago and in France at the University of Aix-Marseilles and has taught at Northwestern University, Yale, and Harvard. He has written a number of books explaining and advocating the approach to philosophy of existentialism and phenomenology. His interests also include philosophic aspects of film and surrealism.

The Selection: Professor Earle puts forward the view that science and the philosophy of science are relatively trivial human activities because they do not and cannot focus on what is most important to us—our lives. It is argued that the central concern of philosophy should be human life, seen not from the point of view of observers but rather from within our lives. Further it is argued that the recommended study of our lives is inherently personal and not amenable to scientific analysis. Such a study reveals our lives to be complexes that are filled with choice, value, and anticipations of the future. The selection is moderately demanding.

We have all heard the story once too often: science is knowledge about what is; the scientific method is self-correcting, its results cumulative, and is in fact the only way in which we can achieve publicly warrantable assertions about things in the world. If in the popular phrase, "Science says it is," then it *is*; and if Science says it

From William A. Earle, "Science and Philosophy," in *Science, Philosophy and our Educational Tasks*, eds. John P. Anton and George Kimball Plochmann, Buffalo Studies (Buffalo: University Council for Educational Administration and School of Education, State University of New York at Buffalo), vol. 2, no. 2 (July 1966), 59–67.

isn't, then it isn't. Science therefore is knowledge. But philosophy also claims to be knowledge; and yet it obviously isn't any experimental or observational science at all. Philosophy will therefore be *analytic;* it will analyze the synthetic conceptual compositions of science, render clear the method of science, its language, how it forms concepts, how it verifies them, etc. In short, we are already on that particular toboggan which carries philosophy downhill until it reaches dead rest in the form of the philosophy of science, art, religion, history, namely, the philosophy of something which is already in operation, living its own life. . . . [I]s it not time that we examine the question whether philosophy must inherently be the analysis and reflection upon the ongoing activities of others, or whether in fact it has not always had another aim, another method, if it has any at all, and its *own* proud independence from *science* and also all other forms of mind. Our question, then, is what can philosophy do that nothing else can do; and secondly, whether science, as well as the philosophy of science, should not always inherently be a derived, and secondary theme for philosophy? I am here arguing that philosophy is the king of the humanities, not a handmaiden of the sciences. . . .

[Philosophy] has as one of its *central* concerns life, and not every form and mode of life but *human* life, namely, our own; and further, not our own lives as seen from any and every possible perspective, such as the biological, sociological, psychological, but our lives seen from the point of view of the very men living them, ourselves, as we live them, in our own living present. Speaking in and about life so considered is a possible mode of expression; the truth is, that it is what lies closest to us as living human beings. It is, if you like, a possible "subject-matter," it has its own aims, its own forms of excellence, and it is essential, I believe, to recognize that it is inherently not a subject-matter for science, nor is its excellence that of scientific method, and its goal is certainly not that of publicly warrantable assertions. It is least of all the analysis of sentences uttered by scientists. But human life so considered is that which is closest to us in every way: since it is our life, we are speaking about ourselves, and speaking about not so much what we may or may not know about nature, but about what we have done and are about to do, what we choose, what consent to, what revolt against; instead of a purportedly value-free discourse in "law-like" sentences about what is inherently not ourselves, it is at least in effort, the attempt to gain whatever clarification might be gained about a certain perpetual problem: how to live. The clarification is not of something called "humanity," but remains personal; it is not a clarification of its problem through laws or generalities, but rather through a rendering explicit of the existing singular; its utility is not in predicting the future but in rendering evident the problem and alternatives of the perpetual present. It hardly aspires to neutral, value-free observations or descriptions, but is expressive and hortatory—if we can deprive the latter term of its empty politico-religious connotations. Now, if such an effort at articulation, exhortation, clarification of ultimate horizons in life, is not warrantable public assertion, then with *that* stipulation for "knowledge," philosophy is not knowledge. It might even aspire to be wisdom. But the capturing of the term "knowledge" by science does have the disastrous effect of leaving us with no term to characterize that philosophy which is not science except as empty emotion, attitude, or posturing. But if philosophy has always sought wisdom, whatever wisdom is, it has something to do with knowing, and if the knowing in question is not scientific knowing, then it is knowing of another sort. The wise man can hardly be regarded as a fool.

I have been trying to point to a domain which I should maintain (following Karl Jaspers [1883–1969]) is absolutely not a province to be explored by any science, since its very character is inherently not subject to either observation or experiment. Further it is not some curious corner, left over from science, of merely private or personal concern; a somewhat messy corner, where anything can be said, so long as it is said in an urgent tone. This particular domain, I believe, happens to be nothing short of our lives, and far from being undisciplined, merely emotional, a matter of guesses and hunches, is in fact the sole domain of the arts and of philosophy, when that discourse understands itself. If it is not explorable by any natural science, and if it touches precisely what we are, then the natural sciences and philosophy conceived as an analysis of the work of natural scientists, both recede into the somewhat secondary curiosities which I believe they inherently are. It is all a question of principle, and not the "present state" of science; it is not possible in principle for psychology, sociology, or cybernetics to clarify this domain, and thereupon render its philosophical clarification either superfluous, or scientifically false or true. The domains are kept distinct; and the remainder of my remarks will be an effort to make plausible this distinctness of domain, of method, and of goal. Science has virtually nothing to do with life as it is lived, its methods and attitudes. Observation, experiment, impersonal materiality transferred to life would amount to a destruction of the appropriate attitudes we entertain towards one another, and its goal of prediction through law utterly irrelevant. Yet, this domain is where we are so long as we exist. Meanwhile, although in contrast to science, it is sometimes thought that the humanistic-philosophical clarification of existence lags behind the sciences, makes no dramatic "breakthroughs," is in effect something rather apologetic and retrospective, defining itself only negatively against the brillance of modern physics, I should like to give some evidence that the domain of life has in fact been explored with a nuance and precision not merely unattained but wholly unattainable in the natural sciences, and that its expression in poetry and philosophy represents the *clearest* form of knowledge we do or could possess. But it is not publicly warrantable assertion, additive or cumulative.

The natural sciences, first of all, must gather data, pertinent to whatever problem they wish to pose. These data obviously must be experienceable; imagined or dreamed of experiences, or experiences which in principle only a single man could have, would hardly supply a very firm foundation for publicly warrantable assertions. And so with experiments. Both observation and experiment must be experiences of something; they must, secondly, be repeatable experiences, repeatable by a "standard observer." As we all know, the aim of the repeatable experience is to settle some problem, and the problem is, typically, to answer the question of either how things work or why they work this particular way, in a word, a law which will describe or explain the experienced; and that law again is for the purpose of predicting the character of future experiences under similar circumstances. Some such thing I would suppose to be the method of the natural sciences, and no doubt it is remarkably successful for its proper domain, nature. But its success there is a correlate to its absolute failure elsewhere, namely, in the domain of our living existence. For, first of all, it needs experienceable data of some sort. But now, if we turn that same experiencing mode of consciousness *within*, the first thing we find is that there is *nothing* there to be experienced; secondly, that my *awareness* of my present existence is not an *experience* of it at all, but rather a *reflexive* [= mediated] *consciousness* of it. The essential characteristic of anything that should be called experience is that it is a mediated awareness of an *independent object;* my perception of the stone is not the stone itself, but rather a perception of it from where I am, with my organs of perception, operating through their own appropriate media and distances. It is precisely due to this mediated character of the perceived thing, that one and the same thing could in principle simultaneously be perceived by another, and therefore supply us with a something or other which in principle could be public and repeatable, hence a fit object for scientific observation. For if anything is clear it is that my *perceptions* cannot be perceived by another, are not themselves perceivable objects, and therefore my awareness of my own perceptions is not itself another perception but a reflexive awareness in which I am *immediately* aware of my own perceptions. Hence it is false to say that we experience our experiences or that we perceive our perceptions; we are indeed *aware* of performing these acts, but not by either experience or perception, whichever term is preferred. Accordingly, acts of consciousness *as* they are enacted by the consciousness, are not fit objects for either observation or experiment. This hardly implies that we are unconscious of them; but rather that our consciousness of them is immediate, and reflexive. And, since they are given immediately to consciousness itself, there is no possibility of repeatability. Another act may be performed very much like the first; but since these acts do not have a thing-like character, the only witness to the similarity would have to be the consciousness immediately having them; and in any event, similarity between two singular acts is radically distinct from the simultaneous perspectives which a plurality of observers can take on a single, perceived thing or event.

The first reason, then, why our existence as we exist in it is not a fit object for science is that it is *wholly* inaccessible to observation and experiment. . . .

Now if we turn our reflexive consciousness to our own living present, what do we find? I said before that we find nothing. We certainly do not find something called a mind, namely our own, painted over with certain *states* or *qualities* like "pain," "pleasure," colors, shapes, etc.; instead we find ourselves *in act;* we have just come from somewhere and are going somewhere; consciousness is as it were in flight, always aimed at something which is not the flight itself, but something in its own future. We are, in this sense, always about to become something; but we never can settle into being that thing. [Jean Paul] Sartre [b. 1905] has described this aspect of consciousness in great detail. Consciousness is inherently intentional, and projective. And so no wonder if we find nothing there but a restlessness. This supplies [a second] very good reason why there can be no natural science of consciousness; so long as we exist, we never *are* anything to be observed. We can certainly recall what we have done; and we can imagine what we are about to do; but the present is torn between the two, a flight from one *to* the other, hence not a thing with thing-like properties. Hence even our reflexive awareness of our lives is nothing like staring within at a datum, but is an awareness of an inner projection toward what we are about to become, our possible alternatives. Or, since existence in this sense is not a collective or public project, a projection toward what *I* am about to become. But what I am *about* to do, I have *not yet* done; I must choose it, decide it, affirm it, consent to it. And, since it appears to me in the light of a *possible* act, and not already *necessarily* implicated by my present, it is of such a sort that it could either be or not; I can always say yes or no to it. I remain free, I choose what inherently depends upon my choice for its existence; and my choice of this rather than that is identical with conferring "value" upon it. The predictability from the outside of my choice has no bearing on this internal lived freedom whatsoever; if I invariably keep my promises, in short, if I am a man of character, "reliable," then indeed I can be depended upon, I act "predictably"; but I am hardly less free from choosing consistently than in being erratic, undependable. Hence, if natural science seeks a law governing experienceables according to which the future can be predicted, nothing would prevent it, so far as I can see, from finding such a law for us. But it hardly means that it has thereby disproven our freedom; it would have established nothing more than that freedom can choose coherently and consistently, and it most frequently does that when it is satisfied with its values, and can see no reason for change. Further, if natural science now turned into psychology and sociology, should find the law, it had better keep this a well-hidden secret; knowing what it was, what would prevent any of us from violating it out of spite?

To bring these remarks together: There is a domain in which the methods of the natural sciences are inapplicable, the domain of our own lives so long as we are alive, and alive for us, not for an external observer. This domain is accessible to us in the form of reflection and not observation or experiment. And our most immediate reflection upon it uncovers it as inherently characterized by singularity, freedom, projectedness, choice, and value. . . .

Why, then, is it outrageous if a philosopher attempts to think through to the bottom his own life, in its depth and in its singularity, and bring us something which might elucidate possibilities in our own existence? . . . If someone should ask, Why should anyone else be interested in the merely autobiographical, what contribution would it make to the universal science of man, the appropriate reply, I suppose, would be: Why should anyone be interested in *anything else* but a singular man who is or was, who is not mankind but only himself, and perhaps, if he is or was wise enough could elucidate some possibilities of our own, so that he could help by having been there before? Considered in this light, both the natural sciences and the philosophy of science must be considered interesting curiosities but existentially irrelevant; philosophy itself is rather a passionate attempt to explore the passionate possibilities which offer themselves to passionate men. It is autobiographical, inseparable from values and urgencies, provided with its own distinctive clarity, and for these reasons above all inherently *closest* to us.

Reading Questions

1. How have many philosophers been persuaded that the only task of philosophy is the analysis of concepts found in fields outside philosophy?
2. What is Earle's conception of a main concern of philosophy?
3. Why can the domain of philosophy (consciousness) not be explored by science?
4. Why is the special value of philosophy autobiographical rather than general?

Questions for Reflection and Research

1. What kinds and sources of knowledge are there? Is science the only source?
2. Would hard or soft determinists be convinced by Earle's defense of free will? (See selection #17 by Minton.)
3. Which answer to the body-mind problem seems to be assumed by Earle? (See selection #11 by Edwards.)
4. Are the findings of the recommended study of consciousness of much greater value than those of science?
5. Why is such self-reflection not itself an observing of something of possible scientific use or merit?
6. If consciousness is inherently personal, how can we be confident that each person's use of language to characterize his consciousness will mean the same to others?
7. What should be the goal of the philosophy of science?

Scientific Methodology

Why should we bother to ask what science is? If we happened to be unfamiliar with the word and wished to know what it meant, we might be interested in its definition. Robert Fischer (in selection #25) gives his own definition of *science* and then compares it with other definitions offered by philosophers and scientists. Surely, however, he and the others who have tried to define science are not seeking to help those who are unfamiliar with the word *science*.

Some would say they seek definitions of *science* simply out of curiosity. They wonder how science is distinguished from other human activities. And perhaps they wonder what the activities of chemists, sociologists, biologists, and anthropologists have in common.

Others might say that besides enjoying the search, they think there are important reasons to seek and establish the correct definition of *science*—reasons having nothing to do with helping people who are unfamiliar with the word. A definition could be used to weed out false candidates for the title *science*. Because of the obvious successes of physics, chemistry, and biology in helping us understand nature, to call an activity a science is now to bestow honor on it. But are library science, secretarial science, and fire science sciences? Is psychic research a science? Are medical doctors scientists? At various times social and behavioral sciences have been challenged as being nonsciences. (For example, see selection #38 by A. R. Louch.) Are they actually sciences?

The correct definition of *science* might help us answer these questions. Further, there is a very practical reason to want to find a way to weed out some of the nonsciences. Some imposter sciences corrupt society by greatly misleading people about the world and by taking gullible people's money through alleged health cures or supposed miracle gadgets. (Such pseudo-sciences are discussed by Martin Gardner in selection #50.)

There is a more positive reason for wanting an accurate definition of the word *science*. Many sciences have succeeded. If it were possible to determine what the sciences share when they are being conducted successfully, then we would have a set of guidelines for improving all science. That is, if sciences share some ingredient that leads to success in learning about the world, the isolation of this ingredient could lead to the improvement of science. If workers in the established sciences had clear knowledge of what constitutes science, they could proceed more carefully in their work. They would fail less often. Further, new sciences for the study of heretofore incompletely understood phenomena could be established and developed with confidence.

Thus, the correct definition of *science* seems to promise dividends. It would help us to get rid of phony sciences, help make existing legitimate sciences more efficient, and lead to the founding of legitimate new sciences. Unfortunately, no definition of *science* has yet won wide support. Furthermore, the thought that we might be able to find such a definition can be challenged.

Often a definition attempts to describe the features common to those things to which the word refers. But perhaps some words name things that do not share common features. Perhaps the activities that we call science do not share common features. Perhaps, that is, a definition of *science* cannot be found.

It is clear, however, that a number of thinkers have assumed *science* to be a common-feature word—and have assumed that the sciences share at least one ingredient. This ingredient has come to be known as the scientific method. Selection #26 by Robert Pirsig (from the book *Zen and the Art of Motor Cycle Maintenance*) offers one version of the scientific method as it might be used to diagnose a motorcycle malfunction. The influential philosopher of science Carl G. Hempel offers another account of the scientific method in selection #27. Both of these accounts will probably strike readers as familiar and as similar to accounts of science offered at the beginning of some science courses.

But are these accounts correct? A chemist and historian of science, James B. Conant, argues (in selection #28) that the various sciences have procedures and objects of study that are so different that their sharing a method is not at all likely.

Whether or not there is a definition of science and whether or not it includes something like a scientific method, scientists do sometimes put forward conjectures about nature and devise experiments seeking to test them. Attempts to relate experimental data or statistical data to conjectures have interested philosophers of science. How much and what kind of evidence is needed to confirm a conjecture or hypothesis? How are we to reason from data about some small number of cases to the whole class of events or things under study? Such questions belong to what is sometimes called confirmation theory. Unfortunately, efforts to explain and clarify the role data play in establishing scientific hypotheses and generalizations face a number of obstacles, two of which are touched on in the readings. Selection #30 by Baruch Brody briefly details Nelson Goodman's "new riddle of induction." Goodman, a philosopher, argues that any data that seem to support generalizations of interest to scientists must be regarded as also supporting certain kinds of generalizations (specified by Goodman) that seem obviously false. A confirmation theory must seek to show that the data do not really support such false generalizations.

One who is interested in confirmation theory, if he or she can figure out a way to resolve Goodman's riddle, must next attempt to select the best of three alternative interpretations of statistical or probabilistic scientific data. Edward Madden in selection #29 explains how the three interpretations are defended and describes some of the problems that result, should any one of them be chosen.

Those who believe that there is a scientific method, and that confirmation procedures are part of it, must face other difficulties besides those already mentioned. These difficulties concern alleged inadequacies of versions of the scientific method presented by Pirsig and Hempel and by a group of philosophers and scientists known as the Vienna Circle.

Beginning in the 1920s members of the Vienna Circle became convinced that science was the main (and almost only) road to truth. The views of these thinkers eventually developed into what is called logical positivism. Selection #32 by philosopher of science Ernan McMullin details recent reactions to the logical positivists' conception of science. Emerging from these reactions is a new conception of progress in science, regarding it as depending much less on the scientific method or rational decision procedures.

The most influential of these critics of the positivist conception of science has been Thomas S. Kuhn, who argues from the perspective of one trained in physics and in the history of science. He contends (see selection #31) that the ideas many philosophers and scientists get about the nature of science originate in science textbooks. But science textbooks are not written to give us an accurate idea of the nature of science; rather, they are written to teach us the findings of the sciences. A study of the history of science, he asserts, reveals how much less tidy science is than is portrayed in science texts. This untidiness is particularly evident during scientific revolutions, periods when scientists are asked to give up much of (what Kuhn calls) their paradigm for their science—i.e., their training and assumptions about their science—and are asked to accept a new paradigm. When scientists face such a decision, the scientific method plays little role, and other more personal factors influence whether the new paradigm will be accepted.

According to the survey of the recent history of the philosophy of science by McMullin there is not full agreement on the legitimacy of the criticisms by Kuhn and others. However, many philosophers of science have become convinced that a more careful study of the history of science is important before one attempts to generalize about the nature of science.

Further Reading: The Nature of Science

1. *The Encyclopedia of Philosophy*, ed. PAUL EDWARDS, 8 vols. (New York: Macmillan Publishing Co., 1967). For a historical survey of conceptions of science and problems of the philosophy of science see "Philosophy of Science, History of" by R. HARRÉ. For discussions that focus in some way on the nature of science see "Confirmation: Qualitative Aspects" by CARL G. HEMPEL; "Confirmation: Quantitative Aspects" by FREDERIC SCHICK; "Operationalism" by G. SCHLESINGER; "Probability" by MAX BLACK; and "Scientific Method" by PETER CAWS.

2. *Conceptual Foundations of Scientific Thought: An Introduction to the Philosophy of Science*, MARX W. WARTOFSKY (New York: Macmillan Publishing Co., 1968) has an excellent bibliography on many topics in the philosophy of science.

3. "Thomas S. Kuhn: Revolutionary Theorist of Science" by NICHOLAS WADE, *Science* 197 (July 8, 1977): 143–45. This brief article gives an overview of reactions to and developments from Kuhn's book.

4. "The Search for Philosophic Understanding of Scientific Theories" by FREDERICK SUPPE in *The Structure of Scientific Theories*, ed. Frederick Suppe (Urbana, Ill.: University of Illinois Press, 1974), pp. 3–232. This is a more complete account of the recent history of the philosophy of science than found in the McMullin selection (#32).

Definitions of Science

The Author: Robert B. Fischer (b. 1920) is a chemist who received his education at Wheaton College in Illinois and the University of Illinois. He has taught at Indiana University and California State University at Dominguez Hills, where he is now Dean of the School of Natural Sciences and Mathematics.

The Selection: *Science* is defined by the author as "the body of knowledge obtained by methods based upon observation." The definition is clarified and compared with a number of other definitions of *science* offered by scientists and philosophers.

[W]e will assume the following as the working definition of the word science: **Science is the body of knowledge obtained by methods based upon observation.**

This definition is consistent with, but more specific than, the concept represented by the Latin word *scientia*. It also incorporates the meaning of the German word *Wissenschaft*—the phrase "body of knowledge" is meant to convey the sense that there is some organization of the bits of knowledge, just as a human body is an organized assemblage of its component parts.

No restriction to the realm of nature or of matter is specifically stated, but the essentiality of observation is specified. Indeed, it is the realm of nature, of matter both living and non-living, that can be observed. To be sure, people can be observed, individually and

From *Science, Man, and Society,* 2nd ed., by Robert B. Fischer (Philadelphia: W. B. Saunders Co., 1975), pp. 3–10. Reprinted by permission of W. B. Saunders Co. and Robert B. Fischer.

collectively. Therefore, science as defined here includes much of what is commonly considered to be the social and behavioral sciences, and it is precisely for this reason and to this extent that these areas of knowledge are within the subject matter of science.

The inclusion in our definition of the words "methods" and "observation" places stress upon the dynamic nature of the knowledge that is science. As long as persons can continue to observe and to utilize the methods, science is dynamic and not static, both in principle and in practice.

This definition carries several implications. Let us list four of the most significant ones.

1. *The practice of science is a human activity.* Human beings do the observing, employ the methods and gain the body of knowledge.

2. *There is an inherent limitation of science.* Anything that is outside of or beyond the senses with which people can observe is, in principle, outside of or beyond the bounds of science.

3. *There is an authority in science.* The practical authority is observation, and the underlying authority is that which is observed.

4. *There is a building upon the authority.* The methods are based upon, not limited to, observation. . . .

Numerous definitions and descriptions of the word science have been written, and little or nothing would be gained by a lengthy tabulation of a large number of them. Nevertheless, a brief sampling of some selected published statements can be of value in reinforcing our working definition, and in both amplifying and providing contrast to its several parts.

The "man in the street," according to [James B.] Conant [b. 1893], considers science to be "the activity of people who work in laboratories and whose discoveries have made possible modern industry and medicine." This statement, although it may appear to be true to many lay persons, is seriously deficient as a meaningful description of what science is. For example, many persons who clearly must qualify as scientists do not work in laboratories, and many of the discoveries of people who are scientists do not have any demonstrable applicability in either modern industry or medicine. However, this concept serves to illustrate the importance of attempting to define significant words in order to clarify just what the concepts really are.

[Norman] Campbell [1880–1949] describes science as consisting of two forms: (a) science is a body of useful and practical knowledge and a method of obtaining it; (b) science is a pure intellectual activity. A justification of the inclusion of the role of the intellect in science and the distinction between the pure and the applied are surely in order. However, it hardly seems appropriate or valid either to separate the "useful and practical" from the intellectual activity or to separate the pure from the "knowledge and a way of obtaining it." . . . [T]here really is no sharp distinction between pure science and applied science. What distinctions there are, moreover, often concern motivation of the scientist rather than what he does or the subject matter of the field in which he works.

There has been considerable controversy over the relative merits of defining science on the basis of knowledge or on the basis of the methodology used in acquiring that knowledge. Some authors use both of these approaches. On the one hand, [Leonard K.] Nash [b. 1918], a chemist, emphasizes that science is a process: "Science is a way of looking at the world." On the other hand, [Eugene P.] Wigner [b. 1902], a physicist, defines "our science" as "our store of knowledge of natural phenomena." Note that Wigner's definition also includes designation of the general subject area of this knowledge—natural phenomena. . . .

The biologist T. H. Huxley [1825–1895] has described science by saying, "Science is organized common sense." This straightforward statement effectively illustrates the reasonableness and the rationality of scientific knowledge and thus aids in dispelling some of the aura of mysticism that so often surrounds science. But, like numerous other simple and straightforward statements, it can be misleading if read too literally, that is, if taken too seriously. Some authors have pointed out that some parts of scientific knowledge, including Einstein's relativity concepts, are not amenable to the physical models that are inevitably a part of common sense thinking. It is interesting to note, however, that [Albert] Einstein [1879–1955] himself said, "The whole of science is nothing more than a refinement of everyday thinking."

A significant definition of science has been presented by [R. H.] Bube [b. 1927], a solid-state physicist, who stated that science is "knowledge of the natural world obtained by sense interaction with that world." This statement provides an interesting elaboration on two aspects of how observation occurs: (a) the observation of natural phenomena, which is the authoritative basis upon which scientific knowledge stands, is through one's mind and senses; (b) the process of observation involves two-way interaction between the observer and that which is observed. Always in principle, and often in practice, the mere process of observation is a two-way street: the observer is affected or caused to respond through his senses; the object or phenomenon being observed is also acted upon and may be changed. . . .

Several published definitions of the word science include some detail as to the methods of using observation in gaining knowledge. . . . For example, [John G.] Kemeny [b. 1926], a philosopher, defines science as "all knowledge collected by means of the scientific method." He hastens to explain that this is not a circular definition, even though the word scientific is used in defining science, for he has earlier defined the scientific method to be a "cycle of induction, deduction, verification and eternal search for improvement of theories which are only tentatively held."

Conant, an organic chemist who maintained a measure of active participation in science even while filling high-level academic and governmental administrative positions, writes, "Science is an inter-connected series of concepts and conceptual schemes that have de-veloped as a result of experimentation and observation and are fruitful of further experimentation and observations." This defini-tion, in addition to describing something about scientific methods, stresses the dynamic character of scientific knowledge by designat-ing the present state of knowledge as the basis for further opera-tions.

[A. Cornelius] Benjamin [b. 1897], a philosopher, gives the fol-lowing definition: "Science is that mode of inquiry which attempts to arrive at knowledge of the world by the method of observation and by the method of confirmed hypothesis on what is given in ob-servation." Note that this definition is based upon method, or "mode of inquiry," but that the method is, in effect, not separable from the knowledge to be gained.

An additional point appears in the definition by [W. C.] Dampier [1867–1952], a historian of science. He wrote, "Science is the or-dered knowledge of natural phenomena and the rational study of the relations between the concepts in which these phenomena are expressed." Here we note that science is not only orderly know-ledge but also rational study—it is coherent and intellectually self-consistent. The practice of science is, indeed, an intellectual activ-ity.

It is often helpful in defining or describing a term to include statements of what it is *not*, as well as of what it is. [Warren] Weaver [b. 1894], a well-known mathematician and science administrator, has used this technique in attempting to explain what science is: "Science is not technology, nor does it consist of technological gadgetry. Science is not black-magic, nor is it a universal snake oil to cure all diseases." Weaver further circumscribed science, but not rigidly, by stating that it is "a way of solving problems, not all prob-lems, but . . . those in which the predominant factors are subject to the basic laws of logic and are usually quantitative in character," and by stating that "Science is not an arrogant dictator in the whole arena of life but rather a democratic companion of philosophy, of art, of religion and of other valid alternative approaches to reality."

[Jacob] Bronowski [1908–1974], who is a scientist and a philosopher of science, has defined science in this way: "Science is the organization of our knowledge in such a way that it commands more of the hidden potential in nature." This definition em-phasizes first the processes of organization and second, the belief or the "faith" that progress is possible because there is more in nature than we already know.

Each of these definitions and descriptive statements reinforces or elaborates upon one or more aspects of the definition [given earlier].

Reading Questions

1. What limitation on science is implicit in the definition?
2. Why does Fischer claim we need a definition of *science* or of any significant word?
3. Compare and contrast the definitions given for their similarities and differences.

Questions for Reflection and Research

1. What are definitions for? How can we tell when a definition is a good one?
2. List all the human activities we call sciences. Do they all fit Fischer's definition?
3. Think of bodies of knowledge that satisfy Fischer's definition. Are all usually regarded as sciences?
4. Is a definition of *science* an attempt to describe what all sciences have in common? Do all sciences have anything in common? (See selection #28 by Conant.)
5. Should scientists care about the correct definition of science? Why or why not?

selection 26.

A Motorcyclist's Version of the Scientific Method

The Author: Robert M. Pirsig (b. 1928) was educated at the University of Minnesota and thereafter taught rhetoric at Montana State University and the University of Illinois, Chicago. He became a technical writer in the Minneapolis area and also grew interested in Zen Buddhism. His book, from which the selection is taken, is autobiographical and has been highly praised by book reviewers.

The Selection: Pirsig's book recounts the story of a father and son riding West on a motorcycle seeking release from various problems and pressures. The father becomes involved in complex reflections, which often involve using the motorcycle as an analogy. In this particular passage the author likens a motorcycle mechanic's attempt to identify the source of a problem to the scientist's use of the scientific method to resolve a scientific problem. In so doing Pirsig explains induction and deduction and gives a six-step account of the scientific method.

Now we follow the Yellowstone Valley right across Montana. It changes from Western sagebrush to Midwestern cornfields and back again, depending on whether it's under irrigation from the river. Sometimes we cross over bluffs that take us out of the irrigated area, but usually we stay close to the river. We pass by a marker saying something about Lewis and Clark. One of them came up this way on a side excursion from the Northwest Passage. . . .

I want to pursue further now that same ghost that Phaedrus

pursued—rationality itself, that dull, complex, classical ghost of underlying form.

This morning I talked about hierarchies of thought—the system. Now I want to talk about methods of finding one's way through these hierarchies—logic.

Two kinds of logic are used, inductive and deductive. Inductive inferences start with observations of the machine and arrive at general conclusions. For example, if the cycle goes over a bump and the engine misfires, and then goes over another bump and the engine misfires, and then goes over another bump and the engine misfires, and then goes over a long smooth stretch of road and there is no misfiring, and then goes over a fourth bump and the engine misfires again, one can logically conclude that the misfiring is caused by the bumps. That is induction: reasoning from particular experiences to general truths.

Deductive inferences do the reverse. They start with general knowledge and predict a specific observation. For example, if, from reading the hierarchy of facts about the machine, the mechanic knows the horn of the cycle is powered exclusively by electricity from the battery, then he can logically infer that if the battery is dead the horn will not work. That is deduction.

Solution of problems too complicated for common sense to solve is achieved by long strings of mixed inductive and deductive inferences that weave back and forth between the observed machine and the mental hierarchy of the machine found in the manuals. The correct program for this interweaving is formalized as scientific method.

Actually I've never seen a cycle-maintenance problem complex enough really to require full-scale formal scientific method. Repair problems are not that hard. When I think of formal scientific method an image sometimes comes to mind of an enormous juggernaut, a huge bulldozer—slow, tedious, lumbering, laborious, but invincible. It takes twice as long, five times as long, maybe a dozen times as long as informal mechanic's techniques, but you know in the end you're going to *get* it. There's no fault isolation problem in motorcycle maintenance that can stand up to it. When you've hit a really tough one, tried everything, racked your brain and nothing works, and you know that this time Nature has really decided to be difficult, you say, "Okay, Nature, that's the end of the *nice* guy," and you crank up the formal scientific method.

For this you keep a lab notebook. Everything gets written down, formally, so that you know at all times where you are, where you've been, where you're going and where you want to get. In scientific work and electronics technology this is necessary because otherwise the problems get so complex you get lost in them and confused and forget what you know and what you don't know and have to give up. In cycle maintenance things are not that involved, but when confusion starts it's a good idea to hold it down by making everything formal and exact. Sometimes just the act of writing down the problems straightens out your head as to what they really are.

The logical statements entered into the notebook are broken down into six categories: (1) statement of the problem, (2) hypotheses as to the cause of the problem, (3) experiments designed to test each hypothesis, (4) predicted results of the experiments, (5) observed results of the experiments and (6) conclusions from the results of the experiments. This is not different from the formal arrangement of many college and high-school lab notebooks but the purpose here is no longer just busywork. The purpose now is precise guidance of thoughts that will fail if they are not accurate.

The real purpose of scientific method is to make sure Nature hasn't misled you into thinking you know something you don't actually know. There's not a mechanic or scientist or technician alive who hasn't suffered from that one so much that he's not instinctively on guard. That's the main reason why so much scientific and mechanical information sounds so dull and so cautious. If you get careless or go romanticizing scientific information, giving it a flourish here and there, Nature will soon make a complete fool out of you. It does it often enough anyway even when you don't give it opportunities. One must be extremely careful and rigidly logical when dealing with Nature: one logical slip and an entire scientific edifice comes tumbling down. One false deduction about the machine and you can get hung up indefinitely.

In Part One of formal scientific method, which is the statement of the problem, the main skill is in stating absolutely no more than you are positive you know. It is much better to enter a statement "Solve Problem: Why doesn't cycle work?" which sounds dumb but is correct, than it is to enter a statement "Solve Problem: What is wrong with the electrical system?" when you don't absolutely *know* the trouble is *in* the electrical system. What you should state is "Solve Problem: What is wrong with cycle?" and *then* state as the first entry of Part Two: "Hypothesis Number One: The trouble is in the electrical system." You think of as many hypotheses as you can, then you design experiments to test them to see which are true and which are false.

This careful approach to the beginning questions keeps you from taking a major wrong turn which might cause you weeks of extra work or can even hang you up completely. Scientific questions often have a surface appearance of dumbness for this reason. They are asked in order to prevent dumb mistakes later on.

Part Three, that part of formal scientific method called experimentation, is sometimes thought of by romantics as all of science itself because that's the only part with much visual surface. They see lots of test tubes and bizarre equipment and people running around making discoveries. They do not see the experiment as part of a larger intellectual process and so they often confuse experiments with demonstrations, which look the same. A man conducting a gee-whiz science show with fifty thousand dollars' worth of Frankenstein equipment is not doing anything scientific if he knows beforehand what the results of his efforts are going to be. A motorcycle mechanic, on the other hand, who honks the horn to see if the battery works is informally conducting a true scientific experiment. He is testing a hypothesis by putting the question to nature. The TV scientist who mutters sadly, "The experiment is a failure; we have failed to achieve what we had hoped for," is suffering mainly from a bad scriptwriter. An experiment is never a failure solely because it fails to achieve predicted results. An experiment is a failure only when it also fails adequately to test the hypothesis in question, when the data it produces don't prove anything one way or another.

Skill at this point consists of using experiments that test only the hypothesis in question, nothing less, nothing more. If the horn honks, and the mechanic concludes that the whole electrical system is working, he is in deep trouble. He has reached an illogical conclusion. The honking horn only tells him that the battery and horn are working. To design an experiment properly he has to think very rigidly in terms of what directly causes what. This you know from the hierarchy. The horn doesn't make the cycle go. Neither does the battery, except in a very indirect way. The point at which the electrical system *directly* causes the engine to fire is at the spark plugs, and if you don't test here, at the output of the electrical system, you will never really know whether the failure is electrical or not.

To test properly the mechanic removes the plug and lays it against the engine so that the base around the plug is electrically grounded, kicks the starter lever and watches the spark-plug gap for a blue spark. If there isn't any he can conclude one of two things: (a) there is an electrical failure or (b) his experiment is sloppy. If he is experienced he will try it a few more times, checking connections, trying every way he can think of to get that plug to fire. Then, if he can't get it to fire, he finally concludes that *a* is correct, there's an electrical failure, and the experiment is over. He has proved that his hypothesis is correct.

In the final category, conclusions, skill comes in stating no more than the experiment has proved. It hasn't proved that when he fixes the electrical system the motorcycle will start. There may be other things wrong. But he does know that the motorcycle isn't going to run until the electrical system is working and he sets up the next formal question: "Solve problem: What is wrong with the electrical system?"

He then sets up hypotheses for these and tests them. By asking the right questions and choosing the right tests and drawing the right conclusions the mechanic works his way down the echelons of the motorcycle hierarchy until he has found the exact specific cause or causes of the engine failure, and then he changes them so that they no longer cause the failure.

An untrained observer will see only physical labor and often get the idea that physical labor is mainly what the mechanic does. Actually the physical labor is the smallest and easiest part of what the mechanic does. By far the greatest part of his work is careful observation and precise thinking. That is why mechanics sometimes seem so taciturn and withdrawn when performing tests. They don't like it when you talk to them because they are concentrating on mental images, hierarchies, and not really looking at you or the physical motorcycle at all. They are using the experiment as part of a program to expand their hierarchy of knowledge of the faulty motorcycle and compare it to the correct hierarchy in their mind. They are looking at underlying form.

Reading Questions

1. What is the difference between induction and deduction?
2. Will the scientific method always eventually lead to the resolution of a problem?
3. What care must be taken in stating the problem (step 1) and stating the conclusion of an experiment (step 6)?
4. Is there any method given for devising hypotheses (step 2)?
5. Of what value are experiments that do not result in what is hoped for?
6. Where are induction and deduction employed in the six steps?

Questions for Reflection and Research

1. Study the history of some scientific breakthrough(s). Did the scientists involved use the method described by Pirsig?
2. Would the method as described actually *guarantee* success in resolving a problem in science? Why or why not?
3. What other accounts of the scientific method have been given? (See, for example, selection #27 by Hempel.) Do the accounts agree?
4. Must all sciences use the same method? Why or why not? (See selection #28 by Conant.)
5. When scientific revolutions occur, do the scientists who bring them about succeed because they have used the scientific method more carefully than their predecessors? (See selection #31 by Kuhn.)

A Philosopher of Science Gives His Account of the Scientific Method

The Author: Carl G. Hempel (b. 1905) was born and educated in Germany, receiving his doctorate from the University of Berlin. His original training was in physics and mathematics, but he eventually turned to philosophy, making contributions in logic, philosophy of mathematics, and philosophy of science. He has taught at Yale and Princeton Universities.

The Selection: The procedures used to determine the cause of childbed fever are described as an example of a scientific approach to a problem. Patterns of deductive reasoning that play a role in scientific thinking are spelled out. The claim that the scientific method uses inductive inference in its first step is examined and rejected. Finally it is argued that even though there are procedures that can be described as the scientific method, there is nevertheless no correct procedure for discovering promising hypotheses for scientific testing.

As a simple illustration of some important aspects of scientific inquiry let us consider Semmelweis' work on childbed fever. Ignaz Semmelweis [1818–1865], a physician of Hungarian birth, did this work during the years from 1844 to 1848 at the Vienna General Hospital. As a member of the medical staff of the First Maternity Division in the hospital, Semmelweis was distressed to find that a large proportion of the women who were delivered of their babies in that division contracted a serious and often fatal illness known as puerperal fever or childbed fever. In 1844, as many as 260 out of

From Carl G. Hempel, *Philosophy of Natural Science*, © 1966, pp. 3–18. Reprinted and adapted by permission of Prentice-Hall, Inc., Englewood Cliffs, N.J.

3,157 mothers in the First Division, or 8.2 per cent, died of the disease; for 1845, the death rate was 6.8 per cent, and for 1846, it was 11.4 per cent. These figures were all the more alarming because in the adjacent Second Maternity Division of the same hospital, which accommodated almost as many women as the First, the death toll from childbed fever was much lower: 2.3, 2.0, and 2.7 per cent for the same years. In a book that he wrote later on the causation and the prevention of childbed fever, Semmelweis describes his efforts to resolve the dreadful puzzle.

He began by considering various explanations that were current at the time; some of these he rejected out of hand as incompatible with well-established facts; others he subjected to specific tests.

One widely accepted view attributed the ravages of puerperal fever to "epidemic influences", which were vaguely described as "atmospheric-cosmic-telluric changes" spreading over whole districts and causing childbed fever in women in confinement. But how, Semmelweis reasons, could such influences have plagued the First Division for years and yet spared the Second? And how could this view be reconciled with the fact that while the fever was raging in the hospital, hardly a case occurred in the city of Vienna or in its surroundings: a genuine epidemic, such as cholera, would not be so selective. Finally, Semmelweis notes that some of the women admitted to the First Division, living far from the hospital, had been overcome by labor on their way and had given birth in the street: yet despite these adverse conditions, the death rate from childbed fever among these cases of "street birth" was lower than the average for the First Division.

On another view, overcrowding was a cause of mortality in the First Division. But Semmelweis points out that in fact the crowding was heavier in the Second Division, partly as a result of the desperate efforts of patients to avoid assignment to the notorious First Division. He also rejects two similar conjectures that were current, by noting that there were no differences between the two Divisions in regard to diet or general care of the patients.

In 1846, a commission that had been appointed to investigate the matter attributed the prevalence of illness in the First Division to injuries resulting from rough examination by the medical students, all of whom received their obstetrical training in the First Division. Semmelweis notes in refutation of this view that (a) the injuries resulting naturally from the process of birth are much more extensive than those that might be caused by rough examination; (b) the midwives who received their training in the Second Division examined their patients in much the same manner but without the same ill effects; (c) when, in response to the commission's report, the number of medical students was halved and their examinations of the women were reduced to a minimum, the mortality, after a brief decline, rose to higher levels than ever before.

Various psychological explanations were attempted. One of them noted that the First Division was so arranged that a priest bearing the last sacrament to a dying woman had to pass through five wards before reaching the sickroom beyond: the appearance of the priest, preceded by an attendant ringing a bell, was held to have a terrifying and debilitating effect upon the patients in the wards and thus to make them more likely victims of childbed fever. In the Second Division, this adverse factor was absent, since the priest had direct access to the sickroom. Semmelweis decided to test this conjecture. He persuaded the priest to come by a roundabout route and without ringing of the bell, in order to reach the sick chamber silently and unobserved. But the mortality in the First Division did not decrease.

A new idea was suggested to Semmelweis by the observation that in the First Division the women were delivered lying on their backs; in the Second Division, on their sides. Though he thought it unlikely, he decided "like a drowning man clutching at a straw", to test whether this difference in procedure was significant. He introduced the use of the lateral position in the First Division, but again, the mortality remained unaffected.

At last, early in 1847, an accident gave Semmelweis the decisive clue for his solution of the problem. A colleague of his, Kolletschka, received a puncture wound in the finger, from the scalpel of a student with whom he was performing an autopsy, and died after an agonizing illness during which he displayed the same symptoms that Semmelweis had observed in the victims of childbed fever. Although the role of microorganisms in such infections had not yet been recognized at the time, Semmelweis realized that "cadaveric matter" which the student's scalpel had introduced into Kolletschka's blood stream had caused his colleague's fatal illness. And the similarities between the course of Kolletschka's disease and that of the women in his clinic led Semmelweis to the conclusion that his patients had died of the same kind of blood poisoning: he, his colleagues, and the medical students had been the carriers of the infectious material, for he and his associates used to come to the wards directly from performing dissections in the autopsy room, and examine the women in labor after only superficially washing their hands, which often retained a characteristic foul odor.

Again, Semmelweis put his idea to a test. He reasoned that if he were right, then childbed fever could be prevented by chemically destroying the infectious material adhering to the hands. He therefore issued an order requiring all medical students to wash their hands in a solution of chlorinated lime before making an examination. The mortality from childbed fever promptly began to decrease, and for the year 1848 it fell to 1.27 per cent in the First Division, compared to 1.33 in the Second.

In further support of his idea, or of his *hypothesis,* as we will also say, Semmelweis notes that it accounts for the fact that the mortality in the Second Division consistently was so much lower: the patients there were attended by midwives, whose training did not include anatomical instruction by dissection of cadavers.

The hypothesis also explained the lower mortality among "street births": women who arrived with babies in arms were rarely examined after admission and thus had a better chance of escaping infection.

Similarly, the hypothesis accounted for the fact that the victims of childbed fever among the newborn babies were all among those whose mothers had contracted the disease during labor; for then the infection could be transmitted to the baby before birth, through the common bloodstream of mother and child, whereas this was impossible when the mother remained healthy.

Further clinical experiences soon led Semmelweis to broaden his hypothesis. On one occasion, for example, he and his associates, having carefully disinfected their hands, examined first a woman in labor who was suffering from a festering cervical cancer; then they proceeded to examine twelve other women in the same room, after only routine washing without renewed disinfection. Eleven of the twelve patients died of puerperal fever. Semmelweis concluded that childbed fever can be caused not only by cadaveric material, but also by "putrid matter derived from living organisms."

We have seen how, in his search for the cause of childbed fever, Semmelweis examined various hypotheses that had been suggested as possible answers. How such hypotheses are arrived at in the first place is an intriguing question which we will consider later. First, however, let us examine how a hypothesis, once proposed, is tested.

Sometimes, the procedure is quite direct. Consider the conjectures that differences in crowding, or in diet, or in general care account for the difference in mortality between the two divisions. As Semmelweis points out, these conflict with readily observable facts. There are no such differences between the divisions; the hypotheses are therefore rejected as false.

But usually the test will be less simple and straightforward. Take the hypothesis attributing the high mortality in the First Division to the dread evoked by the appearance of the priest with his attendant. The intensity of that dread, and especially its effect upon childbed fever, are not as directly ascertainable as are differences in crowding or in diet, and Semmelweis uses an indirect method of testing. He asks himself: Are there any readily observable effects that should occur if the hypothesis were true? And he reasons: *If* the hypothesis were true, *then* an appropriate change in the priest's procedure should be followed by a decline in fatalities. He checks this implication by a simple experiment and finds it false, and he therefore rejects the hypothesis.

Similarly, to test his conjecture about the position of the women during delivery, he reasons: *If* this conjecture should be true, *then* adoption of the lateral position in the First Division will reduce the mortality. Again, the implication is shown false by his experiment, and the conjecture is discarded.

In the last two cases, the test is based on an argument to the effect that *if* the contemplated hypothesis, say *H*, is true, *then* certain observable events (e.g., decline in mortality) should occur under specified circumstances (e.g., if the priest refrains from walking through the wards, or if the women are delivered in lateral position); or briefly, if *H* is true, then so is *I*, where *I* is a statement describing the observable occurrences to be expected. For convenience, let us say that *I* is inferred from, or implied by, *H*; and let us call *I* a *test implication of the hypothesis H*. . . .

In our last two examples, experiments show the test implication to be false, and the hypothesis is accordingly rejected. The reasoning that leads to the rejection may be schematized as follows:

> If *H* is true, then so is *I*.
> 2*a*]   But (as the evidence shows) *I* is not true.
> ―――――――――――――――――――――――
> *H* is not true.

Any argument of this form . . . is deductively valid; that is, if its premises (the sentences above the horizontal line) are true, then its conclusion (the sentence below the horizontal line) is unfailingly true as well. Hence, if the premises of (2*a*) are properly established, the hypothesis *H* that is being tested must indeed be rejected.

Next, let us consider the case where observation or experiment bears out the test implication *I*. From his hypothesis that childbed fever is blood poisoning produced by cadaveric matter, Semmelweis infers that suitable antiseptic measures will reduce fatalities from the disease. This time, experiment shows the test implication to be true. But this favorable outcome does not conclusively prove the hypothesis true, for the underlying argument would have the form

> If *H* is true, then so is *I*.
> 2*b*]   (As the evidence shows) *I* is true.
> ―――――――――――――――――――――――
> *H* is true.

And this mode of reasoning, which is referred to as the *fallacy of affirming the consequent,* is deductively invalid, that is, its conclusion may be false even if its premises are true. This is in fact illustrated by Semmelweis' own experience. The initial version of his account of childbed fever as a form of blood poisoning presented infection with cadaveric matter essentially as the one and only source of the disease; and he was right in reasoning that if this hypothesis should be true, then destruction of cadaveric particles by antiseptic washing should reduce the mortality. Furthermore, his experiment did show the test implication to be true. Hence, in this case, the premisses of (2*b*) were both true. Yet, his hypothesis was false, for as he later discovered, putrid material from living organisms, too, could produce childbed fever.

Thus, the favorable outcome of a test, i.e., the fact that a test implication inferred from a hypothesis is found to be true, does not prove the hypothesis to be true. Even if many implications of a hypothesis have been borne out by careful tests, the hypothesis may still be false. The following argument still commits the fallacy of affirming the consequent:

If H is true, then so are $I_1, I_2, \ldots, I_n$.

2*c*]   (As the evidence shows) $I_1, I_2, \ldots, I_n$ are all true.

H is true.

This, too, can be illustrated by reference to Semmelweis' final hypothesis in its first version. As we noted earlier, his hypothesis also yields the test implications that among cases of street births admitted to the First Division, mortality from puerperal fever should be below the average for the Division, and that infants of mothers who escape the illness do not contract childbed fever; and these implications, too, were borne out by the evidence—even though the first version of the final hypothesis was false.

But the observation that a favorable outcome of however many tests does not afford conclusive proof for a hypothesis should not lead us to think that if we have subjected a hypothesis to a number of tests and all of them have had a favorable outcome, we are no better off than if we had not tested the hypothesis at all. For each of our tests might conceivably have had an unfavorable outcome and might have led to the rejection of the hypothesis. A set of favorable results obtained by testing different test implications, $I_1, I_2, \ldots, I_n$, of a hypothesis, shows that as far as these particular implications are concerned, the hypothesis has been borne out; and while this result does not afford a complete proof of the hypothesis, it provides at least some support, some partial corroboration or confirmation for it. The extent of this support will depend on various aspects of the hypothesis and of the test data. . . .

We have considered [a] scientific [investigation] in which a problem was tackled by proposing tentative answers in the form of hypotheses that were then tested by deriving from them suitable test implications and checking these by observation or experiment. But how are suitable hypotheses arrived at in the first place? It is sometimes held that they are inferred from antecedently collected data by means of a procedure called *inductive inference,* as contradistinguished from deductive inference, from which it differs in important respects.

In a deductively valid argument, the conclusion is related to the

premisses in such a way that if the premisses are true then the conclusion cannot fail to be true as well. This requirement is satisfied,
for example, by any argument of the following general form:

If p, then q.
It is not the case that q.
_____
It is not the case that p.

Brief reflection shows that no matter what particular statements
may stand at the places marked by the letters 'p' and 'q', the conclusion will certainly be true if the premisses are. In fact, our schema
represents the [valid] argument form . . . to which we referred earlier.

Another type of deductively valid inference is illustrated by this
example:

Any sodium salt, when put into the flame of a Bunsen burner,
turns the flame yellow.
This piece of rock salt is a sodium salt.
_____
This piece of rock salt, when put into the flame of a Bunsen
burner, will turn the flame yellow.

Arguments of the latter kind are often said to lead from the general (here, the premiss about all sodium salts) to the particular (a
conclusion about the particular piece of rock salt). Inductive inferences, by contrast, are sometimes described as leading from premisses about particular cases to a conclusion that has the character
of a general law or principle. For example, from premisses to the
effect that each of the particular samples of various sodium salts
that have so far been subjected to the Bunsen flame test did turn
the flame yellow, inductive inference supposedly leads to the general conclusion that all sodium salts, when put into the flame of a
Bunsen burner, turn the flame yellow. But in this case, the truth of
the premisses obviously does *not* guarantee the truth of the conclusion; for even if it is the case that all samples of sodium salts
examined so far did turn the Bunsen flame yellow, it remains quite
possible that new kinds of sodium salt might yet be found that do
not conform to this generalization. Indeed, even some kinds of
sodium salt that have already been tested with positive result might
conceivably fail to satisfy the generalization under special physical
conditions (such as very strong magnetic fields or the like) in which
they have not yet been examined. For this reason, the premisses of
an inductive inference are often said to imply the conclusion only
with more or less high probability, whereas the premisses of a deductive inference imply the conclusion with certainty.

The idea that in scientific inquiry, inductive inference from antecedently collected data leads to appropriate general principles is

clearly embodied in the following account [by the economist Albert B. Wolfe (1876–1967)] of how a scientist would ideally proceed:

If we try to imagine how a mind of superhuman power and reach, but normal so far as the logical processes of its thought are concerned, . . . would use the scientific method, the process would be as follows: First, all facts would be observed and recorded, *without selection* or *a priori* guess as to their relative importance. Secondly, the observed and recorded facts would be analyzed, compared, and classified, *without hypothesis* or *postulates* other than those necessarily involved in the logic of thought. Third, from this analysis of the facts generalizations would be inductively drawn as to the relations, classificatory or causal, between them. Fourth, further research would be deductive as well as inductive, employing inferences from previously established generalizations.

This passage distinguishes four stages in an ideal scientific inquiry: (1) observation and recording of all facts, (2) analysis and classification of these facts, (3) inductive derivation of generalizations from them, and (4) further testing of the generalizations. The first two of these stages are specifically assumed not to make use of any guesses or hypotheses as to how the observed facts might be interconnected; this restriction seems to have been imposed in the belief that such preconceived ideas would introduce a bias and would jeopardize the scientific objectivity of the investigation.

But the view expressed in the quoted passage—I will call it *the narrow inductivist conception of scientific inquiry*—is untenable, for several reasons. A brief survey of these can serve to amplify and to supplement our earlier remarks on scientific procedure.

First, a scientific investigation as here envisaged could never get off the ground. Even its first phase could never be carried out, for a collection of *all* the facts would have to await the end of the world, so to speak; and even all the facts *up to now* cannot be collected, since there are an infinite number and variety of them. Are we to examine, for example, all the grains of sand in all the deserts and on all the beaches, and are we to record their shapes, their weights, their chemical composition, their distances from each other, their constantly changing temperature, and their equally changing distance from the center of the moon? Are we to record the floating thoughts that cross our minds in the tedious process? The shapes of the clouds overhead, the changing color of the sky? The construction and the trade name of our writing equipment? Our own life histories and those of our fellow investigators? All these, and untold other things, are, after all, among "all the facts up to now".

Perhaps, then, all that should be required in the first phase is that all the *relevant* facts be collected. But relevant to what? Though the author does not mention this, let us suppose that the inquiry is concerned with a specified *problem*. Should we not then begin by collecting all the facts—or better, all available data—relevant to that problem? This notion still makes no clear sense. Semmelweis sought to solve one specific problem, yet he collected quite different kinds of data at different stages of his inquiry. And rightly so; for what particular sorts of data it is reasonable to collect is not determined by the problem under study, but by a tentative answer to it that the investigator entertains in the form of a conjecture or hypothesis. Given the conjecture that mortality from childbed fever was increased by the terrifying appearance of the priest and his attendant with the death bell, it was relevant to collect data on the consequences of having the priest change his routine; but it would have been totally irrelevant to check what would happen if doctors and students disinfected their hands before examining their patients. With respect to Semmelweis' eventual contamination hypothesis, data of the latter kind were clearly relevant, and those of the former kind totally irrelevant.

Empirical "facts" or findings, therefore, can be qualified as logically relevant or irrelevant only in reference to a given hypothesis, but not in reference to a given problem.

Suppose now that a hypothesis H has been advanced as a tentative answer to a research problem: what kinds of data would be relevant to H? Our earlier examples suggest an answer: A finding is relevant to H if either its occurrence or its nonoccurrence can be inferred from H. . . .

In sum, the maxim that data should be gathered without guidance by antecedent hypotheses about the connections among the facts under study is self-defeating, and it is certainly not followed in scientific inquiry. On the contrary, tentative hypotheses are needed to give direction to a scientific investigation. Such hypotheses determine, among other things, what data should be collected at a given point in a scientific investigation.

It is of interest to note that social scientists trying to check a hypothesis by reference to the vast store of facts recorded by the U.S. Bureau of the Census, or by other data-gathering organizations, sometimes find to their disappointment that the values of some variable that plays a central role in the hypothesis have nowhere been systematically recorded. This remark is not, of course, intended as a criticism of data gathering: those engaged in the process no doubt try to select facts that might prove relevant to future hypotheses; the observation is simply meant to illustrate the impossibility of collecting "all the relevant data" without knowledge of the hypotheses to which the data are to have relevance.

The second stage envisaged in our quoted passage is open to similar criticism. A set of empirical "facts" can be analyzed and classified in many different ways, most of which will be unilluminating for the purposes of a given inquiry. Semmelweis could have classified the women in the maternity wards according to criteria such as age, place of residence, marital status, dietary habits, and so forth; but information on these would have provided no clue to a patient's prospects of becoming a victim of childbed fever. What Semmelweis sought were criteria that would be significantly connected with those prospects; and for this purpose, as he eventually found, it was illuminating to single out those women who were attended by medical personnel with contaminated hands; for it was with this characteristic, or with the corresponding class of patients, that high mortality from childbed fever was associated.

Thus, if a particular way of analyzing and classifying empirical findings is to lead to an explanation of the phenomena concerned, then it must be based on hypotheses about how those phenomena are connected; without such hypotheses, analysis and classification are blind.

Our critical reflections on the first two stages of inquiry as envisaged in the quoted passage also undercut the notion that hypotheses are introduced only in the third stage, by inductive inference from antecedently collected data. But some further remarks on the subject should be added here.

Induction is sometimes conceived as a method that leads, by means of mechanically applicable rules, from observed facts to corresponding general principles. In this case, the rules of inductive inference would provide effective canons of scientific discovery; induction would be a mechanical procedure analogous to the familiar routine for the multiplication of integers, which leads, in a finite number of predetermined and mechanically performable steps, to the corresponding product. Actually, however, no such general and mechanical induction procedure is available at present; otherwise, the much studied problem of the causation of cancer, for example, would hardly have remained unsolved to this day. Nor can the discovery of such a procedure ever be expected. For—to mention one reason—scientific hypotheses and theories are usually couched in terms that do not occur at all in the description of the empirical findings on which they rest, and which they serve to explain. For example, theories about the atomic and subatomic structure of matter contain terms such as 'atom', 'electron', 'proton', 'neutron', 'psi-function', etc.; yet they are based on laboratory findings about the spectra of various gases, tracks in cloud and bubble chambers, quantitative aspects of chemical reactions, and so forth—all of which can be described without the use of those "theoretical terms". Induction rules of the kind here envisaged would therefore have to provide a mechanical routine for constructing, on the basis of the given data, a hypothesis or theory stated in terms of some quite novel concepts, which are nowhere used in the description of the data themselves. Surely, no general mechanical rule of procedure can be expected to achieve this. . . .

To be sure, mechanical procedures for inductively "inferring" a hypothesis on the basis of given data may be specifiable for situations of special, and relatively simple, kinds. For example, if the length of a copper rod has been measured at several different temperatures, the resulting pairs of associated values for temperature and length may be represented by points in a plane coordinate system, and a curve may be drawn through them in accordance with some particular rule of curve fitting. The curve then graphically represents a general quantitative hypothesis that expresses the length of the rod as a specific function of its temperature. But note that this hypothesis contains no novel terms; it is expressible in terms of the concepts of temperature and length, which are used also in describing the data. Moreover, the choice of "associated" values of temperature and length as data already presupposes a guiding hypothesis; namely, that with each value of the temperature, exactly one value of the length of the copper rod is associated, so that its length is indeed a function of its temperature alone. The mechanical curve-fitting routine then serves only to select a particular function as the appropriate one. This point is important; for suppose that instead of a copper rod, we examine a body of nitrogen gas enclosed in a cylindrical container with a movable piston as a lid, and that we measure its volume at several different temperatures. If we were to use this procedure in an effort to obtain from our data a *general* hypothesis representing the volume of the gas as a function of its temperature, we would fail, because the volume of a gas is a function both of its temperature and of the pressure exerted upon it, so that at the same temperature, the given gas may assume different volumes.

Thus, even in these simple cases, the mechanical procedures for the construction of a hypothesis do only part of the job, for they presuppose an antecedent, less specific hypothesis (i.e., that a certain physical variable is a function of one single other variable), which is not obtainable by the same procedure.

There are, then, no generally applicable "rules of induction", by which hypotheses or theories can be mechanically derived or inferred from empirical data. The transition from data to theory requires creative imagination. Scientific hypotheses and theories are not *derived* from observed facts, but *invented* in order to account for them. They constitute guesses at the connections that might obtain between the phenomena under study, at uniformities and patterns that might underlie their occurrence. "Happy guesses" of this kind require great ingenuity, especially if they involve a radical departure from current modes of scientific thinking, as did, for example, the theory of relativity and quantum theory. The inventive effort required in scientific research will benefit from a thorough familiarity with current knowledge in the field. A complete novice will hardly make an important scientific discovery, for the ideas that may occur to him are likely to duplicate what has been tried before or to run afoul of well-established facts or theories of which he is not aware.

Nevertheless, the ways in which fruitful scientific guesses are arrived at are very different from any process of systematic inference. The chemist [Friedrich] Kekulé [1829–1896], for example, tells us that he had long been trying unsuccessfully to devise a structural formula for the benzene molecule when, one evening in 1865, he found a solution to his problem while he was dozing in front of his fireplace. Gazing into the flames, he seemed to see atoms dancing in snakelike arrays. Suddenly, one of the snakes formed a ring by seizing hold of its own tail and then whirled mockingly before him. Kekulé awoke in a flash: he had hit upon the now famous and familiar idea of representing the molecular structure of benzene by a hexagonal ring. He spent the rest of the night working out the consequences of this hypothesis.

This last remark contains an important reminder concerning the objectivity of science. In his endeavor to find a solution to his problem, the scientist may give free rein to his imagination, and the course of his creative thinking may be influenced even by scientifically questionable notions. Kepler's study of planetary motion, for example, was inspired by his interest in a mystical doctrine about numbers and a passion to demonstrate the music of the spheres. Yet, scientific objectivity is safeguarded by the principle that while hypotheses and theories may be freely invented and *proposed* in science, they can be *accepted* into the body of scientific knowledge only if they pass critical scrutiny, which includes in particular the checking of suitable test implications by careful observation or experiment. . . .

Scientific knowledge, as we have seen, is not arrived at by applying some inductive inference procedure to antecedently collected data, but rather by what is often called "the method of hypothesis", i.e. by inventing hypotheses as tentative answers to a problem under study, and then subjecting these to empirical test. It will be part of such test to see whether the hypothesis is borne out by whatever relevant findings may have been gathered before its formulation; an acceptable hypothesis will have to fit the available relevant data. Another part of the test will consist in deriving new test implications from the hypothesis and checking these by suitable observations or experiments. As we noted earlier, even extensive testing with entirely favorable results does not establish a hypothesis conclusively, but provides only more or less strong support for it. Hence, while scientific inquiry is certainly not inductive in the narrow sense we have examined in some detail, it may be said to be *inductive in a wider sense*, inasmuch as it involves the acceptance of hypotheses on the basis of data that afford no deductively conclusive evidence for it, but lend it only more or less strong "inductive support", or confirmation. And any "rules of induction" will have to be conceived . . . as canons of validation rather than of discovery. Far from generating a hypothesis that accounts for given empirical findings, such rules will presuppose that both the empirical data forming the "premisses" of the "inductive argument" and a tentative hypothesis forming its "conclusion" are *given*. The rules of induction would then state criteria for the soundness of the argument. According to some theories of induction, the rules would determine the strength of the support that the data lend to the hypothesis, and they might express such support in terms of probabilities. . . .

Reading Questions

1. What emerges from the discussion of the childbed fever case as the author's conception of the scientific method?
2. Why is evidence showing that a test implication is true not proof that the original hypothesis is true?
3. What is the difference between induction and deduction?
4. What objections are there to the narrow inductivist conception of scientific inquiry?
5. Can a discovery procedure be devised for uncovering correct or promising hypotheses?
6. What role, if any, does induction play in scientific inquiry?

Questions for Reflection and Research

1. Does this account of the scientific method agree with other accounts? (See, for example, selection #26 by Pirsig.)
2. What point could there be to trying to determine the nature of the method?
3. Compare Hempel's account of the difficulties of devising hypotheses with that of Pirsig in selection #26 and Russell in selection #1.
4. If the implications of a hypothesis have thus far tested out, how can one determine the extent to which the positive results confirm the original hypothesis? (For some relevant considerations see selections #30 by Brody and #29 by Madden.)
5. See the previous selection (#26) for some further related questions for reflection and research.

There Is No Scientific Method

The Author: James B. Conant (b. 1893) was educated at Harvard University and taught at Harvard as a chemist. From 1939 to 1953 he was president of Harvard. Besides working as a chemist he has worked in the history of science, educational theory, and served as ambassador to Germany. He has won many honors and has been a well-known advocate of widening public understanding of science.

The Selection: In the brief excerpt it is contended that gaining scientific knowledge from science textbooks misleads one about the actual methods used by scientists. The study of real scientific investigations reveals great variety in approaches by the various sciences. Thus there is no one scientific method.

The stumbling way in which even the ablest of the scientists in every generation have had to fight through thickets of erroneous observations, misleading generalizations, inadequate formulations, and unconscious prejudice is rarely appreciated by those who obtain their scientific knowledge from textbooks. It is largely neglected by those expounders of the alleged scientific method who are fascinated by the logical rather than the psychological aspects of experimental investigations. Science as I have defined the term represents one segment of the much larger field of accumulative knowledge. The common characteristic of all the theoretical and practical investigations which fall within this framework—a sense of progress—gives no clue as to the *activities* of those who have ad-

From *Science and Common Sense* by James B. Conant (New Haven: Yale University Press, 1951), pp. 44–45.

vanced our knowledge. To attempt to formulate in one set of logical rules the way in which mathematicians, historians, archaeologists, philologists, biologists, and physical scientists have made progress would be to ignore all the vitality in these varied undertakings. Even within the narrow field of the development of "concepts and conceptual schemes from experiment" (experimental science) it is all too easy to be fascinated by oversimplified accounts of the methods used by the pioneers.

To be sure, it is relatively easy to deride any definition of scientific activity as being oversimplified, and it is relatively hard to find a better substitute. But on one point I believe almost all modern historians of the natural sciences would agree and be in opposition to Karl Pearson [1857–1936]. There is no such thing as *the* scientific method. If there were, surely an examination of the history of physics, chemistry, and biology would reveal it. For . . . few would deny that it is the progress in physics, chemistry, and experimental biology which gives everyone confidence in the procedures of the scientist. Yet, a careful examination of these subjects fails to reveal any *one* method by means of which the masters in these field broke new ground.

Reading Questions

1. What aspects of science are left out of science textbooks? What are the bad consequences of learning science only from science texts?
2. What reasons does the author give for his belief that there is no scientific method?

Questions for Reflection and Research

1. In the previous selection (#27) Hempel describes what he regards as the scientific method. Is Conant's view actually in conflict with Hempel's?
2. Is mathematics a science? Is archaeology? Is philology?
3. Read relevant portions of Conant's book to determine whether the evidence he gives in support of his view is convincing.
4. Would it be disturbing if there were no scientific method? Why or why not?
5. Are "science" and "the scientific method" family-resemblance concepts? Would Conant think so? [See Ludwig Wittgenstein, *Philosophical Investigations* (New York: The Macmillan Company, 1958), pp. 31–32.]

Science and Probability

The Author: Edward H. Madden (b. 1925) received his education at Oberlin College and the University of Iowa and has taught at Brown University, Amherst College, and the State University of New York at Buffalo. He has written widely on issues in the philosophy of science and philosophical problems in psychology and is an expert on the thought of the American philosopher and mathematician Chauncey Wright (1830–1875).

The Selection: When thinking about how evidence in science helps confirm theories or conjectures, philosophers have often appealed to ideas involving probability and statistics. This selection describes three theories about the meaning of the words *probable* and *probability.* According to the classical view the probability of an event's occurrence is a ratio of the event to all equiprobable events. The frequency theory regards the probability of an event's occurrence as a conclusion derived from statistical evidence indicating what percentage of the specified kind of events turned up in the past. According to the inductive theory past evidence should be regarded as lending support or disconfirming a hypothesis. The author hints he believes that there are normally three different uses of *probability* and that each theory ignores the diversity. The selection is moderately demanding.

The word 'probable' has many uses in everyday life and science and it is difficult to disentangle and properly relate them, or—as some writers say—to find a common meaning among them. Consider these examples of probability statements:

1) The probability of a thrown die turning up face 3 is 1/6.

From Edward H. Madden, "Probability Notions: Introduction," in *The Structure of Scientific Thought: An Introduction to Philosophy of Science,* ed. Edward H. Madden (Boston: Houghton Mifflin Co.; Cambridge, Mass.: Riverside Press, 1960), pp. 243–49.

2) The probability of a thirty-year-old person living in the United States surviving his thirty-first birthday is .945.

3) The probability of the general theory of relativity is greater than it was thirty-five years ago.

We must be clear, of course, that these three examples are *types* of probability statements; we would have little difficulty in thinking up three equally good examples to mark off the three-way distinction we are beginning to make: for example, 1′) the probability of a tossed coin turning up heads is 1/2; 2′) The probability of a thirty-year-old person living in Florida surviving his thirty-first birthday is .999; 3′) The theory of evolution has a much higher probability than the theory of special creation. But what differences do these types of examples signify? Everything I have to say below will help explain this three-way difference in one way or another, but let us note several points by way of a beginning. First, the examples in 1) and 1′) are taken from games of chance; 2) and 2′) from insurance statistics and 3) and 3′) from science. Now these three types of examples have given rise to the three most influential views about the meaning of 'probable' and 'probability'; they are called, respectively, the classical, the frequency, and the inductive theories of probability—although you must realize that 'theory' here refers to the meaning of a word, not to a scientific theory about the physical world. In what follows I will examine these three views in turn, pointing out along the way their many conflicts and relationships.

THE CLASSICAL THEORY

Pierre Simon, Marquis de Laplace, in the early part of the nineteenth century . . . propounded, in its most complete form, the "classical" view of probability. Recall the example of a thrown die. 'The probability of a thrown die turning up face 3 is 1/6.' Laplace analyzed this sort of statement in the following way. When a die is thrown, any one of the six faces of the die might turn up, and each of these events is *equiprobable*. By 'equiprobable' Laplace meant that any face of the die, as far as we know, has just as much chance to turn up as any other. We know certainly that one of the six faces will turn up but since our knowledge, or ignorance, of which one it will be is equally divided, we have no more or less reason for expecting one rather than another. Thus, as far as we know, they are equiprobable. With the introduction of this key notion of equiprobability, Laplace was able to state his view in a simple way: The probability of an event is a fraction whose numerator is the event in question and whose denominator is the total number of equiprobable events. Hence, in our example, the probability of a thrown die turning up face 3 is 1/6. Or [as W. S. Jevons (1835–1882) has noted], "if the letters of the word *Roma* be thrown down casually in a row, what is the probability that they will form a significant Latin word? The possible arrangements of four letters are 4 × 3 × 2 × 1, or 24 in number and if all the arrangements be examined, seven of these will be found to have meaning, namely, *Roma, ramo, oram, mora, maro, armo,* and *amor.* Hence the probability of a significant result is 7/24."

Several corollaries of particular interest follow from this classical definition of probability. First, this theory is *a priori,* by which I mean that one calculates the probability of an event without collecting any factual information of a statistical sort about how often the event has occurred in the past. I do not need to know how often face 3 turns up in a long series of throws in order to calculate its chances of turning up on any given one; I need to know only a few antecedent facts, that the die has six faces and each one has an equal chance to turn up.

Second, according to this view, 'probable' does not refer to an objective property of events themselves but is a measure of the degree of rational belief. Take any specific throw. There is nothing probable about the event itself; either a 3 will turn up or not. 'Probable' refers, rather, to our rational expectation that it has 1/6 of a chance to come up on this throw.

Third, according to this view, a probability judgment is *relative* to some specifiable set of evidence or knowledge; when the set changes, the probability judgment changes. If I know a die is loaded in favor of face 4, I will expect the chance of face 3 turning up to be much less than 1/6. Or, say, a steamship is missing; some people think she has sunk in mid-ocean, others not. Now the probability of the event's having occurred will vary from day to day, and from mind to mind, as the evidence changes or increases, with the addition of the slightest information regarding vessels met at sea, prevailing weather, condition of vessel, sign of wreck, etc.

Numerous criticisms have been advanced through the years against the classical view, but we will examine only a few of them here. First, it is difficult to see how most probability statements can be analyzed in terms of 'equiprobable events.' If a die is loaded, it is no longer possible to specify the total number of equiprobable events in the denominator of the required ratio. Even more apparent, it is impossible to specify the equiprobable events in any statistical probability statement like 'the probability of a thirty-year-old man living another year is .945.' [As Ernest Nagel (b. 1910) has pointed out:] "It is absurd to interpret such a statement as meaning that there are a thousand possible eventuations to a man's career, 945 of which are favorable to his surviving at least another year. Moreover, the Laplacian definition requires a probability coefficient to be a rational number. But irrational numbers frequently occur as values for such coefficients, and there is no way of interpreting them as ratios of a number of alternatives."

Second, a paradox results from considering probability judgments as *a priori*. Consider the possibility that a person should always throw a coin head uppermost and appear unable to get a tail by chance. On the classical view the probability judgment would remain steadfastly 1/2; experience does not change it. This *a priori* judgment, Jevons wrote, would not be falsified, "because the classical theory contemplates the possibility of the most extreme runs of luck. Our actual experience might be counter to all that is probable; the whole course of events might seem to be in complete contradiction to what we should expect." Jevons, however, wished to minimize this paradox; coincidences of this sort are so "unlikely," he wrote, "that the whole duration of history . . . does not give any appreciable probability of their being encountered."

The probability that any extreme runs of luck will occur is so excessively slight, that it would be absurd seriously to expect their occurrence. It is almost impossible, for instance, that any whist player should have played in any two games where the distribution of the cards was exactly the same, by pure accident. Such a thing as a person always losing at a game of chance, is wholly unknown. Coincidences of this kind are not impossible, as I have said, but they are so unlikely that the lifetime of any person, or indeed the whole duration of history, does not give any appreciable probability of their being encountered. Whenever we make any extensive series of trials of chance results, as in throwing a die or coin, the probability is great that the results will agree nearly with the predictions yielded by theory.

Unfortunately, however, Jevons' use of 'unlikely' and 'probability' in the minimizing of the paradox cannot be given a classical interpretation and appears to be a poorly concealed concession to the fundamental role of empirical information and a consequent abandonment of pure *a priorism*.

Finally, the classical view that 'probable' always refers to the degree of rational belief and never to an objective property of the event in question runs into difficulty again with statistical probability statements. The statement, 'The probability of a thirty-year-old man living at least another year is .945' apparently refers to an empirical fact, a statistical one, to be sure, namely that out of the whole class of thirty-year-olds 945 of every 1000 have been found to survive their next birthday.

THE FREQUENCY THEORY

This view, as I suggested at the beginning, grew out of statistical probability statements like the one we just considered. John Venn [1834–1923] and Charles Peirce [1839–1914], two nineteenth-century authors, were primarily responsible for this view, while Richard Von Mises [1883–1953] and Hans Reichenbach [1891–1953], among others in the present century, have made the viewpoint more precise and acceptable.

These men regarded probability as the measure of the relative frequency with which the members of a specified class of objects or events exhibit a certain property. In our example, an actuary observes the *class* of thirty-year-old men in the United States and discovers that for every 1000 men in this class, 945 exhibit the *property* of surviving their next birthday. The value .945 indicates, then, the precise numerical frequency which the property of surviving exhibited *relative to* the class of thirty-year-old American males. This numerical value, however, must not be determined on a small amount of evidence. The value, after many instances are investigated, may still fluctuate considerably; but when our evidence mounts into the thousands and millions, then fluctuations become fewer and fewer until in the long run the value tends to become fixed. But these notions of "long run" and "tend to become fixed" are exceedingly vague and imprecise. Peirce was one of the first to replace them by the precise notion of a mathematical limit. . . .

Several corollaries of particular interest follow from the frequency view. First, the theory is *empirical,* by which I mean that one calculates the probability of an event by collecting factual information about how often it has occurred in the past. To be sure, one might, in some cases, deduce from certain information what the relative frequency of an event will be; but even here the actual empirical count is necessary to *test* the deduction—perhaps the premises from which it was drawn are false. For example, knowing that pennies are symmetrical, and having a knowledge of mechanics, I might infer that the forces which make a head or a tail turn up will eventually cancel each other out, and hence infer that in the long run the relative frequency of either head or tail will approximate .5. But if pennies never *did* approximate this value, I would have to conclude that something was false about my premises, not ignore the value of the actual series.

Second, 'probable' refers to an objective property of events themselves, not to a degree of rational belief. The numerical values of probability statements refer to the number of times *the members of a specified class of objects or events exhibit a certain property.* Third, a probability judgment is *relative* to some specified set of objects or events. The frequency with which the property 'swarthy' occurs is much greater relative to the class of Spaniards than to the class of Swedes. Fourth, to talk, except in an elliptical fashion, of the probability of an *individual* event is meaningless, for frequency judgments refer only to the relative occurrence of a property in a class of events. Consequently a statement like 'The probability of getting a head on this toss is .5' must be interpreted as an ellipitical [= shortened] way of saying; 'The relative frequency with which the property heads occurs in the class of coin tosses approximates, in the long run, .5.'

Numerous criticisms have been leveled against the frequency view. . . . I shall only say enough about them here to acquaint you with certain types of recurring criticisms. First, the concepts of 'long run' and 'limit' have not gone unchallenged. Consider this situation. Suppose we throw a die a hundred times and get one hundred 3's. Since the relative frequency of 3's is 1 instead of approximating 1/6, should we conclude the die is loaded? Not necessarily, since the frequency theory simply states that the correct frequency will occur in the long run, and apparently one hundred throws is not long enough. But how long must the series be? Well, of course, we can never know for certain, some philosophers say, since a radical variation is always *logically* possible. And this fact leads to a further difficulty. If no series, however long, can falsify an expected ratio, then no series can confirm an expectation either. If, in a thousand throws, the series approximates 1/6 for 3's, this fact does not confirm our expectation since 1000 throws need not be considered a "long run"; and so it is possible in subsequent series that the ratio will change significantly, and so on for any length of series. These puzzles are not unique to the frequency view of probability, however; they occur in any inductive context. Essentially the problem, wherever it occurs, is the same: what is the justification for extrapolating 'X *is* always the case' or 'X *is* the case 90% of the time' into 'X *will be* the case always or 90% of the time' or 'X is the case always or 90% of the time in *unobserved instances*'? This puzzle is the famous "problem of induction". . . .

Second, the inability to explain probability statements which are clearly about individual events certainly restricts the frequency theory. Some probability statements about individual events, to be sure, can be interpreted simply as elliptical ways of referring to relative frequencies. But this sort of analysis hardly applies to a statement like this, 'It is probable that even if Napoleon had been victorious at Waterloo, he would have been unable to remain Emperor of France for much longer,' since Napoleon and the battle of Waterloo are events which are unique and not repeatable. True, one might say there is a class of generals and a class of battles, to which Napoleon and Waterloo belong, etc., but you want to ask yourself seriously if this sort of reply does not strain the statistical concept at the heart of the frequency theory.

THE INDUCTIVE THEORY

This theory can be either a simple straightforward notion or a highly complex one. According to the simple version, the meaning of 'probability' is 'weight or amount of evidence confirming a hypothesis, theory, or statement.' Thus, a theory with much evidence is 'highly probable'; a theory with some evidence is 'more or less probable'; and a theory with little evidence is 'improbable.' On this version, the use of 'probable' is qualitative and unanalyzable but nonetheless important for that. It coincides simply with the logic of the confirmation of hypotheses. . . . The probability of a hypothesis increases, but not in any quantitative way, when each additional consequence is confirmed and alternative hypotheses eliminated; decreases under the opposite condition; and remains constant while no new consequences are deduced from any of the rival hypotheses.

Some writers, however, have tried to make "weight" of evidence more than a metaphor; they have advanced an inductive theory of probability in which weight or amount of evidence of a theory receives a numerical value. . . , although this numerical value has a meaning quite different from the numerical ratios of the frequency theory. For example, "If the weather man were to venture to say that the probability of rain tomorrow was 4/10, he would not be describing a statistical fact but would simply mean that, should you bet on it raining tomorrow, you had better ask for odds of 4 to 6." . . .

[T]hrough the nineteenth and twentieth centuries, philosophers like John Venn, Karl Popper [b. 1902], and Hans Reichenbach have insisted that any inductive theory of probability is gratuitous since the frequency theory already accounts for the use of 'probability' in statements like 'The probability of the general theory of relativity is greater than it was thirty-five years ago.' . . .

Numerous ingenious methods have been used to prove this claim; yet, I think, for several reasons it is false. Peirce made one of these points quite nicely. We cannot, after all, pick universes out of a grab-bag and find in what proportion of them a law or theory holds good! Peirce, however, concluded that since the frequency theory cannot explain the use of 'probable' in reference to scientific theories, then this use is nonsense. But clearly we do so talk, and it is not apparent nonsense; in fact, it is only nonsense if one insists on stretching the frequency view to cover all the uses of 'probable.' But why do this? We had better restrict the theory to what it explains and admit that there are other legitimate meanings of 'probable.'

Another reason for insisting on the separateness of frequency and inductive statements of probability, it seems to me, is that evidence affects the two types of statements in very different ways. In inductive probability statements, evidence increases or decreases the probability, while in frequency statements evidence either confirms or changes the probability. For example, if a physicist should deduce a new consequence from the general theory of relativity, test it, and find it to hold in fact, we would say that this new confirming evidence increases the probability of the theory, while dis-confirming evidence—that is, a negative result—would decrease the probability. On the other hand, recall the frequency statement, 'The probability of a man surviving his thirty-first birthday is .945.' Here further statistical evidence about how many men live beyond their thirty-first birthdays does not increase or decrease the probability in question but simply either confirms or changes it. If the further evidence still approximates .945, then this evidence confirms the statement; if the evidence approximates, say, .900 instead, then the value of the original statement *changes* to this new number.

CONCLUSION

Out of this welter of claims and criticisms, what *can* one conclude? Well, of course, you will have to decide your own position after weighing what I have written and carefully reading the following essays [in Madden's book]—and even then you will have barely started on what is indeed a very complex topic. You may find it helpful, however, in doing your own thinking to know the climate of opinion of experts in this field. They have, by and large, dismissed the classical theory. . . . Some of them accept the frequency theory only; some accept an inductive theory only; but others, not the least in number, accept both of the views, insisting that neither of these senses of 'probable' is reducible to the other. . . .

Reading Questions

1. Why are probability theories put forward?
2. What criticisms have been leveled at each theory?
3. Devise a variety of probability statements and attempt to explain them in terms of each theory.
4. Which theory, if any, does the author favor?

Questions for Reflection and Research

1. Of what importance is this issue to science?
2. The inductivist view seems easiest to apply to scientific hypotheses. Is it crucial that the inductivist view be made numerical? What advantage would it have?
3. Would any of the theories find that the new riddle of induction presents a problem? (See selection #30 by Brody.)
4. What efforts have been made to fully work out a theory of hypothesis confirmation? Which efforts are most widely accepted?

selection 30.

Confirming a Scientific Hypothesis:
The New Riddle of Induction

The Author: Baruch A. Brody (b. 1943) studied at Brooklyn College, Princeton University, and Oxford University in England. He has edited or written works on the philosophy of science, ethics, the philosophy of Thomas Reid (1710–1796), and logic. In addition to his research he has taught philosophy at Massachusetts Institute of Technology and Rice University.

Nelson Goodman (b. 1906), whose views are discussed in this selection, was educated at Harvard University. He has distinguished himself with his writings as a philosopher of science and philosopher of language. He has taught at the University of Pennsylvania and Brandeis University.

The Selection: This excerpt briefly explains a problem raised by Nelson Goodman. Goodman pointed out that for a given hypothesis one can divise another similar but quite unlikely hypothesis that seems to be supported by all the evidence that supports the original hypothesis. Any attempt to explain how experiments support hypotheses must be able to exclude these hypotheses. Brody mentions some attempts to resolve this new riddle of induction.

[There] is one fundamental problem that [Nelson] Goodman has raised which needs to be elaborated upon. . . . Consider the hypothesis "all emeralds are green." It seems natural to suppose that the observation of green emeralds confirms that hypothesis, and that, given the fact that people have observed emeralds under

From Baruch Brody, "The Confirmation of Scientific Hypotheses: Introduction," in *Readings in the Philosophy of Science,* ed. Baruch A. Brody (Englewood Cliffs, N.J.: Prentice-Hall, Inc., 1970), p. 379. Reprinted and adapted by permission of Prentice-Hall, Inc.

216

many diverse conditions and found them all green, the hypothesis in question has a high degree of confirmation. But now consider the hypothesis that "all emeralds are grue," where *grue* means "examined before *t* and green or not examined before *t* and blue" (where *t* is some time after now). Since all the emeralds that we have examined are grue as well as green, it looks as though we are forced to conclude against our intuitions that our observations of emeralds confirm the grue hypothesis as well as the green hypothesis, and that the grue hypothesis has the same high degree of confirmation as the green hypothesis. Goodman points out, however, that this highly counter-intuitive result leads to the disastrous consequence that the observations we make offer an equal degree of confirmation to any prediction we care to make about any object or event. Any theory of confirming evidence or of degrees of confirmation must, therefore, find a way to prevent hypotheses like the grue hypothesis from being confirmed in the same way that ordinary hypotheses are confirmed. Goodman calls this problem the *new riddle of induction*.

Most philosophers considering this problem have attempted to solve it by finding some significant distinction between the predicates "green" and "grue" which can serve as the basis for ruling out the confirmation of hypotheses containing predicates like "grue" in the distinguishing respect. . . . Recently . . . [it has been] argued that there is . . . an important sense in which "grue," but not "green," is a temporal predicate. Their point is that in order to apply "grue," but not "green," to a particular object, one must know what the date is, and it is in this sense that "grue," but not "green," is a temporal predicate. Goodman, while rejecting this argument, agrees that the way to solve the problem is to distinguish between types of predicates. In his book, *Fact, Fiction, and Forecast*, he tries to draw the distinction in terms of the extent to which the predicates in question (or predicates co-extensive with them) have been previously used in other hypotheses.

Not all philosophers have agreed that the way to solve Goodman's problem is to distinguish between types of predicates. Perhaps the best critique of this approach is found in [a] recent article [by Professor Haskell Fain (b. 1926)]. He suggests, as an alternative approach, that the problem can be solved only if we allow for a difference in the initial probability of the two hypotheses, and this can only be justified in light of other information. . . .

Reading Questions

1. Why are the grue and green hypotheses equally confirmed by observation of emeralds?

2. Why do we not like the fact that the grue hypothesis seems as highly confirmed as the green hypothesis?
3. What approaches have been suggested to eliminate the problem?

Questions for Reflection and Research

1. Why would one want to develop a theory of degrees of confirmation?
2. What is the solution to the problem?
3. Is there any resemblance between the old and the new problems of induction? (See selection #21 by Black for an account of the old problem of induction.)
4. Is there any evidence that Goodman has ignored?

selection 31.

Science Does Not Develop by Accumulation

The Author: Thomas S. Kuhn (b. 1922) was educated at Harvard University in physics and has taught at Harvard, the University of California at Berkeley, and Princeton University. He has won numerous awards and served as editor for scientific publications. As noted in the selection, Kuhn's interest in physics gradually widened to an interest in the history and philosophy of science.

The Selection: This excerpt is from the opening of one of the most influential works in the history and philosophy of science in the last twenty-five years. Kuhn here describes the view he is opposed to: science moves closer and closer to the truth by slow accumulation of improved theories, laws, and information. He asserts that a careful study of its history reveals that only during periods of normal science might science seem to fit the picture of advance by accumulation. During revolutionary periods in science, older theories and data are rejected. Furthermore, the revolutions provide a new conception of what nature is, a paradigm. Rejected paradigms become regarded as myths or superstitions—but the author contends they are no less scientific than their replacements. The selection is demanding reading.

PREFACE

The essay that follows is the first full published report on a project originally conceived almost fifteen years ago. At that time I was a graduate student in theoretical physics already within sight of the

From Thomas S. Kuhn, *The Structure of Scientific Revolutions*, 2nd ed. enlarged, International Encyclopedia of Unified Science, Otto Neurath ed., vol. 2, no.2, pp. v, 1-8, 10-13. © 1962, 1970 by The University of Chicago Press. All rights reserved. Second Edition, enlarged 1970.

end of my dissertation. A fortunate involvement with an experimental college course treating physical science for the non-scientist provided my first exposure to the history of science. To my complete surprise, that exposure to out-of-date scientific theory and practice radically undermined some of my basic conceptions about the nature of science and the reasons for its special success.

Those conceptions were ones I had previously drawn partly from scientific training itself and partly from a long-standing avocational interest in the philosophy of science. Somehow, whatever their pedagogic utility and their abstract plausibility, those notions did not at all fit the enterprise that historical study displayed. Yet they were and are fundamental to many discussions of science, and their failures of verisimilitude [= truth] therefore seemed thoroughly worth pursuing. The result was a drastic shift in my career plans, a shift from physics to history of science and then, gradually, from relatively straightforward historical problems back to the more philosophical concerns that had initially led me to history. . . . In some part [this essay] is an attempt to explain to myself and to friends how I happened to be drawn from science to its history in the first place. . . .

1. INTRODUCTION: A ROLE FOR HISTORY

History . . . could produce a decisive transformation in the image of science by which we are now possessed. That image has previously been drawn, even by scientists themselves, mainly from the study of finished scientific achievements as these are recorded in the classics and, more recently, in the textbooks from which each new scientific generation learns to practice its trade. Inevitably, however, the aim of such books is persuasive and pedagogic [=educational]; a concept of science drawn from them is no more likely to fit the enterprise that produced them than an image of a national culture drawn from a tourist brochure of a language text. This essay attempts to show that we have been misled by them in fundamental ways. Its aim is a sketch of the quite different concept of science that can emerge from the historical record of the research activity itself.

Even from history, however, that new concept will not be forthcoming if historical data continue to be sought and scrutinized mainly to answer questions posed by the unhistorical stereotype drawn from science texts. Those texts have, for example, often seemed to imply that the content of science is uniquely exemplified by the observations, laws, and theories described in their pages. Almost as regularly, the same books have been read as saying that scientific methods are simply the ones illustrated by the manipulative techniques used in gathering textbook data, together with the logical operations employed when relating those data to the textbook's theoretical generalizations. The result has been a concept of science with profound implications about its nature and development.

If science is [regarded as] the constellation of facts, theories, and methods collected in current texts, then scientists [will be regarded as] the men who, successfully or not, have striven to contribute one or another element to that particular constellation. Scientific development becomes the piecemeal process by which these items have been added, singly and in combination, to the ever growing stockpile that constitutes scientific technique and knowledge. And history of science [comes to be regarded as] the discipline that chronicles both these successive increments and the obstacles that have inhibited their accumulation. Concerned with scientific development, the historian then appears to have two main tasks. On the one hand, he must determine by what man and at what point in time each contemporary scientific fact, law, and theory was discovered or invented. On the other, he must describe and explain the congeries of error, myth, and superstition that have inhibited the more rapid accumulation of the constituents of the modern science text. Much research has been directed to these ends, and some still is.

In recent years, however, a few historians of science have been finding it more and more difficult to fulfill the functions that the concept of development-by-accumulation assigns to them. As chroniclers of an incremental process, they discover that additional research makes it harder, not easier, to answer questions like: When was oxygen discovered? Who first conceived of energy conservation? Increasingly, a few of them suspect that these are simply the wrong sorts of questions to ask. Perhaps science does not develop by the accumulation of individual discoveries and inventions. Simultaneously, these same historians confront growing difficulties in distinguishing the "scientific" component of past observation and belief from what their predecessors had readily labeled "error" and "superstition." The more carefully they study, say, [the] dynamics [of Aristotle (384-322 b.c.)], phlogistic chemistry, or caloric thermodynamics, the more certain they feel that those once current views of nature were, as a whole, neither less scientific nor more the product of human idiosyncrasy than those current today. If these out-of-date beliefs are to be called myths, then myths can be produced by the same sorts of methods and held for the same sorts of reasons that now lead to scientific knowledge. If, on the other hand, they are to be called science, then science has included bodies of belief quite incompatible with the ones we hold today. Given these alternatives, the historian must choose the latter. Out-of-date theories are not in principle unscientific because they have been discarded. That choice, however, makes it difficult to see scientific development as a process of accretion [= accumulation]. The same historical research that displays the difficulties in isolating individual inventions and discoveries gives ground for profound doubts about the cumulative process through which these individual contributions to science were thought to have been compounded.

The result of all these doubts and difficulties is a historiographic revolution [= a revolution in historical research] in the study of science, though one that is still in early its early stages. Gradually, and often without entirely realizing they are doing so, historians of science have begun to ask new sorts of questions and to trace different, and often less than cumulative, developmental lines for the sciences. Rather than seeking the permanent contributions of an older science to our present vantage, they attempt to display the historical integrity of that science in its own time. They ask, for example, not about the relation of . . . views [of Galileo (1564-1642)] to those of modern science, but rather about the relationship between his views and those of his group, i.e., his teachers, contemporaries, and immediate successors in the sciences. Furthermore, they insist upon studying the opinions of that group and other similar ones from the viewpoint—usually very different from that of modern science—that gives those opinions the maximum internal coherence and the closet possible fit to nature. Seen through the works that result, works perhaps best exemplified in the writings of Alexandre Koyré [b. 1892], science does not seem altogether the same enterprise as the one discussed by writers in the older historiographic tradition. By implication, at least, these historical studies suggest the possibility of a new image of science. This essay aims to delineate that image by making explicit some of the new historiography's implications.

What aspect of science will emerge to prominence in the course of this effort? First, as least in order of presentation, is the insufficiency of methodological directives, by themselves, to dictate a unique substantive conclusion to many sorts of scientific questions. Instructed to examine electrical or chemical phenomena, the man who is ignorant of these fields but who knows what it is to be scientific may legitimately reach any one of a number of incompatible conclusions. Among those legitimate possibilities, the particular conclusions he does arrive at are probably determined by his prior experience in other fields, by the accidents of his investigation, and by his own individual makeup. What beliefs about the stars, for example, does he bring to the study of chemistry or electricity? Which of the many conceivable experiments relevant to the new field does he elect to perform first? And what aspects of the complex phenomenon that then results strike him as particularly relevant to an elucidation of the nature of chemical change or of electrical affinity? For the individual, at least, and sometimes for the scientific community as well, answers to questions like these are often essential determinants of scientific development. We shall note, for example, . . . that the early developmental stages of most sciences have been characterized by continual competition between a number of distinct views of nature, each partially derived from, and all roughly compatible with, the dictates of scientific observation and method. What differentiated these various schools was not one or another failure of method—they were all "scientific"—but what we shall come to call their incommensurable [= non-equivalent] ways of seeing the world and of practicing science in it. Observation and experience can and must drastically restrict the range of admissible scientific belief, else there would be no science. But they cannot alone determine a particular body of such belief. An apparently arbitrary element, compounded of personal and historical accident, is always a formative ingredient of the beliefs espoused by a given scientific community at a given time.

That element of arbitrariness does not, however, indicate that any scientific group could practice its trade without some set of received beliefs. Nor does it make less consequential the particular constellation to which the group, at a given time, is in fact committed. Effective research scarcely begins before a scientific community thinks it has acquired firm answers to questions like the following: What are the fundamental entities of which the universe is composed? How do these interact with each other and with the senses? What questions may legitimately be asked about such entities and what techniques employed in seeking solutions? At least in the mature sciences, answers (or full substitutes for answers) to questions like these are firmly embedded in the educational initiation that prepares and licenses the student for professional practice. Because that education is both rigorous and rigid, these answers come to exert a deep hold on the scientific mind. That they can do so does much to account both for the peculiar efficiency of the normal research activity and for the direction in which it proceeds at any given time. When examining normal science . . . we shall want finally to describe that research as a strenuous and devoted attempt to force nature into the conceptual boxes supplied by professional education. Simultaneously, we shall wonder whether research could proceed without such boxes, whatever the element of arbitrariness in their historic origins and, occasionally, in their subsequent development.

Yet that element of arbitrariness is present, and it too has an important effect on scientific development. . . . Normal science, the activity in which most scientists inevitably spend almost all their time, is predicated on the assumption that the scientific community knows what the world is like. Much of the success of the enterprise derives from the community's willingness to defend that assumption, if necessary at considerable cost. Normal science, for example, often suppresses fundamental novelties because they are necessarily subversive of its basic commitments. Nevertheless, so long as those commitments retain an element of the arbitrary, the very nature of normal research ensures that novelty shall not be suppressed for very long. Sometimes a normal problem, one that ought to be solvable by known rules and procedures, resists the reiterated onslaught of the ablest members of the group within whose competence it falls. On other occasions a piece of equipment designed and constructed for the purpose of normal research fails to perform in the anticipated manner, revealing an anomaly that cannot, despite repeated effort, be aligned with professional expectation. In these and other ways besides, normal science repeatedly goes astray. And when it does—when, that is, the profession can no longer evade anomalies that subvert the existing tradition of scientific practice—then begin the extraordinary investigations that lead the profession at last to a new set of commitments, a new basis for the practice of science. The extraordinary episodes in which that shift of professional commitments occurs are the ones known in this essay as scientific revolutions. They are the tradition-shattering complements to the tradition-bound activity of normal science.

The most obvious examples of scientific revolutions are those famous episodes in scientific development that have often been labeled revolutions before. Therefore . . . where the nature of scientific revloutions is first directly scrutinized, we shall deal repeatedly with the major turning points in scientific development associated with the names of [Nicolaus] Copernicus [1473–1543], [Isaac] Newton [1642–1727], [Antoine] Lavoisier [1743–1794], and [Albert] Einstein [1879–1955]. More clearly than most other episodes in the history of at least the physical sciences, these display what all scientific revolutions are about. Each of them necessitated the community's rejection of one time-honored scientific theory in favor of another incompatible with it. Each produced a consequent shift in the problems available for scientific scrutiny and in the standards by which the profession determined what should count as an admissible problem or as a legitimate problem-solution. And each transformed the scientific imagination in ways that we shall ultimately need to describe as a transformation of the world within which scientific work was done. Such changes, together with the controversies that almost always accompany them, are the defining characteristics of scientific revolutions.

These characteristics emerge with particular clarity from a study of, say, the Newtonian or the chemical revolution. It is, however, a fundamental thesis of this essay that they can also be retrived from the study of many other episodes that were not so obviously revolutionary. For the far smaller professional group affected by them, [the] equations [of James Clerk Maxwell (1831–1879)] were as revolutionary as Einstein's, and they were resisted accordingly. The invention of other new theories regularly, and appropriately, evokes the same response from some of the specialists on whose are of special competence they impinge. For these men the new theory implies a change in the rules governing the prior practice of normal science. Inevitably, therefore, it reflects upon much scientific work they have already successfully completed. That is why a new theory, however special its range of application, is seldom or never just an increment to what is already known. Its assimilation requires the reconstruction of prior theory and the re-evaluation of prior fact, an intrinsically revolutionary process that is seldom completed by a single man and never overnight. No wonder historians have had difficulty in dating precisely this extended process that their vocabulary impels them to view as an isolated event.

Nor are new inventions of theory the only scientific events that have revolutionary impact upon the specialists in whose domain they occur. The commitments that govern normal science specify not only what sorts of entities the universe does contain, but also, by implication, those that it does not. It follows, though the point will require extended discussion, that a discovery like that of oxygen or X-rays does not simply add one more item to the population of the scientist's world. Ultimately it has that effect, but not until the professional community has re-evaluated traditional experimental procedures, altered its conception of entities with which it has long been familiar, and, in the process, shifted the network of theory through which it deals with the world. Scientific fact and theory are not categorically separable, except perhaps within a single tradition of normal-scientific practice. That is why the unexpected discovery is not simply factual in its import and why the scientist's world is qualitatively transformed as well as quantitatively enriched by fundamental novelties of either fact or theory.

This extended conception of the nature of scientific revolutions is the one delineated in the pages that follow. Admittedly the extension strains customary usage. Nevertheless, I shall continue to speak even of discoveries as revolutionary, because it is just the possibility of relating their structure to that of, say, the Copernican revolution that makes the extended conception seem to me so important. . . .

II. THE ROUTE TO NORMAL SCIENCE

In this essay, 'normal science' means research firmly based upon one or more past scientific achievements, achievements that some particular scientific community acknowledges for a time as supplying the foundation for its further practice. Today such achievements are recounted, though seldom in their original form, by science textbooks, elementary and advanced. These textbooks expound the body of accepted theory, illustrate many or all of its successful applications, and compare these applications with exemplary observations and experiments. Before such books became popular early in the nineteenth century (and until even more recently in the newly matured sciences), many of the famous classics of science fulfilled a similar function. Aristotle's *Physica*, . . . *Almagest* [by Ptolemy (2nd century A.D.)], Newton's *Principia* and Op-*ticks*, . . . *Electricity* [by Benjamin Franklin (1706–1790)], Lavoisier's *Chemistry*, and . . . *Geology* [by Charles Lyell (1797-1875)]—these and many other works served for a time implicitly to define the legitimate problems and methods of a research field for succeeding generations of practitioners. They were able to do so because they shared two essential characteristics. Their achievement was sufficiently unprecedented to attract an enduring group of adherents away from competing modes of scientific activity. Simultaneously, it was sufficiently open-ended to leave all sorts of problems for the redefined group of practitioners to resolve.

Achievements that share these two characteristics I shall henceforth refer to as 'paradigms,' a term that relates closely to 'normal science.' By choosing it, I mean to suggest that some accepted examples of actual scientific practice—examples which include law, theory, application, and instrumentation together—provide models from which spring particular coherent traditions of scientific research. These are the traditions which the historian describes under such rubrics as 'Ptolemaic astronomy' (or 'Copernican'), 'Aristotelian dynamics' (or 'Newtonian'), 'corpuscular optics' (or 'wave optics'), and so on. The study of paradigms, including many that are far more specialized than those named illustratively above, is what mainly prepares the student for membership in the particular scientific community with which he will later practice. Because he there joins men who learned the bases of their field from the same concrete models, his subsequent practice will seldom evoke overt disagreement over fundamentals. Men whose research is based on shared paradigms are committed to the same rules and standards for scientific practice. That commitment and the apparent consensus it produces are prerequisites for normal science, i.e., for the genesis and continuation of a particular research tradition. . . .

If the historian traces the scientific knowledge of any selected group of related phenomena backward in time, he is likely to encounter some minor variant of a pattern here illustrated from the history of physical optics. Today's physics textbooks tell the student that light is photons, i.e., quantum-mechanical entities that exhibit some characteristics of waves and some of particles. Research proceeds accordingly, or rather according to the more elaborate and mathematical characterization from which this usual verbalization is derived. That characterization of light is, however, scarcely half a century old. Before it was developed by [Max] Planck [1858-1947], Einstein, and others early in this century, physics texts taught that light was transverse wave motion, a conception rooted in a paradigm that derived ultimately from the optical writings of [Thomas] Young [1773-1829] and [Augustin] Fresnel [1788-1827] in the early nineteenth century. Nor was the wave theory the first to be embraced by almost all practitioners of optical science. During the eighteenth century the paradigm for this field was provided by Newton's *Opticks*, which taught that light was material corpuscles. At that time physicists sought evidence, as the early wave theorists had not, of the pressure exerted by light particles impinging on solid bodies.

These transformations of the paradigms of physical optics are scientific revolutions, and the successive transition from one paradigm to another via revolution is the usual developmental pattern of mature science. It is not, however, the pattern characteristic of the period before Newton's work, and that is the contrast that concerns us here. No period between remote antiquity and the end of the seventeenth century exhibited a single generally accepted view about the nature of light. Instead there were a number of competing schools and subschools, most of them espousing one variant or another of Epicurean, Aristotelian, or Platonic theory. One group took light to be particles emanating from material bodies; for another it was a modification of the medium that intervened between the body and the eye; still another explained light in terms of an interaction of the medium with an emanation from the eye; and there were other combinations and modifications besides. Each of the corresponding schools derived strength from its relation to some particular metaphysic, and each emphasized, as paradigmatic observations, the particular cluster of optical phenomena that its own theory could do most to explain. Other observations were dealt with by *ad hoc* elaborations [= by somewhat arbitrary hypotheses], or they remained as outstanding problems for further research.

At various times all these schools made significant contributions to the body of concepts, phenomena, and techniques from which Newton drew the first nearly. uniformly accepted paradigm for physical optics. Any definition of the scientist that excludes at least the more creative members of these various schools will exclude their modern successors as well. Those men were scientists. Yet anyone examining a survey of physical optics before Newton may well conclude that, though the field's practitioners were scientists, the net result of their activity was something less than science. Being able to take no common body of belief for granted, each writer on physical optics felt forced to build his field anew from its foundations. In doing so, his choice of supporting observation and experiment was relatively free, for there was no standard set of methods or of phenomena that every optical writer felt forced to employ and explain. Under these circumstances, the dialogue of the resulting books was often directed as much to the members of other schools as it was to nature. That pattern is not unfamiliar in a number of creative fields today, nor is it incompatible with significant discovery and invention. It is not, however, the pattern of development that physical optics acquired after Newton and that other natural sciences make familiar today. . . .

Reading Questions

1. What meaning does Kuhn give to *paradigm, normal science,* and *revolution?*
2. What is the difference between the picture of science derived from science textbooks and that derived from careful scrutiny of the history of science?
3. Can the scientific method decide between competing paradigms? If it cannot, how are the decisions made?
4. What kind of work is carried on in science during periods of normal science?
5. What disrupts normal science and leads to scientific revolutions?
6. Once a new paradigm is accepted, what happens to the theories and facts collected under the old paradigm?
7. What connection is there between education and paradigms in science?
8. What occurs in scientific fields in preparadigm stages of development?

Questions for Reflection and Research

1. What criticisms can be made of Kuhn's theory? (For some relevant considerations see selection #32 by McMullin.)
2. Would the scientific methods described in selections #26 and #27 be able to decide between competing paradigms?
3. Which scientific fields seem to be in preparadigm stages of development?
4. Does Kuhn's account of science make science ultimately irrational?
5. What procedure should be used to confirm or refute Kuhn's theory?
6. Does Kuhn's theory apply to itself? Is he offering a paradigm for the study of the history of science?

Reactions to the Logical Positivist Conception of Science

The Author: Ernan McMullin (b. 1924) was born in Ireland and was educated there and in Belgium at the University of Louvain. He has taught philosophy at Notre Dame University as well as served as visiting professor at a number of colleges. The recipient of many honors, he has published widely in the philosophy of science. In addition he served as president of the Metaphysical Society of America. The following selection is part of his presidential address to that organization.

The Selection: The excerpt offers a succinct summary of some of the main currents in the philosophy of science from 1950 to 1974. The author begins with an account of the program of the Vienna Circle, a group of philosphers and scientists in Vienna who argued that true knowledge was restricted to science, logic, and mathematics. This program came to be known as logical positivism. Short accounts are given of reactions to positivism by a number of prominent philosophers: Wittgenstein, Polanyi, Hanson, Kuhn, Toulmin, and Feyerabend. The author also briefly alludes to other challenges to the positivist's program from those who regard the social sciences as different from the natural sciences—and from Marxists who claim science is a product of socioeconomic conditions. The selection is very demanding reading.

In 1950, academic philosophy in the United States was coming increasingly under the influence of logical positivism; philosophical discussion tended more and more to be limited to the groove laid down for it twenty years before by the Vienna Circle, with their uncomfortably narrow criteria of meaning and verification. . . .

From "The Faces of Science" by Ernan McMullin. Originally published in *The Review of Metaphysics*, vol. 27, no. 4 (June 1974): 655-67. Reprinted with permission.

Most of the original members of the Vienna Circle had been trained as scientists. And they were deeply influenced by the critical reflections on science of [Ernest] Mach [1836–1916] and [Albert] Einstein [1879-1955]. No one could charge them with displaying a naive outsiders' view of how scientists actually proceed. Yet what took precedence before all else was their deeply-felt conviction that most of what went on in post-Hegelian [= after the death of the German philosopher Georg W. F. Hegel (1770–1831)] German philosophy was disreputable, and sometimes dangerous, nonsense. What was needed was a new Reformation, a sweeping away of pseudo-speech and empty rhetoric masquerading as responsible world-view. Like the nominalists of the fourteenth century, like [David] Hume in the eighteenth, they rejected the overweening thought-constructions of the metaphysicians. It was obvious where the antidote could be found: in the intellectual sobriety and demanding techniques of the scientist and the logician. Natural science had proved itself a reliable means to the steady accumulation of truth. What better model could one propose for knowledge generally? With science, one knew where one was: one began from the facts of observation, and making use only of tested modes of inference, one moved cautiously and tentatively to the level of generalization. Why not insist on a mode of verification at least *analogous* with this for any assertion laying claim to truth about the world? Then if the assertion could not meet this challenge, one would be entitled to set it aside as meaningless, or at best as evocative expression [= expression that expresses or provokes emotion] of a kind proper to the arts but improper where cognitive [= knowledge] claims are concerned. Metaphysics, in short, could be relegated to the category of bad music!

Notice the pattern here. It is, technically, a "foundationalist" one: one begins from an unproblematic foundation, the observation-statements, themselves in no need of further validation; then by means of equally unproblematic rules of inference, one generates laws or tests hypotheses. There are two quite distinct historical strands interwoven here, one traceable to [Ludwig] Wittgenstein [1889-1951] and [Bertrand] Russell [1872-1970] and the other to Mach and ultimately Hume. In the *Tractatus*, Wittgenstein took the apparatus of the *Principia Mathematica* [written by Russell and A. N. Whitehead (1861-1947)], the atomic propositions and the truth-functional connectives, and sought to discover how well [the apparatus] would serve as a theory of language. If one could but assume that the atomic propositions corresponded to atomic facts, and that propositions other than declarative ones could be set aside, then the business of the world could be transacted in PM-ese [= the language of special logical symbols introduced in *Principia Mathematica*], and the troubling question of the relation between language and that world could perhaps be shelved. In retrospect, it is not difficult to see that the *Tractatus* was proposed as a myth, a "what if?", and not as an assertion. The author had already grasped that there are questions to which saying is not the appropriate response.

But the Vienna Circle took this "what if?" and made assertion of it by interpreting the atomic propositions as reports of sensory observations, linked ostensively and non-problematically to the contents of those observations. Whether the protocol sentences [= atomic propositions regarded as reports of sensory observations] corresponded to sense data [= perceptions], after the tradition of March and Hume, or to traits of physical objects, as [Rudolph] Carnap [1891-1970] came to hold, the essential point was that lines had now been lowered from the constituents of the idealized language directly into the world (or at least, into our experience of the world). Correspondence rules ensured the meaningfulness as well as the truth of the basic propositions, each of them a singular report of an observation. Science simply consisted in enlarging our stock of such propositions, and linking them together to form more complex propositions. Verification reduced either to truth-functional testing or to estimates of probability based on inductive rule.

It was, perhaps, the most ambitious foundationalism in the entire history of philosophy, outdoing even that of Aristotle [384-322 B.C.]. And as we all know, it collapsed. That collapse was engineered rather more by philosophers of science than by the beleaguered metaphysicians themselves [whose views were regarded as meaningless by the positivists]. And the battles thus mounted have made philosophy of science perhaps the liveliest part of the broad domain of philosophy over the past decade or more. . . .

From what sources did the critique of the positivist reduction of science come?

There was Wittgenstein, first and foremost, who by the 1930's had already carried the dialectic of the *Tractatus* a stage further, and could now criticize the assumptions underlying the theory of language explored there: above all the reduction of the diversity of discourse to categorical atomic statements linked truth-functionally. Even worse in his eyes was the one-to-one correlation of these statements with sense-data, a mistake that the *Tractatus* had never made. The inquiries that subsequently took shape as the *Philosophical Investigations* were not primarily a philosophy of science, but they enjoined upon philosophers of science some clear lessons: to take account of the fine texture of language usage and to be wary of devices that claimed to put the elements of language in unproblematic conjunction with the elements of reality. Thus both of the main theses of the Vienna Circle were impugned: in science, as elsewhere, there are no atomic propositions, and the connections of language, far from being truth-functional, are almost endlessly diverse, even where the validation of assertions about the world are concerned.

From another quarter, [Karl] Popper [b.1902] attacked the verificationist emphasis of the positivist program, as well as the attempt to cast the inferential structure of science in an inductive mold. [See selection #21 by Black for a fuller account of Popper's view.—ED.] And also in the 1950's, [Willard V.O.] Quine [b. 1908] was drawing attention to the weakness of a distinction that was altogether crucial to the positivist enterprise, that between the analytic and the synthetic, on which their sharp separation of formal science and factual science rested. But it was in the late nineteen-fifties that the onslaught began in earnest. I want to single out four moments, four points of attack, in the battle that followed.

First, in 1958, came the Polanyi-Hanson raid, right into the enemy's heartland. Between them, they knocked out the sharp distinction between theoretical and observational terms on which the hopes of a foundationalist-inductivist account must ultimately rest. Using analogies drawn from Gestalt psychology, they argued that observation reports are shaped by the conceptual scheme and the expectations of the observer, and are, therefore, to use the later cliché, theory-laden. There is no wholly neutral observation-language; there are no pre-theoretical correspondence-rules. Nor are there sense *data* (in the sense of something *given,* to which the observer has not already contributed). [Immanuel] Kant [1724–1804] had, of course, said as much, but the merit of . . . *Patterns of Discovery* [by Norwood Russell Hanson (b. 1924)] and . . . *Personal Knowledge* [by Michael Polanyi (b. 1891)] was the wealth of example drawn from science and from everyday practice to help make the point. . . .

The second wave of the attack was led by Thomas Kuhn [b.1922]. Kuhn argued that the patterns of logicality imposed by the positivists on modes of validation in science held only during periods of "normal" science, periods defined by the general acceptance of a paradigm, that is, a common ideal of explanation, a set of symbolic forms, a model, a group of problem-solving methods used in the training of students. . . . During the period of revolution, on the other hand, there is a multiplicity of competing paradigms; there are no agreed logical or methodological structures available in terms of which assent to one of these paradigms rather than to another can be enforced. Thus adherence to one rather than to another is, in part at least, a matter of commitment, personal or group-based. And the shift from one paradigm to another, which constitutes a "revolution," in Kuhn's sense, cannot be described or evaluated in purely logical terms. Rather, the analogies must be drawn (and here we are reminded once again of Polanyi) from Gestalt psychology or even from the language of religious conversion, that is, from contexts where one way of seeing is suddenly replaced by another. There is no small sequence of shifts, each explicable in terms of what went before, but rather a massive all-at-once switch. After the switch, another period of normal science follows, within which the criteria of logicality once again apply, but of course not at all in the definitive way the positivists had supposed, since another revolution will one day sweep away the theoretical structures that made this particular state of logicality possible.

It should be noticed that the perspective from which Kuhn speaks is at once historical and sociological; if he is right, no longer can one carry on the philosophy of science without taking account of the history of science and the sociology of scientists. In their pursuit of logicality, the Vienna Circle had drawn a sharp line between the contexts of discovery and of validation in science, and had insisted that only the timeless logical structures of validation were of philosophic concern; the temporal contingencies of discovery were somewhat disdainfully relegated to the historian, the psychologist, and the sociologist. Kuhn now challenged this, as indeed a host of nineteenth century theorists of science (including even Mach himself) would have done. His account of scientific revolutions was based on a historical investigation of what actually goes on in science, on the criteria that seem to govern those theory-changes which have been most significant in shaping the science we know. This was science, not as it might have been, or should be, but as it is. Secondly, Kuhn emphasized that science is the work of a rather special social group, with an extremely complex community structure. The adoption of a new paradigm is "a reconstruction of group commitments," and it cannot be understood without reference to the diversity of factors, psychological, sociological, as well as logical, involved in such reconstruction. [See selection #31 for Kuhn's own account.—ED.]

A third line of attack can be discerned at its sharpest in the work of Stephen Toulmin [b. 1922]. Like Kuhn, he looked to the *history* of science for clues to its characteristic patterns of rationality; like him, he stressed the importance of viewing science as the product of a particular profession, whose role he compared to that of the judge in constitutional legal cases. But he rejected the distinction between normal and revolutionary science, arguing instead for a continuing more-or-less steady transformation of concepts. He was thus led to adopt a theory of conceptual evolution patterned rather closely on the biological theory, one in which the units of variation are individual concepts (not theories or paradigms). The details of this much-debated evolutionary metaphor need not concern us; what we are interested in is the antithesis we find here to the foundationalist view from which we began. Since concepts are constantly shifting, there can be no foundational propositions of any sort. We judge the rationality of a man's conduct by considering, not the consistency or adequacy of his *habitual* beliefs and practices, but rather the way in which he modifies his position in the face of new and unforeseen experiences. Likewise, we must seek the structures of scientific rationality, not in the day-to-day operations, in the puzzle-solving, but in the moments of conceptual stress and shift. And in these moments, logical criteria are not of service. . . .

Kuhn was quite prepared to concede a role to logicalist analysis in the understanding of *normal* science, and furthermore insisted that normal science is in some respects the basic kind of science. But Toulmin cannot permit this. Since the primary structures of science are, in his view, displayed only in the processes leading to conceptual change, and since the application of logical criteria presuppose conceptual stability, these criteria have no relevance to science as such. Yet he by no means wants to lapse into the sort of relativism that this immediately suggests. And so he calls on a broader concept of *rationality* (to be contrasted with "logicality"), stated in rather vague terms of "appraisal" and "richer modes of understanding." Conceptual change, no matter how revolutionary or sudden it may be, is thus rational; indeed, this is *definitionally* true, since it is in such change that human rationality in its highest form is exhibited.

This brings us finally to Paul Feyerabend [b. 1924], bringing up the other end of the battle line, a one-man army happily hurling challenges at all comers. His first target was the . . . deductivist model of explanation, the flagship of the logical empiricist fleet [see selection #35 by Martin for an account of this model]. More generally, he opposed the basic positivist assumption that competing theories can always be put into formal comparison with one another with a view to the acceptance of the one and the rejection of the other. Indeed, he urged (here following Popper), it is desirable that no one theory, no Kuhnian "normal science," ever be allowed to take possession of a field; a plurality of alternatives must always be kept in contention, so that every opening will be tested, every configuration tried. Testing is never a matter of comparing one theory with experience, but rather of seeing how a variety of mutually incompatible theories fare, no one of which is ever adequate to all of the "facts."

Against the entire foundationalist approach, he argues:

> The influence upon our thinking of a comprehensive scientific theory . . . goes much deeper than is admitted by those who would regard it as a convenient scheme for the ordering of facts only. . . . Scientific theories are ways of looking at the world; and their adoption affects our general beliefs and expectations, and thereby also our experiences and our conception of reality.

Hence, the assumption of the meaning-invariance of the terms used in observation-statements, the assumption on which the entire foundationalist program rested, is a mistaken one. There is no neutral set of "facts" or observation-statements, to be accounted for by one or other theory, which would permit us to content ourselves with the question: which of them does the logically better job? Instead, since the adoption of a particular theory ordinarily alters the meaning of the observation-term, that is, alters the facts to be accounted for, we have to recognize (and here he goes beyond

Polanyi and Hanson) that competing theories are, in general, *incommensurable* with one another; there is no way to put them in logical correspondence. In particular, the demand that a theory should be consistent with earlier successful theories in the same domain can be shown to be unfulfillable. An inductive logic that allegedly validates ever broader empirical generalizations is, therefore, a myth. Our only way out, he concludes, is:

> to abandon the idea that theories can be "established" by experience and (to admit) that insofar as they go beyond the facts, we have no means whatever (except perhaps psychological ones) to guarantee their trustworthiness.

In later articles, he has carried these themes much further, under the inspiration (in part) of a deeply-felt liberationist anthropology. To lay claim to a *method* is to claim a special hold on truth, and such absolutism, whether theological or political or scientific, ultimately must diminish man, his hopes and his possibilities. And so he opposes the "experts," the main enemies of the free society, in his view. Against them, he proclaims: "There is no method, and there is no authority." . . .

And he has attempted to back [his view] up by case-histories drawn from science, notably by an extensive analysis of . . . successful advocacy of the Copernican theory [by Galileo (1564–1642)]. There was no question, he argues, of Galileo's *establishing* the new theory, as the [positivist] view of science would presume him to have done, or at least attempted to do. The Copernican theory was at variance with the facts in important respects; it lacked adequate optical and physiological theories in terms of which the telescopic observations alleged on its behalf could be secured against attack. It had no persuasive successes to claim over its rival in the way of prediction. So what Galileo had to fall back on was essentially *propaganda;* he had to persuade people to see the world differently, without realizing that they were doing so. He had to establish "fake connections" between what were in fact "refutable theories," and "distort" the evidence by clever omissions and inventions. In short, he had to know how to exploit "the valuable weaknesses of human thinking." It was his unparalleled talent for doing this that made him the great scientist he was. For this is what science at its best amounts to; its manner of imposing coherence on a chaos is much closer to the spirit of poetry than it is to the logical patterns in which philosophers put their trust. Thus far Feyerabend.

And it *is* pretty far! Think of those dear dead days when science was supposed to provide a nice tight model of what knowledge *ought* to look like: objective, empirically-grounded, progressive, all of the things metaphysics quite evidently was not. . . .

I have been cataloguing the ways in which philosophy of science has contributed to the breaking-down of the stereotype of scientific method advanced by the Vienna Circle. There are several other challenges to this stereotype I could also mention. Some philosophers of the social sciences have argued for a separation between the methods of the natural and social sciences, on such grounds as the special role of *interpretation* in the social sciences, for example. [See selection #39 by Nagel for a discussion of this view.—ED.] This would entail a denial of the unity-of-science thesis of positivism, and in practice also involves a rejection of the foundationalist and logicist model, for the social sciences at least. Or again, we could turn to neo-Marxism, with its claim that all science is "interest"-bound. If "interest" may be interpreted as instrumental control, then this is compatible with a purely positivist view of the *natural* sciences, allied with an extremely anti-positivist theory of the social sciences. . . . If on the other hand, even the natural sciences are held to be an expression of class-consciousness, in need of a subtle theory of mediations linking socio-economic base and conceptual superstructure, then the positivist model would have to be rejected for all parts of science. One recent defender of this view . . . assails Kuhn for limiting his sociological treatment of science to the study of scientists as a professional group, instead of focussing on the socio-economic conditions that [in this critic's view] affect *all* science, even the most mathematicized and apparently objective. I must, however, be content with this brief reference to the important work now in progress in the philosophy of the social sciences, which has raised new questions about the positivist account of science, though perhaps from a more expectable quarter.

Reading Questions

1. What was the program of the Vienna Circle?
2. Why was the positivist program called a foundationalist program?
3. In what way did the later views of Wittgenstein tend to undermine positivist views?
4. What main objection was put forward by Polanyi and Hanson?
5. What is Kuhn's account of the nature of both normal and revolutionary science? What is a paradigm?
6. How do positivists and Toulmin differ with regard to scientific concepts?
7. How, according to Feyerabend, do scientists select a winner from competing scientific theories?

Questions for Reflection and Research

1. How did Quine's attacks on the analytic-synthetic distinction help to undermine logical positivism?

2. From the author's accounts of the views of Polanyi-Hanson, Kuhn, Toulmin, and Feyerabend, which authors would be inclined to reject the idea that there is a scientific method of the sort described in selection #26 by Pirsig and selection #27 by Hempel?
3. What objections can you think of to Feyerabend's views? To Toulmin's?
4. What is the conception of science promoted by Marxist philosophers?
5. How does a scientist's conception of the nature of science influence what he does as a scientist?
6. Select an event in the history of science with which you are familiar and attempt to describe it as it would be described by the main critics of positivism mentioned in the selection.

Explanation

Some observers of contemporary American life have been concerned about the decline in reading and writing skills among students of college age. How can the decline be explained? Some say that watching television is the cause.

But what kind of explanation is this? If it is said that event A caused event B, just what is being claimed about A and B? For instance, is it being asserted that in addition to the watching of television and the poor showing on reading and writing tests, another factor (the cause) has passed between the two, leaving the first and producing the second? David Hume (1711–1776) would respond in the negative to this question. He argued that casual explanations are not claims about the existence of entities called causes. Rather such explanations are actually assertions about correlations. (See selection #33 by Eugene Troxell and William Snyder for an account of Hume's view of causes.)

Hume would claim that if we find that watching television causes reduced reading and writing skills, we have found nothing more than that the former regularly precedes or accompanies the latter. His can be regarded as one of the ancestors of widely accepted recent accounts of causal explanations. These accounts, sometimes called covering-law models of causation, are explained in selection #35 by Michael Martin and, more briefly, in selection #36 by John Hospers.

The covering-law model protrays the casual explanation of an event as an effort to show that the event is subsumed under (= is an instance of) a law or generalization. The laws or generalizations are regarded as correlations of one kind of event with another kind of event.

If it is true that causal explanations do in some way involve the subsumption of events under correlating laws, those who seek such explanations have other philosophical challenges about explanation to reckon with:

(1) One event can seem to have a multiplicity of causes. The car accident was caused by drunken driving, and by the brakes

being applied too slowly, and by the bartender's failure to refuse to serve the drinker, and by the driver's friends who did
not try to stop him from driving, and by the manufacturer who
produces cars that can travel at speeds so much over the speed
limit. Which of these is *the* cause of the accident?

(a) Is it, as Hospers contends in selection #36, that these causes
might all be part of the one overall causal explanation, which is
quite complex?

(b) Or is it wrong to think there must be just one causal explanation of an event? Perhaps there can be multiple causes.
Hospers considers this possibility too.

(c) Or is it that what is counted as a cause varies with a person's
interest in the event? If so, one cannot claim that an event has
some one explanation—but rather an indefinite number. For
each different kind of interest people can have in an event,
there will be a different cause. Troxell and Snyder in selection
#33 seem to favor this alternative.

(2) Consider another way in which an event may seem to have multiple causes. Human behavior is examined by a number of sciences; the human body, including the brain, is studied in other
sciences. Suppose that we seek to know why a certain person,
Matilda, is listening to a particular piece of music. A sociologist
tells us that Matilda's behavior is caused by her culture's standards of what is acceptable music; a psychologist claims that the
behavior is caused by musical conditioning by means of a system of rewards and punishments; and a physical scientist asserts that her conduct is the result of the interaction of stimuli
impinging on the chemical and electrical structures in the
brain. Which scientist is correct? Which one seeks the real cause
of human behavior? Are they competitors in the search for the
real cause—or should their answers be added together, each
providing only a piece of the correct answer?

Selection #34 by Carl Hempel introduces another way of
thinking about the relations of the sciences. Perhaps the sciences are neither in competition nor aiding in one overall com-
posite search for understanding. It could be that some sciences
and their explanations are superfluous. For example, since we
are all composed of the entities and energy units studied in
physics, it is possible that physics is the only science. According
to this view the laws of all sciences can be shown to be derivable
from those of physics, and all scientific explanations should
thus be regarded as really based on the laws of physics. Some
contend that the "reduction" of chemistry, and even of biology,
to physics is well along already.

(3) The view that explanations involve subsuming events under
laws is not directly challenged by the two preceding considerations. No matter how one came to terms with the multiplicity of

explanations of an event, one could still hold that any explanations involved conformed to the covering-law model. The
covering-law model has had its critics, especially among
philosophers interested in the behavioral sciences.

(a) A. R. Louch in selection #38 asserts that explanations of
human behavior do not need to appeal to general laws. Rather,
when we explain human conduct our explanations are not
general—they are for the particular case alone, what Louch
calls ad hoc explanations. Furthermore, explanations of human
behavior usually are quite unlike explanations found in the
physical and biological sciences. Explanations of human behavior are attempts to justify the behavior. If we actually try to
explain behavior in terms of general laws, we end up with uninformative platitudes at best.

(b) Ernest Nagel in selection #39 examines the view of some
philosphers who claim that to understand and explain human
behavior, we must study human purposes and other subjective
states. These philosophers claim that such states require a different method than those used in the nonbehavioral sciences.
Nagel argues that these philosophers are mistaken.

Both Louch and those whom Nagel criticizes are open to
the idea that the social sciences cannot be modeled on the natural sciences. Nagel disagrees, as does Hospers (in selection
#36). Hospers asserts that laws regarding purposes (and,
hence, sciences of human behavior) are quite conceivable.

(4) If in science some events are explained by subsuming them
under laws, how then are laws to be explained? If, as is usually
claimed, this also is done by subsumption under more general
laws, we are led to the question of whether we must eventually
arrive at laws that we cannot explain. Hospers (selection #36)
reasons that there probably are some facts and laws that we
must just accept as given—brute facts. We cannot explain everything. He also concludes that even though we might not be
able to provide an explanation for a particular law, this failure
would not invalidate explanations in which the law was used.

In conclusion, we have seen that despite fairly widespread agreement in the philosophy of science that explanations in the physical and
biological sciences involve subsuming events and laws under laws, there
remain philosophical problems about explanations. How are we to think
about the fact that some events can be explained in a number of different ways, possibly by a number of different sciences? Can explanations of
human behavior that mention purposes be regarded as similar to those
given in the physical and biological sciences? And are there, in explanations, scientific laws that cannot themselves be explained?

Another issue concerns how science can be explained to nonscientists. Susan Stebbing in selection #37 argues that it is exceedingly
difficult to translate the findings of science from scientific vocabulary to

ordinary concepts. She criticizes a well-known popularization of physics by Arthur Eddington.

It may be helpful to note at this point some other relevant selections in this book. All the selections in Section 3 on possible limits of science raise questions about limits of scientific explanations. Selection #7 by Ian Barbour addresses questions about the relation of religious explanations to scientific explanations, while selection #22 discusses the role of theoretical entities in scientific explanations. Section 6 on science and ethics raises again (by implication) the question of whether science can explain everything. The selections on science and ethics, that is, may lead one to ask whether science can explain which kinds of behavior are the right kinds.

Reflection on how we resolve moral and ethical questions leads one quite naturally to the realization that there are many things science cannot explain, that many explanations do not involve science at all. For example, no science need be involved in explaining the point of a joke, or how to play checkers, or why a person should vote for a particular political candidate, or what to listen for in a new piece of music.

Further Reading: Explanation

1. *The Encyclopedia of Philosophy*, ed. PAUL EDWARDS, 8 vols. (New York: Macmillan Publishing Co., 1967). For entries primarily devoted to the covering-law model of explanation see "Explanation in Science" by JAEGWON KIM, "Historical Explanation" by RUDOLPH H. WEINGARTNER, and "Laws and Theories" by MARY HESSE. In the Hesse entry see especially the subsection "The Structure of Theories." For a discussion of causation see "Causation" by RICHARD TAYLOR. For a discussion of whether causal explanations and those in terms of purposes are the same see "Reasons and Causes" by KEITH S. DONNELLAN. Questions of reduction within the social sciences are discussed in "Holism and Individualism in History and Social Sciences" by W. H. DRAY. A general discussion of why we ask why-questions is found in the entry "Why" by PAUL EDWARDS.

2. *Conceptual Foundations of Scientific Thought: An Introduction to the Philosophy of Science* by MARX WARTOFSKY (New York: The Macmillan Company, 1968). This volume contains an excellent bibliography covering topics on causation, explanation, reduction, and philosophy of the behavioral sciences.

3. *The Philosophy of the Social Sciences* by ALAN RYAN (New York: Pantheon Books, Random House, 1970). Issues in the philosophy of the social sciences are succinctly presented including discussions of reduction and explanation.

Causes and David Hume

The Authors: Eugene A. Troxell (b. 1937) received his undergraduate education at Gonzaga University and his graduate education at the University of
Chicago. Ethics and the later philosophy of Ludwig Wittgenstein are two of his
philosophical interests. He teaches philosophy at San Diego State University.

William S. Snyder (b. 1927) also teaches at San Diego State. He was educated as an undergraduate at Temple University and as a graduate student at
Princeton University. Two of his special interests in philosophy include
metaphysics and the relation of philosophy to literature.

David Hume (1711–1776) and his views on causation form a central focus
for this selection. This well-known philosopher from Scotland wrote his major
philosophic works before he was fifty, thereafter concentrating on writing in history, economics, and politics. One of the most famous of empiricist philosophers
he wrote widely on philosophical topics.

The Selection: Two different points about causal explanations are explained.
First it is noted that any particular event can be regarded as having a number of
causes. What is counted as a cause depends on the interests of those concerned
about the event. Second, David Hume's views on causes are explained. Hume
argued that when we describe one event as causing another we are correleating
the events and not claiming there is an entity in the world connecting the events.
That is, Hume argues that the word *cause* (unlike the word *red*) is not used to
refer to something in the world. Thus when we explain events in terms of causes,
we are merely calling attention to correlations we have noticed. The constant association of events in the world makes us *feel* there is a necessary connection between them, even though there is no such necessary connection.

From *Making Sense of Things: An Invitation to Philosophy* by Eugene A. Troxell and William S.
Snyder (New York: St. Martin's Press, Inc., 1976), pp. 54–59. Reprinted by permission of
St. Martin's Press, Inc.

The next interesting philosophical idea we will consider is David Hume's idea concerning causality. Hume's idea has been a major source of interest for philosophers and other intellectuals for the past 250 years. . . . However, it is not easily stated. We will attempt a formulation, but the reader should be cautioned that the formulation will contain misleading elements. The idea should become more clear as we get into making sense out of it in terms of our own everyday experience.

According to Hume, our common ideas concerning causality are due to intellectual habits. That is, we do not *perceive* causes and effects in the world around us. We perceive different events taking place and we intellectually relate some of these events to each other by *thinking* of certain events as being causes or effects of other events. Our thinking in terms of causes and effects is due simply to the way in which our minds function, rather than our perception of causes and effects in our environment.

Causality, of course, is extremely fundamental to the entire Western scientific way of making sense out of our environment. It is so fundamental, in fact, that it seems quite apparent to many people that we are simply "aware" of it taking place in the world around us. Hume's idea seems to suggest that the causality arises out of our own minds rather than actually being there independent of our minds. . . .

We would like to approach Hume's idea by inviting the reader to attempt to become vividly aware of the difference between what we actually *see* or *hear* and what we intellectually supply as we make sense out of what we see or hear. . . . Imagine there has been a fire in a nearby residence. The fire has been put out, after it has caused considerable damage, and an investigation is being conducted to determine its cause. Soon it is determined that the fire was caused by children playing with matches in the garage. After a bit of questioning, little Bobby Jones confesses his guilt amid a flood of tears. Let us, for the sake of our imaginary example, pretend that the investigation has correctly determined the cause of the fire. If we had been able to see everything that happened immediately prior to the fire, we would agree that the fire was caused by Bobby Jones and Jimmy Smith playing with matches in the garage. The fire fighters write up their report, putting down "children playing with matches" as the cause of the fire, and return to the station.

Now let us take a closer look at the circumstances surrounding the beginning of the fire and see if we can think of any other ways to describe the fire's cause. We could perhaps say the fire was caused by a match being placed very close to some old newspaper, which was, in turn, next to some cardboard boxes. Possibly, a physicist would have included mention of these factors in a description of the fire's cause. But these details were not of great concern to the fire fighters. Their determination of the fire's cause would have ot deny that the children playing with matches more directly caused the fire, any more than the fire fighters would deny that the fire's cause could be described as a lighted match coming into contact with newspaper. But just as the fire fighters might contend that in order for a fire to be produced by a match coming into contact with newspaper, other conditions must be present, and it is these other conditions that are of interest to them, similarly our antismoking campaigner could contend that in order for children to start a fire by playing with matches, other conditions must be present. If the children had no access to matches, they couldn't play with them.

At this time, it is apparent that we could also refer to a large number of other events or conditions as causes of the fire. We could say that the fire was caused by Bobby's father and mother fornicating six years earlier, since if that had not happened Bobby would

not have been born, and if Bobby had not been born the fire would
not have occurred. (A fundamentalist preacher might attempt to
make such a case.) Or, we could say the fire was caused by the invention of matches or the fact that Bobby's tricycle was broken,
since we could make a good case for saying that if either of these
events had not occurred, the fire would not háve occurred.

But the mere fact that we can regard many different events as the
cause of the fire does not mean that it makes no difference which of
these events the fire fighters choose as the fire's cause. The fire
fighters have specific purposes for attempting to establish the fire's
cause. These purposes play a part in determining which event they
will establish as that cause. For example, at least one of their purposes is prevention of future fires. Consequently, they will look for
some factor that is frequently associated with fires and that can possibly be curtailed or avoided as a step in avoiding future fires. Bobby's birth, or the invention of matches, will be completely useless
for this purpose. People are not going to stop having children or
using matches simply in order to avoid fires. But they may attempt
to keep their children from playing with matches.

Now what happens when we think of an event such as Bobby's
birth as the cause of a fire that occurs five years later? Do we suddenly notice something about the birth that we had never noticed
before? Of course not. The birth event is just the same whether or
not we think of it as the cause of a later fire. Thinking of Bobby's
birth as the cause of a later fire could not be the result of any difference that our senses reveal between Bobby's birth and anyone
else's. Or, to put it in a different way, we are not aware of any way
of distinguishing, at the time of birth, between those babies who
will turn out to cause fires and those who will not. Our thinking of
the birth event as a cause of the fire is not based upon anything that
our senses reveal to us. It is based simply on our intellectually relating this event to another event as part of the manner in which we
are making sense out of the other event. And in this respect our
thinking of the birth event as a cause is not different from our
thinking of the playing-with-matches event as a cause. Not every
case of playing with matches, nor even every case of a lighted match
coming into contact with newspaper, results in a fire. The difference between those which do and those which do not is not that one
event somehow contains a "causality" element and the other
doesn't. Or, at least if it does, the causality element is not detectable
through our senses.

At this point, it will be worthwhile to remind ourselves exactly
what interesting philosophic idea we are attempting to make sense
out of. Hume's idea is just that our senses do not reveal causes or
effects to us. Rather, our senses reveal events that we think of as
causes or effects of other events. The example Hume used to demonstrate what he meant was what we would ordinarily describe as

one billiard ball hitting a second billiard ball and thus causing the second billiard ball to begin moving. Hume pointed out that all we actually see in a case like this is one billiard ball moving up to a second, and then the second moving away. We can further observe that when we see one billiard ball moving toward a second, we *expect* the second to begin moving—so that if it did not begin moving immediately after the first reached it, we would be surprised. This expectation, in Hume's opinion, is very important to our ordinary ideas concerning causality. Because we have such an expectation, we think that the one observed event (the first billiard ball moving up to the second) is somehow "necessarily connected" to the second observed event (the second billiard ball moving away). The expectation, or idea of a necessary connection, arises, in Hume's opinion, because whenever we observed an event of the first type in the past, it was always—or almost always—followed by an event of the second type. Because of this past experience, our minds have related the first type of event to the second type, and we express the relationship that our minds have formed by saying that the first event causes the second. Hume does not say we are wrong in expressing the relationship in this way, or that it is somehow not the case that the one event causes the other. He is simply pointing out what he believes he has observed concerning our idea of causality. In his opinion, our idea of causality does not simply arise from anything we observe in the world around us. Rather, it arises out of the way we have become accustomed to make sense out of what we observe.

From our point of view, the important thing once again is simply to become aware that when we consider the world in a certain way, we can make sense out of what Hume is talking about—which, of course, is not the same as deciding whether or not what Hume says about causality is true. We can roughly describe this way of considering the world as one in which we concentrate on the *difference* between what we perceive and what we intellectually supply as we make sense out of what we perceive.

Many people assume that if what Hume says about causality is correct, we are somehow wrong or unjustified in talking about the causes of anything. Hume clearly did not believe this was the case. He thought we were virtually forced to assume that every event has a cause in order to make any sense at all of the world. He discusses at some length the factors that shape our causal judgments and suggests rules to aid us in these judgments. He views himself as seeking to understand what we mean by causality and thinks that he has discovered that one part of what we have traditionally considered causality to be (necessary connection) is supplied by the way the mind operates rather than by what we observe.

Provoked to a large extent by Hume, philosophers have continued to explore the nature of causality for the past 200 years. Some have proceeded a bit further along the path that Hume entered by considering causality to be only one among several possible intellectual tools that we may use to establish connections between features of the world. Looking at causality from this point of view emphasizes the possibility that it may not be the best intellectual tool for understanding certain different aspects of the world which we have traditionally attempted to understand with this tool. Whether or not this is really the case we don't know. There are still many more aspects and possibilities of this subject to be explored. But it can be interesting to realize that once one begins looking at things from a certain point of view, such possibilities begin to make good sense. . . .

Reading Questions

1. What was the real cause of the fire?
2. What does Hume think we see when we regard one event as causing another, and what does he think we supply?
3. If causes, in some sense, are in our minds, should we stop speaking of them?

Questions for Reflection and Research

1. Sociologists, psychologists, linguists, and brain physiologists might all be able to contribute different answers to the question: What caused X (some person) to say "I refuse!"? Would their explanations conflict with each other, or are they to be added together? That is, are the sciences in competition? (For a related topic see selection #34 on reduction by Hempel.)
2. Since every cause itself seems to have a cause, can we ever really find *the* cause of an event? (See selection #36 by Hospers for some relevant remarks.)
3. Do scientists seek causal explanations? If so, what other kinds of explanations are there that are not involved in science?
4. Is Hume right about causes? Why should we want to find out?

Reducing One Science to Another

The Author: Carl G. Hempel (b. 1905). For biographical information see selection #27 on the scientific method.

The Selection: There are, it seems, separate sciences such as chemistry, biology, psychology, and so on. Some philosophers and scientists have suggested that some sciences are more basic than others. The main focus in this selection is on the controversy between those who think biological principles can be explained in terms of ("reduced to") findings of chemistry and physics (the mechanist view) and those who think they cannot (the neo-vitalist view). Some suggestions as to how one must envision such a reduction are given. Another focus in the selection is the idea that psychology can be reduced to biology or to physics and chemistry. This topic leads to the body-mind question and eventually to the final point that the social sciences (sociology, economics, history, and so on) might each be reducible to psychology. This selection is demanding reading.

[T]he basic neo-vitalistic idea [is] that biological systems and processes differ in certain fundamental respects from purely physico-chemical ones. This view is opposed by the so-called mechanistic claim that living organisms are nothing else than very complex physico-chemical systems (though not, as the old-fashioned term 'mechanism' would suggest, purely mechanical ones). These conflicting conceptions have been the subject of an extensive and heated debate, whose details we cannot consider here. But evidently, the issue can be fruitfully discussed only if the mean-

From Carl G. Hempel, *Philosophy of Natural Science,* © 1966, pp. 101–110. Reprinted and adapted by permission of Prentice-Hall, Inc., Englewood Cliffs, N.J.

ing of the opposing claims can be made sufficiently clear to show what sorts of argument and evidence can have a bearing on the problem and how the controversy might be settled. It is this characteristically philosophical problem of clarifying the meanings of the conflicting conceptions that we shall now consider; the result of our reflections will also have certain implications concerning the possibility of settling the issue.

Ostensibly, the controversy concerns the question whether or not living organisms are "merely", or exclusively, physico-chemical systems. But just what would it mean to say that they are? . . . We might construe the doctrine of mechanism as making this twofold claim: (M_1) all the characteristics of living organisms are physico-chemical charactersitics—they can be fully described in terms of the concepts of physics and chemistry; (M_2) all aspects of the behavior of living organisms that can be explained at all can be explained by means of physico-chemical laws and theories.

As for the first of these assertions, it is clear that at present, at any rate, the description of biological phenomena requires the use not only of physical and chemical terms, but of specifically biological terms that do not occur in the physico-chemical vocabulary. Take the statement that in the first stage of mitosis, there occurs, among other things, a contraction of the chromosomes in the nucleus of the dividing cell; or take the much less technical statement that a fertilized goose egg, when properly hatched, will yield a gosling. Thesis M_1 implies that the biological entities and processes here referred to—goslings, goose eggs, cells, nuclei, chromosomes, fertilization, and mitosis—can all be fully characterized in physico-chemical terms. The most plausible construal of this claim is that the corresponding biological terms, 'gosling', 'cell', etc., can be *defined* with the help of terms taken from the vocabulary of physics and chemistry. Let us refer to this more specific version of M_1 as M_1'. Similiarly, if all biological phenomena—and thus, in particular, all the uniformities expressed by biological laws—are to be explainable by means of physico-chemical principles, then all the laws of biology will have to be derivable from the laws and theoretical principles of physics and chemistry. The thesis—let us call it M_2'—that this is indeed the case may be regarded as a more specific version of M_2.

Jointly, the statements M_1' and M_2' express what is often called the thesis of *reducibility of biology to physics and chemistry*. This thesis concerns both the concepts and the laws of the disciplines concerned: reducibility of the concepts of one discipline to those of another is construed as definability of the former in terms of the latter; reducibility of the laws is analogously construed as derivability. Mechanism may thus be said to assert the reducibility of biology to physics and chemistry. The denial of this claim is sometimes referred to as the thesis of the *autonomy of biology* or, better, of biological

concepts and principles. Neovitalism thus affirms the autonomy of
biology and supplements this claim with its doctrine of vital forces.
Let us now consider the mechanistic theses in more detail.

The thesis M_1' concerning the definability of biological terms is
not meant, of course, to assert the possibility of assigning physico-
chemical meanings to biological terms by arbitrary stipulative
definitions. It takes for granted that the terms in the vocabulary of
biology have definite technical meanings but claims that, in a sense
we must try to clarify, their import can be adequately expressed
with the help of physical and chemical concepts. The thesis, then,
affirms the possibility of giving what we broadly called "descriptive
definitions" of biological concepts in physico-chemical terms. But
the definitions in question could hardly be expected to be analytic
[=equivalent in meaning]. For it would obviously be false to claim
that for every biological term—for example, 'goose egg', 'retina',
'mitosis', 'virus', 'hormone'—there exists an expression in physico-
chemical terms that has the same meaning in the sense in which
'spouse' may be said to have the same meaning as, or to be
synonymous with, 'husband or wife'. It would be very difficult to
name even one biological term for which a physico-chemical
synonym can be specified; and it would be preposterous to saddle
mechanism with this construal of its claim. But descriptive definition may also be understood in a less stringent sense, which does
not require that the definiens [=the explanation given of the word
or phrase] have the same meaning . . . as the definiendum [=the
word or phrase being defined], but only that it have the same extension or application. The definiens in this case specifies conditions that, as a matter of fact, are satisfied by all and only those instances to which the definiendum applies. A traditional example is
the definition of 'man' by 'featherless biped'; it does not assert that
the word 'man' has the same meaning as the expression 'featherless
biped', but only that it has the same extension, that the term 'man'
applies to all and only those things that are featherless bipeds, or
that being a featherless biped is both a necessary and sufficient
condition for being a man. Statements of this kind might be referred to as *extensional definitions;* they can be schematically expressed
in the form

————has the same extension as———

The definitions to which a mechanist might point to illustrate
and support his claim concerning biological concepts are of this extensional type: they express necessary and sufficient physico-
chemical conditions for the applicability of biological terms, and
they are therefore the results of often very difficult biophysical or
biochemical research. This is illustrated by the characterization of
substances such as penicillin, testosterone, and cholesterol in terms
of their molecular structures—an achievememt that permits the

"definition" of the biological terms by means of purely chemical ones. But such definitions do not purport to express the *meanings* of the biological terms. The original meaning of the word 'penicillin', for example, would have to be indicated by characterizing penicillin as an antibacterial substance produced by the fungus *penicillium notatum;* testosterone is originally defined as a male sex hormone, produced by the testes; and so forth. The characterization of these substances by their molecular structure is arrived at, not by meaning analysis, but by chemical analysis; the result constitutes a biochemical discovery, not a logical or philosophical one; it is expressed by empirical laws, not by statements of synonymy . . . .

The establishment of such definitions requires empirical research. We must conclude therefore that, in general, the question whether a biological term is "definable" by means of physical and chemical terms alone cannot be settled by just contemplating its meaning, nor by any other nonempirical procedure. Hence, the thesis M_1 cannot be established or refuted on *a priori* grounds, i.e., by considerations that can be developed "prior to"—or better, independently of—empirical evidence.

We turn now to the second thesis, M_2', in our construal of mechanism—the thesis asserting that the laws and theoretical principles of biology are derivable from those of physics and chemistry. It is clear that logical deductions from statements couched exclusively in physical and chemical terms will not yield characteristically biological laws, since these have to contain also specifically biological terms. To obtain such laws, we will need some additional premisses that express connections between physico-chemical characteristics and biological ones. The logical situation here is the same as in the explanatory use of a theory, where bridge principles are required, in addition to internal theoretical principles, for the derivation of consequences that can be expressed exclusively in pretheoretical terms. The additional premisses required for the deduction of biological laws from physico-chemical ones would have to contain both biological and physico-chemical terms and would have the character of laws connecting certain physico-chemical aspects of phenomenon with certain biological ones. A connective statement of this kind might take the special form of the laws we have just considered, which afford a basis for an extensional definition of biological terms. Such a statement asserts, in effect, that the presence of certain physico-chemical characteristics (e.g., a substance being of such and such a molecular structure) is both necessary and sufficient for the presence of a certain biological characteristic (e.g., being testosterone). Other connective statements might express physico-chemical conditions that are necessary but not sufficient, or conditions that are sufficient but not necessary, for a given biological characteristic. The generalizations 'where there is vertebrate life there is oxygen' and 'any nerve fiber conducts electric impulses' are of the former kind; the statement that the nerve gas tabun (characterized by its molecular structure) blocks nervous activity and thus causes death in man is of the second kind. Connective statements of various other types are also conceivable.

One very simple form that the derivation of a biological law from a physico-chemical one might take can be schematically described as follows: Let 'P_1', 'P_2' be expressions containing only physico-chemical terms, and let 'B_1', 'B_2' be expressions containing one or more specifically biological terms (and possibly physico-chemical ones as well). Let the statement 'all cases of P_1 are cases of P_2' be a physico-chemical law—we will call it L_p—and let the following connecting laws be given: 'All cases of B_1 are cases of P_1' and 'All cases of P_2 are cases of B_2' (the first states that physico-chemical conditions of kind P_1 are necessary for the occurrence of the biological state or condition B_1; the second, that physico-chemical conditions P_2 are sufficient for biological feature B_2). Then, as is readily seen, a purely biological law can be logically deduced from the physico-chemical law L_p in conjunction with the connecting laws; namely, 'all cases of B_1 are cases of B_2' (or: 'Whenever the biological features B_1 occur then so do the biological features B_2').

Generally, then, the extent to which biological laws are explainable by means of physico-chemical laws depends on the extent to which suitable connecting laws can be established. And that, again, cannot be decided by *a priori* arguments; the answer can be found only by biological and biophysical research.

The physical and chemical theories and the connecting laws available at present certainly do not suffice to reduce the terms and laws of biology to those of physics and chemistry. But research in the field is rapidly advancing and is steadily expanding the reach of a physico-chemical interpretation of biological phenomena. One might therefore construe mechanism as the view that in the course of further scientific research, biology will eventually come to be reduced to physics and chemistry. But this formulation calls for a word of caution. In our discussion, we have assumed that a clear distinction can be drawn between the terms of physics and chemistry on one hand and specifically biological terms on the other. And indeed, if we were presented with any scientific term currently in use, we would probably not find it difficult to decide in an intuitive fashion whether it belonged to one or to the other of those vocabularies or to neither. But it would be very difficult to formulate explicit general criteria by means of which any scientific term now in use, and also any term that might be introduced in the future, could be unequivocally assigned to the specific vocabulary of one particular discipline. Indeed, it may be impossible to give such criteria. For in the course of future research, the dividing line between biology and physics-and-chemistry may become as blurred as that between physics and chemistry has become in our time. Future theories might well be couched in novel kinds of terms functioning in comprehensive theories that afford explanations both for phenomena now called biological and for others now called physical or chemical. To the vocabulary of such a comprehensive unifying theory, the division into physico-chemical terms and biological terms might no longer be significantly applicable, and the notion of eventually reducing biology to physics and chemistry would lose its meaning.

Such a theoretical development, however, is not at hand as yet; and in the meantime, mechanism is perhaps best construed, not as a specific thesis or theory about the character of biological processes, but as a heuristic maxim, as a principle for the guidance of research. Thus understood, it enjoins the scientist to persist in the search for basic physico-chemical theories of biological phenomena rather than resign himself to the view that the concepts and principles of physics and chemistry are powerless to give an adequate account of the phenomena of life. Adherence to this maxim has certainly proved very successful in biophysical and biochemical research—a credential that cannot be matched by the vitalistic view of life.

The question of reducibility has been raised also for scientific disciplines other than biology. It is of particular interest in the case of psychology, where it has a direct bearing on the famous psycho-physical problem, i.e., the question of the relationship between mind and body. A reductionist view concerning psychology holds, roughly speaking, that all psychological phenomena are basically biological or physico-chemical in character; or more precisely, that the specific terms and laws of psychology can be reduced to those of biology, chemistry, and physics. Reduction is here to be understood in the sense defined earlier, and our general comments on the subject apply also to the case of psychology. Thus, the reductive "definition" of a psychological term would require the specification of biological or physico-chemical conditions that are both necessary and sufficient for the occurrence of the mental characteristic, state, or process (such as, intelligence, hunger, hallucination, dreaming) for which the term stands. And the reduction of psychological laws would require suitable connecting principles containing psychological terms as well as biological or physico-chemical ones.

Some such connecting principles, expressing sufficient or necessary conditions for certain psychological states are indeed available: depriving an individual of food or drink or opportunity for rest is sufficient for the occurrence of hunger, thirst, fatigue; the administration of certain drugs is perhaps sufficient for the occurrence of hallucinations; the presence of certain nerve connections is necessary for the occurrence of certain sensations and for visual perception; proper oxygen supply to the brain is necessary for mental activity and indeed for consciousness.

One especially important class of biological or physical indicators of psychological states and events consists in the publicly observable behavior of the individual to whom those states or events are ascribed. Such behavior may be understood to include both large-scale, directly observable manifestations, such as body movements, facial expressions, blushing, verbal utterances, performance of certain tasks (as in psychological tests), and subtler responses such as changes in blood pressure and heartbeat, skin conductivity, and blood chemistry. Thus, fatigue may manifest itself in speech utterances ("I feel tired", etc.), in a decreasing rate and quality of performance at certain tasks, in yawning, and in physiological changes; certain . . . emotional processes are accompanied by changes in apparent skin resistance, as measured by "lie detectors": the preferences and values a person holds express themselves in the way he responds when offered certain relevant choices: his beliefs, in verbal utterances that may be elicited from him, and also in the ways he acts—for example, a driver's belief that a road is closed may show itself in his taking a detour.

Certain characteristic kinds of "overt" (publicly observable) behavior that a subject in a given psychological state, or with a given psychological property, tends to manifest in appropriate "stimulus" or "test" situations are widely used in psychology as operational criteria for the presence of the psychological state or property in question. For intelligence or for introversion, the test situation might consist in presenting the subject with appropriate questionnaires; the response, in the answers the subject produces. The intensity of an animal's hunger drive will manifest itself in such behavioral features as salivation, the strength of the electric shock that the animal will take to reach food, or the amount of food it consumes. To the extent that the stimuli and the responses can be described in biological or physico-chemical terms, the resulting criteria may be said to afford partial specifications of meaning for psychological expressions in terms of the vocabularies of biology, chemistry, and physics. Though they are often referred to as operational definitions, they do not actually determine necessary and sufficient conditions for the psychological terms: the logical situation is quite similar to the one we encountered in examining the relation of biological terms to the physical and chemical vocabulary.

Behaviorism is an influential school of thought in psychology which, in all its different forms, has a basically reductionist orientation: in a more or less strict sense, it seeks to reduce discourse about psychological phenomena to discourse about behavioral phenomena. One form of behaviorism, which is especially concerned to ensure the objective public testability of psychological hypotheses and theories, insists that all psychological terms must have clearly specified criteria of application couched in behavioral terms, and that psychological hypotheses and theories must have test implications concerning publicly observable behavior. This school of thought rejects, in particular, all reliance on methods such as introspection, which can be used only by the subject himself in [an] exploration of his mental world; and it does not admit as psychological data any of the "private" psychological phenomena—such as sensations, feelings, hopes, and fears—that introspective methods are said to reveal.

While behaviorists are agreed in their insistence on objective behavioral criteria for psychological characteristics, states, and events, they differ (or are noncommittal) on the question whether or not psychological phenomena are distinct from the corresponding, often very subtle and complex, behavioral phenomena—whether the latter are only their public manifestations, or whether psychological phenomena are, in some clear sense, identical with certain complex behavioral properties, states, or events. One recent version of behaviorism, which has exerted a strong influence on the philosophical analysis of psychological concepts, holds that psychological terms, though ostensibly referring to mental states and to processes "in the mind", serve, in effect, simply as a means of speaking about more or less intricate aspects of behavior—specifically, about propensities or dispositions to behave in characteristic ways in certain situations. On this view, to say of a person that he is intelligent is to say that he tends to act, or has a disposition to act, in certain characteristic ways; namely, in ways that we would normally qualify as intelligent action under the circumstances. . . .

This conception, which has contributed greatly to clarifying the role of psychological concepts, is evidently reductionist in tenor; it presents the concepts of psychology as affording an effective and convenient way of speaking about subtle patterns of behavior. . . .

Another discipline to which it has been thought that psychology might eventually be reduced is that of physiology, and especially neurophysiology; but again, a full reduction in the sense we specified earlier is not remotely in sight.

Questions of reducibility arise also with respect to the social sciences, particularly in connection with the doctrine of methodological individualism, according to which all social phenomena should be described, analyzed, and explained in terms of the situations of the individual agents involved in them and by reference to the laws and theories concerning individual behavior. The description of an agent's "situation" would have to take into account his motives and beliefs as well as his physiological state and various biological, chemical, and physical factors in his environment. The doctrine of methodological individualism may therefore be viewed as implying the reducibility of the specific concepts and laws of the social sciences (in a broad sense, including group psychology, the theory of economic behavior, and the like) to those of individual psychology, biology, chemistry, and physics. The problems raised by this claim . . . belong to the philosophy of the social sciences and have been mentioned here . . . as a further illustration of the problem of theoretical reducibility and as an example of the many logical and methodological affinities between the natural and the social sciences.

Reading Questions

1. In general what must be accomplished if we are to say one science has been reduced to another?
2. Why does the author reject the view that reduction requires analytic definitions of one science's vocabulary in terms of the other science's vocabulary? What kind of definition seems more reasonable?
3. Why is the question of the reducibility of biology to chemistry and physics an empirical question? What sorts of empirical data must be sought to accomplish the reduction?
4. Why might the idea of reducing biology to chemistry and physics eventually lose its meaning?
5. What would be involved in reducing psychology to biology or sociology to psychology? Why might these reductions seem plausible?

Questions for Reflection and Research

1. How do neo-vitalists defend their view?
2. If any of the reductions described in the selection can be accomplished, what implications (especially philosophical implications) will the reductions have?
3. Compare Hempel's discussion of the reduction of psychology with the body-mind selection by Edwards (#11) and the life-after-death selection by Ducasse (#13). Does either selection provide reasons to doubt the success of such a reduction?
4. What considerations can be advanced against methodological individualism?
5. How do we now distinguish between the sciences?
6. If all sciences are reducible to physics, will this mean humans are nothing but complex machines?

Two Models for Explanation in the Sciences

The Author: Michael Martin (b. 1932) was educated at Arizona State University, the University of Arizona, and Harvard University. His research interests have been in the philosophy of science, philosophy of psychology, and philosophy of law. He has taught at the University of Colorado and Boston University.

The Selection: A description is given of two different models of causal explanation that have been accepted by many philosophers of science. The deductive-nomological model involves universal causal laws and results in deductively certain conclusions. The occurrence of laws in such explanations has led to their being called nomological explanations—for *nomological* means containing laws. The statistical-probabilistic model uses statistical causal laws and leads to explanations that are only probable. It is stressed that these models may not be explicitly used in science, but they do provide standards for complete causal explanations. The selection is demanding reading.

THE DEDUCTIVE-NOMOLOGICAL MODEL OF EXPLANATION

One attempt to formulate a formal notion of causal explanation is the so-called *deductive-nomological* (D–N) model of explanation. This model has played an extremely important role in recent philosophical discussions of explanation in science. It has been expounded by many well-known philosophers of science, such as [Carl G.] Popper [b. 1902], [Carl] Hempel [b. 1905], and [Ernest]

From *Concepts of Science Education: A Philosophical Analysis* by Michael Martin, pp. 50–58. Copyright © 1972 by Scott, Foresman and Company. Reprinted by permission.

Nagel [b. 1901], and discussion of this model by way of either criticism or defense has dominated recent philosophical literature on
the topic of explanation in science.

Stated informally, the model is this: A causal explanation of some
event is achieved when that event is subsumed under some causal
law. Thus someone might ask why a particular substance conducts
electricity. The answer might be that the substance in question is
copper and that all copper conducts electricity. This subsumption
constitutes the explanation of the phenomenon in question. Again,
someone might ask why a rod lengthened. The answer might be
that the rod is made of copper and that the rod was heated and
copper expands when it is heated. Again the phenomenon to be
explained is being brought under a causal law.

Put in the form of an argument, the two explanations would look
like this:

(1) All copper conducts electricity.
     This substance is copper.
     ∴ This substance conducts electricity.

(2) All copper expands when heated.
     This rod is made of copper.
     ∴ This rod expands.

[The three dots are a symbol meaning "therefore": the line sepa-
rates the premises and conclusion of an argument.—ED.] It should
be noted that both of these explanatory arguments have the same
general characteristics. At least one of the premises is a causal law;
all the others are statements describing particular conditions that
hold in a given situation. The conclusion which describes the event
to be explained follows deductively from the premises.

Thus the general form of explanation, according to the D–N
model, is this: Given a certain set of causal laws and statements of
what have been called initial conditions, a statement describing the
event to be explained follows. Put in a diagrammatic way, a D–N
explanation would look like this:

$$\text{deduction} \begin{bmatrix} L_1 \ \& \ L_2 \ldots L_n & \text{causal laws} \\ C_1 \ \& \ C_2 \ldots C_n & \text{statements of initial conditions} \\ E \end{bmatrix}$$

The laws and the sentences stating the initial conditions have to
meet certain . . . requirements:

R_1 All the laws and initial conditions have to be essential for
the deduction.

R_2 All the sentences have to be testable.

R_3 E must logically follow from the statement of initial conditions and laws.

There has been some disagreement over a fourth requirement.
Some philosophers have argued:

R_4 All the sentences in the explanation must be true.

Others have argued:

R'_4 All the sentences in the explanation must be well confirmed relative to available evidence.

It should be clear that R_4 and R'_4 are logically independent requirements—neither requirement entails the other. Some sentences might be true without the available evidence confirming them. On the other hand, some sentences might be well confirmed by the available evidence and yet be false. In the first case, a scientist would have no justification for supposing he had a true explanation; in the second case the scientist would be justified in supposing that the explanation was true although the explanation was not true. In any case, it appears that there is no real disagreement here since two different formal notions of causal explanation are at issue. R_1, R_2, R_3, R_4 specify the requirements for a *true causal explanation;* R_1, R_2, R_3, R'_4 specify the requirements for a *justified causal explanation.*

Let us consider one of the examples already given in the light of these requirements, namely, the explanation of why the rod lengthened as expressed in argument (2) above. The first requirement, R_1, is certainly fulfilled. The law and statements of initial conditions are essential for the deduction; none of these statements can be omitted if the conclusion is to follow. The second requirement, R_2, holds also since these sentences are testable. R_3 holds, for the conclusion "This rod expands" logically follows from the premises. Furthermore, R'_4 holds, for in the light of the available evidence the law and initial conditions are well confirmed. So argument (2) is a justified causal explanation of why the rod expanded. Moreover, according to confirmation theorists, R'_4 gives us good reason to suppose that R_4 holds. Hence, in their view we have good reason to suppose that this is a true causal explanation.

. . . It should be stressed that pragmatic considerations may make it unnecessary or undesirable for the actual discourse of one who explains something causally to someone to conform exactly to the D–N model. For example, Jones may explain the lengthening of the rod to Smith by saying, "You see, the rod was heated." This may be all that is necessary or desirable to say to Smith. Nevertheless, Jones' discourse would be explanatory . . . only because other things were tacitly assumed, namely, that the rod was made out of copper, that the law holds, and that the description of the event explained can be deduced from the law and the statement of initial conditions. The D–N model thus clarifies the tacit assumptions that must be made in an explanatory activity if its discourse is to be logically and epistemologically adequate.

The above point has often been misunderstood in criticism of the

D–N model. Some philosophers of science have seemed to assume that, because the actual explanatory discourse of scientists does not conform to the requirement of the model, the model is incorrect. But the D-N model does not purport to reflect the actual explanatory discourse of the scientist. . . . The D–N model purports to specify epistemological and logical requirements for explanatory discourse abstracted from practical considerations. . . .

To be sure, the requirements specified by the model might be wrong, and arguments might be offered which show that one or more of these requirements should be changed. However, merely showing that scientists do not put their explanatory discourse into D–N form, or that doing so would be inconvenient for scientists, is . . . irrelevant to showing that the D–N model is incorrect. . . . .

In any case, one of the major advantages claimed by advocates of the D–N model is its ability to indicate the logical and epistemological problems in explanations. Consider, for example, the following piece of explanatory discourse:

> The causal factor responsible for the extinction of the large reptiles of antiquity–commonly known as dinosaurs–was the change in vegetation brought about by a change in climate. The plant-eating dinosaurs could not eat the tougher vegetation and died out. The flesh-eating dinosaurs who preyed on the plant-eating ones perished in turn.

What assumptions are being made by the speaker and what factual support is there for them? Perhaps these assumptions can be spelled out and their backing elaborated. If so, we might have a full-fledged D–N explanation. However, if they cannot be, this discourse will simply be an outline or a sketch of a causal explanation–what has been sometimes called an *explanation sketch*. That the discourse as it stands needs to be filled in in accordance with the D–N model is made clear by the following:

SKETCH OF D–N EXPLANATION I

Laws assumed.	?
Statement of initial conditions apparently assumed.	C_1 Some dinosaurs are plant eaters.
	C_2 During a certain period of time, $t_1 - t_2$, plants in the dinosaurs' environment become tougher.
Other statements of initial conditions.	?

∴ Plant-eating dinosaurs died off during period $t_1 - t_2$.

SKETCH OF D–N EXPLANATION II

Laws assumed.		?
Statement of initial conditions apparently assumed.	C_1'	Some dinosaurs were flesh eaters.
	C_2'	The flesh-eating dinosaurs preyed on the plant-eating dinosaurs.
	C_3'	Plant-eating dinosaurs died off during period t_1-t_2.
	C_4'	Flesh-eating dinosaurs could find no other animals to prey on that would sustain them.
Other statements of initial conditions.		?

∴ Flesh-eating dinosaurs died off during period t_1-t_2.

Putting the explanatory discourse into D–N form exposes the logical gaps and makes explicit what assumptions are being made and what others may have to be made. One can begin to see possible weak spots in the explanatory argument. For example, is C_2 true? If so, why weren't the plants too tough for other plant eaters to eat? It is clear that not all the plant-eating animals died out during this period. Is C_4' true? (This condition surely must be assumed, for unless it is there would seem to be no reason why the flesh-eating dinosaurs could not have survived on nondinosaurs.) What is the supporting evidence? If there is none, this is a weak spot in the sketch. What laws are assumed by the explanation? What is the supporting evidence for these alleged laws?

Bringing questions like these to the fore has at least two values. First, it provides the scientific investigator with some guidelines for research in filling in the details of the sketch and producing a more complete explanatory argument. Secondly, it provides the science teacher or student of science with insight and understanding into the gaps in our scientific knowledge. . . .

THE STATISTICAL–PROBABILISTIC (S–P) MODEL OF EXPLANATION

So far we have assumed that the explanatory discourse should be evaluated in terms of the D–N model. Such a model assumes that general laws are necessary for a full-fledged explanation. Thus we have assumed that the laws presupposed in the explanation would have the form "All A and B." For example, perhaps a rough statement of a law presupposed in I above is:

L_1 All plant-eating land animals die when they no longer are able to eat the plants within a radius of two thousand miles from where they live.

However, this is not the only possible reconstruction of explanatory discourse. Perhaps instead of general laws being assumed, statistical laws are assumed. Such a reconstruction has certain advantages. Perhaps L_1 as it stands is false. Perhaps some land animals might be capable of traveling long distances to new environments where they can eat the vegetation. A more plausible assumption might be:

L_2 Most plant-eating land animals die when they no longer are able to eat the plants within a radius of two thousand miles from where they live.

Now such a statistical law could not explain—even when combined with appropriate initial conditions—why all dinosaurs died out; at most it would explain why most of them did. However, this incompleteness may suggest that more laws—either general or statistical—are needed for a complete explanation.

In any case, the consideration of statistical laws suggests a different formal model of explanation. Let us call this model the *statistical–probabilistic* (S–P) model. This model is like the D–N model except for two things: (1) The laws in the premises of an explanatory argument are statistical laws rather than general laws. An example of such a law would be L_2 above. Such laws might be stated in a precise quantitative form, e.g., 90 percent of A's are B, or in a less precise way, e.g., Most A's are B, or Nearly all A's are B, or The proportion of A's that are B is close to 1, or Any A has a good chance of being B. (2) The relation between the premises and the sentences describing the event, state, or process to be explained is probabilistic rather than deductive. Consider, for example, the following S–P explanation. We will assume that the premises of the argument are true.

Nearly all people having streptococcal infections who are treated with penicillin recover.
Jones had a streptococcal infection and was treated with penicillin.

∴ Jones recovered.

Now the conclusion cannot be logically deduced from the premises as in a D–N explanation. For the premises are true and yet the conclusion could be false. However, in a valid deductive argument if the premises are true, the conclusion must be true also. Nevertheless, the conclusion is probable relative to these premises. From this example we can abstract the general form of S–P explanations and diagram this form as follows:

probable	L_1 & $L_2 \ldots L_n$	statistical laws
	C_1 & $C_2 \ldots C_n$	statements of initial conditions
inference	E	statement describing event to be explained. . . .

It is possible in branches of science in which statistical laws are used that these statistical laws will someday be replaced by general laws. Thus the statistical laws of evolutionary theory may someday be replaced by general laws. Such a replacement might involve, for example, discovering some additional property of organisms or of their environments which, when combined with the organisms' advantageous characteristics, would provide a nomologically sufficient condition for survival. The general form of a replacement would be this:

(1) Original statistical law:
For every x, if x has A, then with frequency F x has B.
(2) Replaced by general law:
For every x, if x has A and P, then x has B

The replacement would turn on finding a suitable property P. Thus the use of statistical laws in science is logically compatible with the existence and eventual discovery of such a property P, and with the existence and eventual discovery of general laws. Whether such general laws do exist and whether, if they do, they will ever be discovered is another question.

Reading Questions

1. What is the D–N model of explanation? How does it differ from the S–P model?
2. What requirements must a legitimate D–N explanation meet? What difference is there between the two versions of the fourth requirement?
3. Should scientists always try to formulate their explanations to conform to one of the two models? What advantages are claimed for explanations that conform to the models?
4. What is an explanation sketch?
5. What changes could lead one to change an explanation in the S–P form to a D–N form?

Questions for Reflection and Research

1. Is the goal of science description or explanation or prediction or something else?

2. Can human behavior be explained using either model? (See selection #36 by Hospero, #38 by Louch, and #39 by Nagel.)

3. Are there other kinds of explanations than causal ones? If so, are the noncausal explanations inferior? Are all scientific explanations causal explanations? (See selections #33 by Troxell and Snyder and #36 by Hospers.)

4. How are laws explained? (See selection #36 by Hospers and #34 by Hempel.)

5. Can science explain everything? (For relevant considerations see selections #19 by Russell, #23 by Thompson, #24 by Earle, #36 by Hospers, and #38 by Louch.)

6. If every explanation uses premises, which it doesn't explain, does such an explanation explain anything?

What Is Explanation?

The Author: John Hospers (b. 1918) was educated at Central College, Iowa State University, and Columbia University. He has taught at a number of American universities, most recently at the University of Southern California. His publications are well known and are concerned primarily with topics in ethics, aesthetics, and the theory of knowledge.

The Selection: The author rejects the view that explaining is a matter of connecting the unfamiliar to the familiar. He asserts that to explain an event is to show how the event is an instance of a natural law. Questions about regressions of explanations, multiple explanations, explanations in terms of purposes, and ultimate explanations are all explored, with Hospers clearly expressing his position on each topic. He also points out a number of pitfalls that should be avoided when offering or discussing explanations. The selection is moderately demanding.

[One] account of the nature of explanation is that an event has been explained when it has been shown to be an instance of some class of events which is already familiar to us. For example, when a person's behaviour seems strange to us, we are satisfied when it is 'explained' to us as being really impelled by the same sort of motives and desires as occur in us, and are therefore familiar to us.

From "What Is Explanation?" by John Hospers, originally published in the *Journal of Philosophy*, 1946. The selection is from the revised version found in *Essays in Conceptual Analysis*, ed. Antony Flew (London: Macmillan & Co., Ltd.; New York: St. Martin's Press, 1956), pp. 94–119. Reprinted by permission of Macmillan & Co., Ltd., London and Basingstoke.

'Why is he introducing the man he hates to the woman he loves?'
'Because he wants them to fall in love with each other' would not
generally be accepted as an explanation, for this very reason. When
we observe that a balloon ascends rather than descends, unlike
most objects, and it is made clear to us that air has weight and that
the gas inside the balloon weighs less than would an equal volume
of air, we are satisfied; the phenomenon has been 'reduced' to
something already familiar to us in everyday experience, such as a
dense object sinking in water while a hollow one floats. The event is
no longer unusual, strange, or unique; it has been shown to illustrate a principle with which we were already acquainted. When we
want to know why gases diffuse when released into a chamber from
which the air has been pumped out, the explanation offered by the
kinetic theory of gases is satisfactory to us because it asserts that
molecules behave *like* particles with which we are already acquainted in our everyday experience. . . . .

Professor [P.W.] Bridgman [1882–1962]holds [in *The Logic of
Modern Physics*] that all explanation is of this kind:

I believe that examination will show that the essence of an explanation consists in reducing a situation to elements with which we are so familiar that
we accept them as a matter of course, so that our curiosity rests. . . .

And yet I am sure that such a view as this must be mistaken. In
the *first* place, we may seek explanations for the most familiar
events as well as of those unfamiliar to us. We may ask why stones
fall as well as why aeroplanes rise, and be curious for an answer
equally in both cases. True, our motivation for asking the latter
question is probably greater because the kind of phenomenon in
question is (or was) less familiar; most people would not think to
ask it about stones because the falling of stones is familiar and
usual—but the question can as legitimately be asked in the one case
as in the other. In the *second* place, the explanation may not be
familiar at all: it may be far less familiar than the event to be
explained. The discoloration of a painted kitchen wall when gas
heat is used may be a familiar phenomenon to the housewife—
surely more familiar than its explanation in terms of the chemical
combination of sulphur in the gas fumes with elements in the paint,
producing a compound that is dark in colour. Yet this is the true
explanation. If the explanation is not familiar, one is tempted to
say, it ought to be, as long as it is true. Surely its familiarity is irrelevant to its validity as an explanation. Familiarity is, in any case, a
subjective matter—what is familiar to you may not be familiar to
me; and yet the explanation, if true, is as true for me as for you.

The only grain of truth in the view that explaining is rendering
familiar seems to be this: the law that does the explaining may not
be familiar, *but* the fact that the phenomenon in question, such as
the flight of an aeroplane, *can* be subsumed under a law—the fact
that the behaviour *is* lawlike and hence predictable—tends to make
it less mysterious, less like a miracle, and thus in a sense more famil-

iar. To show that the behaviour of something is lawlike is to show it
to be a part of the order of nature, and in that sense familiar, although the particular law or laws stating the uniformity may be
quite unfamiliar.

In what, then, *does* explanation consist? The answer, I think, is
quite simple: . . . to explain an event is simply to bring it under a
law, and to explain a law is to bring it under another law. . . .

In saying that explanation is in terms of laws, I use the word 'law'
in a wider sense than is sometimes employed: in the sense I mean,
any uniformity of nature is a law. Thus, it is a law that iron rusts,
and it is a law that iron is magnetic—although both of these are
usually listed in textbooks as 'properties of iron' rather than as laws.
In this sense, it seems to me that explaining why something occurs
always involves a law. . . . .

Sometimes, I should add, all we have available is a 'statistical
law'—a law not of the form 'All A is B' or 'Whenever A, then B',
but, *e.g.,* '75 per cent of A is B'. Can such a 'law' constitute an explanation? I should be inclined to say that it is, although we would
still want an explanation of why 25 per cent of A's are *not* B's. If
water did not always boil at 212° F. but did so only 75 per cent of
the time, we might explain the boiling of this kettle of water by saying that its temperature had reached 212°, though we would still
want an explanation of why the kettle of water next to it, which had
also reached 212°, did not boil. In other words, our statistical law
would still not answer the question 'Why this and not that?' and in
order to answer *this* question, we would need a non-statistical law of
the form, 'Under such-and-such conditions, water always boils at
212° F., but under such-and-such other conditions, it does not'. It
would seem, then, that a statistical has in turn to be explained by a
non-statistical one, although of course we may not, at any given
stage in the progress of science, know of any non-statistical law by
which to explain the statistical one. . . .

Whether a statistical law can *always* be explained in terms of a
non-statistical one depends not only on our powers of discovery but
upon the nature of the universe. It is certainly no *a priori* truth that
nature's uniformities are all of the 100 per cent variety instead of
75 percent . . . .

So much for a general statement of what explanation consists of.
I should like now to append some comments and to answer some
questions to which the above account may give rise.

[i] Thus far we have been content to answer the question 'Why
does A do B?' by saying 'Because all A's do B'. But there are those
who say that such an answer is no explanation at all. 'To say that all
gases expand when heated', says Norman Campbell [1880-1949]
(*What Is Science?* . . .) 'is not to explain why hydrogen expands
when heated; it merely leads us to ask immediately why all gases
expand. An explanation which leads immediately to another question of the same kind is no explanation at all.'

I want to insist that the answer given *is* an explanation of the occurrence in question; to say 'Hydrogen is a gas, and all gases expand when heated' is a perfectly satisfactory answer to the question
why hydrogen expands when heated. But it is *not*, of course, an
answer to *another* question—Why do all gases expand when
heated?—and this is probably the question which the person meant
to ask in the first place. These questions must not be confused with
each other; I believe Campbell's position is the result of this confusion. It is fatally easy to telescope (unconsciously) two questions into
one, and then be dissatisfied with the answer. . . .

The situation may be illustrated in [the following] way. If I ask,
'Why did the water-pipes in my basement burst last night?' someone may answer that it is because the basement got too cold, and
another may answer that it is because water expands when it
freezes, while yet another may say that we do not know the 'real
explanation' unless we can state why water expands when it freezes.
Here, again we must separate the questions:

QUESTION 1. Why did the water-pipes break?
EXPLANATION. They always do when the temperature falls to below $32.°$
QUESTION 2. Why do they break when the temperature falls . . . etc.?
EXPLANATION. Because the water in them expands when it freezes, and
the water on expanding breaks the pipes.
QUESTION 3. Why does water expand when it freezes?
EXPLANATION. Here we try to answer in terms of the structure of the
water-molecule.

But to say that we have not explained (1) until we have explained
(3) is grossly to underestimate the number of phenomena for which
we do have perfectly satisfactory explanations. That is, we *do* have
explanations for (1) and (2), and our having them is *not* contingent
upon having an explanation for (3) . . . .

[ii] Can an event have *two* explanations? Why not? Let us suppose
that we want to explain an event E, and that we have a law saying
that every time conditions A are fulfilled, E happens, and another
law saying that every time conditions B are fulfilled, E happens. A
will then be a complete explanation for the occurrence of E, and B
will also be a complete explanation. Whether any such state of affairs actually occurs in the world is, of course, another question.
Most of the suggested double explanations of events are in fact
parts of a single explanation. Thus, for example, if we are asked to
explain why the burglar committed the robbery last night, the detective may explain it in terms of his expertness at picking locks, the
butler may explain it in terms of the family being out of the room,
the maid may say it was because the bedroom window was open, the
policeman may say it was because the night was foggy and visibility
at a minimum, the sociologist may explain it in terms of the criminal's background of slum conditions, and the psychologist may
explain it in terms of pseudo-aggressive impulses dating from a

childhood period marked by intense family quarrels. All these explanations are probably correct enough as far as they go. It may well be that in the absence of any one of these factors the burglary would not have occurred. But these are, it would surely seem, parts and aspects of *one* complete explanation—and in explaining human actions the whole explanation may be inconceivably complex. Still, the possibility remains that in *some* cases there may be two separate and complete explanations for an occurrence: at least it cannot be ruled out *a priori*. . . .

[iii] In evaluating the extent to which proffered explanations yield us genuine empirical knowledge (*i.e.* are real empirical laws), much care is required, for in this field the verbal booby-traps in our way are numerous and intricate.

If someone asked, 'Why is this object spherical?' and the reply were given, 'Because it's globular', everyone would recognize the answer to be trivial because it is analytic [= because it substitutes different words for the same idea]. Many so-called explanations do not give much more information than this, although even very bad ones are not usually quite as empty as this one. Even when one says that opium produces sleep because of its dormitive power, we are at least told that it is because of something within it that sleep is produced, not by some outside factor such as the atmosphere. When we ask why hydrogen combines with oxygen to form water, and are told that it is because hydrogen has an *affinity* for oxygen, again the reply is relatively empty: it tells us only that under certain conditions hydrogen does combine with oxygen but tells us nothing of why hydrogen rather than some other substances does this; but at least we know from the answer that there *is* a law relating the combination of elements to some set of conditions, though we do not yet know what this law is. And if we ask why the mother cat takes care of her kittens and fights to defend them, and are told that it is ᐧbecause she has a *maternal instinct*, at least we know that the activity is not a learned one—and this is indeed something—although again the answer may not give us the kind of thing we were asking for. Most explanations in terms of instinct, tendency, affinity, power, and faculty are of this next-to-worthless kind, conveying only a minimum of information, and leading us to ask a why-question of the explanation given.

Let us observe how easily the invention of a name may make us assume that an explanation has been given. If it is asked, 'Why is iron magnetic?' and we answer, 'Because iron, cobalt, and nickel are magnetic', no one would think much of this as an explanation; but the moment we give a name to the behaviour of these metals, and call them, say, 'fero-affinitive', then when someone asks why iron is magnetic, we can say, 'Why, because it's a fero-affinitive metal, that's why'. And yet no more has been said in the second case than in the first. Similarly, if we had a name for the tendency of seeds to sprout upwards to reach the surface of the ground, people would be readier to say that their tendency to rise could be *explained* by the presence of this property. Yet a name for what it does is a different thing from an explanation of why it does what it does. . . .

[iv] No mention has thus far been made of explanation in terms of *purpose*. And yet this is the oldest concept of explanation and still the one most frequently employed by primitive peoples. And there are contexts in which we still employ the concept of purpose in giving explanations—for example, when we say that my purpose in going to the store was to do some Christmas shopping, and that this is *why* I went.

The word 'purpose' is, of course, ambiguous. (*a*) Most frequently in ordinary usage a purpose is something of which I am conscious—a conscious intent to do something. The conscious intent is not the *whole* of the purpose: part of the criterion of whether it is my purpose to do X is whether I am disposed towards doing X, whether I take steps towards X and do X if I have the chance. (*b*) Some tendencies to act are not accompanied by any state of awareness; and here psychologists speak of *un*conscious purposes. We need not stop here over the exact interpretation of this way of speaking; let us simply say that one is said to have X as his unconscious purpose if he consistently acts, without intending it, so as to bring about X. (*c*) We speak of inanimate objects as having purposes—for example, the purpose of a hammer is to drive nails. This of course is not a purpose consciously envisaged by the hammer. All we mean here is that the mechanical object *reflects* the conscious purposes of its makers. *We* had a conscious purpose in making the hammer, and thus we speak elliptically of the hammer as having that purpose. Strictly speaking, of course, the purpose is ours and not the hammer's.

In all of these cases a purpose implies a purposer, or someone to have the purpose. We do sometimes use the word 'purpose' in another sense which carries no such implication, (*d*) when we say, 'What is the purpose of the heart?' 'To pump blood through the body.' Here purpose simply means function—*i.e.* what does it *do*? what part does it play in the bodily economy? If the word 'purpose' is used here I would view it as a 'degenerate' usage—a misleading locution in which another word, 'function', would serve much better. It is true that someone, in asking the purpose of the heart, might have in mind a theological question, 'What purpose did God have in endowing us with this organ?' but if this is meant, we are back again to purpose in sense 1, in which purpose implies a purposer and the word 'purpose' refers to conscious intent—the only difference now being that it is God's intent and not ours that is in question. But this, of course, is not what medical men generally have in mind when they ask purpose-questions about parts of organisms; else every such medical question would be a disguised theological question.

Having disentangled these senses of 'purpose', let us ask about the legitimacy of purposive explanations. Briefly I think it comes to this: explanations require laws, and if there are laws *about* purposes, there is no reason why they cannot figure in some explanations just as laws about falling bodies figure in other explanations. To the extent that laws about purposes have been established, they can be used as explanations like any other laws. Unfortunately the only laws (if any) that we are in a position to make about purposes are about human ones. Explanations in terms of divine purposes cannot be employed because no laws about divine purposes have ever been established. Even explanations of biological events in terms of animal purposes is frowned upon: we do not count it an explanation if it is said that the hen sits on her eggs *in order to* hatch chicks, because we have no indication that the hen does so with this purpose in mind; even if this is true, we do not know it, and therefore we cannot use it as a law in our explanation. In the human realm alone we know that purposes exist, and only there can we therefore employ them in explanations. We can even deduce conclusions from them, thus:

People act so as to fulfill their purposes, unless prevented by external circumstances.

My purpose was to go shopping, and I was not prevented . . . etc.

Therefore, I went shopping.

This way of putting it may sound rather silly, as the deductive model often does, but at any rate a deduction can be achieved from premises which are in all probability true.

The chief mistake which people are in the habit of making with regard to purposive explanation is probably that of wanting an answer to a why-question in terms of purpose when the conditions under which a purpose-answer is legitimate are not fulfilled. People extend their questioning unthinkingly from areas in which purposive explanation is in order into areas in which it is not. Thus: 'Why did he go to New York?' 'Well, in response to impulses from certain centres in his brain, some muscles in his arms and legs started moving towards the airport and . . .' 'No, that's not what I mean. I mean, why did he go? what did he go for? what purpose did he have in view?' 'He went in order to see some operas.' Contrast this with the following: 'Why did he die?' 'Well, a bullet entered his lung, puncturing some blood vessels, and the blood filled his lung so that he couldn't breathe any more, and . . .' 'No, that's not what I mean. I mean, *why* did he die?' But here we can no longer give an answer in terms of purpose—unless, that is, our talk is rooted in a theological context and we are willing to say that, just as the first person went to New York because he wanted to see operas, so the second person died because God had some purpose (intent) in seeing to it that he was murdered. If this is what is meant, one could try to answer the question in the theistic context of divine purposes; but if this context is rejected, the why-question demanding an answer in terms of purpose is meaningless, because an answer is being demanded when the only conditions under which the question is meaningful are not fulfilled.

This point is worth emphasizing because it is so often ignored in practice. Having received answers to why-questions when these questions were meaningful and explanations could be given, people continue to use why-questions even when they no longer know what they are asking for. One need not be surprised that no answer is forthcoming to such questions. And in our discouragement with such questions we are all too prone to make a mistake ourselves and terminate an exasperating series of why-questions with a remark such as, 'That's just something we don't know,' as if it were like cases where something definite is being asked but we do not yet know the laws which explain the phenomena we are asking about. If something in the case is not known, there must be something in the case which we could fail to know. If we are to ask a meaningful question, we must know what it is that we are asking for; only then can we recognize an answer as being one when we do find it.

[v] This leads us directly into an important question, How far can explanation go? We may explain an event in terms of a law, and this law in terms of other laws, and so on? but must we not finally come to a stop? The bursting of the pipes is explained by the expansion of water on freezing; let us assume that water expands on freezing because the water-molecule has such-and-such a structure; now why does the water-molecule have this structure? Perhaps this can some day be explained by reference to electron-proton arrangements within the atom, and this in turn by reference to the disposition of more minute particles (if they can be called such) yet to be discovered; but sooner or later must we not say, 'That's just the way things are—this is just an ultimate law about the universe. We can explain other things in terms of it, but it we cannot explain'? Are there ultimate laws, laws which explain but cannot even in principle be explained?

In practice we come rather quickly to laws which cannot be explained further. Laws about atomic structure are typical of such laws. Laws of psycho-physical correlation are another example. *Why* do I have a certain colour-sensation which I call red, indescribable but qualitatively different from all others, when light within a certain range of wave-length impinges upon my retina, and another indescribably different sensation which I call yellow when rays of another wave-length strike the retina? That this wave-length is correlated with this visual experience seems to be sheer 'brute fact'—a law which cannot be explained in terms of anything more ultimate than itself.

At the same time, we should be careful in dismissing any uniformity we cannot explain as a 'brute fact' or 'basic law'. Many things, such as why this element has this melting-point and these spectral lines, were once considered basic and unexplainable properties of the element, but have since been explained in terms of the intramolecular structure of the element. No matter how much at a loss we may be for an explanation, we can always ask and speculate. If it had been accepted as a basic law that water starts to expand when it gets below 39° F., we would never have gone on to discover anything about the structure of the water-molecule. Fruitful scientific procedure depends on assuming that no given law is basic; if scientists did not continue always to ask the question 'Why?' the process of scientific enquiry would stop dead in its tracks.

Thus, if there *are* basic laws, it seems that we cannot know of any given law that it is one. We can know that it is *not*, by explaining it in terms of other laws; but how could we know that it *is*? Discovering basic laws is . . . similar to discovering uncaused events: if there are uncaused events, we can never know that there are, for all we can safely say is that we have not yet found causes for them.

One further point about basic or ultimate laws: If a law is really a basic one, any request for an explanation of it is self-contradictory. To explain a law is to place it in a context or network of wider and more inclusive laws; a basic law is by definition one of which this cannot be done; therefore to ask of an admittedly basic law that it be explained is implicitly to deny that it is basic and thus to deny the very premise of the argument. It is a request for explanation in a situation where by one's own admission no more explaining can be done.

Like so many others, this point may seem logically compelling but psychologically unsatisfying. Having heard the above argument, one may still feel inclined to ask, 'Why are the basic uniformities of the universe the way they are, and not some other way? Why should we have just *these* laws rather than other ones? I want an *explanation* of why they are as they are.' I must confess here, as an autobiographical remark, that I cannot help sharing this feeling: I want to ask why the laws of nature, being contingent, are as they are, even though I cannot conceive of what an explanation of this would be like, and even though by my own argument above the request for such an explanation is self-contradictory. The fact is, as we saw above, that why-questions have had answers so many times that we tend automatically to ask them here even when they can have no answers because we have ripped them out of the only context in which they have meaning—like the situation of the child who, being told what is above the table and above the ceiling of his room and above the house and above the earth, now asks what is above the universe. The question has now gone outside the context of meaningful discourse, and so has the request for the explanation of a basic law. We should remember: to explain is to explain *in terms of something,* and if *ex hypothesi* [=by hypothesis] there is no longer any something for it to be explained in terms of, then the request for an explanation is self-contradictory: it demands on the one hand that you explain X in terms of a Y while insisting simultaneously that there is no Y. . . .

Reading Questions

1. Why does Hospers reject the familiarity theory of explanation?
2. Think of some quite ordinary explanations and attempt to explain the same events by bringing them under laws. Are the two kinds of explanations considerably different?
3. Why does Campbell want to reject some explanations that Hospers does not? How does Hospers defend his position?
4. Does Hospers explain how he knows when multiple explanations should be regarded as part of one overall explanation?
5. What are the various almost worthless explanations that Hospers points out?
6. Does Hospers have any reservations about allowing explanations in terms of purposes?
7. How far can explanation go?

Questions for Reflection and Research

1. Are the accounts of explanation in selections #35 by Martin and #38 by Louch in agreement with Hospers?
2. Think up a number of explanations people might offer in quite different circumstances. Can they all be brought into harmony with Hospers' views?
3. If there are "brute facts" in the universe that we cannot explain, would this mean that the universe is ultimately mysterious?
4. Carefully read through some sections of science books in controversial areas of science (for example, sociobiology or some areas of psychology). Do any of the explanations offered in the science books exhibit the defects Hospers warns against?
5. Is Hospers' position implicitly a reductionist one? (See selection #34 by Hempel for an explanation of reductionism.)
6. Are requests for justification of conduct really requests for explanations? (For one answer see selection #38 by Louch.)

Explanations of Science to Nonscientists

The Author: L. Susan Stebbing (1885–1943) was born in London, England, and was educated in philosophy and logic at Cambridge University. She taught for many years at Bedford College, London. Her interests were issues in the foundations of science and metaphysical questions that seem to be forced on us by logic.

Arthur Eddington (1882–1944) is criticized in this selection. He was educated at Cambridge University and later taught astronomy there. His contributions to physics and astronomy won him several awards. He was knighted in 1930.

The Selection: Eddington not only was a well-known and respected scientist, he also attempted to popularize the findings of physics and to explain their philosophical implications. Stebbing's book, *Philosophy and the Physicists*, is a sustained attack on confusions involved in attempts by Eddington and others to popularize physics. In this excerpt she begins by calling attention to one of Eddington's analogies: that stepping on a plank is like stepping on a swarm of flies, that the plank has no solidity. She notes that this way of speaking is quite misleading and is not successful in explaining physicists' findings to nonphysicists.

Imagine the following scene. You are handed a dish containing some apples—rosy-cheeked, green apples. You take the one nearest to you, and realize that you have been 'had'. The 'apple' is too hard and not heavy enough to be really an apple; as you tap it with your finger-nail it gives out a sound such as never came from

From L. Susan Stebbing, *Philosophy and the Physicists* (London: Methuen & Co., Ltd., 1937; New York: Dover Publications, Inc., 1958), pp. 46–53. Reprinted by permission of Methuen & Co., Ltd.

tapping a 'real' apple. You admire the neatness of the imitation. To sight the illusion is perfect. It is quite sensible to contrast this ingenious fake with a 'real' apple, for a 'real' apple just is an object that *really* is an apple, and not only *seems* to be one. This fake is an object that looks to your eyes to be an apple, but neither feels nor tastes as an apple does. As soon as you pick it up you know that it is not an apple; there is no need to taste it. We should be speaking in conformity with the rules of good English if we were to say that the dish contained real apples and imitation apples. But this mode of speaking does not lead us to suppose that there are two varieties of *apples*, namely real and imitation apples, as there are Bramley Seedlings and Blenheim pippins. Again, a shadow may be thrown on a wall, or an image may be thrown through a lantern on to a screen. We distinguish the shadow from the object of which it is the shadow, the image from that of which it is the image. Shadow and image are apprehensible only by sight; they really are visual, i.e. *seeable*, entities. I can see a man, and I can see his shadow; but there is not both a *real* man and a *shadow* man; there is just the shadow of the man.

This point may seem to have been unduly laboured. It is, however, of great importance. The words "real" and "really" are familiar words; they are variously used in every-day speech, and are not, as a rule, used ambiguously. The opposition between a *real* object and an *imitation* of a real object is clear. So, too, is the opposition between 'really seeing a man' and having an illusion. We can speak sensibly of the distinction between 'the real size' and 'the apparent size' of the moon, but we know that both these expressions are extremely elliptical. The significance of the words "real" and "really" can be determined only by reference to the context in which they are used. Nothing but confusion can result if, in one and the same sentence, we mix up language used appropriately for the furniture of earth and our daily dealings with it with language used for the purpose of philosophical and scientific discussion.

A peculiarly gross example of such a linguistic mixture is provided by one of Eddington's most picturesque passages:

I am standing on a threshold about to enter a room. It is a complicated business. In the first place I must shove against an atmosphere pressing with a force of fourteen pounds on every square inch of my body. I must make sure of landing on a plank travelling at twenty miles a second round the sun—a fraction of a second too early or too late, the plank would be miles away. I must do this whilst hanging from a round planet head outward into space, and with a wind of aether blowing at no one knows how many miles a second through every interstice of my body. The plank has no solidity of substance. To step on it is like stepping on a swarm of flies. Shall I not slip through? No, if I make the venture one of the flies hits me and gives me a boost up again; I fall again and am knocked upwards by another fly; and so on. I may hope that the net result will be that I remain steady; but if unfortunately I should slip through the floor or be boosted too violently up to the ceiling the occurrence would be, not a violation of the laws of Nature, but a rare coincidence. (*Nature of the Physical World,* p. 342)

Whatever we may think of Eddington's chances of slipping through the floor, we must regard his usage of language in this statement as gravely misleading to the common reader. I cannot doubt that it reveals serious confusion in Eddington's own thinking about 'the nature of the physical world'. Stepping on a plank is not in the least like 'stepping on a swarm of flies'. This language is drawn from, and is appropriate to, our daily intercourse with the familiar furniture of earth. We understand well what it is like to step on to a solid plank; we can also imagine what it would be like to step on to a swarm of flies. We know that two such experiences would be quite different. The plank is solid. If it be securely fixed, it will support our weight. What, then, are we to make of the comparison of stepping on to a plank with stepping on to a swarm of flies? What can be meant by saying that 'the plank has no solidity of substance'?

Again, we are familiar with the experience of shoving against an obstacle, and with the experience of struggling against a strong head-wind. We know that we do not have 'to shove against an atmosphere' as we cross the threshold of a room. We can imagine what it would be like to jump on to a moving plank. We may have seen in a circus an equestrian acrobat jump from the back of a swiftly moving horse on to the back of another horse moving with approximately the same speed. We know that no such acrobatic feat is required to cross the threshold of a room.

I may seem too heavy-handed in my treatment of a picturesque passage, and thus to fall under the condemnation of the man who cannot see a joke and needs to be 'in contact with merry-minded companions' in order that he may develop a sense of humour. But the picturesqueness is deceptive; the passage needs serious criticism since Eddington draws from it a conclusion that is important. 'Verily,' he says, 'it is easier for a camel to pass through the eye of a needle than for a scientific man to pass through a door. And whether the door be barn door or church door it might be wiser that he should consent to be an ordinary man and walk in rather than wait until all the difficulties involved in a really scientific ingress [= act of entering] are resolved.' It is, then, suggested that an ordinary man has no difficulty in crossing the threshold of a room but that 'a really scientific ingress' presents difficulties. The suggested contrast is as absurd as the use of the adjective 'scientific' prefixed to 'ingress', in this context, is perverse. Whatever difficulties a scientist, by reason of his scientific knowledge, may encounter in becoming a member of a spiritual church, these difficulties bear no comparison with the difficulties of the imagined acrobatic feat. Consequently, they are not solved by the consideration that Eddington, no less than the ordinary man, need not hesitate to cross the threshold of his room. The false emotionalism of the picture is reminiscent of [James] Jeans's picture of human beings standing on 'a microscopic fragment of a grain of sand'. It is open to a similar criticism.

If Eddington had drawn this picture for purely expository purposes, it might be unobjectionable. The scientist who sets out to give a popular exposition of a difficult and highly technical subject must use what means he can devise to convey to his readers what it is all about. At the same time, if he wishes to avoid being misunderstood, he must surely warn his readers that, in the present stage of physics, very little can be conveyed to a reader who lacks the mathematical equipment required to understand the methods by which results are obtained and the language in which these results can alone find adequate expression. Eddington's picture seems to me to be open to the objection that the image of a swarm of flies used to explain the electronic structure of matter is more appropriate to the old-fashioned classical conceptions that found expression in a model than to the conceptions he is trying to explain. Consequently, the reader may be misled unless he is warned that nothing resembling the spatial relations of flies in a swarm can be found in the collection of electrons. No concepts drawn from the level of common-sense thinking are appropriate to sub-atomic, i.e. microphysical, phenomena. Consequently, the language of common sense is not appropriate to the description of such phenomena. Since, however, the man in the street tends to think in pictures and may desire to know something about the latest developments of physics, it is no doubt useful to provide him with some rough picture. The danger arises when the scientist uses the picture for the purpose of making explicit denials, and expresses these denials in common-sense language used in such a way as to be devoid of sense. This, unfortunately, is exactly what Eddington has done in the passage we are considering, and indeed, in many other passages as well.

It is worth while to examine with some care what exactly it is that Eddington is denying when he asserts that 'the plank has no solidity of substance'. What are we to understand by "solidity"? Unless we do understand it we cannot understand what the denial of solidity to the plank amounts to. But we can understand "solidity" only if we can truly say that the plank is solid. For "solid" just is the word we use to describe a certain respect in which a plank of wood resembles a block of marble, a piece of paper, and a cricket ball, and in which each of these differs from a sponge, from the interior of a soap-bubble, and from the holes in a net. We use the word "solid" sometimes as the opposite of "empty", sometimes as the opposite of "hollow", sometimes as the opposite of "porous". We may also, in a very slightly technical usage, contrast "solid" with "liquid" or with "gaseous". There is, no doubt, considerable variation in the precise significance of the word "solid" in various contexts. Further, as is the case with all words, "solid" may be misused, and may also be used figuratively. But there could not be a *misuse*, nor a *figurative* use, unless there were some correct and literal usages. The point is that the common usage of language enables us to attribute a meaning to the phrase "a solid plank"; but there is no common usage of language that provides a meaning for the word "solid" that would make sense to say that the plank on which I stand is not *solid*. We oppose the solidity of the walls of a house to the emptiness of its unfurnished rooms; we oppose the solidity of a piece of pumice-stone to the porous loofah sponge. We do not deny that the pumice-stone is to some degree porous, that the bricks of the wall have chinks and crevices. But we do not know how to use a word that has no sensible opposite. If the plank is non-solid, then what does "solid" *mean*? In [a] companion passage to the one quoted above, . . . Eddington depicts the physicist, about to enter a room, as reflecting that 'the plank is not what it appears to be—a continuous support for his weight'. This remark is absurd. The plank appears to be capable of supporting his weight, and, as his subsequent entry into the room showed, it *was* capable of supporting his weight. If it be objected that the plank is 'a support for his weight' but not 'a *continuous* support', I would reply that the word "continuous" is here used without any assigned meaning. The plank appears *solid* in that sense of the word "solid" in which the plank is, in fact, solid. It is of the utmost importance to press the question: If the plank appears to be *solid*, but is really *non-solid*, what does "solid" mean? If "solid" has no assignable meaning, then "non-solid" is also without sense. If the plank is non-solid, then where can we find an example to show us what "solid" means? The pairs of words "solid"—"empty", "solid"—"hollow", "solid"—"porous", belong to the vocabulary of common-sense language; in the case of each pair, if one of the two is without sense, so is the other.

This nonsensical denial of solidity is very common in popular expositions of the physicist's conception of material objects. . . .

Reading Questions

1. What is the point of the discussion of the word *real*?
2. What criticisms are leveled against the swarm-of-flies comparison?
3. What is wrong with using ordinary concepts to explain findings of subatomic physics?
4. Why is Eddington's denial of solidity senseless?

Questions for Reflection and Research

1. Can Russell in selection #19 also be charged with using ordinary concepts in peculiar ways?
2. Is there any way scientific findings can be conveyed accurately to nonscientists?
3. Summarize the main objections Stebbing makes in her book to popularizations of physics.
4. Read a current book or article that attempts to explain scientific findings to nonscientists. Does it mislead?
5. What reasons are there to want nonscientists informed of scientific findings? (See selections in Section 7.)

Human Conduct Requires Ad Hoc Explanations

The Author: A. R. Louch (b.1927) is a member of the philosophy faculty at Claremont Graduate School. He was educated at the University of California at Berkeley and Cambridge University in England. In addition to philosophy of the social sciences and philosophy of psychology, he has a special interest in philosophy of mind and theory of knowledge.

The Selection: It is pointed out that in ordinary life we succeed in explaining our behavior without resorting to generalizations and laws about human behavior. Nevertheless social scientists and psychologists have been persuaded that such ad hoc explanations usually are not really sufficient, and they seek explanations of conduct in terms of laws and generalizations. According to Louch such explanations turn out to be either irrelevant or uninformative. He asserts that when we seek explanations of human behavior, what we want to know is whether the behavior is justified. That is, explanations of behavior, unlike explanations of physical phenomena, are moral explanations. For such explanations ad hoc accounts are appropriate. As a consequence, the social and behavioral sciences are confused in their efforts. The selection is moderately demanding.

In daily life we succeed in accounting for our actions without recourse to general theories or statistical regularities. When we appeal to wants, plans, schemes, desires, intentions and purposes we render our actions intelligible to ourselves and our everyday auditors [= listeners]. More often than not, it would seem absurd to ren-

From *Explanation and Human Action* by A. R. Louch (Berkeley and Los Angeles: University of California Press, 1966), pp. 1–5. Copyright © 1966 by A. R. Louch, reprinted by permission of the University of California Press.

der our accounts explicit; they are implied in the ways we observe and describe behaviour. A student in my office reaches for a cigarette and matches, he strikes a match and lights the cigarette, inhales and exhales the smoke. It would not occur to me to accompany this set of observations of his actions with further comments designed to explain what he did. If I had to do so, I should appeal to his reaching for a cigarette as indicating a desire to smoke, and the rest of his actions as contributing to the same end. It would not occur to me or to my interlocutors [=questioners] to offer or demand general laws from which this action can be shown to follow, or regularities of which the connexion of this action and its motive would be an instance.

'Behavioural scientists' (i.e. psychologists and social scientists) and philosophers have put obstacles in the way of *ad hoc* explanations [=explanations for the particular case alone] by demanding that any explanation lean on generalities for its support. When these demands of philosophers of science or 'methodologists' are taken seriously, as they are very frequently by psychologists and sociologists, theories are developed which meet the formal requisite of generality, but which pay the price for it rather heavily. For these theories are often redundant and platitudinous or totally irrelevant to the behaviour they are designed to explain. When we say that a man seeks food because he is hungry, or kills his father because he has been cut out of the will, or equally, when we say that men band together in economic or political enterprises and religious and social ceremonies because of their beliefs, needs, or roles, we are offering explanations of cases which do not require the support of general or theoretical statements. Often enough, of course, patient and detailed observation is necessary to describe adequately what we wish to explain; but no further research of generalizing technique is required to add an explanation to this description. It is true that men generally seek food when hungry, but it would hardly be necessary or relevant to establish or invoke this generalization in order to proffer the claim that hunger led me to cook my dinner. . . .

But philosophers are inveterate generalizers . . . , and *ad hoc* answers thus leave qualms. The qualms grow as we extend the discussion to more complicated questions. If someone asks me why I took up philosophy it might seem reasonably decisive to say that I became concerned with conceptual difficulties that stand in the way of empirical discoveries. But if an unflattering psychiatrist should suggest that I was temperamentally unfitted for the more arduous work of the laboratory or market place I should find it difficult to challenge him with my *ad hoc* reasons. In some sense my reason is the reason, yet in a sense that leaves open a host of alternative explanations.

Moreover, it is not only professional or professed scientists who find themselves ready and able to challenge *ad hoc* reasons. The accounts we give of our own behaviour are frequently challenged in an unanswerable way by wives and mothers and friends. A wife scorns her husband's account of his night of drinking (a business deal, of course) or his animated conversation with a pretty girl at a party (her intelligent conversation) as transparent rationalizations. But we don't know when to speak of his excuses as reasons and when as rationalizations. It may be that a new contract as well as a headache was the consequence of the evening's entertainment, and that the girl had brains as well as looks, though nothing is remembered of what she said. Quite outside the needs expressed by philosophers and scientists, to tidy up or generalize or verify our hypotheses, we do want to accept some reasons as appropriate or plausible or correct, and reject others as rationalizations. But we are in a quandary if we attempt to draw the line, or frame criteria which would enable us to draw the line, between reasons and rationalizations.

We are tempted in such circumstances to deny the propriety of reason-giving accounts altogether, and suppose that human nature must await, as the sociologists say, its Galileo. Much of the rationale of work in the behavioural sciences has to do with this sort of expectation, and so it is that psychologists and sociologists feel their actions justified if they spend lifetimes collecting statistics and framing indices, computing the mathematical values of correlations and devising hypothetical constructs: it will all bear on the Galilean revolution in the human sciences just as Brahe's tables of planetary motion contributed to Kepler's hypotheses. [See selection # 1 for an account of early astronomy.—Ed.]

Still, much of the time our reasons are not challenged. At least some of the time such accounts must stand; otherwise we should hardly have grounds for singling out some instances as rationalizations. If I said I enjoyed complicated fiction like that of [Marcel] Proust [1871–1922] or [William] Faulkner [1897–1962] as an explanation for having their volumes on my shelves, yet when alone ferret out whodunits and scatological [=obscene] tracts, I should be rationalizing my possession of solemn novels. By the same token I should be giving an adequate account of my possession of whodunits and salacious [=obscene] paperbacks if I said I enjoyed them. So we distinguish between good and bad, or better and worse reasons; the problem is to see them formulated in such a way as to make clear why some of them are good and others are bad. And this is the difficulty.

How, then, can an explanation be adequate and yet have no implications beyond the case? One solution, quite popular among philosophers of history around the turn of the century, preserves *ad hoc* accounting, but does so by shrouding the business of explanation in mystery. According to the advocates of this kind of view, explaining human action is a matter of plumbing motives by means of a hypothetical experiment enabling the historian or sociologist to relive the actions of those whose lives he investigates. It is not at all clear, however accurate an account this may be of the historian's procedure, how successful divinations can be distinguished from the failures. . . .

The mystical and divinatory excesses of these philosophers have contributed much to the power of the opposite thesis that all explanation is general and theoretical in nature. Sometimes the advocates of this view follow a . . . line [similar to that of David Hume (1711–1776)], according to which the strategy of any explanation consists in an appeal to regularities. At others·it is supposed that explanation consists in bringing an event under a law, without claiming that the law is descriptive. An adequate explanation, on either form of this account, is one that can be shown to extend the account beyond the case in question, which, in its most usual form, is to predict. If either the inductive or the hypothetico-deductive strategies [See selection #35.—ED.] are taken as paradigm [=standards], something must be done about putative *ad hoc* accounts. Sometimes they are dismissed as irrelevant, being treated as rather trivial and uninteresting approximations of knowledge. At other times it is supposed that they disguise generalizations which could be brought forward in their defence, but which, because of their transparency or unimportance, do not need to be.

Neither of these alternatives, it seems to me, does justice to the business of *ad hoc* explanation. History, anthropology, journalism and our day-to-day observations attest the prevalence and importance of *ad hoc* accounts. We have, in fact, a rather rich knowledge of human nature which can only be assimilated to the generality pattern of explanation by invoking artificial and ungainly hypotheses about which we are much less secure than we are about the particular cases the generalizations are invoked to guarantee. Moreover, when we move . . . to a review of attempts by psychologists and sociologists to seek law-like explanations, we shall discover that these attempts normally result in redundancy and platitude, or else are irrelevant to the behaviour to be explained. . . .

The thesis I shall advance . . . and work out in detail in the remainder of the book, is simply this: when we offer explanations of human behaviour, we are seeing that behaviour as justified by the circumstances in which it occurs. Explanation of human action is moral explanation. In appealing to reasons for acting, motives, purposes, intentions, [and] desires . . . which occur in both ordinary and technical discussions of human doings, we exhibit an action in the light of circumstances that are taken to entitle or warrant a person to act as he does. . . .

The behavioural sciences have become established features of academic life. They play a crucial role in the political and social strategy of governments. Experts in these disciplines are looked to for professional advice. To oppose their influence is thus to find oneself opposed to intelligent action in government and social policy. And if one denies to them the right to frame hypotheses and form laws of human behaviour, one undercuts their status as scientists and experts.

But the truth, I think, is somewhat different. The intelligent and well-informed rearing of children, treatment of the mentally ill, and fashioning of policy is, no doubt, highly to be desired. But the observations pertinent to these areas are piecemeal, the conclusions tentative, and dependent upon a moral point of view. The machinery that behavioural scientists bring to bear on human action is, in contrast, general and theoretical, and in principle free of the context of moral discussion. Consequently, I will suggest, their efforts pass by the problems to which they are ostensibly addressed. Behavioural scientists are forced into a mistaken view of their subject-matter as a result of their preoccupation with a method they take to be necessary to any respectable inquiry.

Reading Questions

1. Why are general laws or regularities said not to be needed in explaining our conduct?
2. What problems beset attempts to explain behavior in terms of general laws?
3. What factors tend to make us receptive to the idea that our everyday ad hoc explanations are inadequate?
4. What is the author's conception of a moral explanation?

Questions for Reflection and Research

1. Does Louch think the social sciences and psychology have any useful role to play? If so, should their studies be classifiable as science? (See Louch's book.)
2. In what ways does Louch disagree with the views put forward in selections #35 by Martin, #36 by Hospers, and #39 by Nagel? Is there any area of agreement?
3. How does Louch develop his views in his book?
4. What critical responses have there been to Louch's conclusion by philosophers of science, psychologists, and social scientists?

Social Science Defended

The Author: Ernest Nagel (b.1901) was born in Czechoslovakia and came to the United States when ten years old. During his education at the City College of New York and Columbia University, his interests moved from mathematics to philosophy. He is one of the main figures in the philosophy of science in the twentieth century. For many years he taught at Columbia and served as the editor of two philosophy journals.

The Selection: The author first sets out the reasoning of those who argue that there can be no social sciences or that the social sciences are very different from the natural sciences. Those who hold such views assert that the explanation of human conduct involves values and/or psychological states that are not open to public observation. Is it true, however, that the study and explanation of human conduct must rely entirely on concepts that are "subjective"? A number of examples are cited in which non-subjective factors are needed to properly explain certain kinds of behavior. Even assuming that researchers must consider subjective states, it is not true that researchers are limited to studying their own imaginative reconstructions of others' feelings. Researchers can obtain objective data by observing behavior (including verbal responses). This selection is demanding reading.

A set of related methodological questions is raised by the familiar claim that objectively warranted explanations of social phenomena are difficult if not impossible to achieve, because those phenomena have an essentially "subjective" or "value-impregnated" aspect.

Excerpted from *The Structure of Science* (pp. 473–76, 480–85) by Ernest Nagel, © 1961 by Harcourt Brace Jovanovich, Inc. and reprinted with their permission.

The subject matter of the social sciences is frequently identified as purposive human action, directed to attaining various ends or "values," whether with conscious intent, by force of acquired habit, or because of unwitting involvement. A somewhat more restrictive characterization limits that subject matter to the responses men make to the actions of other men, in the light of expectations and "evaluations" concerning how these others will respond in turn. On either delimitation of that subject matter, its study is commonly said to presuppose familiarity with the motives and other psychological matters that constitute the springs of purposive human behavior, as well as with the aims and values whose attainment is the explicit or implicit goal of such behavior.

According to many writers, however, motives, dispositions, intended goals, and values are not matters open to sensory inspection, and can be neither made familiar nor identified by way of an exclusive use of procedures that are suitable for exploring the publicly observable subject matters of the "purely behavioral" (or natural) sciences. On the contrary, these are matters with which we can become conversant solely from our "subjective experience." Moreover, the distinctions that are relevant to social science subject matter (whether they are employed to characterize inanimate objects, as in the case of terms such as 'tool' and 'sentence,' or to designate types of human behavior, as in the case of terms such as 'crime' and 'punishment') cannot be defined except by reference to "mental attitudes" and cannot be understood except by those who have had the subjective experience of possessing such attitudes. To say that an object is a tool, for example, is allegedly to say that it is *expected* to produce certain effects by those who so characterize that object. Accordingly, the various "things" that may need to be mentioned in explaining purposive action must be construed in terms of what the human actors *themselves believe* about those things, rather than in terms of what can be discovered about the things by way of the objective methods of the natural sciences. As one proponent of this claim states the case, "A medicine or a cosmetic, e.g., for the purposes of social study, are not what cures an ailment or improves a person's looks, but what people think will have that effect." And he goes on to say that, when the social sciences explain human behavior by invoking men's knowledge of laws of nature, "what is relevant in the study of society is not whether these laws of nature are true in any objective sense, but solely whether they are believed and acted upon by the people."

In short, the categories of description and explanation in the social sciences are held to be radically "subjective," so that these disciplines are forced to rely on "nonobjective" techniques of inquiry. The social scientist must therefore "interpret" the materials of his study by imaginatively identifying himself with the actors in social processes, viewing the situations they face as the actors themselves view them, and constructing "models of motivation" in which springs of action and commitments to various values are imputed to these human agents. The social scientist is able to do these things, only because he is himself an active agent in social processes, and can therefore understand in the light of his own "subjective" experiences the "internal meanings" of social actions. A purely "objective" or "behavioristic" social science is in consequence held to be a vain hope; for to exclude on principle every vestige of subjective, motivational interpretation from the study of human affairs is in effect to eliminate from such study the consideration of every genuine social fact.

This account of social science subject matter raises many issues, but only the following . . . will receive attention in the present context: [A] Are the distinctions required for exploring that subject matter exclusively "subjective"? . . . [B] Do imputations of "subjective" states to human agents fall outside the scope of the logical canons [=principles] employed in inquiries into "objective" properties?

[A] It is beyond dispute that human behavior is frequently purposive; and it is likewise beyond question that when such behavior is described or explained, whether by social scientists or by laymen, various kinds of "subjective" (or psychological) states are commonly assumed to underlie its manifestations. Nevertheless, as is evident from the biological sciences, many aspects of goal-directed activities can frequently be investigated without requiring the postulation of such states. But what is more to the point, even when the behaviors studied by the social sciences are indisputably directed toward some consciously entertained ends, the social sciences do not confine themselves to using only distinctions that refer to psychological states exclusively; nor is it clear, moreover, why these disciplines should place such restrictions upon themselves. For example, in order to account for the adoption of certain rules of conduct by a given community, it may be relevant to inquire into the ways in which members of the community cultivate the soil, construct shelters, or preserve food for future use; and the overt behaviors these individuals exhibit in pursuing these tasks cannot be described in purely "subjective" terms.

Furthermore, even though purposive action is sometimes partly explained with the help of assumptions concerning dispositions, intentions, or beliefs of the actors, other assumptions concerning matters with which the actors are altogether unfamiliar may also contribute to the explanation of their action. Thus, as the passage quoted above makes clear, if we wish to account for the behavior of men who believe in the medicinal properties of a given substance, it is obviously important to distinguish between the question whether that belief has any influence upon the conduct of the believers, and the question whether the substance does in fact have the assumed medicinal properties. On the other hand, there appear to be excellent reasons for rejecting the conclusion, alleged to follow from this distinction, that in explaining purposive behavior the social scientist must use no information available to himself but not available to those manifesting the behavior. For example, southern cotton planters in the United States before the Civil War were certainly unacquainted with the laws of modern soil chemistry, and mistakenly believed that the use of animal manure would preserve indefinitely the fertility of the cotton plantations. Nevertheless, a social scientist's familiarity with those laws can help explain why, under that treatment, the soil upon which cotton was grown gradually deteriorated, and why in consequence there was an increasing need for virgin land to raise cotton if the normal cotton crop was not to decrease. It is certainly not evident why such explanations should be ruled out from the social sciences. But if they are not ruled out, and since they patently involve notions not referring to the "subjective" states of purposive agents, it does become evident that the categories of description and explanation in those sciences are not exclusively "subjective" ones. . . .

[B] [L]et us assume that the distinctive aim of the social sciences is to "understand" social phenomena in terms of "meaningful" categories, so that the social scientist seeks to explain such phenomena by imputing various "subjective" states to human agents participating in social processes. The crucial question that thus remains to be examined is whether such imputations involve the use of logical canons which are different from those employed in connection with the imputation of "objective" traits to things in other areas of inquiry.

It will be helpful in discussing this issue to have before us some examples of "meaningful" explanations of human actions. Let us begin with a simple one, in which the writer stresses the essential difference

between a paper flying before the wind and a man flying from a pursuing crowd. The paper knows no fear and the wind no hate, but without fear and hate the man would not fly nor the crowd pursue. If we try to reduce fear to its bodily concomitants [=to bodily changes that accompany it] we merely substitute the concomitants for the reality expressed as fear. We denude the world of meanings for the sake of a theory, itself a false meaning which deprives us of all the rest. We can interpret experience only on the level of experience.

. . . But the example that has come to serve as the classical model for "meaningful" explanations of social phenomena is [the] carefully worked out account of modern capitalism [of Max Weber (1864–1920)], in which he attributes the development of this type of economic enterprise at least in part to the spread of the religious beliefs and the precepts of practical conduct associated with ascetic forms [=forms that practice self-denial] of Protestantism. Weber's discussion is too detailed to permit brief summary. However, the structure of his argument (and of other "meaningful" explanations) can be represented by the following abstract schema. Suppose a social phenomenon E (e.g., the development of modern capitalistic enterprise) is found to occur under a complex set of social conditions C (e.g., widespread membership in certain religious groups, such as those professing Calvinistic Protestantism), where some of the individuals participating in C generally also participate in E. But individuals who participate in E are assumed to be committed to certain values (or to be in certain "subjective" states) V_E (e.g., they prize honesty, orderliness, and abstemious [=avoiding self-indulgence] labor); and individuals who participate in C are assumed to be in the subjective state V_C (e.g., they believe in the sacredness of a worldly calling). However, V_C and V_E are also alleged to be "meaningfully" related, in view of the motivational patterns we find in our own personal experiences—for example, by reflecting on how our own emotions, values, beliefs, and actions hang together, we come to recognize an intimate connection between believing that one's vocation in life is consecrated by divine ordinance, and believing that one's life should not be marked by indolence or self-indulgence. Accordingly, by imputing subjective states to the agents engaged in E and C, we can "understand" why it is that E occurs under conditions C, not simply as a mere conjuncture or succession of phenomena, but as manifestations of subjective states whose interrelations are familiar to us from a consideration of our own affective [=emotional] and cognitive states.

These examples make it clear that such "meaningful" explanations invariably employ two types of assumptions which are of particular relevance to the present discussion: an assumption, singular in form, characterizing specified individuals as being in certain psychological states at indicated times (e.g., the assumption, in the . . . quotation above, that members of the crowd hated the man they were pursuing); and an assumption, general in form, stating the ways such states are related to one another as well as to certain overt behaviors. . . .

However, neither of such assumptions is self-certifying, and evidence is required for each of them if the explanation of which they are parts is to be more than an exercise in uncontrolled imagination. Competent evidence for assumptions about the attitudes and actions of other men is often difficult to obtain; but it is certainly not obtained merely by introspecting one's own sentiments or by examining one's own beliefs as to how such sentiments are likely to be manifested in overt action—as responsible advocates of "interpretative" explanations have themselves often emphasized (e.g., with vigor and illumination by Max Weber). We may identify ourselves in imagination with a trader in wheat, and conjecture what course of conduct we would adopt were we confronted with some problem requiring decisive action in a fluctuating market for that commodity. But conjecture is not fact. The sentiments or envisioned plans we may impute to the trader either may not coincide with those he actually possesses, or even if they should so coincide may eventuate in conduct on his part quite different from the course of action we had imagined would be the "reasonable" one to adopt under the assumed circumstances. The history of anthropology amply testifies to the blunders that can be committed when categories appropriate for describing familiar social processes are extrapolated without further scrutiny to the study of strange cultures. Nor is the frequent claim well founded that relations of dependence between psychological processes with which we have personal experience, or between such processes and the overt actions in which they may be manifested, can be comprehended with a clearer "insight" into the reasons for their being what they are than can any relations of dependence between nonpsychological events and processes. Do we really understand more fully and with greater warranted certainty why an insult tends to produce anger, than why a rainbow is produced when the sun's rays strike raindrops at a certain angle?

Moreover, it is by no means obvious that a social scientist cannot account for men's actions unless he has experienced in his own person the psychic states he imputes to them or unless he can successfully recreate such states in imagination. Must a psychiatrist be at least partly demented if he is to be competent for studying the mentally ill? Is a historian incapable of explaining the careers and social changes effected by men like Hitler unless he can recapture in imagination the frenzied hatreds that may have animated such an individual? Are mild-tempered and emotionally stable social scientists unable to understand the causes and consequences of mass hysteria, institutionalized sexual orgy, or manifestations of pathological lusts for power? The factual evidence certainly lends no support to these and similar suppositions. Indeed, *discoursive* knowledge—i.e., knowledge statable in *propositional form,* about "common-sense" affairs as well as about the material explored by the specialized procedures of the natural and social sciences—is not a matter of *having* sensations, images, or feelings, whether vivid or faint: and it consists neither in identifying oneself in some ineffable manner with the objects of knowledge, nor in reproducing in some form of direct experience the subject matter of knowledge. On the other hand, discoursive knowledge is a *symbolic* representation of only certain selected phases of some subject matter; it is the product of a process that deliberately aims at formulating relations between traits of a subject matter, so that one set of traits mentioned in the formulations can be taken as a reliable sign of other traits mentioned; and it involves as a necessary condition for its being warranted, the possibility of verifying these formulations through controlled sensory observation by anyone prepared to make the effort to verify them.

In consequence, we can *know* that a man fleeing from a pursuing crowd that is animated by hatred toward him is in a state of fear, without our having experienced such violent fears and hatred or without imaginatively recreating such emotions in ourselves—just as we can *know* that the temperature of a piece of wire is rising because the velocities of its constituent molecules are increasing, without having to imagine what it is like to be a rapidly moving molecule. In both instances "internal states" that are not directly observable are imputed to the objects mentioned in explanation of their behaviors. Accordingly, if we can rightly claim to *know* that the individuals do possess the states imputed to them and that possession of such states tends to produce the specified forms of behavior, we can do so only on the basis of evidence obtained by observation of "objective" occurrences—in one case, by observation of overt human behavior (including men's verbal responses), in the other case, by observation of purely physical changes. To be sure, there are important differences between the specific characters of the states imputed in the two cases: in the case of the human actors the states are psychological or "subjective," and the social scientist making the imputation may indeed have first-hand personal experience of them, but in the case of the wire and other inanimate objects they are not. Nevertheless, despite these differences, the crucial point is that the logical canons employed by responsible social scientists in assessing the objective evidence for the imputation of psychological states do not appear to differ essentially (though they may often be applied less rigorously) from the canons employed for analogous purposes by responsible students in other areas of inquiry.

In sum, the fact that the social scientist, unlike the student of inanimate nature, is able to project himself by sympathetic imagination into the phenomena he is attempting to understand, is pertinent to questions concerning the *origins* of his explanatory hypotheses but not to questions concerning their validity. His ability to enter into relations of empathy with [=to identify with] the human actors in some social process may indeed be heuristically important in his efforts to *invent* suitable hypotheses which will explain the process. Nevertheless, his empathic identification with those individuals does not, by itself, constitute *knowledge*. The fact that he achieves such identification does not annul the need for objective evidence, assessed in accordance with logical principles that are common to all controlled inquiries, to support his imputation of subjective states to those human agents.

Reading Questions

1. How do Nagel's opponents think the study of human conduct must be carried on? How do they think the methods needed differ from those needed for the natural sciences?

2. What kinds of factors does the author cite that are both nonsubjective and necessary for the explanation and understanding of some kinds of human conduct?
3. What objections does Nagel have to the view that understanding others' behavior must be based solely on observers' introspecting their own sentiments?

Questions for Reflection and Research

1. Read Max Weber's *The Theory of Social and Economic Organization* or Peter Winch's *The Idea of a Social Science*. Has Nagel fairly represented the authors' views?
2. Is the following true: When we learn our native language, we learn to understand human beings? If it is true, why should we need social and behavioral sciences?
3. Are the social and behavioral sciences modeled on the physical sciences? Should they be? (See selections #36 by Hospers and #38 by Louch for some opinions on this.)
4. Do contemporary practicing psychologists and social scientists agree with views of the sort attacked by Nagel? If you are a student, ask faculty members in psychology and the social sciences to comment.
5. Do Nagel's views contain any explicit or implicit answer to the views of Louch in selection #38?
6. Compare Hospers' comments on purpose in selection #36 with Nagel's views.

Science and Ethics

Ethics is the branch of philosophy devoted to questions about which kinds of conduct are best. It examines and attempts to clarify such moral concepts as good, right, rights, duties, responsibility, and justice. There are at least three ways in which science and ethics interact.

1. It has been thought by some that science can help decide questions in ethics. As long ago as the time of Socrates in the fifth century B.C. philosophers were interested in the foundation of moral or ethical judgments. If stealing is wrong, why is it wrong? Is there any way to prove that stealing and lying and cruelty are wrong? Attempts by philosophers to justify moral standards have included appeals to religion (God forbids such conduct); appeals to self-interest (Avoiding such conduct will win others' approval and avoid feelings of guilt); appeals to intuition or self-evidence (We hold these truths to be self-evident . . .); appeals to love for our fellow human beings (Do the loving thing!); appeals to universalization (What if everyone did it?); and more.

Opposed to these attempts to provide objective foundations for morality has always been the view called ethical or moral relativism. Protagoras, a philosophic opponent of Socrates, is one of the earliest advocates of this view. He is recorded as having said "Man is the measure of all things. . . ." This saying has been interpreted to mean, among other things, that what is right and wrong in conduct depends only on what people say is right and wrong. Thus, if one culture approves of a certain kind of conduct and another disapproves, there is no way to settle the difference. Values are arbitrary inventions.

In the twentieth century, as the science of anthropology matured, one of its leading figures, Ruth Benedict, argued that anthropology had shown the relativist ethical theory to be correct. Investigations of various cultures very different from Western culture revealed, she claimed, that values are merely customs. Since cultures sometimes have conflicting customs, she concluded that there is no correct set of values. Some of Benedict's views are given in selection #40.

Selection #41 provides a rebuttal to Benedict's arguments and conclusions. Its author, the philosopher John W. Cook, argues that she has
misdescribed the practices of other cultures and has failed to see that
customs are the subject of moral scrutiny. Cook, then, is not persuaded
that moral relativism is true, nor is he persuaded that science can provide proof or disproof of the moral-relativity thesis.

If, as Cook holds, moral relativism is an incorrect doctrine, there
still remains the question of what the foundation of morality is. However, it has not usually been thought that this question might be settled
by scientific investigation. For it has been asserted that science merely is
concerned with observable facts, and from facts one cannot infer values.
One cannot derive an "ought" (what we *ought* to do) from an "is" (what *is*
factually true). Thus, it is held that if morality has a foundation, it will
not be established by science but rather by philosophical reflection.

There are some other basic moral issues on which scientific findings
seem to have a bearing, however. One is whether moral appraisals
should be made at all. If human beings are merely complex stimulus-
response machines, creatures whose conduct is entirely the product of
genetic and environmental factors, then it has seemed to some
philosophers that humans are never free. If it is true that humans are
not free, praising or condemning their conduct is improper. Those who
do good and those who do evil cannot help acting as they do; thus, they
deserve neither praise nor blame. A number of selections in Section 3
discuss the relevance of scientific findings to the issue of free will.

Another basic issue in ethics that scientific findings may help to
resolve is the extent of moral equality among living things. In the not-
too-distant past and in the present some people have found reason to
suppose that people of a different race, or of a different sex, or children,
or animals need not be regarded as moral equals with the privileged
members of the culture. They have claimed that one or more of these
groups differ in important respects from the morally privileged—in respect of intelligence, or strength, or emotional character, or in capacity
to understand the world, or in some other way. In opposition to such
reasoning, of course, is the view that differences in capacities are irrelevant to what rights individuals have.

Science can be appealed to determine whether morally relevant
differences exist (assuming it can be settled which differences are morally
relevant). Unfortunately, when science has attempted to study the differences between races or sexes, the scientists involved have often been
charged with injecting biased views into their studies. Selection #48 by
psychologist Robert Williams argues that racism has infected attempts to
determine human intelligence differences. Selection #49 by psychologist
Naomi Weisstein similarly argues that those scientists who have made
pronouncements on male/female differences have all too often based
their pronouncements on faulty methodology.

Selections #48 and #49, and selection #46 about animals by Peter
Singer (and many selections in Section 3), do point to the potential role

science can play in helping us to see whether any group of living beings can be justly treated differently in any respect. But selections #48 and #49 also warn us that despite the commonly held views that science is objective, its practitioners can and do contaminate their findings with biases of various sorts.

2. Science, thus, may be able to help in the resolution of some issues in ethics. A second way in which science and ethics interact is within science. Scientists must resolve ethical issues that crop up in the preparation for or the performance of their research. Under the influence of the doctrine that an "ought" cannot be derived from an ·"is," some philosophers have concluded that science is value-free and tended to think that ethics and science cannot connect.

Those who assert that value judgments are part of science are in general not attempting to derive values from facts. They wish only to call attention to how factual and ethical concerns can and do intermingle in the actual practice of science. Selection #42 by the philosopher and logician Nicholas Rescher spells out a variety of ethical decisions practicing scientists must make. How should funds be allocated among competing scientific projects and researchers? How is scientific credit for discoveries to be apportioned? When should findings be shared with other researchers?

If investigators plan to experiment using animals or humans, they must consider some moral questions. The biologist George H. Kieffer discusses (in selection #45) factors that can tempt some researchers to ignore the welfare and rights of their human subjects. And the moral and political philosopher Peter Singer argues in selection #46 that many animals are grievously mistreated by scientific researchers. He argues that higher animals are entitled to the same kind of treatment as human infants are. If researchers would not perform an experiment on a baby, they should not be willing to do so on an animal.

3. Science and ethics interact in a third way when the products or results of science create new ethical problems for us. Gordon Rattray Taylor (in selection #43) reminds us how advances in biology and medicine have created and will continue to create new moral issues. We must now face a variety of moral issues having to do with human reproduction, organ transplants, the prolongation of life, the control and change of psychological characteristics, and mercy killings. Taylor is not optimistic that we can handle these new decisions well.

Another science that has raised new moral issues is nuclear physics. Nuclear power, as a source both of electrical and mechanical energy and of weapons, has forced moral questions on us that continue to perplex us. Selection #44, from a play by a former medical doctor, Heinar Kipphardt, dramatically portrays the struggle of one scientist who tried to decide whether he should feel responsibility for possible evil uses of his scientific work. The scientist portrayed is J. Robert Oppenheimer, sometimes referred to as the father of the atomic bomb. The selection thus shows both how science can create new moral problems and how moral issues can intrude in science.

Selection #47 also reveals a number of ways science and ethics can interact. It describes and gives some arguments in favor of an experiment proposed by psychologist Harris Rubin at Southern Illinois University. Rubin proposed to study the effects of the use of marijuana on sexual arousal. The study would involve showing pornographic movies to male volunteers (some of whom had smoked marijuana) and measuring their arousal by sensors attached to their penises. The experimenters, the subjects, and those who decide on funding of the experiment must consider a number of moral and ethical questions. Is it wrong to smoke marijuana? Is it wrong to view pornographic movies? Is it wrong to conduct an experiment with public funds if many taxpayers regard the experiment as involving immoral conduct? If the experimental results turn out to show that marijuana increases sexual arousal, should this finding be made known—especially if it is clear that such a finding would increase the use of marijuana? The public reaction to the proposed experiment has by and large been one of distress [a common reaction to sex studies, beginning with the studies of Sigmund Freud (1856–1939)].

We must conclude, then, that science, despite its reputation to the contrary, is a human activity that has many connections with ethics. It may help in the resolution of ethical problems, and its practitioners must consider ethical matters ranging from ethical treatment of their fellow scientists to fair treatment of experimental subjects. Any student preparing for a career in the sciences or allied fields, then, might profit from further study in the field of ethics.

Further Reading: Science and Ethics

1. *The Encyclopedia of Philosophy*, 8 vols., ed. PAUL EDWARDS (New York: Macmillan Publishing Co., 1967). To gain a better understanding of the controversy over ethical relativism see "Ethical Relativism" by RICHARD BRANDT. To become better acquainted with some objective ethical theories see "Ethical Naturalism" and "Ethical Objectivism" both by JONATHAN HARRISON. The ethical theory subscribed to by many members of the scientific and philosophical movement known as logical positivism is described in the entry "Emotive Theory of Ethics" by BRANDT. The question of whether values should or do have a role in science is discussed in the two entries "Economics and Ethical Neutrality" by KURT KLAPPHOLZ and "History and Value Judgments" by W. H. DRAY.

2. *Animal Liberation* by PETER SINGER (New York: New York Review, 1975). This book includes a more thorough treatment of issues discussed by Singer in

selection #46. Also look for reviews of the book for scientists' reactions to
the arguments presented against the use of animals in experiments.

3. Biomedical ethics: Three books covering a variety of ethical topics created by
   advances in biology and medicine are given below. This field is growing
   rapidly, with much new material being published.
   (a) *Ethics and the New Medicine* by HARMON L. SMITH (Nashville, Tenn.:
       Abingdon Press, 1970).
   (b) *Bioethics*, ed. THOMAS A. SHANNON (New York: Paulist Press, 1976).
   (c) *Bioethics: A Textbook of Issues* by GEORGE H. KIEFFER (Reading, Mass.:
       Addison-Wesley Publishing Co., Inc., forthcoming). Selection #45 is de-
       rived from an early version of this book.

4. Sexism and Science: For a brief account of sexism in medical fields see *Witches,
   Midwives, and Nurses: A History of Women Healers* by BARBARA EHRENREICH
   and DEIRDRE ENGLISH (Old Westbury, N.Y.: Feminist Press, 1973). For an
   engrossing account of sexism in late nineteenth-century biology, see "Science Corrupted: Victorian Biologists Consider 'The Woman Question' " by
   SUSAN SLEETH MOSEDALE in *Journal of the History of Biology*, vol. 11, no. 1
   (Spring 1978), pp. 1–55. See the journal *Signs* for helpful guides to literature on sexism in the sciences.

5. Many ethical issues involving science are discussed in certain science periodicals. In addition, books on ethical issues and science are reviewed in the
   periodicals. The following are especially helpful: *The Bulletin of the Atomic
   Scientists, The Hastings Center Report, Psychology Today, Science,* and *Scientific
   American.*

selection 40.

Anthropology and Moral Relativism

The Author: Ruth Benedict (1887–1948) was educated in English literature at Vassar College and in anthropology at Columbia University. Later she also taught at Columbia. Until the 1930s she wrote under the pseudonym Anne Singleton. Her most famous work, *Patterns of Culture* (1934), derived in part from her field work among Indian tribes in southwestern United States. Her theories in the area of culture and personality in the field of cultural anthropology have had a profound influence.

The Selection: It is contended that the science of anthropology has shown that concepts of what is right and wrong or normal and abnormal vary from culture to culture—and thus no culture's values can be considered correct. As evidence for this theory some seemingly odd and distressing practices of some other cultures are described and compared with the practices of our culture. The main focus is on the culture of the Dobu and the Kwakiutl. This selection is moderately demanding.

In how far are such categories [as normal-abnormal] culturally determined, or in how far can we with assurance regard them as absolute? In how far can we regard inability to function socially as diagnostic of abnormality, or in how far is it necessary to regard this as a function of the culture?

As a matter of fact, one of the most striking facts that emerge from a study of widely varying cultures is the case with which our abnormals function in other cultures. It does not matter what kind

From "Anthropology and the Abnormal" by Ruth Benedict in the *Journal of General Psychology* 10 (1934): 59–80. Reprinted by permission of The Journal Press.

of "abnormality" we choose for illustration, those which indicate extreme instability, or those which are more in the nature of character traits like sadism or delusions of grandeur or of persecution. There are well-described cultures in which these abnormals function at ease and with honor, and apparently without danger or difficulty to the society.

The most notorious of these is trance and catalepsy. Even a very mild mystic is aberrant [=regarded as abnormal] in our culture. But most peoples have regarded even extreme psychic manifestations not only as normal and desirable, but even as characteristic of highly valued and gifted individuals. This was true even in our own cultural background in that period when Catholicism made the ecstatic experience the mark of sainthood. It is hard for us, born and brought up in a culture that makes no use of the experience, to realize how important a role it may play and how many individuals are capable of it, once it has been given an honorable place in any society. . . .

The most spectacular illustrations of the extent to which normality may be culturally defined are those cultures where an abnormality of our culture is the cornerstone of their social structure. . . . A recent study of an island of northwest Melanesia . . . describes [the Dobu] society [which is] built upon traits . . . we regard as beyond the border of paranoia [=a personality disorder involving delusions of persecution]. In this tribe the [various] groups look upon each other as prime manipulators of black magic, so that one marries always into an enemy group which remains for life one's deadly and unappeasable foes. They look upon a good garden crop as a confession of theft, for everyone is engaged in making magic to induce into his garden the productiveness of his neighbors'; therefore no secrecy in the island is so rigidly insisted upon as the secrecy of a man's harvesting of his yams. Their polite phrase at the acceptance of a gift is, "And if you now poison me, how shall I repay you this present?" Their preoccupation with poisoning is constant; no woman ever leaves her cooking pot for a moment untended. . . . They . . . people the whole world outside their own quarters with such malignant spirits that all-night feasts and ceremonials simply do not occur here. They have even rigorous religiously enforced customs that forbid the sharing of seed even in one family group. Anyone else's food is deadly poison to you, so that communality of stores is out of the question. . . .

Now in this society where no one may work with another and no one may share with another . . . [there was an] individual who was regarded by all his fellows as crazy. He was not one of those who periodically ran amok and, beside himself and frothing at the mouth, fell with a knife upon anyone he could reach. Such behavior they did not regard as putting anyone outside the pale. They did not even put the individuals who were known to be liable to these attacks under any kind of control. They merely fled when they saw the attack coming on and kept out of the way. "He would be all right tomorrow." But there was one man of sunny, kindly disposition who liked work and liked to be helpful. The compulsion was too strong for him to repress it in favor of the opposite tendencies of his culture. Men and women never spoke of him without laughing; he was silly and simple and definitely crazy. Nevertheless, to the ethnologist used to a culture that has, in Christianity, made his type the model of all virtue, he seemed a pleasant fellow.

An even more extreme example, because it is of a culture that has built itself upon a more complex abnormality, is that of the North Pacific Coast of North America. The civilization of the Kwakiutl, at the time when it was first recorded in the last decades of the nineteenth century, was one of the most vigorous in North America. It was built up on an ample economic supply of goods, the fish which furnished their food staple being practically inexhaustible and obtainable with comparatively small labor, and the wood which furnished the material for their houses, their furnishings, and their arts being, with however much labor, always procurable. They lived in coastal villages that compared favorably in size with those of any other American Indians and they kept up constant communication by means of sea-going dug-out canoes.

It was one of the most vigorous and zestful of the aboriginal cultures of North America, with complex crafts and ceremonials, and elaborate and striking arts. It certainly had none of the earmarks of a sick civilization. The tribes of the Northwest Coast had wealth, and exactly in our terms. That is, they had not only a surplus of economic goods, but they made a game of the manipulation of wealth. It was by no means a mere direct transcription of economic needs and the filling of those needs. It involved the idea of capital, of interest, and of conspicuous waste. It was a game with all the binding rules of a game, and a person entered it as a child. His father distributed wealth for him, according to his ability, at a small feast or potlatch, and each gift the receiver was obliged to accept and to return after a short interval with interest that ran to about 100 per cent a year. By the time the child was grown, therefore, he was well launched, a larger potlatch had been given for him on various occasions of exploit or initiation, and he had wealth either out at usury [=out gathering interest] or in his own possession. Nothing in the civilization can be enjoyed without validating it by the distribution of this wealth. Everything that was valued, names and songs as well as material objects, were passed down in family lines, but they were always publicly assumed with accompanying sufficient distributions of property. It was the game of validating and exercising all the privileges one could accumulate from one's various forbears, or by gift, or by marriage, that made the chief interest of the culture. Everyone in his degree took part in it, but many, of course, mainly as spectators. In its highest form it was played out between rival chiefs representing not only themselves and their family lines but their communities, and the object of the contest was to glorify oneself and to humiliate one's opponent. On this level of greatness the property involved was no longer represented by blankets, so many thousand of them to a potlatch, but by higher units of value. These higher units were like our bank notes. They were incised copper tablets, each of them named, and having a value that depended upon their illustrious history. This was as high as ten thousand blankets, and to possess one of them, still more to enhance its value at a great potlatch, was one of the greatest glories within the compass of the chiefs of the Northwest Coast. . . .

The drives [in this contest] were those which in our own culture we should call megalomaniac [=disorder involving delusions of grandeur]. There was an uncensored self-glorification and ridicule of the opponent that it is hard to equal in other cultures outside of the monologues of the abnormal. . . .

[Further] all of existence was seen in terms of insult. Not only derogatory acts performed by a neighbor or an enemy, but all untoward events, like a cut when one's axe slipped, or a ducking when one's canoe overturned, were insults. All alike threatened first and foremost one's ego security, and the first thought one was allowed was how to get even, how to wipe out the insult.

In their behavior at great bereavements this set of the culture comes out most strongly. Among the Kwakiutl it did not matter whether a relative had died in bed of disease, or by the hand of an enemy, in either case death was an affront to be wiped out by the death of another person. The fact that one had been caused to mourn was proof that one had been put upon. A chief's sister and her daughter had gone up to Victoria, and either because they drank bad whiskey or because their boat capsized they never came back. The chief called together his warriors. "Now I ask you, tribes, who shall wail? Shall I do it or shall another?" The spokesman answered, of course, "Not you, Chief. Let some other of the tribes." Immediately they set up the war pole to announce their intention of wiping out the injury, and gathered a war party. They set out, and found seven men and two children asleep and killed them. "Then they felt good when they arrived at Sebaa in the evening."

The point which is of interest to us is that in our society those who on that occasion would feel good when they arrived at Sebaa that evening would be the definitely abnormal. There would be some, even in our society, but it is not a recognized and approved mood under the circumstances. On the Northwest Coast those are favored and fortunate to whom that mood under those circumstances is congenial, and those to whom it is repugnant are unlucky. . . .

This head-hunting that takes place on the Northwest Coast after a death is no matter of blood revenge or of organized vengeance. There is no effort to tie up the subsequent killing with any responsibility on the part of the victim for the death of the person who is being mourned. A chief whose son has died goes visiting wherever his fancy dictates, and he says to his host, "My prince has died today, and you go with him." Then he kills him. In this, according to their interpretation, he acts nobly because he has not been downed. He has thrust back in return. The whole procedure is meaningless without the fundamental paranoid reading of bereavement. Death, like all the other untoward accidents of existence, confounds man's pride and can only be handled in the category of insults.

Behavior honored upon the Northwest Coast is one which is recognized as abnormal in our civilization, and yet it is sufficiently close to the attitudes of our own culture to be intelligible to us and to have a definite vocabulary with which we may discuss it. The megalomaniac paranoid trend is a definite danger in our society. It is encouraged by some of our major preoccupations, and it confronts us with a choice of two possible attitudes. One is to brand it as abnormal and reprehensible, and is the attitude we have chosen in our civilization. The other is to make it an essential attribute of ideal man, and this is the solution in the culture of the Northwest Coast.

These illustrations, which it has been possible to indicate only in the briefest manner, force upon us the fact that normality is culturally defined. An adult shaped to the drives and standards of either of these cultures, if he were transported into our civilization, would fall into our categories of abnormality. He would be faced with the psychic dilemmas of the socially unavailable. In his own culture, however, he is the pillar of society, the end result of socially inculcated mores [= customs], and the problem of personal instability in his case simply does not arise.

No one civilization can possibly utilize in its mores the whole potential range of human behavior. Just as there are great numbers of possible phonetic articulations [= speech sounds], and the possibility of language depends on a selection and standardization of a few of these in order that speech communication may be possible at all, so the possibility of organized behavior of every sort, from the fashions of local dress and houses to the dicta [= pronoun cements] of a people's ethics and religion, depends upon a similar selection among the possible behavior traits. In the field of recognized economic obligations or sex tabus this selection is as nonrational and subconscious a process as it is in the field of phonetics. It is a process which goes on in the group for long periods of time and is historically conditioned by innumerable accidents of isolation or of contact of peoples. In any comprehensive study of psychology, the selection that different cultures have made in the course of history within the great circumference of potential behavior is of great significance.

Every society, beginning with some slight inclination in one direction or another, carries its preference farther and farther, integrating itself more and more completely upon its chosen basis, and discarding those types of behavior that are uncongenial. Most of those organizations of personality that seem to us most uncontrovertibly abnormal have been used by different civilizations in the very foundations of their institutional life. Conversely the most valued traits of our normal individuals have been looked on in differently organized cultures as aberrant. Normality, in short, within a very wide range, is culturally defined. It is primarily a term for the socially elaborated segment of human behavior in any culture; and abnormality a term for the segment that that particular civilization does not use. The very eyes with which we see the problem are conditioned by the long traditional habits of our own society.

It is a point that has been made more often in relation to ethics than in relation to psychiatry. We do not any longer make the mistake of deriving the morality of our locality and decade directly from the inevitable constitution of human nature. We do not elevate it to the dignity of a first principle. We recognize that morality differs in every society, and is a convenient term for socially approved habits. Mankind has always preferred to say, "It is morally good," rather than "It is habitual," and the fact of this preference is matter enough for a critical science of ethics. But historically the two phrases are synonymous.

The concept of the normal is properly a variant of the concept of the good. It is that which society has approved. A normal action is one which falls well within the limits of expected behavior for a particular society. Its variability among different peoples is essentially a function of the variability of the behavior patterns that different societies have created for themselves, and can never be wholly divorced from a consideration of culturally institutionalized types of behavior. . . .

Reading Questions

1. What traits that we regard as abnormal are asserted to be normal in some other cultures?
2. Why do the Dobu tend to distrust everyone?
3. Why do members of Kwakiutl tribes hold potlatches? When do they feel justified in killing innocent people?

4. According to Benedict, why do different cultures evolve different customs and practices?
5. What is anthropology thought to have shown about ethics and morality?

Questions for Reflection and Research

1. Is there any other way to explain the difference between our culture and the culture of the Dobus and the Kwakiutl? That is, do they really have different concepts of ethics and normality—or is it rather that they have different beliefs about the world? (See selection #41 by Cook for a number of criticisms of Benedict's reasoning.)
2. Is anthropology a science?
3. Can we conclude that there are no correct evaluations because people differ in their evaluations? Think of activities that involve evaluation (for example, evaluation in engineering work, aesthetics, economics, learning, and so on).
4. Is the question of whether morality is relative a scientific issue? How do we decide the issue?
5. Compare the views of Whorf (selection #18) on linguistic relativity with those of Benedict.

selection 41.

Is There Evidence for Moral Relativism?

The Author: John W. Cook (b. 1930) received his undergraduate education at the University of Minnesota and graduate education at the University of Nebraska. In teaching philosophy at Lake Forest College and later at the University of Oregon he has been especially interested in topics in the philosophy of mind, metaphysics, theory of knowledge, and moral philosophy.

The Selection: Moral relativism (as advocated by Ruth Benedict in the preceding selection) is criticized. A question is raised about how morality can be merely a matter of customs if customs are the kinds of things that are evaluated morally. Cook argues that the false theory (moral relativism) results from anthropologists being misled by superficial similarities between cultures. Several instances are cited in which anthropologists misdescribe other cultures and thereby lead themselves to think the other cultures regard as right what we regard as wrong.

Moral relativism, as a precept of anthropology, is a product of the last century. It developed as a reaction against cultural comparisons, made by Europeans, in which known cultures were ranked as higher or lower, as more or less civilized, depending on how closely they resembled the culture of Western Europe. Among the points of comparison was the 'morality' of the cultures being ranked, and under this heading sexual conduct held a prominent place. Thus, if monogamy was strictly practiced, adultery and in-

---

The selection derives from an unpublished paper, "Relativism," by John W. Cook. It was revised for this volume by the author. Reprinted by permission of the author.

cest strictly forbidden, and modesty strictly enforced, a culture was given high marks; otherwise it was placed somewhere down the scale. Such comparisons fell into disfavor, however, when anthropologists began to regard their discipline as a science. Their reasoning, perhaps, ran somewhat as follows: "If such comparisons were to be made by members of some other culture, they would arrive at a different set of rankings. Such rankings, then, can hardly be thought of as models of scientific objectivity. They are, rather, models of ethnocentrism [= cultural bias] and have no place in a scientific anthropology."

This no doubt was a rather sensible conclusion, but it was soon generalized into a philosophical theory which came to be known as "moral (or cultural) relativism." It was seen by anthropologists not merely as a means of ridding anthropology of provincialism but as a weapon with which to undercut by a single stroke all forms of intolerance of alien cultures. The relativists' argument ran something like this: "There is no real truth in any morality, as can be seen from the fact that different cultures have different moral standards or principles. If men were capable of discerning genuine, universal moral truths, we would not find this diversity among the cultures of the world. But we do find it, and accordingly we must conclude that morality is nothing but socially conditioned habits. What is right or wrong, good or bad is nothing but what a given society says it is."

It is not my intention to discuss here all of the questionable aspects of this piece of reasoning. I will content myself, rather, with making a few observations about its conclusion and will then go on to inquire what has made it so plausible to think that anthropology has provided evidence that supports moral relativism.

Let us turn, then, to the conclusion of the above argument. A version of it is found in Ruth Benedict's essay "Anthropology and the Abnormal" [see the previous selection —ED.], where she writes:

We recognize that morality differs in every society, and is a convenient term for socially approved habits. Mankind has always preferred to say, "It is morally good," rather than "It is habitual".... But historically the two phrases are synonymous.

The first thing to notice about this is that Benedict seems to think that "good" is an important moral term, and in this she would seem to be mistaken. That word turns up in such phrases as "good weather," "good health," and "good soil," but it is difficult to think of many moral contexts in which the word occurs. (Certainly no one ever says, "It is morally good.") The only example that comes to mind is that we might say to someone who has done us a kindness, "It was good of you to do that for me." Now if Benedict's claim were correct, then this would come to the same as saying, "It was habitual for you to do that for me." But this is absurd. A person who expresses her gratitude by saying "It was good of you" is not remarking on her benefactor's habits. Nor for that matter is she saying that her benefactor has acted as most people act. Not only may she have no idea how most people act in such a situation, but it is entirely possible that her benefactor has acted in quite an extraordinary way, that few other people would perform such a kindness.

If, then, Benedict has correctly stated the relativist's conclusion, relativism would seem to be quite obviously false.

There may, of course, be other ways of stating that conclusion, but any version of it must either say or imply that a person's conduct can be morally judged only by comparing it with what is the usual and accepted conduct in that person's society. This would mean, for example, that if someone's actions are morally criticized, he can always defend his actions by pointing out that he has acted as everyone in his society acts in that situation. It would also mean that if I am faced with a moral question and ask myself, "What should I do?," then I must be asking what most people in my society would do. But on both these counts relativism would seem to be quite mistaken. For we may well think that what most people in our society do in a given situation is wrong, i.e., is cruel or unfair or degrading to others or something of the sort. Thus, if a congressman were shown to have accepted bribes in exchange for his vote, we would not think that he could demonstrate the rightness of his actions by demonstrating that most political officeholders have accepted bribes. We would not say to him, "Oh, in that case you certainly did the right thing." Or consider the practice among Russian gentlemen of the last century of always paying off their gambling debts to one another before paying debts to shopkeepers or wages to servants. We can easily imagine some gentleman of the period, such as Tolstoy, suffering a troubled conscience over this and in the end deciding that he ought to pay first the servants and shopkeepers. After all, they are probably more in need of payment, and in any case they have a better claim to it because they have provided goods and services and this is their only livelihood.

We could present many other counterexamples to relativism, examples which show that we do not always (Do we ever?) judge the rightness of a person's conduct by considering what people usually do in our society. I will mention only one more. Since the Middle Ages it has been an accepted practice in Sicily that if a suitor's proposal of marriage were rejected, he could force the young woman to the altar by kidnapping and raping her. For she was then no longer a virgin and no other man would have her. A few years ago a young woman, Franca Viola, refused to be manipulated in this degrading way and brought a criminal charge of rape against the suitor she had rejected. He was convicted, and Franca Viola, despite much public abuse, eventually married another man. —Now although the relativist's theory implies that Franca acted wrongly, because wrong is defined by one's culture, there is surely no relativist who would, in practice, abide by his own theory and declare that Franca acted wrongly. Anyone not blinded by callousness can see that Franca, far from acting wrongly, was courageously refusing to be cruelly manipulated.

What these counterexamples make clear is that our customs, traditions, and practices are among the things about which we raise moral questions. We may sometimes recognize that these are cruel or degrading or unfair even when they are part of our own culture. It cannot be, then, that morality just is a matter of custom or tradition.

There is something plainly wrong, then, with moral relativism. And yet the curious fact is that many people, including many anthropologists, have thought that relativism is not merely true but obviously true. What could be the explanation of this curious fact? That is the question I want now to answer.

The fact that needs explaining is not only that relativists have embraced a theory, a philosophical theory, which flies in the face of the facts, i.e., in the face of counterexamples anyone could think of on his own, but that they believe that their theory is supported by evidence from anthropological studies. This suggests several things that we must bear in mind if we are to understand the relativist's thinking. First, since relativism would not have seemed plausible to anthropologists if, from the outset, they had given due attention to cases like the foregoing counterexamples (indeed, many of them beat a hasty retreat from relativism when the enormity of Nazism became apparent), it must be that their attention was riveted upon examples of some other sort. Second, there must be something about examples of this latter sort (whatever they turn out to be) that leads anthropologists, quite mistakenly, to see them as proof of relativism. Our question, then, is narrowed down to this: What sort of examples are relativists thinking of and why do they mistake them for something they are not?

Fortunately, the answer to this question is not hard to find. In fact it is quite easy to invent examples that meet the above two requirements. And this I will now proceed to do, my aim being to present an example in which the relevant features stand out as clearly as possible.

Suppose then that in a tribe known as the Mobimtu it is the expected thing that when a boy reaches the age of passage his father shall begin to talk a great deal about the boy's greatness and goodness. He is to speak often and even with some exaggeration about his son's prowess, exploits, and possessions. To fail in this parental duty is regarded as a failure to provide the son with the self-confidence that is necessary to meet the rigors of tribal life. Now if we should happen upon this tribe and notice a man going on in this fashion about his son, we might be reminded of some neighbor of ours back home who constantly brags about his children. We might then think: What an obnoxious fellow, always puffing himself up with exaggerated tales about his son! And as we notice more and more of this going on in the tribe, and notice also that no one castigates these men for their constant and (as it seems to us) insufferable bragging, we may conclude that the Mobimtu have no scruples about bragging.

It is at this point that the turn toward relativism may occur. For if we were anthropologists studying the Mobimtu, we would soon recognize that this 'bragging' we had noticed occurs under prescribed circumstances and that it has the social function of preparing boys for adult life. And having recognized this, we might now think: "These people ought not to be scorned or censured for their bragging, for although it sounds vainglorious to our ears, they see nothing wrong in it, and it serves a valuable purpose in their lives. The Mobimtu simply have a different morality from ours: we think that bragging is wrong and they do not."

Here we see the relativist's conclusion, and we can also see why anthropologists would think that they had found evidence for the 'relativity of values.' But I hope it is equally easy to see from this example that the reasoning involves two mistakes. The first of these lies in thinking that these Mobimtu fathers are great braggarts. They are not, of course, for although they talk in ways which, in our culture, would amount to bragging, the Mobimtu are not extolling their sons in order to reflect credit or glory upon themselves. And not only do they have a different purpose, but they are doing only what is expected of them. (There may be braggarts among them, but if so, this would have to show itself in other ways than by their carrying out this parental duty to their sons.) The second mistake compounds the first. It consists of retaining the idea that these men are bragging and then, having noticed that this is prescribed behavior, concluding that bragging is morally accepted (or required) among the Mobimtu. It is here, of course, that one gets the idea that there are different and conflicting moralities.

It is the first of these mistakes that is crucial, for the second would not occur without it. It consists, I think we can say, of being misled by superficial similarities into thinking that, in cases like the above, the behavior that is censured in culture A, when it occurs in A, is the *same* behavior that is accepted without censure (or is even required) in culture B. This mistake can occur even within a culture, as when one person does not understand the other's expectations and so reads the wrong motive into his behavior, but it is a mistake more readily made (for the reason illustrated in my example) if the behavior we are observing occurs on the other side of some cultural divide. This is reason enough, I think, for believing that anthropologists really have been led into relativism by making this mistake. But we need not rest content with thus inferring that they have made this mistake, for as we shall see there are clear instances of it in their own writings.

Consider first a self-confessed instance mentioned by Raymond Firth (in *Elements of Social Organization*, 1951, pp. 190–92). He tells us that early in his study of the Tikopia he "came to the conclusion that there was no such thing as friendship or kindness for its own sake among these people." It seemed to him that, far from offering him assistance, they were constantly demanding that he give them things. Understandably, he took them to be a greedy and calculating people. Later on, however, he realized that he had been mistaken about this. It was not that these people were greedy and lacking in kindness; it was rather that among these people "the most obvious foundation of friendship was material reciprocity." Their constantly asking to be given things was not greediness, as he had thought, but overtures or tests of friendship.

In this instance Firth came to recognize that his initial view of these people's actions was mistaken, and so he did not slip into saying that they have a different morality from ours, that while we value kindness and deplore greed, they do the opposite. But as we shall see, not all anthropologists are as acute as Firth in catching and correcting the first mistake.

It will be useful here to consider several examples from the essay by Ruth Benedict referred to above. Her aim in that essay is to demonstrate that assessment of people's psychological normality (or the lack of it) is 'relative' to a culture. She thinks this is so because she believes she has found cases in which people who are regarded as perfectly normal (or sane) in one culture act no differently from people who are designated as abnormal (or crazy) in some other culture. For instance, she believes that a normal person among the Kwakiutl is indistinguishable from the paranoids [=those with delusions of persecution] and the megalomaniacs [=those with delusions of grandeur] in our culture. Let us consider this.

As proof that the Kwakiutl are, by our standards, megalomaniacs she cites their potlatches and comments that on these occasions "there was an uncensored self-glorification and ridicule of the opponent that it is hard to equal in other cultures outside of the monologues of the abnormal." Now this much, perhaps, we can grant her: the hyperbole of the potlatch, the amassing of blankets and their destruction all bear some resemblance to the ravings and antics of a megalomaniac, perhaps a Texas millionaire whose ostentation has exceeded the bounds of sanity. But is this resemblance more than merely superficial? Benedict is claiming that the Kwakiutl, in the course of their potlatches, are doing the same thing as a Texas oilman gone berserk, that they are, by our standards, insane. But surely this ignores a great deal about both the Kwakiutl and (genuine) megalomaniacs. The latter act as they do because of their neurotic insecurity; they are overcompensating for what they take to be their own insignificance. Is this what the Kwakiutl are doing? Of course not! Their behavior does not develop in them individually, as it does with megalomaniacs. They have been taught since childhood to participate in potlatches, and what they say on these occasions is largely a matter of ritual form. While there may be megalomaniacs among them, this would have to show itself in other ways than by their participation in potlatches, for example, in the way they talk about themselves to their children or other relations, how they comport themselves at tribal meetings, and so on. It is here, and not in their potlatches, that one might find indications of megalomania. Benedict has overlooked all this. She has also neglected the fact that a Kwakiutl is born into a culture in which even minimal self-esteem requires successful participation in potlatches. If he were to give up and drop out of the competition, he would not be at all like a megalomaniac who, perhaps with psychiatric help, abandons his self-congratulatory declamations. The latter is a person who has shed his self-doubts and whose self-esteem has risen to the point where he no longer compulsively overcompensates. By contrast, a Kwakiutl who declined to compete in potlatches would have to be a person whose self-esteem had, by *any* standard, suffered an unhealthy decline, like that of a middle-class American who is a failure at earning a living and supporting his family.

If we bear all of this in mind, we will have no inclination to think that what the Kwakiutl do is also what megalomaniacs do. Benedict has made the mistake here of identifying actions in one culture with those in another culture because of a superficial resemblance in behavior. This in turn leads to her second mistake of thinking that people who are normal among the Kwakiutl are people whom we would regard as abnormal or crazy.

One can find mistakes of this sort throughout Benedict's essay. I will mention briefly two other instances.

As proof that normal people among the Kwakiutl are like our paranoids, she cites the fact that they see "all of existence . . . in terms of insult" and permit themselves to retaliate for all sorts of accidental mishaps. But what does this really prove? Even perfectly normal people among us do not, and are not expected to, suffer insults gladly, and a most common response is some form of retaliation. Thus, if one of us found himself, like the Kwakiutl, thrust into a situation in which he was bombarded with insults, his quite healthy response would be to give as good as he gets, trading insult for insult. In this respect, then, there is no difference between the normal Kwakiutl and the normal Frenchman or American. But what are we to make of the fact that they see insults everywhere? Evidently, Benedict thinks that, by 'our' standards, this calls for a diagnosis of paranoia. Here she is forgetting that it makes a great difference that in the Kwakiutl this is a learned response, and not, as with genuine paranoids, a way of seeing things which each has developed on his own. A Kwakiutl's tendency to see any untoward incident as an insult is not the outcome of some irrational fear or suppressed hostility that betokens a flaw in his ego structure. He is merely living out a pattern which he has learned from his elders. And in view of this we must surely reject Benedict's contention that the Kwakiutl are no different from people whom we diagnose as paranoid. Her account suggests that the Kwakiutl would find the paranoids in our society to be quite sane. But if we could credit the Kwakiutl with the capacity to understand all the facts relevant to our diagnosing someone as paranoid, then surely they would concur that the person is not in sound mental health. Here again Benedict has been tripped up by superficial similarities.

As a final case, let us consider an example that Benedict draws from Fortune's study of the Dobu. These people are believers in black magic and malignant spirits, and since everyone is a potential threat to oneself, especially by means of poisoning, people are constantly vigilant and no one may work with or share food with another person. Among them, however, Fortune found a man of sunny, kindly disposition who kept no vigil against poisoning and offered help to others with their work. The Dobu regarded him as simple and definitely crazy.

Benedict finds clear proof in this that the Dobu do not share our notions of what is normal and abnormal. In fact, the case proves nothing of the sort. Benedict has neglected a crucial detail: Did this man share the others' belief that they were all in constant peril? If, as the Dobu must have assumed, he did believe this, then they were quite right, as we would agree, to regard him as crazy. More than likely, however, he did not share their beliefs, in which case it is no mere cultural bias that we would find his helpfulness to be perfectly sane behavior. (I would surmise that the man was a victim of brain damage and simply did not understand all the fuss about poisoning. The mentally retarded often have sunny dispositions.) Contrary to Benedict, then, there is nothing here to show that assessments of psychological abnormality are "relative" to a culture. Nothing here shows (Could anything show?) that the Dobu think that, to be sane, a person must take precautions where he sees no peril or that we think that a man is of perfectly sound mind although he neglects to take reasonable precautions when faced with clear and present danger.

In these examples we find Benedict making the very mistake which, earlier, I said was the source of the relativist's theory. We may conclude, then, that what anthropologists have presented as evidence of relativism is not evidence at all.

I have argued that the plausibility of moral relativism is the result of mistakenly thinking that, in certain cases, the behavior that is condoned in one culture is the same behavior that is condemned in another. These are, however, special cases. It would not, for instance, be a mistake to say that what those Sicilian men did to the women who rejected them was the same thing (namely, rape) that

we condemn when it occurs in our own culture. What happened to
Franca Viola was not something quite harmless or blameless that
only superficially resembled rape. No, rape is rape and murder is
murder wherever they may occur, and such actions do not become
blameless merely because an entire culture is (or has become) cal-
lous and condones them. (This is what some relativists dimly
realized when confronted with the ugly spectacle of Nazism.) But
sometimes we need to ask a question such as this: Is the head-
hunting practiced by, for instance, the Dyaks plain murder or do
their supernatural beliefs about what they are doing (even if false)
make their head-hunting morally blameless? The point is that if we
decide that the Dyaks are blameless we are deciding that they are
not really murderers; we are certainly not deciding that we must, in
their case, condone murder. The relativist, wanting to hold the
Dyaks blameless, goes about this all wrong by saying that the Dyaks
have a different morality.

Reading Questions

1. What moral purpose does Cook think motivated anthropologists to
   develop and promote moral relativism?
2. According to the author what considerations show that moral relativism is false?
3. Explain the two mistakes it is tempting to make about the Mobimtu.
4. Explain the mistake Raymond Firth was tempted to make.
5. Explain the mistakes the author attributes to Ruth Benedict in his assessments of the Kwakiutl and the Dobu.

Questions for Reflection and Research

1. If morality is not based on custom, on what is it based?
2. Can science decide whether morality is or is not a matter of custom?
3. What methods has Cook used to criticize Benedict? Are his methods
   scientific?
4. In some ways Cook seems to be arguing that once we understand a
   culture we will lose our reasons to condemn it. Does he think cultures
   can be condemned? When?
5. Should science be value-free? Is it value-free? (See selection #42 by
   Rescher.)
6. Compare and contrast Benedict's views about morality with those of
   Mencken (selection #9) about religion.
7. Does morality vary from culture to culture? If not, what does vary?
   (Did the Nazis have a different morality?)

selection 42.

The Ethical Dimension of Scientific Research

The Author: Nicholas Rescher (b. 1928) is a logician as well as a contributor of solutions to problems in metaphysics, theory of knowledge, value theory, and the philosophy of science. He was educated at Queens College and Princeton University and has taught philosophy at Lehigh University and the University of Pittsburgh. A member of a number of philosophical organizations, he has published widely.

The Selection: The view that science is value-free is attacked. Ethical problems are shown to occur at numerous points in the framework of scientific research. For example, the selection of research goals by national and institutional groups and the focus of an individual's own effort often require ethical decisions. Additional ethical problems discussed include those arising in science over research methods, standards of proof, dissemination of findings, restricting pseudo-scientific misinformation, and assigning credit for findings.

It has been frequently asserted that the creative scientist is distinguished by his objectivity. The scientist—so it is said—goes about his work in a rigidly impersonal and unfeeling way, unmoved by any emotion other than the love of knowledge and the delights of discovering the secrets of nature.

This widely accepted image of scientific inquiry as a cold, detached, and unhumane affair is by no means confined to the scientifically uninformed and to scientific outsiders, but finds many of its most eloquent spokesmen within the scientific community itself. . . .

From Nicholas Rescher, "The Ethical Dimension of Scientific Research" in *Beyond the Edge of Certainty: Essays in Contemporary Science and Philosophy*, Robert G. Colodny, editor, © 1965, pp. 261–275. Reprinted and adapted by permission of Prentice-Hall, Inc.

This point of view that science is "value free" has such wide acceptance as to have gained for itself the distinctive, if somewhat awesome, label as the thesis of the *value neutrality of science*.

Now the main thesis that I propose is simply that this supposed division between the evaluative disciplines on the one hand and the nonevaluative sciences on the other is based upon mistaken views regarding the nature of scientific research. In paying too much attention to the abstract logic of scientific inquiry, many students of scientific method have lost sight of the fact that science is a human enterprise, carried out by flesh and blood men, and that scientific research must therefore inevitably exhibit some normative [= evaluative] complexion. It is my aim to examine the proposition that evaluative, and more specifically *ethical*, problems crop up at numerous points within the framework of scientific research. I shall attempt to argue that the scientist does not, and cannot put aside his common humanity and his evaluative capabilities when he puts on his laboratory coat.

ETHICAL ISSUES AND THE COLLECTIVIZATION OF SCIENTIFIC RESEARCH

Before embarking on a consideration of the ethical dimension of scientific research, a number of preliminary points are in order.

In considering ethical issues within the sciences, I do not propose to take any notice at all of the various moral problems that arise in relation to what is *done with* scientific discoveries once they have been achieved. . . . Such questions of what is done with the fruits of the tree of science, both bitter and sweet, are not problems that arise *within* science, and are not ethical choices that confront the scientist himself. This fact puts them outside of my limited area of concern. They relate to the exploitation of scientific research, not to its pursuit, and thus they do not arise *within* science in the way that concerns us here.

Before turning to a description of some of the ethical issues that affect the conduct of research in the sciences, I should like to say a word about their reason for being. Ethical questions—that is, issues regarding the rightness and wrongness of conduct—arise out of people's dealings with each other, and pertain necessarily to the duties, rights, and obligations that exist in every kind of interpersonal relationship. For a Robinson Crusoe, few, if any, ethical problems present themselves. One of the most remarkable features of the science of our time is its joint tendency toward collectivization of effort and dispersion of social involvement. . . . This phenomenon of the collectivization of scientific research leads increasingly to more prominent emphasis upon ethical considerations within science itself. . . .

ETHICAL PROBLEMS REGARDING RESEARCH GOALS

Perhaps the most basic and pervasive way in which ethical problems arise in connection with the prosecution of scientific research is in regard to the choice of research problems, the setting of research goals, and the allocation of resources (both human and material) to the prosecution of research efforts. This ethical problem of choices relating to research goals arises at all levels of aggregation—the national, the institutional, and the individual. I should like to touch upon each of these in turn.

The National Level

As regards the national level, it is a commonplace that the United States government is heavily involved in the sponsorship of research. The current [=1965] level of federal expenditure on research and development is 8.4 billion dollars, which is around 10 per cent of the federal budget, and 1.6 per cent of the gross national product. If this seems like a modest figure, one must consider the historical perspective. The rate of increase of this budget item over the past ten years has been 10 per cent per annum, which represents a doubling time of seven years. . . .

In the Soviet Union, 35 per cent of all research and academic trained personnel is engaged in the engineering disciplines, compared with 10 per cent in medicine and pharmaceutical science. Does this 3.5 to 1 ratio of technology to medicine set a pattern to be adopted by the United States? Just how are we to "divide the pie" in allocating federal support funds among the various areas of scientific work? . . .

These decisions, which require weighing space probes against biological experimentation and atomic energy against oceanography are among the most difficult choices that have to be made by, or on behalf of, the scientific community. The entrance of political considerations may complicate, but cannot remove, the ethical issues that are involved in such choices.

What is unquestionably the largest ethical problem of scientific public policy today is a question of exactly this type. I refer to the difficult choices posed by the fantastic costs of the gadgetry of space exploration. The costs entailed by a systematic program of manned space travel are such as to necessitate major sacrifices in the resources our society can commit both to the advancement of knowledge as such in areas other than space and to medicine, agriculture, and other fields of technology bearing directly upon human welfare. Given the fact, now a matter of common knowledge, that modern science affords the means for effecting an almost infinite improvement in the material conditions of life for at least half the population of our planet, are we morally justified in sacrificing this opportunity to the supposed necessity of producing cold war spectaculars? No other question could more clearly illustrate the ethical character of the problem of research goals at the national level.

The Institutional Level

Let me now turn to the institutional level—that of the laboratory or department or research institute. Here again the ethical issue regarding research goals arises in various ways connected with the investment of effort, or, to put this same matter the other way around, with the selection of research projects.

One very pervasive problem at this institutional level is the classical issue of pure, or basic, versus applied, or practical, research. This problem is always with us and is always difficult, for the more "applied" the research contribution, the more it can yield immediate benefits to man; the more "fundamental," the deeper is its scientific significance and the more can it contribute to the development of science itself. No doubt it is often the case unfortunately that the issue is not dealt with on this somewhat elevated plane, but is resolved in favor of the applied end of the spectrum by the mundane, but inescapable, fact that this is the easier to finance.

I need scarcely add that this ethical issue can also arise at the institutional level in far more subtle forms. For instance, the directorship of a virology laboratory may have to choose whether to commit its limited resources to developing a vaccine which protects against a type of virus that is harmless as a rule but deadly to a few people, as contrasted with a variant type of virus that, while deadly to none, is very bothersome to many.

The Individual Level

The most painful and keenly felt problems are often not the greatest in themselves, but those that touch closest to home. At the level of the individual, too, the ethical question of research goals and the allocation of effort—namely that of the individual himself—can arise and present difficulties of the most painful kind. To cite one example, a young scientist may well ponder the question of whether to devote himself to pure or to applied work. Either option may present its difficulties for him, and these can, although they need not necessarily, be of an ethical nature.

Speaking now just of applied science, it is perfectly clear that characteristically ethical problems can arise for the applied scientist in regard to the nature of the application in question. This is at its most obvious in the choice of a military over against a nonmilitary problem context—A-bombs versus X-rays, poison gas versus pain killers. . . .

ETHICAL PROBLEMS REGARDING THE STAFFING OF RESEARCH ACTIVITIES

The recruitment and assignment of research personnel to particular projects and activities poses a whole gamut of problems of an ethical nature. I will confine myself to two illustrations.

It is no doubt a truism that scientists become scientists because of their interest in science. Devotion to a scientific career means involvement with scientific work: *doing* science rather than *watching* science done. The collectivization of science creates a new species—the science administrator whose very existence poses both practical and ethical problems. Alvin Weinberg [b. 1915], director of the Oak Ridge National Laboratory, has put it this way:

Where large sums of public money are being spent there must be many administrators who see to it that the money is spent wisely. Just as it is easier to spend money than to spend thought, so it is easier to tell other scientists how and what to do than to do it oneself. The big scientific community tends to acquire more and more bosses. The Indians with bellies to the bench are hard to discern for all the chiefs with bellies to the mahogany desks. Unfortunately, science dominated by adminstrators is science understood by administrators, and such science quickly becomes attenuated [= weakened], if not meaningless.

The facts adduced by Weinberg have several ethical aspects. For one thing there is Weinberg's concern with what administrationitis may be doing to science. And this is surely a problem with ethical implications derived from the fact that scientists have a certain obligation to the promotion of science itself as an ongoing human enterprise. On the other hand, there is the ethical problem of the scientist himself, for a scientist turned administrator is frequently a scientist lost to his first love.

My second example relates to the use of graduate students in university research. There seems to me to be a very real problem in the use of students in the staffing of research projects. We hear a great many pious platitudes about the value of such work for the training of students. The plain fact is that the kind of work needed to get the project done is simply not always the kind of work that is of optimum value for the basic training of a research scientist in a given field. Sometimes instead of doing the student a favor by awarding him a remunerative research fellowship, we may be doing him more harm than good. In some instances known to me, the project work that was supposedly the training ground of a graduate student in actuality derailed or stunted the development of a research scientist.

ETHICAL PROBLEMS REGARDING RESEARCH METHODS

Let me now take up a third set of ethical problems arising in scientific research—those having to do with the *methods* of the research itself. Problems of this kind arise perhaps most acutely in biological or medical or psychological experiments involving the use of experimental animals. [See selection #46.—ED.] They have to do with the measures of omission and commission for keeping experimental animals from needless pain and discomfort. In this connection, let me quote Margaret Mead [b. 1901];

The growth of importance of the study of human behavior raises a host of new ethical problems, at the head of which I would place the need for consent to the research by both observer and subject. Studies of the behavior of animals other than man introduced a double set of problems: how to control the tendency of the human observer to anthropomorphize, and so distort his observations, and how to protect both the animal and the experimenter from the effects of cruelty. In debates on the issue of cruelty it is usually recognized that callousness toward a living thing may produce suffering in the experimental subject, but it is less often recognized that it may produce moral deterioration in the experimenter. (From *Science*, Vol. 133 (1961),164.)

It goes without saying that problems of this sort arise in their most acute form in experiments that risk human life, limb, well-being, or comfort. [See selection #45.—ED.]

Problems of a somewhat similar character come up in psychological or social science experiments in which the possibility of a compromise of human dignity or integrity is present, so that due measures are needed to assure treatment based on justice and fair play.

ETHICAL PROBLEMS REGARDING STANDARDS OF PROOF

I turn now to a further set of ethical problems relating to scientific research—those that are bound up with what we may call the standards of proof. These have to do with the amount of evidence that a scientist accumulates before he deems it appropriate to announce his findings and put forward the claim that such-and-so may be regarded as an established fact. At what juncture should scientific evidence be reasonably regarded as strong enough to give warrant for a conclusion, and how should the uncertainties of this conclusion be presented?

This problem of standards of proof is ethical, and not merely theoretical or methodological in nature, because it bridges the gap between scientific understanding and action, between thinking and doing. . . .

Every trained scientist knows, of course, that "scientific knowledge" is a body of statements of varying degrees of certainty—including a great deal that is quite unsure as well as much that is reasonably certain. But in presenting particular scientific results, and especially in presenting his own results, a researcher may be under a strong temptation to fail to do justice to the precise degree of certainty and uncertainty involved.

On the one hand, there may be some room for play given to a natural human tendency to exaggerate the assurance of one's own findings. Moreover, when much money and effort have been expended, it can be embarrassing—especially when talking with the nonscientific sponsors who have footed the bill—to derogate [= take away] from the significance or suggestiveness of one's results by dwelling on the insecurities in their basis. . . .

On the other hand, it may in some instances be tempting for a researcher to underplay the certainty of his findings by adopting an unreasonably high standard of proof. This is especially possible in medical research, where life-risking actions may be based upon a research result. In this domain, a researcher may be tempted to "cover" himself by hedging his findings more elaborately than the realities of the situation may warrant. . . .

ETHICAL PROBLEMS REGARDING THE DISSEMINATION OF RESEARCH FINDINGS

A surprising variety of ethical problems revolve around the general topic of the dissemination of research findings. It is so basic a truth as to be almost axiomatic that, with the possible exception of a handful of unusual cases in the area of national security classification, a scientist has not only the right, but even the duty, to communicate his findings to the community of fellow scientists, so that his results may stand or fall in the play of the open market place of ideas. Modern science differs sharply in this respect from science in Renaissance times [about 1400–1700], when a scientist shared his discoveries only with trusted disciples, and announced his findings to the general public only in cryptogram form, if at all.

This ethical problem of favoritism in the sharing of scientific information has come to prominence again in our day. Although scientists do generally publish their findings, the processes of publication consume time, so that anything between six months and three years may elapse between a scientific discovery and its publication in the professional literature. It has become a widespread practice to make prepublication announcements of findings, or even pre-prepublication announcements. The ethical problem is posed by the extent and direction of such exchanges, for there is no doubt that in many cases favoritism comes into the picture, and that some workers and laboratories exchange findings in a preferential way that amounts to a conspiracy to maintain themselves ahead of the state of the art in the world at large. There is, of course, nothing reprehensible in the natural wish to overcome publication lags or in the normal desire for exchanges of ideas with fellow workers. But when such practices tend to become systematized in a prejudicial way, a plainly ethical problem comes into being.

Let us consider yet another ethical problem regarding the dissemination of research findings. The extensive dependence of science upon educated public opinion, in connection with its support both by the government and the foundations, has already been touched upon. This factor has a tendency to turn the reporting of scientific findings and the discussion of issues relating to scientific research into a kind of journalism. There is a strong incentive to create a favorable climate of public opinion for certain pet projects or concepts. Questions regarding scientific or technical merits thus tend to get treated not only in the proper forum of the science journals, but also in the public press and in Congressional or foundation committee rooms. Not only does this create the danger of scientific pressure groups devoted to preconceived ideas and endowed with the power of retarding other lines of thought, but it also makes for an unhealthy emphasis on the spectacular and the novel, unhealthy, that is, from the standpoint of the development of science itself. For such factors create a type of control over the direction of scientific research that is disastrously unrelated to the proper issue of strictly scientific merits. . . .

ETHICAL PROBLEMS REGARDING THE CONTROL OF SCIENTIFIC "MISINFORMATION"

Closely bound up with the ethical problems regarding the dissemination of scientific information are what might be thought of as the other side of the coin—the control, censorship, and suppression of scientific misinformation. Scientists clearly have a duty to protect both their own colleagues in other specialties and the lay public against the dangers of supposed research findings that are strictly erroneous, particularly in regard to areas such as medicine and nutrition, where the public health and welfare are concerned. And quite generally, of course, a scientist has an obligation to maintain the professional literature of his field at a high level of content and quality. The editors and editorial reviewers in whose hands rests access to the media of scientific publication clearly have a duty to preserve their readership from errors of fact and trivia of thought. But these protective functions must always be balanced by respect for the free play of ideas and by a real sensitivity to the possible value of the unfamiliar.

To give just one illustration of the importance of such considerations, I will cite the example of the nineteenth-century English chemist J. J. Waterston [1811–1883]. His groundbreaking papers on physical chemistry, anticipating the development of thermodynamics by more than a generation, were rejected by the referees of the Royal Society for publication in its *Proceedings*, with the comment (among others) that "the paper is nothing but of nonsense." As a result, Waterston's work lay forgotten in the archives of the Royal Society until rescued from oblivion by [John William] Rayleigh [1842–1919] some forty-five years later. . . .

Many other examples could be cited to show that it is vitally important that the gatekeepers of our scientific publications be keenly alive to the possible but unobvious value of unfamiliar and strange seeming conceptions.

It is worth emphasizing that this matter of "controlling" the dissemination of scientific ideas poses special difficulties due to an important, but much underrated, phenomenon: *the resistivity to novelty and innovation by the scientific community itself. . . .*

The history of science is, in fact, littered with examples of this phenomenon. [Joseph] Lister [1827–1912], in a graduation address to medical students, bluntly warned against blindness to new ideas such as he had himself encountered in advancing his theory of antisepsis. [The] discovery of the biological character of fermentation [by Louis Pasteur (1822–1895)] was long opposed by chemists, . . . and his germ theory met with sharp resistance from the medical fraternity of his day. No doubt due in part to the very peculiar character of [Franz Anton] Mesmer [1734–1815] himself, the phenomenon of hypnosis, or mesmerism, was rejected by the scientifically orthodox of his time as so much charlatanism. At the summit of the Age of Reason [= the eighteenth century in France], the French Academy dismissed the numerous and well-attested reports of stones falling from the sky (meteorites, that is to say) as mere folk stories. And this list could be prolonged *ad nauseam* [= to a sickening degree]. . . .

In summary, the prominence, even in scientific work, of the human psychological tendency to resist new ideas must temper the perspective of every scientist when enforcing what he conceives to be his duty to safeguard others against misinformation and error.

At no point, however, does the ethical problem of information control in science grow more difficult and vexatious than in respect to the boundary line between proper science on the one hand and pseudo-science on the other. The plain fact is that truth is to be found in odd places, and that scientifically valuable materials turn up in unexpected spots.

No one, of course, would for a moment deny the abstract thesis, that there is such a thing as pseudo-science, and that it must be contested and controlled. The headache begins with the question of just what is pseudo-science and what is not. We can all readily agree on some of the absurd cases so interestingly described in Martin Gardner's wonderful book *Fads and Fallacies in the Name of Science*. . . . [See selection #50.—ED.] But the question of exactly where science ends and where pseudo-science begins is at once important and far from simple. There is little difficulty indeed with Wilbur Glenn Voliva, Gardner's Exhibit No. 1, who during the first third of this century thundered out of Zion (Illinois) that "the earth is flat as a pancake." But parapsychology, for example, is another study and a much more complicated one. . . . Nobody in the scientific community wants to let pseudo-science make headway. But the trouble is that one man's interesting possibility may be another man's pseudo-science. . . .

But let us return to the ethical issues involved. These have to do not with the uncontroversial thesis that pseudo-science must be controlled, but with the procedural question of the *means* to be used for the achievement of this worthy purpose. It is with this problem of the means for its control that pseudo-science poses real ethical difficulties for the scientific community.

The handiest instrumentalities to this end and the most temptingly simple to use are the old standbys of thought control—censorship and suppression. But these are surely dire and desperate remedies. It is no doubt highly unpleasant for a scientist to see views that he regards as "preposterous" and "crackpot" to be disseminated and even to gain a considerable public following. But surely we should never lose sensitivity to the moral worth of the methods for achieving our ends or forget that good ends do not justify questionable means. It is undeniably true that scientists have the duty to prevent the propagation of error and misinformation. But this duty has to be acted on with thoughtful caution. It cannot be construed to fit the conveniences of the moment. And it surely cannot be stretched to give warrant to the suppression of views that might prove damaging to the public "image" of science or to justify the protection of one school of thought against its critics. Those scientists who pressured the publisher of [the] fanciful *Worlds in Collision* [of Immanuel Velikovsky (b. 1895)] by threatening to boycott the firm's textbooks unless this work were dropped from its list resorted to measures that I should not care to be called on to defend, but the case is doubtless an extreme one. However, the control exercised by editors and guardians of foundation pursestrings is more subtle, but no less effective and no less problematic.

The main point in this regard is one that needs little defense or argument in its support. Surely scientists, of all people, should have sufficient confidence in the ability of truth to win out over error in the market place of freely interchanged ideas as to be unwilling to forgo the techniques of rational persuasion in favor of the unsavory instrumentalities of pressure, censorship, and suppression.

ETHICAL PROBLEMS REGARDING THE ALLOCATION OF CREDIT FOR SCIENTIFIC RESEARCH ACHIEVEMENTS

The final set of ethical problems arising in relation to scientific research that I propose to mention relate to the allocation of credit for the achievements of research work. Moral philosophers as well as students of jurisprudence [= law] have long been aware of the difficulties in assigning to individuals the responsibility for corporate acts, and thus to allocate to individual wrongdoers the blame for group misdeeds. This problem now faces the scientific community in its inverse form—the allocation to individuals of credit for the research accomplishments resulting from conjoint, corporate, or combined effort. Particularly in this day of collectivized research, this problem is apt to arise often and in serious forms.

Let no one be put off by stories about scientific detachment and disinterestedness. The issue of credit for their findings has for many centuries been of the greatest importance to scientists. Doubts on this head are readily dispelled by the prominence of priority disputes in the history of science. Their significance is illustrated by such notorious episodes as the bitter and long-continuing dispute between [Isaac] Newton [1642–1727] and [Gottfried von] Leibniz [1646–1716] and their followers regarding priority in the invention of the calculus—a dispute that made for an estrangement between English and continental mathematics which lasted through much of the eighteenth century, considerably to the detriment of the quality of British mathematics during that era.

But to return to the present, the problem of credit allocation can come up nowadays in forms so complex and intricate as to be almost inconceivable to any mind not trained in the law. For instance, following out the implications of an idea put forward as an idle guess by X, Y, working under W's direction in Z's laboratory, comes up with an important result. How is the total credit to be divided? It requires no great imagination to think up some of the kinds of problems and difficulties that can come about in saying who is to be credited with what in this day of corporate and collective research. . . .

RETROSPECT ON THE ETHICAL DIMENSION OF SCIENTIFIC RESEARCH

Let us now pause for a moment to survey the road that we have traveled thus far. The discussion to this point has made a guided tour of a major part of the terrain constituting the ethical dimension of scientific research. In particular, we have seen that questions of a strictly ethical nature arise in connection with scientific research at the following crucial junctures:

1. the choice of research goals
2. the staffing of research activities
3. the selection of research methods
4. the specification of standards of proof
5. the dissemination of research findings
6. the control of scientific misinformation
7. the allocation of credit for research accomplishments

In short, it seems warranted to assert that, at virtually every juncture of scientific research work, from initial inception of the work to the ultimate reporting of its completed findings, issues of a distinctively ethical character may present themselves for resolution.

It is a regrettable fact that too many persons, both scientists and students of scientific method, have had their attention focused so sharply upon the abstracted "logic" of an idealized "scientific method" that this ethical dimension of science has completely escaped their notice. This circumstance seems to me to be particularly regrettable because it has tended to foster a harmful myth that finds strong support in both the scientific and the humanistic camps—namely, the view that science is antiseptically devoid of any involvement with human values. Science, on this way of looking at the matter, is so purely objective and narrowly factual in its concerns that it can, and indeed should, be wholly insensitive to the emotional, artistic, and ethical values of human life.

I hope that my analysis of the role of ethical considerations within the framework of science has been sufficiently convincing to show that this dichotomy, with its resultant divorce between the sciences and the humanities, is based on a wholly untenable conception of the actual division of labor between these two areas of intellectual endeavor. It is my strong conviction that both parties to this unasked for divorce must recognize the spuriousness of its alleged reasons for being, if the interests of a wholesome unity of human understanding are to be served properly. . . .

Reading Questions

1. What factors have led to the view that science is value-free?
2. Which ethical problems discussed arise primarily for scientific administrators and which arise primarily for individual scientists?
3. Be able to explain the various kinds of ethical issues enumerated by the author.

Questions for Reflection and Research

1. Are there other kinds of ethical issues within science that Rescher has overlooked?
2. Could it be argued that all the problems mentioned by Rescher are not really problems *within* science?
3. Should scientists be concerned about how animals are used in scientific research? Why or why not? (See selection #46 by Singer.)
4. What kinds of ethical issues confront those scientists whose research requires experimentation on human beings? (See selection #45 by Kieffer.)
5. Read an account of the human factors involved in a scientific discovery. See, for example, *The Double Helix* by James Watson (New York: Atheneum Publishers, 1968). To what extent do the concerns men-

tioned by Rescher intrude in the scientists' lives? If they do not intrude, should they?

6. Compare Rescher's views on pseudo-science with those of Martin Gardner in selection #50.

7. Compare Rescher's account of the issues involved in funding science with those of Robert Fischer in selection #52.

Where Are the Biologists Taking Us?

The Author: Gordon Rattray Taylor (b. 1911) is English and received his education at Cambridge University. He began his career as a newspaper writer and gradually came to specialize in science writing. He has published widely, been involved in television science programs, and has participated in a lecture tour of the United States. The International Science Writers Association was founded by him.

The Selection: It is argued that we are now in the opening stages of a new and extremely profound human revolution: the biological revolution. Advances in biology are beginning to change many aspects of human life. These advances will transform society, create new ethical problems, lend themselves to misuse, and possibly occur too fast for society to accommodate. Changes in biology will involve control of reproduction, organ transplants, lengthening of life, control of moods and feelings, and control of intelligence. The control of biological research and limiting the uses made of new findings must occur to help ensure the survival of civilization.

Two hundred years ago the French Encyclopaedist [Denis] Diderot [1713–1784], in an ironical vision of the future which he called *The Dream of d'Alembert*, described how one day human embryos would be artificially cultivated and their hereditary endowment predetermined. His hero saw 'a warm room with the floor covered with little pots, and on each of these pots a label: soldiers,

From *The Biological Time Bomb* by Gordon Rattray Taylor (Cleveland: New American Library and World Publishing Company, 1968), pp. 9–21. © 1968 by Gordon Rattray Taylor. Printed by permission of Harold Matson Company, Inc.

magistrates, philosophers, poets, potted courtesans, potted kings. . . .'

Today his vision no longer seems entirely fanciful, and some biologists believe that, before the end of the century at latest, it may be realized. Other writers—among them [George Bernard] Shaw [1856–1950] and [H. G.] Wells [1866–1946]—have dreamed of the control of growth, of tampering with memory and of the extension of the human life span to many centuries. None of these seems any longer to be so impossible of achievement. Indeed, some may be alarmingly close.

All these are biological advances. We are now, though we only dimly begin to realize the fact, in the opening stages of the Biological Revolution—a twentieth-century revolution which will affect human life far more profoundly than the great Mechanical Revolution of the nineteenth century or the Technological Revolution through which we are now passing. . . .

The biologists have got up their sleeves discoveries which have just as universal and earth-shaking an effect as those of the chemists and physicists. Attentive readers of the scientific journals have noticed, during the past five years or so [that is, from about 1962 to 1967], the appearance of a series of warning statements by eminent biologists—some made verbally at meetings or symposia, others in special articles or letters—warnings about the direction in which biology is heading. . . .

[P]erhaps the strongest warning has come from the British ethologist Dr. W. H. Thorpe [b. 1902] of Cambridge University, one of the world's leading experts on animal behaviour, who declared recently: 'The ethical problems raised by the population explosion and artificial insemination, by genetics and neurophysiology, and by the social and mental sciences are at least as great as those arising from atomic energy and the H-bomb, from space travel and ultrasonic flight, from telecommunications, computers and automation. There is no doubt in my mind that several of these developments are as epoch-making for mankind as any that have preceded them. They rank at least as high, if not higher, in importance than the discovery of fire, of agriculture, the development of printing and the discovery of the wheel.'

More important than fire, printing and the wheel? One could hardly put it more strongly than that. What induces Dr. Thorpe to make such a sweeping claim?

The discoveries he names have all radically changed man's way of life and the scope of his ability to influence his fellows. What the biologists have in store will certainly change our way of life too. Hitherto, for instance, it has been usual for a child to be born of two parents of differing sex, both of whom were alive at the time of his/her conception. Such tedious limitations are rapidly disappearing, with unforeseeable consequences for marriage and the family as we know it. Thanks to techniques for storing the male seed, it is already the case that a child may be conceived long after the death of the father. And a woman might bear a child to her great-grandfather one day. Indeed, research now in hand may make it possible for a woman to bear a child without male intervention, or even for a child to be born without the comfort of a maternal womb. The parents, if any, may be able to specify the sex of the child in advance, and even change it.

But these are simply advances in the single field of the reproductive process. In the field of ageing, gerontologists foresee both an extension of the life span and the preservation of a degree of youthful vigour into old age. Some even contemplate the possibility of immortality. Neurologists and others are exploring the brain, and hint at raising the level of intelligence, at improvement of memory and the control of moods and feelings. Geneticists are so confident of being able to tamper with heredity that they have begun to warn us to beware of them, while transplantation surgery has already begun to present us with ethical problems. Biochemists have even seriously proposed an attempt to synthesize life from inert materials. All these 'advances', it is evident, would have major social and ethical implications if they are really 'on'.

The difficulty which a writer faces in writing about such developments is that a general statement conveys only a feeble impression of the potentialities of the advance, whereas a concrete one appears hopelessly sensational and even repellent. Thus if I say that grafting techniques may make body parts completely interchangeable I suggest little more than a medical advance. On the other hand, if I say that one day someone might say to you, indicating another person, 'I want you to meet my uncle and niece. They were in a car smash but fortunately the surgeon was able to get one complete body out of the undamaged bits', I am more likely to evoke incredulity [= disbelief] than alarm.

I suspect that the immediate reaction of many people to such forecasts is that, if not downright impossible, they lie so far in the future as to be of no practical importance to people now living. Nothing could be farther from the truth, I regret to say. While some of the possibilities hinted at by biologists, such as the attainment of personal immortality, may lie a century or more in the future, it is certain that much of what they are doing will begin to bear fruit in the lifetime of those now living. For instance, the growing ability to control mental states is *already* facing us with problems such as the inability of young people to make a mature use of LSD. But this is not a once-for-all phenomenon. The hallucinogens are merely one of the first of an indefinitely long series of advances in the direction of mental control, and the present generation will certainly live to see many comparable problems as well as others less definable.

Again, the discovery of oral contraceptives is merely the *beginning* of a new world of expertise in the control of the reproductive process, and the controversies which have raged about the use of such pills will soon be lost in the thunder of even more desperate battles.

No one can say for sure when anything will be discovered, but it is fair to assume that at least *some* of the matters on which biologists all over the world are working will yield breakthroughs in the next five or ten years. For instance, there is an imminent prospect of being able to control the process by which the body rejects grafts of tissue from other organisms; this will make a wide range of transplantation operations possible. The heart transplantations which make news stories today should be viewed simply as the earliest advances in a long campaign. To look on such developments as complete and final is to repeat the complacency of the man who dismissed the automobile with the comment: 'Very clever, but it will never replace the horse.'

The fact is, we are all short on imagination. How many people, looking at a black bakelite telephone or brown bakelite switch-cover, thirty years ago, envisaged the world of brilliantly coloured plastics, both rigid and flexible, which we know today? Equally, it takes uncommon imagination to see in the hard-won and often unsatisfying biological achievements of today the fantastic possibilities which will be taken for granted by the generation of tomorrow. And I don't mean the day *after* tomorrow. Many of the possibilities discussed in this book, incredible as they may seem to some, will become realities only too soon.

It is therefore not merely interesting but socially important to try to evaluate them without delay. . . .

The radical nature of what is happening can perhaps best be conveyed by a comparison. We can now create, on a commercial scale by chemical processes, substances which previously we had to look for in nature, and even substances which never previously existed. Whereas before we had to make do with what nature provided, now we can decide what we want; this may be called chemical control. Similarly, in the coming century, we shall achieve biological control: the power to say how much life, of what sort, shall exist where. We shall even be able to create forms of life which never existed before.

To some the prospect may seem terrifying, but as in all such advances, the new knowledge can be used for good or ill. The first consequences will certainly be a great extension of responsibilities. What was settled before, by chance or ineluctable circumstance, now becomes within our own power to regulate, and presents us with the need to take decisions—a task which many people find burdensome. Constant decision-making is the price of freedom. Part of the problem which faces us is to devise adequate institutions

for taking the broader social decisions with which the mushroom-
ing of biological knowledge most certainly is about to face us.

The mechanical revolution brought new freedoms to the ordinary man. Instead of having to spend his life in the area where he
was born, it became easy for him to visit other parts of the country,
to settle down in a chosen area, and still to maintain contacts with
his family and childhood environment. True, this faced him with
the necessity of actually *deciding* where to live, instead of accepting
what the fates provided, but the responsibility was small compared
with the benefits. Equally, of course, it led to a great deal of unnecessary travel, perhaps not worth the great technological investment which was needed to support it, and it certainly created new
population movements and accelerated the drift to the towns,
creating social problems there. The biological revolution will have
comparable results.

Such knowledge will not only change our lives but will also, in so
doing, change our industries. It will also affect the scale and direction of investment, and even the scale and direction of public taxation. We are now seeing the growth of a science-based industry
which is primarily rooted in physics and, in particular, electronics.
A second wave of science-based industry which is primarily
biochemical, biophysical and biological will follow—where? Its
forerunners are the small but immensely skilled firms which will
now supply, often from stock, the most recondite biochemical substances, and the 'biomedical engineers' who devise ingenious
machines for doctors, from radio pills to artificial kidneys. There
will also be a vast expansion of medicine.

Agriculture will also be affected. The destruction of pests by releasing sterilized males, as was so successfully achieved by Dr. Edward F. Knipling [b. 1909] with the screw-worm fly, which formerly
caused the loss of millions of dollars' worth of livestock every year,
is but a pointer to the things to come.

To take a long look into the crystal ball may therefore be com-
mercially smart as well as socially desirable.

There is also the military aspect. It was the British astronomer
Fred Hoyle [b. 1915] who said to me: 'I wouldn't go into biology if I
were starting my life again now. In twenty years it is the biologists
who will be working behind barbed wire.' The United States and
Britain are known to have considerable establishments for the
study of biological warfare. The American one is at Fort Detrick,
the British at Porton Down. The American army also has plants, at
Edgeworth Arsenal and elsewhere, for the manufacture of biological weapons, and several of these have been used in Vietnam. Such
weapons can be deployed against crops and herds, as well as against
men. How far other countries, and especially Russia and China, are
pursuing similar activities remains shrouded in secrecy. It would be
a pretty safe bet that they are, as may be some of the smaller belli-
cose countries. This might expand into a major branch of warfare.

Parallel with this runs the emergence of neurological war. Many countries are known to be manufacturing nerve-gases. U.S. generals have advocated the use of substances (among them, LSD-25) which may undermine the will to resist, claiming that a humane type of 'bloodless warfare' could be introduced. Important if true,. but some people see another side to the question, and the issue needs clarifying.

All these advances, in fact, pose problems on which society ought to be making up its mind, and it is vital that it should do so before things have gone so far that they cannot be altered. The question of whether to regulate the world population size, and if so how and at what level, is merely one of the first of a great series of universal issues which need to be faced, and most of which are still being ignored.

In short, the biological revolution is certain to affect our lives, our safety and our happiness in a myriad ways.

The biological revolution presents mankind with a group of quite new and extremely pressing questions. It is not often that a writer can use the word 'vital' without exaggeration, but these are truly vital matters—matters which affect our very lives.

Is this new accession of human know-how desirable? Will it actually conduce to greater human happiness? Even if it could, in principle, be so used, will man in fact have the sense to use it wisely or will he, as so often in the past, misuse it, creating biological slums and vital pollution to parallel the physical slums and chemical pollution which were the heavy price of the industrial revolution?

I call these new questions because, until the advent of the atomic bomb, the conviction that all knowledge was to the good and that scientific research promised overwhelming benefits for man was generally held. The idea of forbidding a line of research did not receive serious discussion, nor did anyone hesitate to publish his results for any but reasons of commercial advantage. But today the release of nuclear forces is seen by many people as entailing risks which outweigh any conceivable advantage. And it has actually happened that scientists have avoided publicizing procedures which would bring the power to make nuclear weapons within the reach of small groups.

Some psychologists feel compunction about publicizing all they know about control of the mind, for fear that such knowledge will be abused and used for 'brainwashing' or similiar purposes. Quite a number of the developments I am about to describe [in a part of Taylor's book not included here] could be equally misused, either through malice or stupidity, or both. So the question of whether such work should proceed unsupervised and uncontrolled is real and urgent. There is still time to stop. Soon it will be too late, even if we wish to. These issues must therefore be considered now.

The feeling that some kinds of knowledge are too dangerous for man, at least in his current state of social and intellectual development, is founded, I think, on the belief that he is more likely to use new power for ill than for good. Or perhaps we should say that more people will misuse the new powers, or that they will be misused more often, than they will be used for good. Or, simply, that misuse could have consequences so serious as to outweigh any possible advantages of wise use. This is what we feel about nuclear warfare. The costs and misery caused by a nuclear war would so far outweigh the advantages of cheaper power for civil purposes, that only a vanishingly small risk of misuse is acceptable.

Are the new biological powers of this character? How serious are the consequences of misuse? How likely is misuse to occur? Since only a confirmed optimist would bet on men—some men, somewhere—not misusing powers, the question of whether we could impose some kind of control on biological research is not an academic one.

Apart from the actual misuse of new powers, whether by accident or design, there is a contingent [= factual] question of extreme importance. How great a rate of change can society stand? It takes time to adjust to new social conditions, and when the rate of innovation is rapid, the disruption caused can destroy a culture, as has often been seen when western culture has impinged on technologically primitive societies. (There are curious parallels between the response of western youth to hallucinogenic drugs like LSD and the response of South Sea Islanders to alcohol.) It seems quite possible that the rate of biological innovation may be so high as to destroy western civilization, perhaps even world culture, from within, creating a disorientated, unhappy and unproductive society, unless it is brought under deliberate control.

Control could take two forms. Either the scope and direction of research could be controlled, or research could be left free, but its findings could be placed in the ice-box and brought out for practical application only when and as desired. In practice a combination of both would be needed, since even a rigorous control of research could not prevent the occurrence of unscheduled discoveries. But, of course, both types of control would be immensely difficult to apply, and could very easily be the source of abuse and misjudgment. So much so, that many people would prefer to take a chance on the dangers of uncontrolled research rather than face the limitations of control. Certainly, almost all scientists would take this view.

This being so, we are obliged to face up to the converse set of implications. If the rate of change is to be high, and especially if it is unlimited, could we improve our capacity to adapt? Under present conditions, when an innovation is made, it is launched into use without any preliminary social readjustment. A good example is artificial insemination. This . . . creates problems of a legal kind: for instance, does the child of an artificially inseminated mother inherit property from its legal father? But instead of clarifying the law on this and similar points *before* making the technique available, we have introduced the technique and left the law—to say nothing of the social and personal implications—to sort themselves out as best they can, a process which is now occurring at a considerable cost in time, money, heartbreak and injustice as between different cases.

Having surveyed the work of biologists in many countries, having listened to their own comments on the implications of such work, to me at least it is clear that the social and personal costs of adapting to this new knowledge will be terrifyingly, unacceptably high unless we make a major, conscious effort to regulate the pace and scope of development, instead of letting it control us.

Apparently it is not in human nature to consider making major social adjustments before the shoe actually pinches: indeed, it often has to go on pinching a long time before inertia and vested interest are overcome. A more telling instance than artificial insemination is the need for many more kidney dialysis machines, for lack of which large numbers of people are now dying. Only the first stirrings of a public demand that something be done about this situation are so far felt. One cannot avoid the conclusion that the public will not begin to make provision for the many other strange developments described in this book until the problems are dumped, howling, on their doorstep.

I am therefore forced to the conclusion that society will have to control the pace of research, if it can, and will certainly have to regulate the release of these new powers. There will have to be a biological 'ice-box' in which the new techniques can be placed until society is ready for them. This is not a conclusion to my taste at all. I do not feel in the least optimistic about our prospects of exerting such control without serious muddles and abuses. Nevertheless, the social consequences of what is in the pipeline could be so disastrous—nothing less than the break-up of civilization as we know it—that the attempt must be made. . . .

The writing is on the wall: it is urgently necessary that someone should make an attempt to interpret it.

Reading Questions

1. List all the advances that Taylor foresees in biology. What social and ethical consequences does he predict for each?
2. How will the biological revolution change our industries and thinking on military matters?
3. How and why does Taylor think the scope and direction of biological research should be controlled?

Questions for Reflection and Research

1. Read Taylor's book. To what extent have his conclusions and predictions been borne out by subsequent developments in biology and elsewhere?

2. What ethical problems must people in the health care fields now face that they did not have to face twenty years ago?

3. If there are not enough kidney dialysis machines in a hospital to care for all those who need them, who should decide who gets to use them? What factors are relevant to selecting who gets to use them?

4. What kinds of control are now placed on recombinant DNA research in this country? In other countries? What other kinds of control are being considered or should be considered?

5. Who should decide when death occurs? How should such a decision be made? What role should science play in determining a satisfactory definition for death?

6. Compare the concerns of early nuclear scientists with the concerns of present-day biologists. What are the parallels and differences? (See selection #44 by Kipphardt.)

The Responsibility of Scientists to Humanity

The Author: Heinar Kipphardt (b. 1922) is German and was educated in medicine at a number of German universities. He left the practice of medicine to become a full-time dramatic author. Beginning in 1953 (when his first play was produced in Berlin) his stage and television plays have been well received.

The Selection: The selection is from a play which was based on an actual security hearing that occurred in 1954 in the United States during the Communist scare promoted by Senator Joseph McCarthy. The physicist, J. Robert Oppenheimer (1904–1967), is under examination for possible disloyalty. In the course of the hearing Oppenheimer indicates his part in developing the atomic bomb and in calculating which Japanese cities might be the most devastated by it. At this point in the play he seems to favor the view that it was not his business as a scientist to try to influence decisions about whether the bomb should be produced or used—such decisions are not scientific but political. Implicit in the selection is the issue of the extent to which scientists should concern themselves with the possibility of evil consequences of their research.

PART ONE

The stage is open. Visible spotlights. White hangings separate the stage from the auditorium, sufficiently high for the following documentaries to be projected on them:

A selection from *In the Matter of J. Robert Oppenheimer* by Heinar Kipphardt. Translated by Ruth Speirs. This translation © 1967, 1968 by John Roberts. Originally published in German as *In der Sache J. Robert Oppenheimer.* © 1964 Suhrkamp Verlag, Frankfurt am Main. All rights reserved. Reprinted with the permission of Hill and Wang, now a division of Farrar, Straus & Giroux, Inc., and of Methuen & Co. Ltd.

Scientists in battledress, looking like military personnel, are doing the count-down for test explosions—4–3–2–1–0 (in English, Russian, and French).

Cloud formations caused by atomic explosions unfold in great beauty, watched by scientists through dark filters.

On the wall of a house, radiation shadows of a few victims of the atomic explosion on Hiroshima.

The hangings open.

SCENE 1

Room 2022

A small ugly office; walls of white-washed wooden boards. The room has been temporarily furnished for the purpose of the investigation. On a raised platform, back center, a table and three black leather armchairs for the members of the Board. Behind, on the wall, the Stars and Stripes. In front of the platform, floor level, the stenographers are seated with their equipment. On the right, ROBB *and* ROLANDER, *counsel for the Atomic Energy Commission, are busying themselves with stacks of documents. Opposite* ROBB *and* ROLANDER, *on a raised platform, tables and chairs for* OP-PENHEIMER'S *counsel. In front of the platform, floor level, a small old leather sofa.*

J. ROBERT OPPENHEIMER *enters Room 2022 by a side door on the right. He is accompanied by his two lawyers. An official leads him diagonally across the room to the leather sofa. His lawyers spread out their materials. He puts down his smoking paraphernalia and steps forward to the footlights.*

OPPENHEIMER. On the twelfth of April 1954, a few minutes to ten, J. Robert Oppenheimer, Professor of Physics at Princeton, formerly Director of the Atomic Weapons Laboratories at Los Alamos, and, later, Adviser to the Government on atomic matters, entered Room 2022 in Building T3 of the Atomic Energy Commission in Washington, to answer questions put to him by a Personnel Security Board, concerning his views, his associations, his actions, suspected of disloyalty. The evening before this investigation, Senator McCarthy said in a television interview:

A huge picture of Joseph McCarthy is projected on the white screens at the back. OPPENHEIMER *goes to the leather sofa and fills his pipe. A voice shaking with agitation issues from the loudspeakers.*

McCARTHY'S VOICE. If there are no Communists in our government, why do we delay the hydrogen bomb by eighteen months while our defense services report day after day that the Russians are feverishly stepping up on the H-bomb? Now they've got it! Now our monopoly is gone! When I tell America tonight that our nation may perish, it will perish because of that delay of eighteen months. And, I ask you, who is to blame? Were they loyal Americans or were they traitors, those who deliberately misled our government, who got themselves celebrated as atomic heroes, and whose crimes must at last be investigated.

The members of the Board enter by a small door, back center. Those present rise for a moment. Then everybody sits down.

GRAY. This Board has been appointed by the United States Atomic Energy Commission to investigate Dr. J. Robert Oppenheimer's continued eligibility for clearance. It is composed of the following members: Thomas A. Morgan, Ward V. Evans, and myself, Gordon Gray, Chairman. Counsel for the Atomic Energy Commission are Roger Robb and C. A. Rolander. Dr. Oppenheimer is represented by Lloyd K. Garrison and Herbert S. Marks. Dr. Oppenheimer is present as a witness in his own case. This inquiry is not a trial. It shall be regarded as strictly confidential.

MARKS. May I ask, Mr. Chairman, whether any of you saw the interview with Senator McCarthy last night?

GRAY. I did not see it. Did you, Mr. Morgan?

MORGAN [*looking up from his documents for a moment*]. McCarthy? No.

EVANS. I heard it on the radio. I was greatly surprised. I immediately thought of Oppenheimer.

MARKS. Did you hear the interview, Mr. Robb?

ROBB. No. Senator McCarthy would have to be clairvoyant if he alluded to our proceeding.

MARKS. He was interviewed by Fulton Lewis, Jr. I believe you represented that gentleman at various trials, Mr. Robb.

GRAY. Did you take his remarks as referring to yourself, Dr. Oppenheimer?

OPPENHEIMER. Five or six people called me up. Einstein said: "If I had the choice again I'd rather be a plumber or a pedlar, if only to enjoy some small measure of independence."

MARKS. I mention the interview because it makes me wonder if our proceedings can be kept private, Mr. Chairman.

GRAY. We shall do our best. . . . It is my duty, Dr. Oppenheimer, to ask whether you are satisfied with the composition of the Board.

OPPENHEIMER. Yes. With one general reservation.

GRAY. What is your reservation?

OPPENHEIMER. The Board will examine the complex duties of a physicist in our times; therefore, I would have preferred the members to be scientists. Only Professor Evans is engaged in science, I believe.

EVANS. But I don't know anything about nuclear physics, either. Fortunately. You probably know that we had no choice in this matter here. We were appointed. I wouldn't have chosen it myself.

OPPENHEIMER. Neither would I, I guess.

MARKS. The profession of the members should perhaps be shown in the record.

GRAY. Very well, Mr. Marks. Ward V. Evans . . .

EVANS. Professor of Chemistry, Chicago.

GRAY. Thomas A. Morgan . . .

MORGAN. Chairman of the Board and President of the Sperry Gyroscope Company, atomic equipment. One of the sharks of Big Business. [*He laughs.*]

GRAY. Gordon Gray, newspaper editor, radio station; former Secretary of the Army, Department of Defense.

MORGAN. Information concerning our income is not required?

MARKS. You wouldn't want to disclose yours, Mr. Morgan.

Slight laughter.

GRAY. I would like to ask Dr. Oppenheimer whether he wishes to testify under oath.

OPPENHEIMER. Certainly.

GRAY. You are not obliged to do so.

OPPENHEIMER. I know. [*He rises to his feet.*]

GRAY. Julius Robert Oppenheimer, do you swear that the testimony you are to give the Board shall be the truth, the whole truth, and nothing but the truth, so help you God?

OPPENHEIMER. I do.

GRAY. The proceeding may now commence. May I ask you to take the stand . . . Mr. Robb.

OPPENHEIMER *walks across to a swivel chair which faces the members of the Board. He sits down and lights his pipe.*

ROBB. You have been called the Father of the Atom Bomb, Doctor?

OPPENHEIMER. In magazines. Yes.

ROBB. You would not call yourself that?

OPPENHEIMER. It isn't a very pretty child—and it has about a hundred fathers, if we consider the basic research. In several countries.

ROBB. But the baby was ultimately born in Los Alamos, in the laboratories which you yourself had set up, and of which you were the Director from 1943 to 1945.

OPPENHEIMER. We produced that patent toy, yes.

ROBB. So you are not denying it, Doctor? [OPPENHEIMER *laughs.*] You produced it in a fantastically short time, you tested it, and then you dropped it on Japan, did you not?

OPPENHEIMER. No.

ROBB. You did not?

OPPENHEIMER. The dropping of the atom bomb on Hiroshima was a political decision—it wasn't mine.

ROBB. But you supported the dropping of the atom bomb on Japan. Or didn't you?

OPPENHEIMER. What do you mean by "supported"?

ROBB. You helped to select the targets, did you not?

OPPENHEIMER. I was doing my job. We were given a list of possible targets . . .

ROBB. Would you name them?

OPPENHEIMER. Hiroshima, Kokura, Nigata, Kyoto . . . [*Partial views of these cities are projected on the white screens at the back.*] . . . and we, as experts, were asked which targets would be most suitable for the dropping of the atomic bomb, according to the experience we had gathered from tests.

ROBB. Whom do you mean by "we," Doctor?

OPPENHEIMER. An advisory council of nuclear physicists, appointed for this purpose by the Secretary of War.

ROBB. Who was on that council?

OPPENHEIMER. Fermi, Lawrence, Arthur H. Compton, and myself.
Photographs of these scientists are projected on the screens.
ROBB. And you had to select the targets?
OPPENHEIMER. No. We supplied the scientific data as to the suitability of the targets.
ROBB. What kind of target did you consider to be of the desired suitability?
OPPENHEIMER. According to our calculations, the area had to be at least two miles in diameter, densely built up, preferably with wooden buildings—because of the blast, and the subsequent wave of fire. Also, the selected targets had to be of a high military and strategic value, and unscathed by previous bombardments.
ROBB. Why, Doctor?
OPPENHEIMER. To enable us to measure exactly the effect of a single atomic bomb.
EVANS. These military considerations, I mean, after all, they were the business of the physicists, weren't they, at that time?
OPPENHEIMER. Yes. Because we were the only people who had the necessary experience.
EVANS. I see. I'm rather out of my depth here. How did you feel?
OPPENHEIMER. I asked myself that question, later. I don't know. . . . I was very relieved when the Secretary of War followed our suggestions and crossed the famous temple city, Kyoto, off the list. It was the largest and most vulnerable target.
ROBB. But you did not oppose the dropping of the atom bomb on Hiroshima?
OPPENHEIMER. We set forth arguments against . . .
ROBB. I am asking you, Doctor, whether *you* opposed it.
OPPENHEIMER. I set forth arguments against dropping it.
ROBB. Against dropping the atom bomb?
OPPENHEIMER. Yes, that's right. But I did not press the point. Not specifically.
ROBB. You mean to say that having worked day and night for three or four years to produce the atomic bomb, you then argued it should not be used?
OPPENHEIMER. No. When I was asked by the Secretary of War I set forth the arguments both for and against. I expressed my uneasiness.
ROBB. Did you not also determine the height, Doctor, at which the atomic bomb was to explode in order to produce the maximum effect?
OPPENHEIMER. We, as experts, were doing a job we were asked to do. But this does not mean that we thereby decided that the bomb should in fact be dropped.
ROBB. You knew of course, did you not, that the dropping of the atomic bomb on the target you had selected would kill thousands of civilians?
OPPENHEIMER. Not as many people as we thought, as things turned out.
ROBB. How many were killed?
OPPENHEIMER. Seventy thousand.
ROBB. Did you have moral scruples about that?
OPPENHEIMER. Terrible ones.

ROBB. You had terrible moral scruples?

OPPENHEIMER. I don't know anyone who would *not* have had terrible moral scruples after the dropping of the bomb.

ROBB. Isn't that a trifle schizophrenic?

OPPENHEIMER. What is? To have moral scruples?

ROBB. To produce the thing, to pick the targets, to determine the height at which the explosion has the maximum effect—and then to be overcome by moral scruples at the consequences. Isn't that a trifle schizophrenic, Doctor?

OPPENHEIMER. Yes. . . . It is the kind of schizophrenia we physicists have been living with for several years now.

ROBB. Would you elucidate that?

OPPENHEIMER. The great discoveries of modern science have been put to horrible use. Nuclear energy is not the atomic bomb.

ROBB. You mean it could be exploited industrially, and so forth?

OPPENHEIMER. It could produce abundance, for the first time. It's a matter of cheap energy.

ROBB. Are you thinking of a Golden Age, a Land of Cockaigne, that sort of thing?

OPPENHEIMER. Yes, plenty for all. It is our misfortune that people rather think of the reverse kind of uses.

ROBB. Whom do you mean by "people," Doctor?

OPPENHEIMER. Governments. The world is not ready for the new discoveries. It is out of joint.

ROBB. And you have come along "to set it right," as Hamlet says?

OPPENHEIMER. I can do no such thing. The world itself must do that.

MORGAN. Dr. Oppenheimer, do you mean to tell an old pragmatist like me that you made the atomic bomb in order to create some Land of Cockaigne? Did you not make it in order to use it and win the war with it?

OPPENHEIMER. We made it in order to prevent it being used. Originally, at any rate.

MORGAN. You spent two billion dollars of the taxpayers' money on the bomb in order to prevent it being used?

OPPENHEIMER. To prevent it being used by Hitler. In the end it turned out that there wasn't any German atomic bomb project. . . . But then we used it all the same.

ROLANDER. I beg your pardon, sir, but were you really not asked—at a certain stage in the development of the bomb—were you not asked whether it should be used against Japan?

OPPENHEIMER. We weren't asked *whether* it should be used, but only *how* it should be used in order to produce the maximum effect.

ROLANDER. Is that entirely correct, sir?

OPPENHEIMER. What do you mean?

ROLANDER. Did not the Secretary of War show you the so-called Franck Report, the memorandum by the physicists Szilard, Franck, and others? It strongly opposed the dropping of the bomb on Japan and recommended an internationally public demonstration of the bomb over a desert.

OPPENHEIMER. We were given it to read. That's right. Not officially, I believe.

ROBB. What did you say to that, Doctor?

OPPENHEIMER. That we were in no position to decide this question, that opinion was divided among us. We set forth our arguments—for, and against.

ROBB. Were you against?

OPPENHEIMER. Lawrence was against. I was undecided, I'm afraid. I think we said that the exploding of one of these things as a firecracker over a desert wasn't likely to be very impressive—and, probably, that the overriding consideration should be the saving of lives, by bringing the war to an end as soon as possible.

ROBB. Did this not mean, in effect, Doctor, that you were *against* a demonstration of the weapon—and *for* it being dropped without warning?

OPPENHEIMER. It most certainly did not mean that. No. We were physicists, not the military, not politicians. That was the time of very heavy fighting on Okinawa. It was a horrible decision. . . .

Reading Questions

1. What information and advice did Oppenheimer supply to the government with regard to dropping the atomic bomb on Japan?
2. Why does Robb think Oppenheimer's behavior was somewhat schizophrenic?
3. What, according to Oppenheimer, was given as the initial reason for developing the atomic bomb?

Questions for Reflection and Research

1. Read the entire play and read biographical material on Oppenheimer to find out how he sought to impede development of the hydrogen bomb.
2. Why was the periodical *The Bulletin of the Atomic Scientists* founded? Summarize the contents of some recent issues.
3. What other research by scientists has led to (or has the potential to lead to) great harm to humanity? (See, for example, selection #43 by Taylor.)
4. Should scientists have training in ethics?
5. Is science value-free so that moral or ethical considerations are not relevant to its practice? (See selection #42 by Rescher.)
6. Study the history of the atomic bomb project. What should the physicists have done?
7. Should scientists have helped develop the neutron bomb? Should any government actually produce a neutron bomb for military use?

The Ethics of Experimenting with Human Subjects

The Author: George H. Kieffer (b. 1930) was educated at Concordia Teachers College (Illinois), the University of Colorado, and the University of Arizona. His graduate training was in ecology and cell biology. His present position on the biology faculty of the University of Illinois enables him to pursue research interests in biological education and on ethical problems created by biological findings and research activities.

The Selection: The ethical concern with experimentation on human beings is of relatively recent origin. Reactions to experiments conducted in German concentration camps led to the drafting of the Nuremberg Code of conduct for those who experiment on humans. It stresses that experimentation should not be done unless experimenters obtain fully informed consent of subjects. Kieffer stresses that fully informed consent is difficult to obtain when experimental subjects are ill, or prisoners, or children, or mentally retarded. Further, it is not possible to have experimental subjects fully informed in "double-blind" experiments.

It is fair to say that among all the questions raised by an increasingly skeptical public about science, technology, and medicine, an especially sensitive one deals with biomedical experimentation on humans.

Historically, the ethical issues associated with human experimentation are of recent origin. Concern was generated from events of

By George H. Kieffer, adapted from chapter 7 of a manuscript entitled *Ethics in the Life Sciences*. The manuscript is the basis for a forthcoming book, *Bioethics: A Textbook of Issues*, to be published by Addison-Wesley Publishing Company, Inc. Printed by permission of the author.

World War II and immediately thereafter. At least two can be identified. First, World War II convulsed the world not only physically
but morally as well. World War II marked the first time in the history of warfare that large civilian populations were exposed to the
destructiveness of war. One need only mention such "new"
phenomena as the detonation of the nuclear bomb on civilian
populations of Japan killing hundreds of thousands, the fire bomb-
ing of Dresden with the same devastating results, the horrifying
and dehumanizing events made public by the war crimes trials following the war, the charges of genocide as entire populations of
people were exterminated, and the individual as well as the public
conscience experiences disgust and nausea. Following the war, an
organized effort was made at reassessing the world moral order
and codifying standards of ethical behavior. . . . [An] example
demonstrating this movement was the infamous Nuremburg war
crimes trials, which brought before a world judicial tribunal for the
first time those accused of perpetrating the morally revulsive events
of a war. Defendant after defendant pleaded his innocence, arguing that he was merely implementing the law of the land. The
defendants reasoned that they were in the untenable position of
carrying out the orders issued by others higher in authority, and
that not to do so, seriously threatened their own safety. By only
doing what they were told, and by not initiating any independent
action, they could not be judged guilty. The prosecution countered
that there were basic human rights, self-evident and inviolable, that
all persons owed allegiance to. There are basic values or basic incli-
nations of human nature that need no validation and one is obligated to conform his behavior to these (e.g., protection of the innocent). These sovereign principles must take precedence over any
other considerations; to do less would serve to undermine the
moral basis on which society's very being rests. . . .

One of the more shameful episodes brought out by the Nuremburg trials concerned the matter of human experimentation where
large numbers of concentration camp prisoners were used for purposes of medical experimentation. A great many of those confined
were non-Germans whose incarceration was often tantamount to
death. Certainly it can be assumed that few, if any, volunteered
themselves as experimental subjects. Some of the physicians and
scientists conducting these researches were persons of high standing within the profession, enjoying both national and international
reputations. The standard arguments made in their defense were
first, that they too were simply carrying out orders given them; and
second, that the prisoners were going to die anyway. If that be the
case, why not extract some benefit for humankind from the evil of
their hastened death—an inevitable event in any instance and one
over which the scientists had no control. But more sinister and
threatening to the concept of basic human rights was the defense

argument that the acquisition of knowledge and the advancement of social ends must override the individual. In other words, the welfare of society must take precedence over the welfare of any single person. This was [a] manifestation of science itself becoming prostituted in the cause of knowledge; also, of any means justifying the desired end. The inherent dangers of such an approach are so great that most sane people would recoil in shock and horror, as did those trying the war crimes cases. They asserted that there is a more fundamental morality at stake, one that must be protected from abuse if society is to avert disaster.

After the Nuremberg trials, the judicial tribunal with help of expert physicians drafted a code of conduct, the Nuremberg Code, a landmark document on human experimentation specifying the relationship between experimenter and experimental subject. It is a lengthy document containing some ten propositions. In the main, these can be summarized as follows:

1. The voluntary consent of the human subject is absolutely essential.

2. The experiment should yield fruitful results for the good of society unprocurable by other methods or means of study.

3. The experiment should be designed and based on the results of previously conducted animal experimentation.

4. The experiment should be designed to avoid all unnecessary physical and mental suffering and injury.

5. No experiment should be conducted where there is . . . reason to believe that death or disabling injury will occur.

6. The degree of risk should never exceed the determined humanitarian importance of the problem under investigation.

7. Adequate preparation should be made to protect the experimental subject against even remote possibilities of injury, death, or disability.

8. The experiment should be conducted only by scientifically qualified persons.

9. During the course of an experiment, human subjects should be at liberty to bring the experiment to an end.

10. During the course of an experiment, the scientist in charge must be prepared to terminate the experiment at any stage if in his judgment its continuation is likely to result in injury, disability, or death to the experimental subjects.

The ethical values of human freedom and the inviolability of the human person are the root of this code. Throughout these propositions, emphasis is placed on full disclosure of all experimental details and voluntary informed consent of the human subject. In effect, the Nuremberg Code reaffirmed the great traditional safeguard so long practiced between the physician and his patient: "First of all do not do injury." Just as the welfare of the individual patient must be of basic importance in the physician/patient relationship, so the first responsibility of the researcher is the safety of the human experimental subject. . . .

A second source of concern relative to human experimentation originates from the intensified search for medical knowledge following World War II. There are a number of reasons why this push for new knowledge exacerbated [= aggravated] the general problem. Of primary importance is the enormous and continuing availability of research funds. . . . Since World War II, the United States National Institutes of Health budget for medical research increased a whopping 624-fold. The availability of research funds is further added to by individual or foundation-supported research programs; for example, Jerry Lewis and muscular dystrophy, March of Dimes and research on birth defects, "War on Cancer" programs. The obvious corollary follows—as great sums of money are devoted to medical research, the dangers of ethical error will also increase as larger numbers of experiments are conducted on human subjects.

But the problem is not only one of absolute numbers. Medical schools and university hospitals are dominated by medical investigators. Young scientists know that their professional future in a major institution is determined by their abilities as investigators, and publication is still the measure. Coupling the two factors—the ready availability of money for conducting research and pressure to publish—one can see how great the chances become of committing ethical errors on human subjects. . . .

Although it is nearly axiomatic, it bears emphasizing that even though much testing is carried out with laboratory animals, the ultimate tests must be made on humans. In fact, federal regulations require that these tests be done. There is no way one can extrapolate with certainty from animal experiments to human response. In the end, humans themselves must provide information about themselves. Furthermore, there are many instances where animal experimentation is simply not suitable, for animal models do not exist (e.g., species-specific infection). . . . Thus, a variety of experiments requiring large numbers of human subjects will continue, heightening concern and elevating the clamor for regulation. . . .

How can the rights of individuals as subjects be protected; specifically, how does one obtain meaningful and informed consent? . . . Let's examine several instances where obtaining reasonably informed consent may be questionable. In the first case, [consider experimentation on a] patient. . . . The experimentation may benefit [the patient] directly by alleviating an illness, or the research is used to gain knowledge which may benefit others but not the person being experimented on.

All such requests [made to patients for consent to experiment on them] are filtered through the illness setting; patients generally do not complain or question the physician's judgment. It is of course for the reason of getting well that they have placed themselves under the care of a physician, so that if suitably approached, they will accede on the basis of trust to almost any request the physician may make. If the physician's request is refused, there is the danger that no treatment or only minimal treatment will be given. In this case, the risk of losing treatment outweighs an informed objective choice. Also, the rejection of a proposed therapy can be interpreted as a denial of the physician's wisdom—for our society still clothes the physician with the "mystique of wisdom." . . . Another problem in obtaining informed consent is that many times the patient, unaware of either the real nature of his illness or the proposed therapy, tends to equate research with treatment. This is a particular difficulty since it is the poor, uneducated, or functionally illiterate (e.g., do not understand English, are senile) that comprise over 80 per cent of the human subjects used in experimentation. [The fact that] university and public hospitals [have] a large fraction of patients [who are impoverished] accounts for the disproportionate representation. . . .

Finally, one more factor that complicates this picture is that the experiment is usually free, engendering the very common response [from patients], "What have I got to lose?" It seems to be part of the human psyche [= mind] that monetary cost is somehow equated with value, and although the experimental treatment may involve some risks, the gamble is favorable since there is no money given for the service. Under any of these conditions, it can be seriously questioned whether any genuine and informed consent can be gotten. If these be the circumstances, although no coercion is intended, one might question whether there is any real difference between implied pressure and coercion. . . .

A second instance where obtaining reasonably informed consent may be difficult involves the subject who is not ill. Healthy human subjects are especially necessary for testing the toxicological [= potentially poisonous] effects of drugs and other chemicals. . . .

A particular difficulty arises when it is essential to the success of the experiment that the participant, sometimes even the researcher, be uninformed about certain aspects of the experiment, for example, the control group placebo experiment or the "double blind" experiment. Some have seriously challenged the ethics of these protocols [= experiments], especially in cases where the subject volunteers. [Some feel] . . . [the] sick patient . . . is definitely wronged even when not physically harmed—for such procedures betray the trust of the patient who believes that he is receiving treatment. Even apart from ethics, the practice of deception holds the danger of undermining the faith in legitimate treatment, the very basis of the doctor-patient contract. Clearly the prescription of placebos is intentionally deceptive and makes informed consent impossible. . . .

The use of prisoners as research subjects has raised some of the hottest confrontations over the ethics of human experimentation. While prisoners normally do not lack the capacity to offer a reasonably informed consent, their capacity to do so voluntarily is problematical. Consequently, most states have taken steps to either completely abandon or at least initiate a moratorium on further research until the matter can be more thoroughly studied. Some are calling for an outright ban on all prison research. . . .

Prisoners form the largest pool of potential subjects, especially for drug testing, and most drug companies have working agreements with prisons. Although the extent and nature of experimentation with prisoners cannot be determined, at least 3600 prisoners in the U.S. were used for drug testing during 1975 alone, according to the National Commission for the Protection of Human Subjects. Besides these tests, performed primarily by drug companies, the Commission also determined that the federal government funded a number of other studies in which prisoners were used: within the Public Health Service, 124 biomedical studies and 19 behavioral projects between 1970–75; the Department of Defense sponsored numerous studies for research on infectious diseases; and the former Atomic Energy Commission (now Energy Research and Development Administration) had supported research involving radiation of male prisoners' genitals.

During the year 1975, eight states and six county and municipal prisons were used. One of the largest and most elaborate research facilities is located at the State Prison of Southern Michigan at Jackson. This is a maximum-security prison, one of the biggest penitentiaries in the United States. Of its 5,000 inmates, 800 prisoners form an available pool for research in special facilities built within the walls of the prison by two of the country's largest pharmaceutical manufacturers, Parke-Davis and Upjohn. Between 1964 and 1968, over 100,000 tests on human subjects were performed here. . . .

Prison abuses of all kinds have been widely publicized. Jessica Mitford's recent book on prison conditions, *Kind and Usual Punishment*, points out that some experimentation conducted in prisons is dangerous and has little scientific value. At the Iowa State Prison, the experimental induction of scurvy in eleven prisoners led to acute episodes of swollen and bleeding gums, joint swelling and pain, hemorrhaging, etc. In some, the effects proved to be irreversible (two of the prisoners later escaped). All this was done even though the cause and cure of scurvy are well known. Another example is the infamous Tuskegee syphilis study, where 400 black men with syphilis were not treated so the course of the disease could be followed. Here again, the etiology [= cause] and cure of this affliction is known. The list could be added to almost endlessly from medical literature as well as popular reporting.

However, the personal welfare of the prisoners is not the only ethical consideration. The [question] of whether any nontherapeutic research should be allowed in prisons arises from several factors:

1. The subjects involved are captives of the state and are made available by the permission of the state. . . .

2. The prisoner participants' position of confinement renders their consent to participate questionable; prisoners are not free agents and true consent without overt or implied coercion is impossible in prisons. . . .

3. Research in prisons is carried on in an environment which lacks the kind of peer review or openness found in other research settings. Because such research is not in the public eye, there is the possiblity of abuse even if it is unintended. Such abuse can be easily covered up if negative publicity may result. . . .

The problem of full capacity to render informed consent presents another urgent case when children are the experimental subjects. Present Food and Drug Administration regulations require that drugs be tested on all age groups for whom the drug is intended. This includes tests for safety on normal subjects before the drug can be released for use on patients. In research involving children, the ethical considerations are quite different from the two groups previously discussed; [one must distinguish] between therapeutic and nontherapeutic research. The law states that parents may consent for the child if the treatment is for the child's welfare or benefit, that is, for therapeutic purposes. Proxy consent is permissible here because parents have the obligation to care for and protect the welfare of their children. Parents are frequently called upon to make decisions for their children (e.g., the school attended), and this right is highly praised. However, parents are not morally (or legally) permitted to make decisions for their children that carry with them high risks, only those that will not infringe on the child's welfare. . . . One of the difficulties, though, is how broadly to interpret welfare or benefit. This has generated an important controversy, particularly as it applies to nontherapeutic research on children.

If an experiment is for nontherapeutic purposes, the generally followed guideline stipulates that the child be at least 14 years of age and intelligent and mature enough to understand the nature of the procedure, including potential hazards, and that no coercion be applied or guilt feelings engendered. These conditions satisfied, child consent coupled with parental or guardian permission completes the requirement of the law. In some extreme cases such as organ donation, the age minimum may be lowered to six years if the recipient is a sibling and /or the child understands the procedure including risks and losses. . . .

Lastly, there is the special problem of subjects, again not possessed with full capacity to consent, who are inmates at state nonpenal institutions (e.g., mental hospitals, children's homes). In terms of legal standing, the state has assumed the obligation of ward or guardian. These populations are composed primarily of individuals with mental retardation or physical defects or both, with the largest number being in the first group. According to [one observer], these institutions represent conditions of total deprivation where individuals surrender all control of their lives. Inmates are completely dominated by staff discretion. The mentally retarded especially are frequently treated as subhumans: the design of the institution [according to this observer] is to shorten the lives of those committed and to keep inmates out of the sight of the public. . . . This issue is obvious: is there any way at all for these persons to give informed consent or is it a matter for the state to decide? The clearest example of questionable ethical procedures is the controversial Willowbrook experiments on hepatitis in which institutionalized, mentally retarded children were intentionally given hepatitis. And in fact, according to one source, permission for participation in the experiment was a [condition] for admittance to the hospital. . . . The experiments were defended on the grounds that the children would contract hepatitis normally and getting it under controlled medication was to be preferred. Experiments like this have led to the demand that a permanent prohibition against using such persons be enacted.

Much more discussion could be devoted to the problem of human experimentation and the literature attacking and defending it is voluminous. However, the point has been made. The central ethical issue is this: the welfare of the individual must be of basic importance when he or she is placed in the experimental environment. Can adequate protection of human subjects be effected?

Reading Questions

1. Which two factors in the last 40 years have significantly increased concern about the ethics of experimenting on humans?
2. What reasons have been offered in defense of German concentration camp researchers? Why does Kieffer reject these reasons?
3. What principles are embodied in the Nuremberg code?
4. Why won't animal experiments suffice to test biological or medical hypotheses?
5. What kinds of experimental situations limit the ability of patients to give fully informed consent?

Questions for Reflection and Research

1. Read Kieffer's book and report on the full range of ethical problems confronting biomedical researchers.
2. What kind of training in ethics should people in health-care fields receive?
3. Is research now being carried out on human beings in the university or college with which you are affiliated—or at a nearby university or medical center? What regulations are in effect to protect potential experimental subjects? Are the regulations enforced? Are the regulations sufficient?
4. How does one know what is right and wrong?
5. Can science establish what is right and wrong?
6. Read about Stanley Milgram's well-known experiment in selection #49 by Weisstein. Would Kieffer approve of the experiment? Were the experimental subjects asked for informed consent? Should they have been?
7. How can the desire to advance in a biological or medical field tempt a researcher to use questionable research procedures?
8. Should animals be used for experiments that are intended to reveal facts about humans? Do animals have any rights? (See selection #46 by Singer.)

The Morality of Experimenting with Animals

The Author: Peter Singer (b. 1946), an Australian, was educated at the University of Melbourne in Australia and Oxford University in England. His interests and publications are in the fields of moral and political philosophy. He has taught at Oxford, New York University, and La Trobe University in Australia. The issue of animal rights has been further developed by him in his book *Animal Liberation*.

The Selection: Prior to discussion of the use of animals in experiments, the author seeks to prove that animals that can feel pain should be given moral consideration. It is asserted that what entitles a creature to moral consideration is not intelligence nor bodily form but whether it can suffer. The use of animals for experiments and to test products for possible side effects is condemned and compared to using brain-damaged human infants for experiments.

I

We are familiar with Black Liberation, Gay Liberation, and a variety of other movements. . . . A liberation movement demands an expansion of our moral horizons, so that practices that were previously regarded as natural and inevitable are now seen as intolerable.

Animals, Men and Morals is a manifesto for an Animal Liberation movement. . . . It is a demand that we cease to regard the exploitation of other species as natural and inevitable, and that, instead, we

---

From a review by Peter Singer of the book *Animals, Men and Morals* in *The New York Review of Books*, 20, no. 5 (April 5, 1973): 17-19. Reprinted by permission of the author.

see it as a continuing moral outrage. Patrick Corbett, Professor of Philosophy at Sussex University, captures the spirit of the book in his closing words:

> . . . we require now to extend the great principles of liberty, equality and fraternity over the lives of animals. Let animal slavery join human slavery in the graveyard of the past.

The reader is likely to be skeptical. "Animal Liberation" sounds more like a parody of liberation movements than a serious objective. The reader may think: We support the claims of blacks and women for equality because blacks and women really are equal to whites and males—equal in intelligence and in abilities, capacity for leadership, rationality, and so on. Humans and nonhumans obviously are not equal in these respects. Since justice demands only that we treat equals equally, unequal treatment of humans and nonhumans cannot be an injustice.

This is a tempting reply, but a dangerous one. It commits the non-racist and non-sexist to a dogmatic belief that blacks and women really are just as intelligent, able, etc., as whites and males—and no more. Quite possibly this happens to be the case. Certainly attempts to prove that racial or sexual differences in these respects have a genetic origin have not been conclusive. But do we really want to stake our demand for equality on the assumption that there are no genetic differences of this kind between the different races or sexes? Surely the appropriate response to those who claim to have found evidence for such genetic differences is not to stick to the belief that there are no differences, whatever the evidence to the contrary; rather one should be clear that the claim to equality does not depend on IQ. Moral equality is distinct from factual equality. Otherwise it would be nonsense to talk of the equality of human beings, since humans, as individuals, obviously differ in intelligence and almost any ability one cares to name. If possessing greater intelligence does not entitle one human to exploit another, why should it entitle humans to exploit nonhumans?

[The philosopher] Jeremy Bentham [1748–1832] expressed the essential basis of equality in his famous formula: "Each to count for one and none for more than one." In other words, the interests of every being that has interests are to be taken into account and treated equally with the like interests of any other being. Other moral philosophers, before and after Bentham, have made the same point in different ways. Our concern for others must not depend on whether they possess certain characteristics, though just what that concern involves may, of course, vary according to such characteristics.

Bentham, incidentally, was well aware that the logic of the demand for racial equality did not stop at the equality of humans. He wrote:

The day *may* come when the rest of the animal creation may acquire those rights which never could have been withholden from them but by the hand of tyranny. The French have already discovered that the blackness of the skin is no reason why a human being should be abandoned without redress to the caprice of a tormentor. It may one day come to be recognized that the number of the legs, the villosity [= hairiness] of the skin, or the termination of the *os sacrum* [= last bone of the spine] are reasons equally insufficient for abandoning a sensitive being to the same fate. What else is it that should trace the insuperable line? Is it the faculty of reason, or perhaps the faculty of discourse? But a full-grown horse or dog is beyond comparison a more rational, as well as a more conversable animal, than an infant of a day, or a week, or even a month old. But suppose they were otherwise, what would it avail? The question is not, Can they *reason?* nor Can they *talk?* but, Can they *suffer?*

Surely Bentham was right. If a being suffers, there can be no moral justification for refusing to take that suffering into consideration, and, indeed, to count it equally with the like suffering (if rough comparisons can be made) of any other being.

So the only question is: do animals other than man suffer? Most people agree unhesitatingly that animals like cats and dogs can and do suffer, and this seems also to be assumed by those laws that prohibit wanton cruelty to such animals. Personally, I have no doubt at all about this and find it hard to take seriously the doubts that a few people apparently do have. . . . Nevertheless, because this is such a fundamental point, it is worth asking what grounds we have for attributing suffering to other animals.

It is best to begin by asking what grounds any individual human has for supposing that other humans feel pain. Since pain is a state of consciousness, a "mental event," it can never be directly observed. No observations, whether behavioral signs such as writhing or screaming or physiological or neurological recordings, are observations of pain itself. Pain is something one feels, and one can only infer that others are feeling it from various external indications. The fact that only philosophers are ever skeptical about whether other humans feel pain shows that we regard such inference as justifiable in the case of humans.

Is there any reason why the same inference should be unjustifiable for other animals? Nearly all the external signs which lead us to infer pain in other humans can be seen in other species, especially "higher" animals such as mammals and birds. Behavioral signs—writhing, yelping, or other forms of calling, attempts to avoid the source of pain, and many others—are present. We know, too, that these animals are biologically similar in the relevant respects, having nervous systems like ours which can be observed to function as ours do.

So the grounds for inferring that these animals can feel pain are nearly as good as the grounds for inferring other humans do. Only nearly, for there is one behavioral sign that humans have but nonhumans, with the exception of one or two specially raised chimpanzees, do not have. This, of course, is a developed language. As the quotation from Bentham indicates, this has long been regarded as an important distinction between man and other animals. Other animals may communicate with each other, but not in the way we do. . . . Nevertheless, as Bentham pointed out, this distinction is not relevant to the question of how animals ought to be treated, unless it can be linked to the issue of whether animals suffer. . . .

As Jane Goodall [b. 1934] points out in her study of chimpanzees, when it comes to the expression of feelings and emotions, humans tend to fall back on non-linguistic modes of communication which are often found among apes, such as a cheering pat on the back, an exuberant embrace, a clasp of hands, and so on. Michael Peters [b. 1937] makes a similar point in his contribution to *Animals, Men and Morals* when he notes that the basic signals we use to convey pain, fear, sexual arousal, and so on are not specific to our species. So there seems to be no reason at all to believe that a creature without language cannot suffer. . . .

Behavioral signs and knowledge of the animals's biological similarity to ourselves together provide adequate evidence that animals do suffer. After all, we would not accept linguistic evidence if it contradicted the rest of the evidence. If a man was severely burned, and behaved as if he were in pain, writhing, groaning, being very careful not to let his burned skin touch anything, and so on, but later said he had not been in pain at all, we would be more likely to conclude that he was lying or suffering from amnesia than that he had not been in pain. . . .

The grounds we have for believing that other mammals and birds suffer are, then, closely analogous to the grounds we have for believing that other humans suffer. It remains to consider how far down the evolutionary scale this analogy holds. Obviously it becomes poorer when we get further away from man. To be more precise would require a detailed examination of all that we know about other forms of life. With fish, reptiles, and other vertebrates the analogy still seems strong, with molluscs like oysters it is much weaker. Insects are more difficult, and it may be that in our present state of knowledge we must be agnostic about whether they are capable of suffering.

If there is no moral justification for ignoring suffering when it occurs, and it does occur in other species, what are we to say of our attitudes toward these other species? Richard Ryder [b. 1940], one of the contributors to *Animals, Men and Morals*, uses the term "speciesism" to describe the belief that we are entitled to treat members of other species in a way in which it would be wrong to treat members of our own species. The term is not euphonious [= pleasant sounding], but it neatly makes the analogy with racism.

The non-racist would do well to bear the analogy in mind when he is inclined to defend human behavior toward nonhumans. "Shouldn't we worry about improving the lot of our own species before we concern ourselves with other species?" he may ask. If we substitute "race" for "species" we shall see that the question is better not asked. "Is a vegetarian diet nutritionally adequate?" resembles the slave-owner's claim that he and the whole economy of the South would be ruined without slave labor. There is even a parallel with skeptical doubts about whether animals suffer, for some defenders of slavery professed to doubt whether blacks really suffer in the way that whites do. . . .

II

The logic of speciesism is most apparent in the practice of experimenting on nonhumans in order to benefit humans. This is because the issue is rarely obscured by allegations that nonhumans are so different from humans that we cannot know anything about whether they suffer. The defender of vivisection [= animal experimentation] cannot use this argument because he needs to stress the similarities between man and other animals in order to justify the usefulness to the former of experiments on the latter. The researcher who makes rats choose between starvation and electric shocks to see if they develop ulcers (they do) does so because he knows that the rat has a nervous system very similer to man's, and presumably feels an electric shock in a similar way.

Richard Ryder's restrained account of experiments on animals made me angrier with my fellow men than anything else in this book. Ryder, a clinical psychologist by profession, himself experimented on animals before he came to hold the view he puts forward in his essay. Experimenting on animals is now a large industry, both academic and commercial. . . . We tend to think that this is all for vital medical research, but of course it is not. Huge numbers of animals are used in university departments from Forestry to Psychology, and even more are used for commercial purposes, to test whether cosmetics can cause skin damage, or shampoos eye damage, or to test food additives or laxatives or sleeping pills or anything else.

A standard test for foodstuffs is the "LD50." The object of this test is to find the dosage level at which 50 percent of the test animals will die. This means that nearly all of them will become very sick before finally succumbing or surviving. When the substance is a harmless one, it may be necessary to force huge doses down the animals, until in some cases sheer volume or concentration causes death.

Ryder gives a selection of experiments, taken from recent scientific journals. I will quote two, not for the sake of indulging in gory details, but in order to give an idea of what normal researchers think they may legitimately do to other species. The point is not that the individual researchers are cruel men, but that they are behaving in a way that is allowed by our speciesist attitudes. As Ryder points out, even if only 1 percent of the experiments involve severe pain, that is 50,000 experiments in Britain each year, or nearly 150 every day (and about fifteen times as many in the United States, if Ryder's guess is right). Here then are two experiments:

O. S. Ray and R. J. Barrett of Pittsburgh gave electric shocks to the feet of 1,042 mice. They then caused convulsions by giving more intense shocks through cup-shaped electrodes applied to the animals' eyes or through pressure spring clips attached to their ears. Unfortunately some of the mice who "successfully completed Day One training were found sick or dead prior to testing on Day Two." [*Journal of Comparative and Physiological Psychology*, 1969, Vol. 67, pp. 110-116]

At the National Institute for Medical Research, Mill Hill, London, W Feldberg and S. L. Sherwood injected chemicals into the brains of cats— "with a number of widely different substances, recurrent patterns of reaction were obtained. Retching, vomiting, defaecation, increased salivation and greatly accelerated respiration leading to panting were common features.". . .

The injection into the brain of a large dose of Tubocuraine caused the cat to jump "from the table to the floor and then straight into its cage, where it started calling more and more noisily whilst moving about restlessly and jerkily . . . finally the cat fell with legs and neck flexed, jerking in rapid clonic [= pulsating] movements, the condition being that of a major [epileptic] convulsion . . . within a few seconds the cat got up, ran for a few yards at high speed and fell in another fit. The whole process was repeated several times within the next ten minutes, during which the cat lost faeces and foamed at the mouth."

This animal finally died thirty-five minutes after the brain injection. [*Journal of Physiology*, 1954, Vol. 123, pp. 148–167]

There is nothing secret about these experiments. One has only to open any recent volume of a learned journal, such as the *Journal of Comparative and Physiological Psychology*, to find full descriptions of experiments of this sort, together with the results obtained— results that are frequently trivial and obvious. The experiments are often supported by public funds.

It is a significant indication of the level of acceptability of these practices that, although these experiments are taking place at this moment on university campuses throughout the country, there has, so far as I know, not been the slightest protest from the student movement. Students have been rightly concerned that their universities should not discriminate on grounds of race or sex, and that they should not serve the purposes of the military or big business. Speciesism continues undisturbed, and many students participate in it. There may be a few qualms at first, but since everyone regards it as normal, and it may even be a required part of a course, the student soon becomes hardened and, dismissing his earlier feelings as "mere sentiment," comes to regard animals as statistics rather than sentient beings [= beings capable of feeling] with interests that warrant consideration.

Argument about vivisection has often missed the point because it has been put in absolutist terms: would the abolitionist be prepared to let thousands die if they could be saved by experimenting on a single animal? The way to reply to this purely hypothetical question is to pose another: Would the experimenter be prepared to experiment on a human orphan under six months old, if it were the only way to save many lives? (I say "orphan" to avoid the complication of parental feelings, although in doing so I am being overfair to the experimenter, since the nonhuman subjects of experiments are not orphans.) A negative answer to this question indicates that the experimenter's readiness to use nonhumans is simple discrimination, for adult apes, cats, mice, and other mammals are more conscious of what is happening to them, more self-directing, and, so far as we can tell, just as sensitive to pain as a human infant. There is no characteristic that human infants possess that adult mammals do not have to the same or a higher degree.

(It might be possible to hold that what makes it wrong to experiment on a human infant is that the infant will in time develop into more than the nonhuman, but one would then, to be consistent, have to oppose abortion, and perhaps contraception, too, for the fetus and the egg and sperm have the same potential as the infant. Moreover, one would still have no reason for experimenting on a nonhuman rather than a human with brain damage severe enough to make it impossible for him to rise above infant level.)

The experimenter, then, shows a bias for his own species whenever he carries out an experiment on a nonhuman for a purpose that he would not think justified him in using a human being at an equal or lower level of sentience, awareness, ability to be self-directing, etc. . . .

Reading Questions

1. What is the basis for moral equality? What reasons does Singer give in support of this view?
2. What reasons are given to suppose that animals feel pain?
3. What kinds of testing and experimentation does Singer indicate should be halted? Why?
4. Why does Singer refer to orphaned (and brain-damaged) infants in his arguments against scientific speciesism?
5. What parallels are there between sexism, racism, and speciesism?

Questions for Reflection and Research

1. Read Singer's fuller account of the grounds for treating animals ethically in his book *Animal Liberation* (New York: New York Review, 1975). What additional arguments does he offer? Can they be criticized?

2. Ask professional and student animal experimenters to give their reactions to Singer's views. How do they justify their harming the animals?

3. What objections can be advanced against Singer's views?

4. Is Bentham right in claiming that one deserves moral considerations if one can suffer? What other criteria for the basis of moral consideration seem plausible?

5. Since different cultures value animals differently, does this mean that there is no objective way to determine whether it is right or wrong to experiment with animals? (See selections #40 by Benedict and #41 by Cook.)

6. Are there any moral differences between eating animals and cannibalism?

What Moral Limits Should Be Placed on Science?
The Sex-Pot Study

The Author: John Gardner (b. 1933) is the author of the second portion of this selection. (The first portion was authored by a staff reporter for the periodical *Science*.) Gardner is acclaimed both as a writer of fiction and as a scholar of literature. His education was at DePauw University, Washington University, and the State University of Iowa. He has taught at Southern Illinois University and a number of other American colleges and universities. (He should not be confused with the mystery writer John Gardner nor the founder of the citizens' lobby, Common Cause, whose name is also John Gardner.)

The Selection: Both of the passages below concern a study proposed by the Southern Illinois University psychologist Harris Rubin. He wanted to study whether smoking marijuana influences sexual arousal. The first passage below is from *Science*. It describes the nature of the proposed research and a vote in the House of Representatives to delete funding for the proposal. The second passage was written as a letter to a newspaper editor some months prior to the vote. Gardner defends the sex-pot study as an attempt to resolve a dispute by obtaining the facts. The facts, it is argued, will benefit society no matter what they turn out to be.

HOUSE CHOPS SEX-POT PROBE

In one of the more unusual congressional examples of democracy at work, an Illinois congressman has taken action that could send a sharp twinge of alarm through the nation's scientists. On 13

Gardner's letter appeared in the newspaper *The Southern Illinoisan*, Sept. 15, 1975, and is reprinted by permission of the newspaper and the author. The material from *Science*, 192, no. 4238 (April 30, 1976): 450, is copyright 1976 by the American Association for the Advancement of Science and is reprinted by permission.

April [1976], the House of Representatives passed an appropriations bill for the Department of Labor and Health, Education, and Welfare (HEW) that explicitly cancels funding for an HEW-approved project designed to explore the relation between marijuana use and sexual response.

The action—wiping out a specific project that has been approved through all the normal governmental peer review procedures—is, at the very least, highly unusual and may be unprecedented. A staff member of the Senate Appropriations Committee, which will act on the bill after Easter recess, says he has never heard of such a thing in the 12 years he has been there. Many researchers are appalled—"Implications for the future are just stupefying," says a professor at the Southern Illinois University medical school, where the project is to be carried out under the direction of psychologist Harris Rubin [b.1932].

The 2-year project, slated for a total of $121,000 from the National Institute on Drug Abuse (NIDA), has been the object of continual controversy since last summer. The purpose of the experiment is to develop some objective evidence concerning marihuana's effect on sexual arousal by exposing groups of male pot-smokers to pornographic films and measuring their responses by means of sensors attached to their penises. The control group is to smoke marihuana from which the active agent, tetrahydrocannabinol, has been removed. Rubin explains that most information on marihuana and sexual arousal comes from subjective accounts, and that his project is unique in that it will supply hard data on the topic. . . .

To the editor:

I would like to defend, at least in terms of general theory and moral principal, Professor Rubin's investigation of possible relationships between marijuana use and sexual potency.

Let me say first that, while in the past the general public has not much interested itself in how scientists use tax money, it seems to me quite proper that taxpayers should ask how their money is spent, and they should expect a straight and immediate answer—not only from scientists but from any politician, government agency, or government affiliated institution. In general, our tax dollars are not being wasted by scientists, and the more open scientists are with the public, the sooner the real problems will be clear.

The present outcry against Professor Rubin's study is based, apparently, on fear and moral indignation: both marijuana and sex, misused or treated too casually, might harm individuals, wreck families, even wreck the structure and meaning of our society. But a scientist's purpose is not necessarily moral or immoral; it is to know the truth, because at moments of crisis only knowledge can save individuals, families, and society.

Marijuana use is high in America. Estimates vary, but all who have studied the matter agree that a great many Americans use the stuff, despite the strong likelihood that it is a substance at least as dangerous as tobacco or alcohol. The divorce rate is also frighteningly high in America, and at present the number one cause of divorce is said to be sexual incompatibility—trouble in bed.

A great many young people who use marijuana claim that it does wonderful things for their sexual potency, though in fact there seems to be a very good chance that marijuana seriously decreases potency. For the scientist the question is not moral but factual: which is true? Does marijuana help or hurt in the love relationship?

The important point, of course, is that once the truth is known it may—and almost certainly will—have practical applications. A psychologist or marriage counselor dealing with a troubled marriage certainly needs to know whether sexual failure is a contributing cause, and to convince the troubled couple, if they are devout marijuana users, he needs to know whether marijuana does indeed lead to a measure of impotence. He needs facts to lay before them. Young people not yet interested in love and marriage need to know the truth about what marijuana may do to their lives.

Simply condemning marijuana use on, say, moral or religious grounds will not work. It's been tried. Society has no choice but to hunt down the facts, whether in the end they support or attack popular superstitions about marijuana's wonders. This is the work Professor Rubin and many other scientists in various fields are now doing.

However shocking such work may seem at first glance (its methodology, in point of fact, is about as clinical and clean as one could possibly imagine in an experiment involving human sexual stimulation under drug influence), its goal is the usual goal of science: to replace superstition with objective knowledge. If the result is, as it may well be, the explosion of one of the chief myths favoring marijuana use, Professor Rubin and his assistants will have served the righteous cause of those who most noisily attack him—and will have served it more powerfully than they could ever do themselves. . . .

Taxpayers have a right, as I've said, to ask what they're getting for their money. In this case, it seems, no one is being cheated, and the blind moralistic attacks seem completely unwarranted.

Reading Questions

1. What experiment does Rubin want to conduct?
2. Why are researchers appalled at the action of the House of Representatives?

3. What reasons does Gardner give for concluding that the facts, no matter what they are, will be better for society than our present ignorance of the facts?
4. What are the goals of science claimed to be?

Questions for Reflection and Research

1. What arguments might have been (or were) put forward by opponents of the Rubin experiment?
2. Should science always seek to get the facts no matter what research methods are involved? (See, for example, selections #45 by Kieffer and #46 by Singer. Think also of the research Nazi scientists did on human beings.)
3. Compare the ethical problems described in the selection by Nicholas Rescher (#42) with those raised by the Rubin experiment. Does this experiment reveal other kinds of ethical problems involved in science?
4. How can we determine whether there is anything wrong with the Rubin experiment? Can science tell us? Why or why not?
5. How should decisions on the allocation of research funds be made? (See selections #42 by Rescher and #52 by Fischer.)
6. What is the answer to each of the following questions:
   (a) Is it wrong to smoke marijuana?
   (b) Is it wrong to watch pornographic movies?
   (c) Is it wrong to conduct an experiment with public funds if many taxpayers regard the experiment as involving immoral conduct?

Racism in Science

The Author: Robert L. Williams (b. 1930) was educated at Philander Smith College, Wayne State University, and Washington University and has taught psychology at Washington University. Before beginning his academic career he served as a psychologist in a Veterans Administration hospital and in various other capacities in the field of mental health. He has published widely and was a founder of the Association of Black Psychologists.

The Selection: The IQ test is singled out as an outstanding example of how science, despite its claim to objectivity, has fostered culturally biased conclusions. Evidence is given to show that standard intelligence tests are unfairly conceived, giving great advantage to white middle-class test takers. The Tuskegee syphilis experiment is cited as another example of scientific racism. And recent attempts to link race and intelligence are condemned as yet more racism.

The fundamental, inescapable problem for black people in America is still racism. The civil rights movement of the '60s focused on institutional racism, that oppressive cluster of laws, customs, and practices that systematically support doctrines of superiority and inferiority in America.

Now, blacks suffer another counterforce to survival: scientific racism. It has always been part of the American formula, but recently it has grown more virulent with advances in technology. This cold

From "The Silent Mugging of the Black Community: Scientific Racism and IQ" by Robert L. Williams in *Psychology Today*, 7, no. 12 (May 1974): 32–41, 101. Reprinted from *Psychology Today* magazine. Copyright © 1974 Ziff-Davis Publishing Company.

and inhumane experimentation with, and exclusion of, human beings is insidious because it is housed in universities, nurtured in industry, and cloaked in the language of rational science. An Ashanti proverb warns, "It is the calm and silent waters that drown a man." But the calmness fools no one; scientific racism is part of silent racial war, and the practitioners of it use intelligence tests as their hired guns.

I was almost one of the testing casualties. At 15, I earned an IQ test score of 82, three points above the track of the special education class. Based on this score, my counselor suggested that I take up bricklaying because I was "good with my hands." My low IQ, however, did not allow me to see that as desirable. I went to Philander Smith College anyway, graduating with honors, earned my master's degree at Wayne State University and my Ph.D. at Washington University in St. Louis. Other blacks, equally as qualified, have been wiped out.

The primary issues in the great black-white IQ controversy are not those of cultural test bias, the nature of intelligence, or the heritability of IQ. The issue is admittance to America's mainstream. IQ and achievement tests are nothing but updated versions of the old signs down South that read For Whites Only. University admission policies have required standardized psychological tests such as the Scholastic Aptitude Test (SAT) or the Graduate Record Examination (GRE) as a criterion for admission to colleges, graduate schools, medical or law schools and other professional schools. For blacks, these tests more often mean exclusion. . . .

The American testing industry goes hand-in-hand with the university in fostering the misuse of tests, and it is no mom-and-pop corner store. It is a multimillion-dollar-a-year supermarket of oppression. If the captains of this industry would admit the truth about testing, they would face bankruptcy. But the economic survival of the testing industry depends upon its symbiotic [= mutually beneficial] relationship with educational institutions, and both have constructed elaborate defenses against outside criticism. In spite of arguments to the contrary, test publishers maintain that the tests are neutral. They contend that although test results may be employed in a biased manner, they are not in themselves biased.

The educational institutions argue that testing is the fairest way to determine every child's ability. But no matter which argument one hears or believes, the results are the same. With few recent exceptions, black parents have had no control over whether or not their children were tested and how the test results would be used. Consequently, black children are placed, in disproportionate numbers, in classes for the mentally retarded, special education classes or lower educational tracks.

Such misuse of psychological tests with black children is based upon several misconceptions. First, IQ cannot be inherited. An intelligence quotient (IQ) is nothing more than a score earned on a test. Actual intelligence covers a broad range of human abilities that IQ tests do not even attempt to measure. For example, no test has formally assessed the many verbal and nonverbal skills required to survive in the black community. What we need is a survival quotient (SQ), not an IQ.

Second, IQ tests do not measure the ability to succeed in the world, or even to get along in a different academic environment. Psychologists have designed these tests specifically to predict school success, but children must attend a school that adequately teaches the content of the test in order to score well. Most ghetto schools fail at this task.

A third misconception about the IQ test is its value as a measurement of mental retardation. Illiteracy is frequently equated with mental retardation, but literacy and intellect are not directly correlated. One who is highly literate is not necessarily a wise person or possessed of great intellect. Conversely, an illiterate person is not necessarily mentally retarded. . . .

Finally, IQ tests do not measure one's capacity to learn; a low score does not mean low ability. According to [the psychologist] Bruno Bettelheim [b. 1903], "One boy who came to us diagnosed as feeble-minded today is a professor at Stanford."

Many white researchers have claimed that black children are nonverbal and lack the ability to reason abstractly. There is irony in that view, since the culture of black people is based upon an oral tradition, dating back before Christ, that abounds in abstractions and symbolism. That tradition predates the Gutenberg press by at least 2,000 years. Proverbs, songs, prayers, myths, stories, and legends were at the heart of formal and informal African educational systems.

Although the slave traders ripped the Africans from their native country, many of their customs and folkways survived the Atlantic passage. The slaves transplanted much of their oral traditions to the plantation, and incorporated them into black culture.

Blacks have maintained this African heritage, although Western chauvinism has isolated and belittled it as childlike and simple-minded. As Edmund Leach [b. 1910], the British anthropologist, has pointed out, the white Westerner is taught to believe that logical, mathematical, Aristotelian statements are the path to communication. This narrow perspective encourages reverence for literature and mathematics, and causes scorn for the metaphysical language of myth, which transcends logic. Westerners believe, says Leach, that they practice Aristotelian logic all the time. The truth is more complex, and consistent with the African tradition. Human beings communicate on many channels, with messages penetrating us through our eyes, our ears, our noses, our skin. And communication between human beings is not complete without the nuances of tone of voice, gestures, shared visual perceptions, and prior information held in common.

Black scholars are attempting to reconstruct the essence of the African tradition in a concept known as Ebonics. This concept combines linguistic and paralinguistic features that represent the communicative competence of West African, Caribbean, and United States slave descendants of African ancestors. It includes the various idioms, patois, argots, and social dialects of these regions. It also involves nonverbal cues, such as those referred to by Leach. . . .

Given these differences in black culture, the rationale for a culture-specific intelligence test is clear. If a child can learn certain familiar relationships in his own culture, he can master similar concepts in the school curriculum, so long as the curriculum is related to his background experiences. For the average black child, there is too often a mismatching or discontinuity between the skills acquired from his culture and those required for successful test-taking and in the school curriculum.

L. Wendell Rivers, a black child psychologist and researcher, and I conducted a study to measure the effects of test instructions written in black dialectal language and in standard English on the performance of black children during intelligence testing. We divided 890 black kindergarten, first- and second-grade children into two groups of 445 each. We controlled for the variables of IQ, age, sex, and grade in both the experimental and control groups. We used the standard version of the Boehm Test of Basic Concepts (BTBC), and a nonstandard version that we developed. The BTBC consists of 50 pictorial multiple-choice items involving concepts of space, quantity, and time. Black teachers and graduate students translated the concepts and objects into the black idiom:

STANDARD VERSION	NONSTANDARD
Mark the toy that is *behind the sofa*.	Mark the toy that is *in back of* the *couch*.
Mark the apple that is *whole*.	Mark the apple that is *still all there*.
Mark the boy who is *beginning* to climb the tree.	Mark the boy who is *starting* to climb the tree. (Variations may be used as: about to, getting ready to.)

Children who took the test that was representative of their cultural background, i.e., the nonstandard version, scored significantly higher than the other group. The language of the standard version penalized the children taking the Boehm test.

That study suggested the need to develop a culture-specific test for black children. I conducted another experiment, this time using the Black Intelligence Test of Cultural Homogeneity (The BITCH Test) that I developed. I took 100 vocabulary items from the *Afro-*

American Slang dictionary, my friends, and my personal experiences in working with black people. I gave the test to 100 black and 100 white subjects who were from 16 to 18 years old. Half in each group were from the low socioeconomic level, and half were from the middle. The results showed that blacks scored much higher than whites on a test that was specific to their culture; the black subjects earned a mean score of 87.07, while the whites earned a mean score of 51.07. Clearly, if black children are given a culture-specific test that is representative of their backgrounds, they will do better than white children taking the same test.

The notion of a culture-specific test is not new. The Stanford-Binet, Wechsler Intelligence Scale for Children, and the Peabody Picture Vocabulary Test, among others, are clear examples of culturally specific tests. Representatives of the white middle-class culture contributed the bulk of the test items. White experts determined the correct responses, and all-white populations normalized them. Culture specific tests for *black children* would only continue the tradition. The difference is that those children would not arrive in the classrooms of America with "unteachable" labels pasted, on the bias, to their permanent records. . . .

The implications of the testing controversy should not escape us. Historically, when one group of people has wished to subjugate or exploit another group, they dehumanized them by ascribing derogatory characteristics to the subjects: animalistic, savage, emotional, over-sexed, lazy, unscrupulous, and crazy, to name a few. It was also necessary to impugn the subjects' ability to determine their own destinies; they were described as child-like, immature, backward, simple-minded, illiterate, or of low intelligence.

The black-white IQ controversy presents an analogous situation. When a people is labeled consistently as being of low intellect or simple-minded, the respect among the general populace for their rights to life can and will erode to nothing. It has happened historically, and it has happened here. The black community has become the white researcher's hunting ground, the ideal experimental laboratory.

What we now know of the Tuskegee syphilis experiment is a shocking disclosure of clear-cut scientific racism. During a 40-year, federally funded study, scientists in Alabama used 600 black men as human guinea pigs. The men, victims of syphilis, were denied treatment even after the discovery of penicillin, so that scientists could study the progress of the disease. There is no moral or medical justification for that act alone, but to make this act of moral pauperism worse, scientists already knew the effects of long-term, untreated syphilis from data obtained from a Norwegian study that was conducted from 1891 to 1910. Syphilis is a highly contagious, dangerous, and debilitating disease, that left untreated, can cause sterility, blindness, deafness, bone deterioration, nervous-system degeneration, heart disease, and eventually death. The experimenters tricked these poor black men into participating in the experiment by offering them transportation to and from the hospital, hot lunches, medical care for ailments other than syphilis, and free burial. Malcolm X [1925-1965] reminds us that "a man who tosses worms in the river isn't necessarily a friend to the fish; all the fish who take him for a friend, who think the worm got no hooks in it, usually end up in the frying pan."

Records from the public-health center for disease control in Atlanta disclosed that somewhere between 28 and 100 participants died as a direct result of syphilis. Another 154 persons died of heart disease that may have been caused by syphilis. Unrecorded are the statistics on the many wives and girl friends that the men may have infected.

The Tuskegee experiment underscores the low regard for black lives among some members of the scientific community. This poses a serious threat to the survival of black people in the United States. Approximately 600 psychosurgical operations are performed each year. The subjects are too frequently black and almost invariably poor. Prisoners, especially black ones, seem to be fair game for the psychosurgeon's knife. . . .

It is no coincidence that genetic theories of black IQ deficits are being advanced at this time; blacks are making social and political gains that threaten the racist structure of American society. Arthur Jensen [b. 1923] has suggested that blacks have an IQ deficit, and that this may be inherited; William Shockley [b. 1910] claims that a so-called "dysgenic trend" among blacks threatens to make us a race of idiots. In the minds of black people, both theories lead down one road: genocide. A recent poll . . . found a fear of genocide among blacks. Of 1,890 blacks who were questioned in two cities, 62 percent agreed that, as blacks become more militant, there will be an effort to decrease the black population. And 51 percent agreed that as the need for cheap labor goes down, there will be an effort to reduce the number of blacks. Thirty-nine percent agreed that birth-control programs are a plot to eliminate blacks. . . .

The issue of scientific racism has affected blacks predominantly because we have been the most vulnerable. But those whites who would dismiss this as a worry solely for blacks should remember that poor whites and unaware whites are equally vulnerable. The forced sterilization of welfare mothers in South Carolina included white mothers as well. And poor white children often wind up in special education classes for reasons that are punitive rather than educational. As with every other manifestation of racism, the scientific variety threatens to destroy us all.

Reading Questions

1. Why is the testing industry reluctant to establish culture-specific tests?
2. What kinds of scientific studies are described as evidence of the racism found in science?
3. What is the difference between what IQ tests measure and what intelligence is?
4. What evidence is offered to support the conclusion that standard tests are culturally biased?

Questions for Reflection and Research

1. What is the current status of research attempts to determine whether intelligence is linked to race? Do investigators agree? Have investigators tried to modify intelligence tests to correct the defects Williams points out?
2. What is intelligence? What is the proper way to find out?
3. Is there any way to ensure that racism cannot be perpetuated by science?
4. Do different cultures have different concepts of intelligence? (For relevant considerations see selections #40 by Benedict, #41 by Cook, and #18 by Whorf.)
5. Does sociobiology tend to perpetuate racism? (See selection #14 by Edey and locate publications critical of sociobiology.)

Sexism in Science

The Author: Naomi Weisstein (b. 1939) is a psychologist who was educated at Wellesley College and Harvard University. As a researcher she focuses on the organization of complex perception. She is also an educator, having taught at Loyola University in Chicago and (now) at the State University of New York at Buffalo. She is a member of a variety of professional organizations and honorary societies.

The Selection: Both personality research and clinical psychology are criticized for their willingness to pronounce on the nature of male/female differences without either gathering sufficient evidence or carefully designing experiments to test hypotheses. A number of experiments cited by Weisstein are held to show that people tend to act the way people expect them to act. Thus psychologists' preconceptions about male/female differences can easily contaminate any studies of these differences. This selection is demanding reading.

It is an implicit assumption that the area of psychology which concerns itself with personality has the onerous [= burdensome] but necessary task of describing the limits of human possibility. Thus when we are about to consider the liberation of women, we naturally look to psychology to tell us what "true" liberation would mean: what would give women the freedom to fulfill their own in-

From "Psychology Constructs the Female; or The Fantasy Life of the Male Psychologist (with Some Attention to the Fantasies of His Friends, the Male Biologist and the Male Anthropologist)" by Naomi Weisstein in *Social Education*, 35, no. 4 (April 1971): 362–73. An earlier version of this paper, entitled "Kinder, Küche, and Kirche as Scientific Law: Psychology Constructs the Female," was published by the New England Free Press. Reprinted by permission of the author.

trinsic [= true] natures. Psychologists have set about describing the true natures of women with a certainty and a sense of their own infallibility rarely found in the secular world. Bruno Bettelheim [b. 1903], of the University of Chicago, tells us that

We must start with the realization that, as much as women want to be good scientists or engineers, they want first and foremost to be womanly companions of men and to be mothers.

Erik Erikson [b. 1902] of Harvard University, upon noting that young women often ask whether they can "have an identity before they know whom they will marry, and for whom they will make a home," explains somewhat elegiacally that

Much of a young woman's identity is already defined in her kind of attractiveness and in the selectivity of her search for the man (or men) by whom she wishes to be sought. . .

Mature womanly fulfillment, for Erikson, rests on the fact that a woman's

. . . somatic [= bodily] design harbors an "inner space" destined to bear the offspring of chosen men, and with it, a biological, psychological, and ethical commitment to take care of human infancy.

Some psychiatrists even see the acceptance of woman's role by women as a solution to societal problems. "Woman is nurturance . . . ," writes Joseph Rheingold [b. 1903], a psychiatrist at the Harvard Medical School, ". . . anatomy decrees the life of a woman . . . when women grow up without dread of their biological functions and without subversion by feminist doctrine, and therefore enter upon motherhood with a sense of fulfillment and altruistic [= concern about other people's well-being] sentiment, we shall attain the goal of a good life and a secure world in which to live it."

These views from men who are assumed to be experts reflect, in a surprisingly transparent way, the cultural consensus. They not only assert that a woman is defined by her ability to attract men, they see no alternative definitions. They think that the definition of a woman in terms of a man is the way it should be; and they back it up with psychosexual incantation and biological ritual curses. A woman has an identity if she is attractive enough to obtain a man, and thus, a home; for this will allow her to set about her life's task of "joyful altruism and nurturance.". . .

The central argument of my paper, then, is this. Psychology has nothing to say about what women are really like, what they need and what they want, essentially because psychology does not know. I want to stress that this failure is not limited to women; rather, the kind of psychology which has addressed itself to how people act and who they are has failed to understand, in the first place, why people act the way they do, and certainly failed to understand what might make them act differently.

The kind of psychology which has addressed itself to these questions divides into two professional areas: academic personality research, and clinical psychology and psychiatry. The basic reason for failure is the same in both these areas: the central assumption for most psychologists of human personality has been that human behavior rests on an individual and inner dynamic, perhaps fixed in infancy, perhaps fixed by genitalia, perhaps simply arranged in a rather immovable cognitive network. But this assumption is rapidly losing ground as personality psychologists fail again and again to get consistency in the assumed personalities of their subjects. Meanwhile, the evidence is collecting that what a person does and who she believes herself to be, will in general be a function of what people around her expect her to be, and what the overall situation in which she is acting implies that she is. . . .

Some academic personality psychologists are at least looking at the counter evidence and questioning their theories; no such corrective is occurring in clinical psychology and psychiatry: Freudians [= those who accept the views of Sigmund Freud (1859–1939)] and neo-Freudians, nudie-marathonists and touchy-feelies, classicists and swingers, clinicians and psychiatrists, simply refuse to look at the evidence against their theory and practice. And they support their theory and practice with stuff so transparently biased as to have absolutely no standing as empirical evidence.

⹁ To summarize: the first reason for psychology's failure to understand what people are and how they act is that psychology has looked for inner traits when it should have been looking for social context; the second reason for psychology's failure is that the theoreticians of personality have generally been clinicians and psychiatrists, and they have never considered it necessary to have evidence in support of their theories.

THEORY WITHOUT EVIDENCE

Let us turn to this latter cause of failure first: the acceptance by psychiatrists and clinical psychologists of theory without evidence. If we inspect the literature of personality, it is immediately obvious that the bulk of it is written by clinicians and psychiatrists, and that the major support for their theories is "years of intensive clinical experience." This is a tradition started by Freud. His "insights" occurred during the course of his work with his patients. Now there is nothing wrong with such an approach to theory *formulation*; a person is free to make up theories with any inspiration that works: divine revelation, intensive clinical practice, a random numbers table. But he/she is not free to claim any validity for his/her theory until it has been tested and confirmed. But theories are treated in no such tentative way in ordinary clinical practice. Consider Freud. What he thought constituted evidence violated the most minimal conditions of scientific rigor. In *The Sexual Enlightenment of Children*, the classic document which is supposed to demonstrate empirically the existence of a castration complex and its connection to a phobia, Freud based his analysis on the reports of the father of the little boy, himself in therapy, and a devotee of Freudian theory. I really don't have to comment further on the contamination in this kind of evidence. It is remarkable that only recently has Freud's classic theory on the sexuality of women—the notion of the double orgasm—been actually tested physiologically and found just plain wrong. Now those who claim that fifty years of psychoanalytic experience constitute evidence enough of the essential truths of Freud's theory should ponder the robust health of the double orgasm. Did women, until [the findings of W. H.] Masters [b. 1915] and [V. E.] Johnson [b. 1925], believe they were having two different kinds of orgasm? Did their psychiatrists badger them into reporting something that was not true? If so, were there other things they reported that were also not true? Did psychiatrists ever learn anything different than their theories had led them to believe? If clinical experience means anything at all, surely we should have been done with the double orgasm myth long before the Masters and Johnson studies.

But certainly, you may object, "years of intensive clinical experience" is the only reliable measure in a discipline which relies for its findings on insight, sensitivity, and intuition. The problem with insight, sensitivity, and intuition, is that they can confirm for all time the biases that one started with. People used to be absolutely convinced of their ability to tell which of their number were engaging in witchcraft. All it required was some sensitivity to the workings of the devil.

Years of intensive clinical experience is not the same thing as empirical evidence. The first thing an experimenter learns in any kind of experiment which involves humans is the concept of the "double blind." The term is taken from medical experiments, where one group is given a drug which is presumably supposed to change behavior in a certain way, and a control group is given a placebo. If the observers or the subjects know which group took which drug, the result invariably comes out on the positive side for the new drug. Only when it is not known which subject took which pill, is validity remotely approximated. In addition, with judgments of human behavior, it is so difficult to precisely tie down just what behavior is going on, let alone what behavior should be expected, that one must test again and again the reliability of judgments. How many judges, blind, will agree in their observations? Can they replicate their own judgments at some later time? When, in actual practice, these judgment criteria are tested for clinical judgments, then we find that the judges cannot judge reliably, nor can they judge consistently: they do no better than chance in identifying which of a certain set of stories were written by men and which by women;

which of a whole battery of clinical test results are the products of homosexuals and which are the products of heterosexuals, and which, of a battery of clinical test results *and* interviews (where questions are asked such as "Do you have delusions?") are products of psychotics, neurotics, psychosomatics, or normals. Lest this summary escape your notice, let me stress the implications of these findings. The ability of judges, chosen for their clinical expertise, to distinguish male heterosexuals from male homosexuals on the basis of three widely used clinical projective tests—the Rorschach, the TAT, and the MAP—was *no better than chance*. The reason this is such devastating news, of course, is that sexuality is supposed to be of fundamental importance in the deep dynamic of personality; if what is considered gross sexual deviance cannot be caught, then what are psychologists talking about when they, for example, claim that at the basis of paranoid psychosis is "latent homosexual panic"? They can't even identify what homosexual anything is, let alone "latent homosexual panic." More frightening, expert clinicians cannot be consistent on what diagnostic category to assign to a person, again on the basis of both tests and interviews; a number of normals in [one] study were described as psychotic, in such categories as "schizophrenic with homosexual tendencies" or "schizoid character with depressive trends." But most disheartening, when the judges were asked to rejudge the test protocols some weeks later, their diagnoses of the same subjects on the basis of the same protocol differed markedly from their initial judgments. It is obvious that even simple descriptive conventions in clinical psychology cannot be consistently applied; if clinicians were as faulty in recognizing food from non-food, they'd poison themselves and starve to death. That their descriptive conventions have any explanatory significance is therefore, of course, out of the question.

As a graduate student at Harvard some years ago, I was a member of a seminar which was asked to identify which of two piles of a clinical test, the TAT, had been written by males and which by females. Only four students out of twenty identified the piles correctly, and this was after one and a half months of intensively studying the differences between men and women. Since this result is below chance—that is, the result would occur by chance about four out of a thousand times—we may conclude that there *is* finally a consistency here; students are judging knowledgeably within the context of psychological teaching about the differences between men and women; the teachings themselves are simply erroneous. . . .

THE SOCIAL CONTEXT

Thus, since we can conclude that because clinical experience and tools can be shown to be worse than useless when tested for consistency, efficacy [= success in treatment], agreement, and reliability, we can safely conclude that theories of a clinical nature advanced about women are also worse than useless. I want to turn now to the second major point in my paper, which is that, even when psychological theory is constructed so that it may be tested, and rigorous standards of evidence are used, it has become increasingly clear that in order to understand why people do what they do, and certainly in order to change what people do, psychologists must turn away from the theory of the causal nature of the inner dynamic and look to the social context within which individuals live. . . .

In the first place, it is clear that personality tests never yield consistent predictions; a rigid authoritarian on one measure will be an unauthoritarian on the next. But the reason for this inconsistency is only now becoming clear, and it seems overwhelmingly to have much more to do with the social situation in which the subject finds him/herself than with the subject him/herself.

In a series of brilliant experiments, [Robert] Rosenthal [b. 1933] and his co-workers have shown that if one group of experimenters has one hypothesis about what they expect to find, and another group of experimenters has the opposite hypothesis, both groups will obtain results in accord with their hypotheses. The results obtained are not due to mishandling of data by biased experimenters: rather, somehow, the bias of the experimenter creates a changed environment in which subjects actually act differently. For instance, in one experiment, subjects were to assign numbers to pictures of men's faces, with high numbers representing the subject's judgment that the man in the picture was a successful person, and low numbers representing the subject's judgment that the man in the picture was an unsuccessful person. Prior to running the subjects, one group of experimenters was told that the subjects tended to rate the faces high; another group of experimenters was told that the subjects tended to rate the faces low. Each group of experimenters was instructed to follow precisely the same procedure: they were required to read to subjects a set of instructions, and to say *nothing else*. For the 375 subjects run, the results showed clearly that those subjects who performed the task with experimenters who expected high ratings gave high ratings, and those subjects who performed the task with experimenters who expected low ratings gave low ratings. How did this happen? The experimenters all used the same words; it was something in their conduct which made one group of subjects do one thing, and another group of subjects do another thing.

The concreteness of the changed conditions produced by expectation is a fact, a reality: even with animal subjects, in two separate studies, those experimenters who were told that rats learning mazes had been especially bred for brightness obtained better learning from their rats than did experimenters believing their rats to have been bred for dullness. In a very recent study, Rosenthal and [Lenore] Jacobson . . . extended their analysis to the natural classroom situation. Here, they tested a group of students and reported to the teachers that some among the students tested "showed great promise." Actually, the students so named had been selected on a random basis. Some time later, the experimenters retested the group of students: those students whose teachers had been told that they were "promising" showed real and dramatic increments in their IQs as compared to the rest of the students. Something in the conduct of the teachers towards those who the teachers believed to be the "bright" students, made those students brighter.

Thus, even in carefully controlled experiments, and with no outward or conscious difference in behavior, the hypotheses we start with will influence enormously the behavior of another organism. These studies are extremely important when assessing the validity of psychological studies of women. Since it is beyond doubt that most of us start with notions as to the nature of men and women, the validity of a number of observations of sex differences is questionable, even when these observations have been made under carefully controlled conditions. Second, and more important, the Rosenthal experiments point quite clearly to the influence of social expectation. In some extremely important ways, people are what you expect them to be, or at least they behave as you expect them to behave. Thus, if women, according to Bettelheim, want first and foremost to be good wives and mothers, it is extremely likely that this is what Bruno Bettelheim, and the rest of society, want them to be.

There is another series of brilliant social psychological experiments which point to the overwhelming effect of social context. These are the obedience experiments of Stanley Milgram [b. 1933] in which subjects are asked to obey the orders of unknown experimenters, orders which carry with them the distinct possibility that the subject is killing somebody.

In Milgram's experiments, a subject is told that he/she is administering a learning experiment, and that he/she is to deal out shocks each time the other "subject" (in reality, a confederate of the experimenter) answers incorrectly. The equipment appears to provide graduated shocks ranging upwards from 15 volts through 450 volts; for each of four consecutive voltages there are verbal descriptions such as "mild shock," "danger, severe shock," and, finally, for the 435- and 450-volt switches, a red XXX marked over the switches. Each time the stooge answers incorrectly, the subject is supposed to increase the voltage. As the voltage increases, the stooge begins to cry in pain; he/she demands that the experiment stop; finally, he/she refuses to answer at all. When he/she stops responding, the experimenter instructs the subject to continue increasing the voltage; for each shock administered the stooge shrieks in agony. Under these conditions, about 62-1/2 percent of the subjects administered shocks that they believed to be possibly lethal.

No tested individual differences between subjects predicted how many would continue to obey, and which would break off the experiment. When forty psychiatrists predicted how many of a group of 100 subjects would go on to give the lethal shock, their predictions were orders of magnitude below the actual percentages; most expected only one-tenth of one per cent of the subjects to obey to the end.

But even though *psychiatrists* have no idea how people will behave in this situation, and even though individual differences do not predict which subjects will obey and which will not, it is easy to predict when subjects will be obedient and when they will be defiant. All the experimenter has to do is change the social situation. In a variant of Milgram's experiment, two stooges were present in addition to the "victim": these worked along with the subject in administering electric shocks. When these two stooges refused to go on with the experiment, only 10 percent of the subjects continued to the maximum voltage. This is critical for personality theory. It says that behavior is predicted from the social situation, not from the individual history.

Finally, an ingenious experiment by [Stanley] Schachter [b. 1922] and [Jerome E.] Singer [b. 1934] showed that subjects injected with adrenalin, which produces a state of physiological arousal in all but minor respects identical to that which occurs when subjects are extremely afraid, became euphoric when they were in a room with a stooge who was acting euphoric, and became extremely angry when they were placed in a room with a stooge who was acting extremely angry.

To summarize: If subjects under quite innocuous and non-coercive social conditions can be made to kill other subjects and under other types of social conditions will positively refuse to do so; if subjects can react to a state of physiological fear by becoming euphoric because there is somebody else around who is euphoric, or angry because there is somebody else around who is angry; if students become intelligent because teachers expect them to be intelligent, and rats run mazes better because experimenters are told the rats are bright, then it is obvious that a study of human behavior requires, first and foremost, a study of the social contexts within which people move, the expectations as to how they will behave, and the authority which tells them who they are and what they are supposed to do. . . .

CONCLUSION

. . . My paper began with remarks on the task of the discovery of the limits of human potential. Psychologists must realize that it is they who are limiting discovery of human potential. They refuse to accept evidence, if they are clinical psychologists, or, if they are rigorous, they assume that people move in a context-free ether, with only their innate dispositions and their individual traits determining what they will do. Until psychologists begin to respect evidence, and until they begin looking at the social context within which people move, psychology will have nothing of substance to offer in this task of discovery. I don't know what immutable differences exist between men and women apart from differences in their genitals; perhaps there are some other unchangeable differences; probably there are a number of irrelevant differences. But it is clear that until social expectations for men and women are equal, until we provide equal respect for both men and women, our answers to this question will simply reflect our prejudices.

Reading Questions

1. What is wrong with the evidence usually offered by psychologists to back up their claims about women? What evidence does Weisstein offer to back up her conclusions about the failures of the male psychologists?
2. Why are double-blind procedures important in experiments in science?
3. What evidence is offered to support the contention that people's expectations about others greatly influence others' conduct?

Questions for Reflection and Research

1. Read the full essay by Weisstein. What other sciences does she condemn for sexist bias?
2. Is there any way to repair science so that scientists will not be able to produce illegitimate findings about the nature of male/female differences?
3. To what extent does our language influence our thinking about men and women? (For some relevant considerations see selection #18 by Whorf.)
4. Does anyone contest the experiments Weisstein cites to support the view that expectations influence behavior? If so, what are the reasons for criticizing the experiments?

5. Would those who drafted the Nuremberg Code (see selection #45) approve of the experiments on human beings described toward the end of this selection? Were those experimented on asked for their informed consent? Should they have been?
6. Examine other sciences that study human beings. Is there evidence of sexist bias in them too?
7. How does sexism manifest itself in science (other than by biasing results of scientific inquiry)?
8. To what extent is this text sexist?

Science and Society

The division between this and the preceding section of science and ethics is somewhat artificial. Many ethical problems affect society. The ethical problems created by the atomic bomb and by the recent advances in biological research are obvious examples. The influence of biased results concerning racial and sexual equality is another obvious example. Some ways in which science and society interact, however, do not so fully involve matters of ethics. Some of these topics are included here.

In Section 4 the nature of science is discussed. It is pointed out that the search for a definition of science and the search for the scientific method have sometimes been motivated by a desire to rid the world of imposter sciences, pseudo-sciences. Pseudo-sciences masquerade as sciences, and as a consequence their findings are taken to be trustworthy. Society suffers because its members become misinformed about the world. Some people who are thus misinformed may act in ways detrimental to themselves and society. For instance, those who accept findings of health or food faddists about the value of various food supplements may fail to nourish themselves and their children properly (assuming the health and food faddists are incorrect in their claims).

Society is harmed in other ways by pseudo-science. Resources are siphoned from legitimate research to the fraudulent sciences. Gullible and scientifically uneducated people may purchase products that are alleged to cure diseases, restore hair, find water, and so on. Others may be moved by claims that the government or the scientific establishment is persecuting a pseudo-scientist—and donate money to the pseudo-scientist's cause. Martin Gardner in selection #50 discusses pseudo-scientists and the role publishers play in propagating pseudo-science.

Not only is society being corrupted by pseudo-sciences; it is also under attack from another quarter. Polluted air and water, excessive noise, pesticide residues in food, and dehumanized factory workers are all evidence of the seemingly evil influence of science and technology on society. Novelist Robert M. Pirsig in selection #53 portrays a husband

and wife who use a product of technology, a motorcycle, to escape on weekends what they regard as a menace to them and to humanity: technology.

Is it true that science and technology are evil? Perhaps only technology is. Science, it might be thought, is involved in basic research, while technology often involves the careless practical use of scientific findings. Garvin McCain and Edwin Segal clarify (in selection #51) the distinction between science and technology, noting that at present each depends on the other. Without technology, instruments and synthetic materials would not be available for scientific experimentation. On the other hand many instruments and materials would not exist without the theoretical understanding provided by science. (In earlier ages science and technology existed in greater separation. Inventors often succeeded with little or no scientific training.) If McCain and Segal are correct and science and technology are intermingled now, they are either both to be blamed or both absolved from the charge of corrupting human life.

A physicist, Victor Weisskopf, describes three common conceptions of science in selection #54. The second conception is that science is the source of technology and that technology corrupts. The first is that science is now involved in obscure studies into matters of concern to few people and that such studies are too expensive. The third conception is that science can fix anything and should be set to work on all unresolved problems. Weisskopf argues that science and technology are neither evil, trivial, nor a cure-all. Humans must learn to use them intelligently but not expect science to fix everything.

Society's conception of science influences its willingness to fund science. If science is regarded as a great evil, funds will be cut. If science is regarded as a cure-all, funds will be made available to support scientific studies that promise practical results of interest to members of the society. Robert Fischer in selection #52 points out the many difficult decisions faced by those who administer funds for science. He gives little advice on how these decisions should be made. Since most scientists are not trained to make such decisions, how can we expect scientists to make them well? And if the decisions are left to nonscientists, how can they be trusted to correctly evaluate the merit of scientific requests for funds?

This brings us to consider the education of those in the sciences. Many selections in this volume remind us that scientists' work often raises nonscientific issues. The selections suggest that scientists will enjoy richer lives, and the world will profit more, if they are trained not only as scientists but as widely concerned human beings. And nonscientists will be able both to understand the world better and to keep sciences intelligently in check if they know a fair amount about science. These goals for the education of scientists and nonscientists are approved of by C. P. Snow, the scientist and author of works of fiction. Selection #55 by Dietrich Schroeer describes the warning Snow issued in the 1950s about a split among educated people. In his book *The Two Cultures* Snow argued that those trained in the humanities and those trained in the sciences were almost fully ignorant of each other's fields. They often had contempt for each other. Snow's claims were criticized for being oversimplified.

Are they oversimplified? Consider the people in scientific fields whom you know and those trained in the humanities (literature, philosophy, religion, or the arts). How much do they understand about or care about each other's concerns? If there is a split of the sort mentioned by Snow, educational efforts in universities to require students to broaden their perspectives have failed thus far. Only through students' personal and concerted effort can they hope to be fully and widely educated.

Further Reading: Science and Society

1. *1984 and All That: Modern Science, Social Change, and Human Values*, ed. FRED H. KNELMAN (Belmont, Calif.: Wadsworth Publishing Company, 1971). This is a wide-ranging anthology covering many topics in the sociology of science.
2. *Philosophical Problems of Science and Technology*, ed. ALEX C. MICHALOS (Boston: Allyn & Bacon, 1974). This anthology devotes eight out of twenty-seven selections to issues about science and society.
3. Two books that range over many topics about science and society and that have helpful bibliographies were sources for selections in this section.
    (a) *Science, Man & Society*, 2nd ed., by ROBERT B. FISCHER (Philadelphia: W. B. Saunders Company, 1975).
    (b) *The Game of Science*, 2nd ed., by GARVIN McCAIN and ERWIN M. SEGAL (Belmont, Calif.: Wadsworth Publishing Company, 1973). Especially see chapter 7.
4. Periodicals: Many issues about science and society are discussed in articles in certain science periodicals. These periodicals also include reviews of books about science and society. See especially *The Bulletin of the Atomic Scientists*, *Psychology Today*, *Science*, and *Scientific American*.

How Does One Distinguish Science from Pseudo-Science?

The Author: Martin Gardner (b. 1914) is well known for his monthly "Mathematical Games" column in *Scientific American*, which he began in 1956. Educated at the University of Chicago, he has written a number of books explaining the complexities of modern physics.

The Selection: The reading is an excerpt from an entertaining book filled with detailed examples of incredible theories purported to be scientific. The author argues the rise in prestige of science has attracted promoters of pseudo-science, attempting to capitalize on this prestige. Publishers of books and periodicals are condemned for their willingness to publish unsupported and sensational claims in the name of science. The common characteristics of pseudo-scientists are enumerated.

Since the bomb exploded over Hiroshima, the prestige of science in the United States has mushroomed like an atomic cloud. In schools and colleges, more students than ever before are choosing some branch of science for their careers. Military budgets earmarked for scientific research have never been so fantastically huge. Books and magazines devoted to science are coming off the presses in greater numbers than at any previous time in history. Even in the realm of escape literature, science fiction threatens seriously to replace the detective story.

One curious consequence of the current boom in science is the rise of the promoter of new and strange "scientific" theories. He is

From *Fads and Fallacies in the Name of Science* by Martin Gardner (New York: Dover Publications, 1957), pp. 3-14. Reprinted by permission of the author.

riding into prominence, so to speak, on the coat-tails of reputable investigators. The scientists themselves, of course, pay very little attention to him. They are too busy with more important matters. But the less informed general public, hungry for sensational discoveries and quick panaceas [= cure-alls], often provides him with a noisy and enthusiastic following.

In 1951, tens of thousands of mentally ill people throughout the country entered "dianetic reveries" in which they moved back along their "time track" and tried to recall unpleasant experiences they had when they were embryos. Thousands of more sophisticated neurotics, who regard dianetics as the invention of a mountebank [= fraud], are now sitting in "orgone boxes" to raise their body's charge of "orgone energy." Untold numbers of middle-aged housewives are preparing to live to the age of 100 by a diet rich in yoghurt, wheat-germ, and blackstrap-molasses.

Not only in the fields of mental and physical health is the spurious scientist flourishing. A primitive interpretation of Old Testament miracle tales, which one thought went out of fashion with the passing of William Jennings Bryan [1860-1925], has just received a powerful shot in the arm. Has not the eminent "astrophysicist," Dr. Immanuel Velikovsky [b. 1895], established the fact that the earth stopped rotating precisely at the moment Joshua commanded the sun and moon to stand still? For fifty years, geologists and physicists have been combining forces to perfect complex, delicate instruments for exploring underground structures. They've been wasting their time according to Kenneth Roberts [1885-1957], the well-known novelist. All you need is a forked twig, and he has written a persuasive and belligerent book to prove it.

Since flying saucers were first reported in 1947, countless individuals have been convinced that the earth is under observation by visitors from another planet. Admirers of . . . Behind the Flying Saucers [by Frank Scully (1892–1964)] suspect that the mysterious disks are piloted by inhabitants of Venus who are exact duplicates of earthlings except they are three feet tall. A more recent study by Gerald Heard [1889–1971] makes out an even stronger case for believing the saucers are controlled by intelligent bees from Mars.

In the twenties, newspapers provided a major publicity outlet for the speculations of eccentric scholars. Every Sunday, Hearst's American Weekly disclosed with lurid pictures some outlandish piece of scientific moonshine. The pages of the daily press were spotted with such stories as unconfirmed reports of enormous sea serpents, frogs found alive in the cornerstones of ancient buildings, or men who could hear radio broadcasts through gold inlays in their teeth. But gradually, over the next two decades, an unwritten code of science ethics developed in the profession of news journalism. Wire services hired competent science writers. Leading metropolitan dailies acquired trained science editors. The American Medical Association stepped up its campaign against press publicity for medical quackery, and disciplined members who released accounts of research that had not been adequately checked by colleagues. Today, science reporting in the American press is freer of humbug and misinformation than ever before in history.

To a large extent, the magazine and book publishing firms shared in the forging of this voluntary code. Unfortunately, at the turn of the half-century they began to backslide. *Astounding Science Fiction*, until recently the best of the science fantasy magazines, was the first to inform the public of the great "Dianetic Revolution" in psychiatry. *True* boosted its circulation by breaking the news that flying saucers came from another planet. *Harper's* published the first article in praise of Velikovsky's remarkable discoveries, and similar pieces quickly followed in *Collier's* and *Reader's Digest. The Saturday Evening Post* and *Look* gave widespread publicity to [the] blackstrap-molasses cult [of Gayelord Hauser (b. 1895)] during the same month that the Pure Food and Drug Administration seized copies of his best-seller, *Look Younger, Live Longer*. The government charged that displays of the book next to jars of blackstrap constituted, because of the book's sensational claims, a "mislabeling" of the product.

Many leading book publishers have had no better record. It is true that . . . *Dianetics* [by L. Ron Hubbard (b. 1911)] was too weird a manuscript to interest the larger houses, but Velikovsky's equally preposterous work found two highly reputable publishers. [The] book [of Kenneth Roberts (1885-1957)] on the art of finding water with a dowsing rod, Scully's saucer book, and Heard's even more fantastic study also appeared under the imprints of major houses.

When book editors and publishers are questioned about all this, they have a ready answer. It is a free country, they point out. If the public is willing to buy a certain type of book in great quantities, do they not, as public servants, have every right—perhaps even the obligation—to satisfy such a demand?

No one with any respect for independent thinking would propose that a publishing house or magazine be *compelled*, by any type of government action, to publish only material sanctioned by a board of competent scientists. That, however, is not the issue. The question is whether the voluntary code of ethics, so painstakingly built up during the past two decades, is worth preserving. Velikovsky's book, for example, was widely advertised as a revolutionary astronomical discovery. The publisher, of course, had every legal right to publish such a book. Likewise, the scientists who threatened to boycott the firm's textbooks unless it dropped Velikovsky from its list, were exercising their democratic privilege of organized protest. The issue is not a legal one, or even a political one. It is a question of individual responsibility.

Perhaps we are making a mountain out of a molehill. It is all very amusing, one might say, to titillate public fancy with books about bee people from Mars. The scientists are not fooled, nor are readers who are scientifically informed. If the public wants to shell out cash for such flummery, what difference does it make? The answer is that it is not at all amusing when people are misled by scientific claptrap. Thousands of neurotics desperately in need of trained psychiatric care are seriously retarding their therapy by dalliance with crank cults. Already a frightening number of cases have come to light of suicides and mental crack-ups among patients undergoing these dubious cures. No reputable publisher would think of releasing a book describing a treatment for cancer if it were written by a doctor universally considered a quack by his peers. Yet the difference between such a book and *Dianetics* is not very great.

What about the long-run effects of non-medical books like Velikovsky's, and the treatises on flying saucers? It is hard to see how the effects can be anything but harmful. Who can say how many orthodox Christians and Jews read *Worlds in Collision* and drifted back into a cruder Biblicism because they were told that science had reaffirmed the Old Testament miracles? [H. L.] Mencken [1880–1956] once wrote that if you heave an egg out of a Pullman car window anywhere in the United States you are likely to hit a fundamentalist. That was twenty-five years ago, and times have changed, but it is easy to forget how far from won is the battle against religious superstition. It is easy to forget that thousands of high school teachers of biology, in many of our southern states, are still afraid to teach the theory of evolution for fear of losing their jobs. There is no question but that informed and enlightened Christianity, both Catholic and Protestant, suffered a severe body blow when Velikovsky's book was enthusiastically hailed by the late Fulton Oursler [1892–1953] (in *Reader's Digest*) as scientific confirmation of the most deplorable type of Bible interpretation.

Flying saucers? I have heard many readers of the saucer books upbraid the government in no uncertain terms for its stubborn refusal to release the "truth" about the elusive platters. The administration's "hush hush policy" is angrily cited as proof that our military and political leaders have lost all faith in the wisdom of the American people.

An even more regrettable effect produced by the publication of scientific rubbish is the confusion they sow in the minds of gullible readers about what is and what isn't scientific knowledge. And the more the public is confused, the easier it falls prey to doctrines of pseudo-science which may at some future date receive the backing of politically powerful groups. . . . A renaissance of German quasi-science paralleled the rise of Hitler. If the German people had been better trained to distinguish good from bad science, would they have swallowed so easily the insane racial theories of the Nazi anthropologists?

In the last analysis, the best means of combating the spread of pseudo-science is an enlightened public, able to distinguish the work of a reputable investigator from the work of the incompetent and self-deluded. This is not as hard to do as one might think. Of course, there always will be borderline cases hard to classify, but the fact that black shades into white through many shades of gray does not mean that the distinction between black and white is difficult.

Actually, two different "continuums" are involved. One is a scale of the degree to which a scientific theory is confirmed by evidence. At one end of this scale are theories almost certainly false, such as the dianetic view that a one-day-old embryo can make sound recordings of its mother's conversation. Toward the middle of the scale are theories advanced as working hypotheses, but highly debatable because of the lack of sufficient data. . . . Finally, at the other extreme of the scale, are theories almost certainly true, such as the belief that the earth is round or that men and beasts are distant cousins. The problem of determining the degree to which a theory is confirmed is extremely difficult and technical, and, as a matter of fact, there are no known methods for giving precise "probability values" to hypotheses. . . .

The second continuum is the scale of scientific competence. It also has its extremes—ranging from obviously admirable scientists, to men of equally obvious incompetence. That there are individuals of debatable status—men whose theories are on the borderline of sanity, men competent in one field and not in others, men competent at one period of life and not at others, and so on—all this ought not to blind us to the obvious fact that there is a type of self-styled scientist who can legitimately be called a crank. It is not the novelty of his views or the neurotic motivations behind his work that provide the grounds for calling him this. The grounds are the technical criteria by which theories are evaluated. If a man persists in advancing views that are contradicted by all available evidence, and which offer no reasonable grounds for serious consideration, he will rightfully be dubbed a crank by his colleagues. . . .

A . . . characteristic of the pseudo-scientist . . . is a tendency toward paranoia. This is a mental condition (to quote a recent textbook) "marked by chronic, systematized, gradually developing delusions, without hallucinations, and with little tendency toward deterioration, remission, or recovery." . . . It is easy to understand . . . that a strong sense of personal greatness must be involved whenever a crank stands in solitary, bitter opposition to every recognized authority in his field.

If the self-styled scientist is rationalizing strong religious convictions, as often is the case, his paranoid drives may be reduced to a minimum. The desire to bolster religious beliefs with science can be a powerful motive. For example, in our examination of George McCready Price [1870–1963], the greatest of modern opponents of evolution, we shall see that his devout faith in Seventh Day Adventism is a sufficient explanation for his curious geological views. But even in such cases, an element of paranoia is nearly always present. Otherwise the pseudo-scientist would lack the stamina to fight a vigorous, single-handed battle against such overwhelming odds. If the crank is insincere—interested only in making money, playing a hoax, or both—then obviously paranoia need not enter his make-up. However, very few cases of this sort will be considered.

There are five ways in which the sincere pseudo-scientist's paranoid tendencies are likely to be exhibited.

(1) He considers himself a genius.

(2) He regards his colleagues, without exception, as ignorant blockheads. Everyone is out of step except himself. Frequently he insults his opponents by accusing them of stupidity, dishonesty, or other base motives. If they ignore him, he takes this to mean his arguments are unanswerable. If they retaliate in kind, this strengthens his delusion that he is battling scoundrels.

Consider the following quotation: "To me truth is precious. . . . I should rather be right and stand alone than to run with the multitude and be wrong. . . . The holding of the views herein set forth has already won for me the scorn and contempt and ridicule of some of my fellowmen. I am looked upon as being odd, strange, peculiar. . . . But truth is truth and though all the world reject it and turn against me, I will cling to truth still."

These sentences are from the preface of a booklet, published in 1931, by Charles Silvester de Ford, of Fairfield, Washington, in which he proves the earth is flat. Sooner or later, almost every pseudo-scientist expresses similar sentiments.

(3) He believes himself unjustly persecuted and discriminated against. The recognized societies refuse to let him lecture. The journals reject his papers and either ignore his books or assign them to "enemies" for review. It is all part of a dastardly plot. It never occurs to the crank that this opposition may be due to error in his work. It springs solely, he is convinced, from blind prejudice on the part of the established hierarchy—the high priests of science who fear to have their orthodoxy overthrown.

Vicious slanders and unprovoked attacks, he usually insists, are constantly being made against him. He likens himself to Bruno, Galileo, Copernicus, Pasteur, and other great men who were unjustly persecuted for their heresies. If he has had no formal training in the field in which he works, he will attribute this persecution to a scientific masonry, unwilling to admit into its inner sanctums anyone who has not gone through the proper initiation rituals. He repeatedly calls your attention to important scientific discoveries made by laymen.

(4) He has strong compulsions to focus his attacks on the greatest scientists and the best-established theories. When Newton was the outstanding

name in physics, eccentric works in that science were violently anti-Newton. Today, with Einstein the father-symbol of authority, a crank theory of physics is likely to attack Einstein in the name of Newton. . . .

(5) He often has a tendency to write in a complex jargon, in many cases making use of terms and phrases he himself has coined. Schizophrenics sometimes talk in what psychiatrists call "neologisms"—words which have meaning to the patient, but sound like Jabberwocky to everyone else. Many of the classics of crackpot science exhibit a neologistic tendency.

When the crank's I.Q. is low, as in the case of the late Wilbur Glenn Voliva [1870–1942] who thought the earth shaped like a pancake, he rarely achieves much of a following. But if he is a brilliant thinker, he is capable of developing incredibly complex theories. He will be able to defend them in books of vast erudition, with profound observations, and often liberal portions of sound science. His rhetoric may be enormously persuasive. All the parts of his world usually fit together beautifully, like a jig-saw puzzle. It is impossible to get the best of him in any type of argument. He has anticipated all your objections. He counters them with unexpected answers of great ingenuity. Even on the subject of the shape of the earth, a layman may find himself powerless in a debate with a flat-earther. . . .

Reading Questions

1. Why does the author claim pseudo-science has begun to flourish?
2. What bad consequences are there when pseudo-science is published?
3. How does Gardner suggest we can distinguish science from pseudo-science or the reputable scientists from the pseudo-scientists?

Questions for Reflection and Research

1. Consider what some regard as health fads: Laetrile, vitamin E, vitamin C, and so on. Is the support for them pseudo-scientific?
2. Think of other examples of suspicious science. What makes us suspicious? Are the suspicions confirmable?
3. Could we use either Fischer's definition in selection #25 or the scientific methods described by Pirsig in selection #26 and Hempel in selection #27 to discriminate science from pseudo-science?
4. Read Gardner's book and determine how in each case of a pseudo-science, he is able to distinguish it from science.

5. Is psychology a pseudo-science? Is history? How can we obtain reliable answers to these questions? (For some relevant considerations see selections #36, #38, and #39 by Hospers, Louch, and Nagel, respectively.)

6. Even if there are reasons to wish that pseudo-science not be published, what reasons are there for allowing full freedom of expression?

7. In his time, Galileo was thought to be practicing pseudo-science. Was there any way to tell science from pseudo-science in his case?

8. Is the portrayal of science on popular science-fiction television programs or in films an accurate portrayal? If not, can such popularization of science promote pseudo-science? (See *TV Guide*, February 4–10, 1978 for an article on television and pseudo-science by the astronomer Carl Sagan.)

selection 51.

The Relation between Science and Technology

The Authors: Garvin McCain (b. 1922) was educated in psychology at Washburn University and the University of Texas. He has taught at the University of Texas at Arlington.

Erwin M. Segal (b. 1936) received his training in psychology at the University of Maryland and the University of Minnesota. He has taught at State College of Iowa, Arlington State College, and the State University of New York at Buffalo.

The Selection: A distinction is made between science and technology. It is contended that science and technology mutually benefit each other—even though often the practical value of pure science is at first difficult to guess. The development of the microscope and advances in understanding electricity are used to illustrate the interaction between science and technology. Finally, financial support of science is defended as a means to obtain technological advances.

Science and technology are mutually supportive. Science benefits from technological advances, and much modern technology rests on scientific discovery. Until relatively recently, much of technology developed independently of scientific advances, although much of science depended on the then current technology. Today, however, new technology usually depends on scientific discovery, and this dependency will undoubtedly increase. In the past, technology was relatively simple and utilized readily available materials. This is unlikely to be the case in the future.

Adapted from *The Game of Science* (3rd ed.), by Garvin McCain and Erwin M. Segal. Copyright © 1977 by Wadsworth Publishing Company, Inc. Reprinted by permission of the publisher, Brooks/Cole Publishing Company, Monterey, California.

To illustrate the mutual relationship between science and technology, we might consider the microscope. An early step in the developmental sequence was the invention or discovery of a method of making glass. This event was preceded by the ability to control fire, as well as other necessary antecedents. Early records of the Egyptians indicate that they knew how to make glass, and this knowledge probably came from Asia. But the origins of this major technological development are buried in prehistory.

There is a report that a convex lens made of rock crystal was found among the ruins of the palace of Nimrod (about 1800 B.C.). Certainly, for many centuries prior to scientific research, men had known of the magnifying powers of natural or accidental lenses. A significant step in this history is a book of optics attributed to Ptolemy. Ptolemy did make significant contributions to science. His book on optics (written in the second century A.D.) laid the scientific groundwork for later work (about 1000 A.D.) by Ibn-al-Haytham, who advanced the science of optics through extensive research. Roger Bacon (1270+) was familiar with Ibn-al-Haytham's work and described a telescope, although there is no record that Bacon built one. The first modern convex lens (a simple magnifying glass) was made by grinding (a technological advance) sometime in the late 1200s. A major breakthrough in microscopes occurred about 1590 when Hans and Zacharias Janssen, Dutch spectacle makers, made the first compound microscope. In 1611 Kepler outlined the construction of an improved compound microscope, based on optical theory, and a model was built in 1628 by Christoph Scheiner. This microscope laid the rudimentary pattern for the modern optical microscope. Note that up to this time there was an intermingling of scientific and technological steps: the techniques of glass and lens making were necessary to the science of optics, and the scientific principles of optics were equally important to the design of an advanced microscope.

We could move from the development of the microscope to a discussion of its use, but it is sufficient to say that the microscope plays a very significant role as a tool of both science and technology. . . .

To gain some appreciation of the technological products that rest on a scientific base, one has only to look around. For example, whatever the limitations of fluorescent light, it is vastly superior to kerosene lamps. Consider a few of the basic scientific discoveries necessary to produce this illumination. Again, the rude beginnings go back probably beyond recorded history. There is evidence that about 500 B.C. Thales, a Greek philosopher and scientist, rubbed amber with a cloth and observed that the amber then attracted lightweight objects, such as strands of feathers. Doubtless others, in idle moments, had seen the attraction of amber for other objects, but we have no record of their observations; possibly they only shrugged and went on to more important matters.

The curious behavior of amber was known for about 2200 years before William Gilbert [1540–1603] (an English physician) made an important extension to our knowledge of this peculiar phenomenon. Gilbert found that other substances (such as sulphur and glass) had the same properties as amber. Strangely enough, lodestone seemed to have some of the same characteristics as amber, except that lodestone and amber attracted different bodies. It became clear that scientists could not limit their studies to the attractive qualities of amber. By 1646 Sir Thomas Browne (another English physician) contributed the name "electricity" to the phenomena being observed. . . . Charles Du Fay (a chemist who was also superintendent of gardens to the King of France) studied the attraction and repulsion of charged objects; by 1733 he came up with the idea that there were two kinds of electricity. At this time (around the 1740s), as [Thomas] Kuhn [b. 1922] phrases it, "There were almost as many views about the nature of electricity as there were important experimenters." The first and possibly greatest American scientist, Benjamin Franklin [1706–1790], proposed a concept that organized a large portion of the known data and gave direction to much later research. Franklin concluded that there was only one "electric fluid." This fluid was found in all bodies; those bodies having an excess quantity were positively charged, while those with smaller quantities were negatively charged. The concept was crude and did not account for all the information available at the time, but despite its deficiencies Franklin's way of organizing the data was accepted as being superior to others. Franklin's successors developed his ideas about electrical phenomena in a number of ways, but his concept was a critical beginning. Franklin has been best known popularly for his later experiments and for his explanation of the similarities between static electricity and lightning (particularly the kite experiment, 1752). As ingenious as this later work was, it was not nearly so important as his earlier conceptualization. . . .

In passing we should glance at the work of the Italians Luigi Galvani [1737–1798] (a professor of anatomy) and Alessandro Volta [1745–1827] (physics), if for no other reason than the fact that their work originated in the twitching of frogs' legs. The anatomist concluded that frogs' legs contained electricity that was released when they touched metal. The physicist concluded and demonstrated that the chemical action of moisture and different metals such as iron and copper produced electricity. . . .

In 1820 Hans Christian Oersted (a Danish scientist) showed that an electric current has a magnetic effect. By 1822 André Marie Ampère (a French physicist) worked out the laws on which the present-day concept of electricity is based.

Michael Faraday, the English chemist and physicist, gives a fitting climax to our consideration of the history of electricity. Faraday believed that if electricity could produce magnetism, then magnatism could probably produce electricity. In 1831 he found that relative movement of a magnet and wire loop leads to induction of an electric current. A lesser-known American scientist, Joseph Henry, also discovered this principle in 1831. The principle discovered by Faraday and Henry is the basis of the construction of electric generators and motors. Why is it that this scientific history omits a discussion of [Thomas] Edison [1847–1931]? He can be placed high among the developers of the *uses* of electricity, but his scientific contributions to the *concepts* of electricity are few.

Before drawing any conclusions about the scientific work discussed, let's consider for a moment the technological fallout. Could a modern technological society exist without electricity? It's difficult to see how. Certainly we could have developed alternatives for some things, such as fluorescent lights, but alternatives to radios, telephones, computers, T.V., radar, most internal-combustion engines, and many chemical processes would be out of the question.

From this abbreviated history of electricity we can extract a few points, some of which have probably already occurred to you.

1. Investigation of electricity was truly an international and interdisciplinary endeavor. Greeks, Italians, French, Americans, English, Germans, Danes, and Duch all made significant contributions, as did philosophers, amateur scientists, chemists, anatomists, physicists, physicians, and generalists. . . . [S]cience is an open community, with membership dependent on contributions, not on politics, geography, or professional titles.

2. The pace of the history picks up over time. The history is long, but events come closer and closer together as we approach the modern era. This increasing intensity is in part due to the interdependence of science. Each new discovery or concept suggests additional possibilities or relates prior findings.

3. Curiosity motivated most of the researchers. What distant horizon hid the "practical" applications? Could Thales, Gilbert, Franklin, Galvani, Oersted, or even Faraday have had immediate "practical" applications as their goals? This motivation does not seem even remotely possible. These men had found their game. Our present-day technological fallout is an unsought and unforeseen by-product of their efforts. If their efforts had been directed toward immediate application, where would we be? Not only would we have failed to produce basic scientific knowledge of electricity, but we could not have achieved our present technological development. Had the Roman engineer-administrator outlook dominated our culture, we would doubtless have achieved infinite refinements of existing knowledge and techniques, together with some fortuitous gains. Just how we could have achieved new insights and changes based on abstract principles is impossible to conceive.

4. To restate an earlier point, technology and science have strong mutual influences, even though they have quite different objectives. . . .

Jerome B. Wiesner [b. 1915], Special Assistant for Science and Technology to President Kennedy, displayed courage, wit, and keen insight in his struggle to explain the nature of basic research and its possible relation to technology. Had you been in his position, using the example of electricity, how would you explain to budget administrators or Congressmen your reasons for financial support of Gilbert's amber rubbing, Galvani's frog-leg preparation, or Franklin's kite flying? One's imagination fails at this point. Fortunately Wiesner's did not. His summary of the problem rings with the clarity of a rock-crystal goblet.

The research scientist is primarily motivated by an urge to explore and understand, but society supports fundamental research primarily because experience has demonstrated how essential such work is for continued progress in technology. Halt the flow of new research and the possible scope of technical developments will soon be limited and ultimately reduced to nothing. Incidentally, scientific knowledge need not be exploited immediately once it becomes available. It exists for all to use forever.

Thus, acquiring scientific knowledge is a form of capital investment. Unlike most other capital investments, it does not become obsolete; nor can it be used up. Technological developments are also a form of capital investment, though somewhat less enduring. To be sure, a more efficient process will also yield its benefits endlessly, but usually technological developments tend to become obsolete as better methods, devices, and processes emerge.

Reading Questions

1. What is the authors' conception of the difference between science and technology?
2. In the accounts of the development of electricity and the microscope, which advances were based on technology and which on science?
3. Why do the authors point out that most of the researchers in electricity were motivated by curiosity?

Questions for Reflection and Research

1. Is science different from technology? What is the difference?
2. Do the definitions given in selection #25 by Fischer clearly exclude science from technology?
3. What reasons are there to want to stress the distinction between science and technology?
4. What is the difference between a scientist and an engineer?

5. How should research funds be distributed between science and technology? (See selection #52 by Fischer.)

6. Why do some people regard technology as evil? (See selection #53 by Pirsig.) Is it any more or less evil than science? Is it evil?

7. Who, if anyone, should be held responsible for harm done the world by products of technology? (See selections #43 by Taylor and #44 by Kipphardt.)

Government Support of Research

The Author: Robert B. Fischer (b. 1920). For biographical information see selection #25 on definitions of science.

The Selection: The allocation of funds by the federal government for scientific and technological research is not a simple matter. The percentage of the gross national product to be devoted to research must be decided, and it also must be decided which kinds of research deserve funding; the latter entails a decision about the level of funding for basic research. It is usually not clear what, if any, practical consequences may result from basic research, and there is thus some reluctance to fund it at all. If there is to be basic research, in what areas should it be funded? Should funds go to a few projects that use quite elaborate and expensive equipment—or to many less expensive projects?

One of the most basic issues is that of the extent to which government should be involved in the support of research and deveolpment. . . . [T]his was an issue before the Constitutional Convention, and it has frequently risen to the surface as a matter of deep concern ever since. The urgency and the magnitude of the problem have increased considerably as the nation has changed from an agrarian to an industrial society, and as it is even now in the throes of a further change to a post-industrial society fashioned, to a much greater extent than ever before, by science and by a science-based technology.

From *Science, Man & Society*, 2nd ed., by Robert B. Fischer (Philadelphia: W. B. Saunders Co., 1975), pp. 138-42. Reprinted by permission of W. B. Saunders Co. and Robert B. Fischer.

For two decades following World War II, research and development [in the United States] were almost magic words, the mention of which frequently brought forth additional allocation of funds and attracted capable personnel. The feeling was widespread that most any goal could be accomplished if enough money was made available for the needed research and development. . . . [T]he overall areas of research and development during these years consumed a rapidly increasing fraction of the federal budget. To be sure, research and development did lead to economic gains. So it is even more significant to note that the overall expenditures for research and development were consuming a rapidly increasing percentage of the gross national product. It is obvious that the annual growth rate of funds for research and development could not indefinitely continue to exceed the growth rates of the federal budget and of the gross national product. It was inevitable that there had to be a diminishing growth rate, and a leveling off of funds for research and development relative to the whole of the budget and of the gross national product, even though there seems in retrospect to have been insufficient recognition of this reality during the 1960s.

There has been a significant decrease in the annual growth rate of funds for research and development since 1966. Even though is was inevitable, this leveling off has come much sooner than many persons had expected. There are numerous practical consequences of this most recent trend in overall commitment to these areas. The issue is very significant and urgent, probably more so now than ever before—what should be the overall commitment of society and, in particular, of the Federal Government to research and development?

There is considerable justification for the viewpoint that the answer to this question must be expressed in terms of the gross national product. Even if this principle is accepted, it is very difficult, of course, to quantify it. For the issues remain as to just what percentage of the gross national product should be devoted to research and development, and as to the relative contributions to this total of government through taxation and of industry and other private sources.

Of equal or greater significance is the question of what scientific and technological areas should receive emphasis. There are some areas and types of research and development which it is both appropriate and feasible for industry to undertake, but other scientific and science-related problem areas simply cannot be handled without major support and sponsorship by the Federal Government, such as the development of newer sources of energy, the survival or replacement of urban areas, new forms of transportation, demographic [= population] concerns, problems related to the prediction of earthquakes, tornados and hurricanes and the

minimization of their destructive consequences, and the prevention, treatment and cure of cancer and heart disease, to name a
few.

The knowledge that is obtained and refined by means of basic
research is one of the necessary resources prerequisite to all
applied science and science-based technology. The level of the national commitment to basic research is one of the significant issues
in the area of science and public policy. Perhaps what is needed is
an overall, long-range public policy for basic scientific research as
distinct from a policy for technology.

There has been an understandable tendency over the years for
government officials and members of boards of directors of industrial concerns alike to respond more favorably to requests for funds
when they can anticipate in advance what "useful" product or practical accomplishment will result from it. This tendency has been to
assume that the necessary reservoir of basic scientific knowledge is
available. In addition, however, there has continually been some
recognition of the fact that this reservoir cannot be tapped indefinitely without some definite steps being taken to replenish it, as
illustrated, for example, by the record of the founding and early
development of the Smithsonian Institution. Even though existing
scientific knowledge is "used," and not "used up," continual advancement in basic science is essential to an ongoing technology.
With the increasing tempo of scientific and technological expansion
and with the frequently decreasing "lead-time" between discovery
in basic science and its application in technology, the issue of the
proper level of commitment to basic research is now an extremely
urgent one.

. . . [A]bout 14 to 15 percent of the overall funding for research
and development has been devoted to basic research in recent
years. This figure should be taken only as an approximation, because the dividing lines between basic research and applied research and development are frequently quite diffuse. But what
fraction of the overall funding for research and development really
should be devoted to basic research? There is surely no simple answer to this question. However, the consequences to all people of
much of modern technology are so serious that basic scientific research is surely a high priority item in modern society.

It is generally considered that the government should support
much of the basic research and that industry should directly support relatively more of the applied research and development. The
rationale is primarily that the basic research results in input to the
reservoir of scientific knowledge, which is ideally available to all
peoples, and thus the costs can appropriately be paid by all industries and persons through taxes, whereas a given industrial concern
can be expected to provide financing for applied research intended
to lead more directly to marketable products or processes. The dis-

tinction is, of course, not a sharp one. The government is directly involved in its own applications of knowledge, and there is only a diffuse dividing line between the pure and the applied.

In addition to the issue of the overall level, there is a real issue as to what basic research should be supported. In the sense that all knowledge can be considered to be good . . . and in the sense that it is impossible to specify in advance what practical applications may come of any particular basic knowledge, it would seem that all basic research should be supported. But funding limitations and personnel limitations make this impossible. There simply must be choices among alternative fields and topics of basic research. Priorities must be established, and herein lies a very difficult issue. The magnitude of the problems is great. The views of human beings are widely disparate and fluctuate rapidly.

One aspect of this issue is the competition for funds between "big science" and "small science." The former term refers to scientific research that requires the use of extremely expensive and usually very large equipment installations, such as radio telescopes and high energy accelerators. Large groups of supporting personnel are usually required, in addition to the scientists. Much basic research in experimental astronomy and elementary particle physics comes under this category. By way of contrast, most research in chemistry, in biology and in some areas of physics is "small science," in that individuals or small groups of persons can work on significant problems with equipment that typically costs tens of thousands of dollars rather than millions of dollars, as is the case with "big science." These distinctions lead to very practical problems when, for example, hundreds of small science projects could be supported with the same amount of funding as one or two large science undertakings.

Another aspect of the problem of selectivity in the support of basic research arises from the fact that scientific and/or technological "pay-offs" can often be expected to be greater from some fields of work than from others. Some research problems are more basic and of potentially greater significance to scientific knowledge than are others. Still another basis for assigning priorities among alternative areas of research is their presumed relevance with respect to the solution of problems of society, as those problems are currently being perceived. Research in some areas is more likely to lead to "useful" applications than in other areas. Underlying any such predictions, of course, must be the recognition that they may not turn out to be correct. . . .

Reading Questions

1. Why has the growth rate of federal research funds slowed considerably in recent years?

2. What questions must be answered before allocating government funds for research?
3. What role should the private sector play in funding research?

Questions for Reflection and Research

1. Obtain figures for present United States and worldwide support of research. Compare and contrast levels and distribution of funds.
2. What procedures should be used by government officials to resolve the questions raised by Fischer? Is there a scientific way to resolve the questions?
3. Is economics a science?
4. How should research efforts be structured to ensure maximum funding and greatest efficiency of resources? How should the government be organized to best evaluate and encourage research?
5. Should funding for any kinds of research be limited because of ethical reasons? (See selections #42 by Rescher, #43 by Taylor, #45 by Kieffer, #46 by Singer, and #47 by J. Gardner.)
6. Is basic scientific research responsible for all the advances in technology? Does technology sometimes proceed independently of basic science? Do advances in technology ever lead to advances in basic science? (See selections #51 by McCain and Segal and #54 by Weisskopf.)
7. How was research funded in past centuries before government funding? Who funded the work of Benjamin Franklin, or Newton, or Pasteur?
8. How does the current use of grants as a means of research support tend to discourage questioning of basic theories? Do Kuhn's views (in selection #31) support the view that grants tend to discourage scientific innovations?

Hostility to Technology by Two Who Depend on Technology

The Author: Robert M. Pirsig. For biographical information see selection #26 on the scientific method.

The Selection: Both this and selection #28 are excerpts from an autobiographical work that relates the story of a man and his son as they travel westward on a motorcycle. Part of the way they are accompanied by a married couple, John and Sylvia. The author at first is puzzled by some aspects of his friends' attitudes toward motorcycle maintenance and dripping faucets. Eventually he realizes they hate and fear technology both because it is incomprehensible to them and because it seems to be corrupting the world. The author indicates that his feelings toward technology are more positive.

The Chautauqua [= series of discussions] that is in mind for this trip was inspired by these two [John and Sylvia] many months ago and perhaps, although I don't know, is related to a certain undercurrent of disharmony between them.

Disharmony I suppose is common enough in any marriage, but in their case it seems more tragic. To me, anyway.

It's not a personality clash between them; it's something else, for which neither is to blame, but for which neither has any solution, and for which I'm not sure I have any solution either, just ideas.

The ideas began with what seemed to be a minor difference of opinion between John and me on a matter of small importance: how much one should maintain one's own motorcycle. It seems

Adapted and reprinted by permission of William Morrow and Company, Inc., from *Zen and the Art of Motorcycle Maintenance*, pp. 10–18. Copyright © 1974 by Robert M. Pirsig.

natural and normal to me to make use of the small tool kits and instruction booklets supplied with each machine, and keep it tuned and adjusted myself. John demurs. He prefers to let a competent mechanic take care of these things so that they are done right. Neither viewpoint is unusual, and this minor difference would never have become magnified if we didn't spend so much time riding together and sitting in country roadhouses drinking beer and talking about whatever comes to mind. What comes to mind, usually, is whatever we've been thinking about in the half hour or forty-five minutes since we last talked to each other. When it's roads or weather or people or old memories or what's in the newspapers, the conversation just naturally builds pleasantly. But whenever the performance of the machine has been on my mind and gets into the conversation, the building stops. The conversation no longer moves forward. There is a silence and a break in the continuity. It is as though two old friends, a Catholic and Protestant, were sitting drinking beer, enjoying life, and the subject of birth control somehow came up. Big freeze-out.

And, of course, when you discover something like that it's like discovering a tooth with a missing filling. You can never leave it alone. You have to probe it, work around it, push on it, think about it, not because it's enjoyable but because it's on your mind and it won't get off your mind. And the more I probe and push on this subject of cycle maintenance the more irritated he gets, and of course that makes me want to probe and push all the more. Not deliberately to irritate him but because the irritation seems symptomatic of something deeper, something under the surface that isn't immediately apparent.

When you're talking birth control, what blocks it and freezes it out is that it's not a matter of more or fewer babies being argued. That's just on the surface. What's underneath is a conflict of faith, of faith in empirical social planning versus faith in the authority of God as revealed by the teachings of the Catholic Church. You can prove the practicality of planned parenthood till you get tired of listening to yourself and it's going to go nowhere because your antagonist isn't buying the assumption that anything socially practical is good per se [= good by itself]. Goodness for him has other sources which he values as much as or more than social practicality.

So it is with John. I could preach the practical value and worth of motorcycle maintenance till I'm hoarse and it would make not a dent in him. After two sentences on the subject his eyes go completely glassy and he changes the conversation or just looks away. He doesn't want to hear about it.

Sylvia is completely with him on this one. In fact she is even more emphatic. "It's just a whole other thing," she says, when in a thoughtful mood. "Like garbage," she says, when not. They want *not* to understand it. Not to *hear* about it. And the more I try to fathom what makes me enjoy mechanical work and them hate it so, the more elusive it becomes. The ultimate cause of this originally minor difference of opinion appears to run way, way deep.

Inability on their part is ruled out immediately. They are both plenty bright enough. Either one of them could learn to tune a motorcycle in an hour and a half if they put their minds and energy to it, and the saving in money and worry and delay would repay them over and over again for their effort. And they *know* that. Or maybe they don't. I don't know. I never confront them with the question. It's better to just get along.

But I remember once, outside a bar in Savage, Minnesota, on a really scorching day when I just about let loose. We'd been in the bar for about an hour and we came out and the machines were so hot you could hardly get on them. I'm started and ready to go and there's John pumping away on the kick starter. I smell gas like we're next to a refinery and tell him so, thinking this is enough to let him know his engine's flooded.

"Yeah, I smell it too," he says and keeps on pumping. And he pumps and pumps and jumps and pumps and *I* don't know what more to say. Finally, he's really winded and sweat's running down all over his face and he can't pump anymore, and so I suggest taking out the plugs to dry them off and air out the cylinders while we go back for another beer.

Oh my God no! He doesn't want to get into all that stuff. "All what stuff?" "Oh, getting out the tools and all that stuff. There's no reason why it shouldn't start. It's a brand-new machine and I'm following the instructions perfectly. See, it's right on full choke like they say."

"Full *choke!*"

"That's what the instructions say."

"That's for when it's *cold!*"

"Well, we've been in there for a half an hour at least," he says.

It kind of shakes me up. "This is a hot day, John," I say. "And they take longer than that to cool off even on a freezing day."

He scratches his head. "Well, why don't they tell you that in the instructions?" He opens the choke and on the second kick it starts. "I guess that was it," he says cheerfully.

And the very next day we were out near the same area and it happened again. This time I was determined not to say a word, and when my wife urged me to go over and help him I shook my head. I told her that until he had a real felt need he was just going to resent help, so we went over and sat in the shade and waited.

I noticed he was being superpolite to Sylvia while he pumped away, meaning he was furious, and she was looking over with a kind of "Ye gods!" look. If he had asked any single question I would have been over in a second to diagnose it, but he wouldn't. It must have been fifteen minutes before he got started.

Later we were drinking beer again over at Lake Minnetonka and everybody was talking around the table, but he was silent and I could see he was really tied up in knots inside. After all that time. Probably to get them untied he finally said, "You know . . . when it doesn't start like that it just . . . really turns me into a *monster* inside. I just get paranoic about it." This seemed to loosen him up, and he added, "They just had this *one* motorcycle, see? This *lemon*. And they didn't know what to do with it, whether to send it back to the factory or sell it for scrap or what . . . and then at the last moment they saw *me* coming. With eighteen hundred bucks in my pocket. And they knew their problems were over."

In a kind of singsong voice I repeated the plea for tuning and he tried hard to listen. He really tries hard sometimes. But then the block came again and he was off to the bar for another round for all of us and the subject was closed.

He is not stubborn, not narrow-minded, not lazy, not stupid. There was just no easy explanation. So it was left up in the air, a kind of mystery that one gives up on because there is no sense in just going round and round and round looking for an answer that's not there.

It occurred to me that maybe I was the odd one on the subject, but that was disposed of too. Most touring cyclists know how to keep their machines tuned. Car owners usually won't touch the engine, but every town of any size at all has a garage with expensive lifts, special tools and diagnostic equipment that the average owner can't afford. And a car engine is more complex and inaccessible than a cycle engine so there's more sense to this. But for John's cycle, a BMW R60, I'll bet there's not a mechanic between here and Salt Lake City. If his points or plugs burn out, he's done for. I *know* he doesn't have a set of spare points with him. He doesn't know what points are. If it quits on him in western South Dakota or Montana I don't know what he's going to do. Sell it to the Indians maybe. Right now I know what he's doing. He's carefully avoiding giving any thought whatsoever to the subject. The BMW is famous for not giving mechanical problems on the road and that's what he's counting on.

I might have thought this was just a peculiar attitude of theirs about motorcycles but discovered later that it extended to other things. . . . Waiting for them to get going one morning in their kitchen I noticed the sink faucet was dripping and remembered that it was dripping the last time I was there before and that in fact it had been dripping as long as I could remember. I commented on it and John said he had tried to fix it with a new faucet washer but it hadn't worked. That was all he said. The presumption left was that that was the end of the matter. If you try to fix a faucet and your fixing doesn't work then it's just your lot to live with a dripping faucet.

408

SCIENCE AND SOCIETY

This made me wonder to myself if it got on their nerves, this drip-drip-drip, week in, week out, year in, year out, but I could not notice any irritation or concern about it on their part, and so concluded they just aren't bothered by things like dripping faucets. Some people aren't.

What it was that changed this conclusion, I don't remember . . . some intuition, some insight one day, perhaps it was a subtle change in Sylvia's mood whenever the dripping was particularly loud and she was trying to talk. She has a very soft voice. And one day when she was trying to talk above the dripping and the kids came in and interrupted her she lost her temper at them. It seemed that her anger at the kids would not have been nearly as great if the faucet hadn't also been dripping when she was trying to talk. It was the combined dripping and loud kids that blew her up. What struck me hard then was that she was *not* blaming the faucet, and that she was *deliberately* not blaming the faucet. She wasn't ignoring that faucet at all! She was *suppressing* anger at that faucet and that goddamned dripping faucet was just about *killing* her! But she could not admit the importance of this for some reason.

Why suppress anger at a dripping faucet? I wondered.

Then that patched in with the motorcycle maintenance and one of those light bulbs went on over my head and I thought, Ahhhhhhhh!

It's not the motorcycle maintenance, not the faucet. It's all of technology they can't take. And then all sorts of things started tumbling into place and I knew that was it. Sylvia's irritation at a friend who thought computer programming was "creative." All their drawings and paintings and photographs without a technological thing in them. Of course she's not going to get mad at that faucet, I thought. You always suppress momentary anger at something you deeply and permanently hate. Of course John signs off every time the subject of cycle repair comes up, even when it is obvious he is suffering for it. That's technology. And sure, of course, obviously. It's so simple when you see it. To get away from technology out into the country in the fresh air and sunshine is why they are on the motorcycle in the first place. For me to bring it back to them just at the point and place where they think they have finally escaped it just frosts both of them, tremendously. That's why the conversation always breaks and freezes when the subject comes up.

Other things fit in too. They talk once in a while in as few pained words as possible about "it" or "it all" as in the sentence, "There is just no escape from it." And if I asked, "From what?" the answer might be "The whole thing," or "The whole organized bit," or even· "The system." Sylvia once said defensively, "Well, *you* know how to *cope* with it," which puffed me up so much at the time I was embarrassed to ask what "it" was and so remained somewhat puzzled. I thought it was something more mysterious than technology. But now I see that the "it" was mainly, if not entirely, technology. But, that doesn't sound right either. The "it" is a kind of force that gives rise to technology, something undefined, but inhuman, mechanical, lifeless, a blind monster, a death force. Something hideous they are running from but know they can never escape. I'm putting it way too heavily here but in a less emphatic and less defined way this is what it is. Somewhere there are people who understand it and run it but those are technologists, and they speak an inhuman language when describing what they do. It's all parts and relationships of unheard-of things that never make any sense no matter how often you hear about them. And their things, their monster keeps eating up land and polluting their air and lakes, and there is no way to strike back at it, and hardly any way to escape it.

That attitude is not hard to come to. You go through a heavy industrial area of a large city and there it all is, the technology. In front of it are high barbed-wire fences, locked gates, signs saying No Trespassing, and beyond, through sooty air, you see ugly strange shapes of metal and brick whose purpose is unknown, and whose masters you will never see. What it's for you don't know, and why it's there, there's no one to tell, and so all you can feel is alienated, estranged, as though you didn't belong there. Who owns and understands this doesn't want you around. All this technology has somehow made you a stranger in your own land. Its very shape and appearance and mysteriousness say, "Get out." You know there's an explanation for all this somewhere and what it's doing undoubtedly serves mankind in some indirect way but that isn't what you see. What you see is the No Trespassing, Keep Out signs and not anything serving people but little people, like ants, serving these strange, incomprehensible shapes. And you think, even if I were a part of this, even if I were not a stranger, I would be just another ant serving the shapes. So the final feeling is hostile, and I think that's ultimately what's involved with this otherwise unexplainable attitude of John and Sylvia. Anything to do with valves and shafts and wrenches is part of *that* dehumanized world, and they would rather not think about it. They don't want to get into it.

If this is so, they are not alone. There is no question that they have been following their natural feelings in this and not trying to imitate anyone. But many others are also following their natural feelings and not trying to imitate anyone and the natural feelings of very many people are similar on this matter; so that when you look at them collectively, as journalists do, you get the illusion of a mass movement, an antitechnological mass movement, an entire political antitechnological left emerging, looming up from apparently nowhere, saying, "Stop the technology. Have it somewhere else. Don't have it here." It is still restrained by a thin web of logic that points out that without the factories there are no jobs or standard of living. But there are human forces stronger than logic. There always have been, and if they become strong enough in their hatred of technology that web can break.

Clichés and stereotypes such as "beatnik" or "hippie" have been invented for the antitechnologists, the antisystem people, and will continue to be. But one does not convert individuals into mass people with the simple coining of a mass term. John and Sylvia are not mass people and neither are most of the others going their way. It is against being a mass person that they seem to be revolting. And they feel that technology has got a lot to do with the forces that are trying to turn them into mass people and they don't like it. So far it's still mostly a passive resistance, flights into the rural areas when they are possible and things like that, but it doesn't always have to be this passive.

I disagree with them about cycle maintenance, but not because I am out of sympathy with their feelings about technology. I just think that their flight from and hatred of technology is self-defeating. The Buddha, the Godhead, resides quite as comfortably in the circuits of a digital computer or the gears of a cycle transmission as he does at the top of a mountain or in the petals of a flower. To think otherwise is to demean the Buddha—which is to demean oneself. That is what I want to talk about in this Chautauqua.

We're out of the marshes now, but the air is still so humid you can look straight up directly at the yellow circle of the sun as if there were smoke or smog in the sky. But we're in the green countryside now. The farmhouses are clean and white and fresh. And there's no smoke or smog.

Reading Questions

1. Why do John and Sylvia want to not understand motorcycle maintenance?
2. Why does the author reject the antitechnology view?
3. Is there or is there not an antitechnology movement?

Questions for Reflection and Research

1. How would Weisskopf (in selection #54) classify John and Sylvia?
2. Do people you know in technical and scientific fields tend to distrust those in the arts and the humanities? Is the reverse true? If there is a mutual distrust, is this a failing of Western culture? (See selection #55 by Schroeer.)

3. Read Pirsig's book. How does the main character recommend that difficulties found in technological society be dealt with?
4. Are science and technology ultimately evil, causing more harm than good? (See selections #43 by Taylor, #44 by Kipphardt, and #54 by Weisskopf.)
5. In the Bible (in Genesis, chapter 1) God tells Adam and Eve to "Be fruitful, and multiply, and replenish the earth, and subdue it." To what extent is this injunction responsible for Western technological disregard of nature?

Science: Cure-All, Evil, or Trivial?

The Author: Victor F. Weisskopf (b. 1908), an Austrian, received his Ph.D. in physics from the University of Göttingen in Germany and has received honorary degrees from various foreign and American universities. He is well known as a physicist and has taught at various universities, most recently at the Massachusetts Institute of Technology. His research interests include quantum mechanics, electron theory, and nuclear physics.

The Selection: Three conceptions of current science are outlined and evaluated. Position 1 regards current science as impractical, trying to resolve remote and useless questions. Those who accept this position prefer that science funding be limited to areas that promise practical payoffs. Weisskopf argues that most practical payoffs have come from areas of science that at one time were thought unlikely to have any such payoffs. Position 2 regards science as dangerous because it contributes to environmental degradation, to the development of dreadful weapons, and to the dehumanization of life. Weisskopf acknowledges some truth here, but points to the benefits of science and technology. He also argues that some of the bad consequences of science are the result not of scientific misjudgment but rather of social and political short-comings. Position 3 regards science as the great hope for all problems. Weisskopf concedes that science cannot study all aspects of human experience, but it can be used more intelligently to improve life.

The development of science and technology during the last centuries has been very fast and overwhelming. All aspects of human society have been deeply influenced by it, the quality of life has

From "The Significance of Science" by Victor F. Weisskopf in *Science* 176, no. 4031 (April 14, 1972): 138-42, 146. Copyright 1972 by the American Association for the Advancement of Science. Reprinted by permission.

been changed and often gravely disturbed. Today we have become very sensitive to the problems raised by this fast development, and we are faced with important questions regarding the role of science in society.

Science is under severe attack from some quarters; it is considered a panacea [=a remedy] for the cure of all ills by others. I will sketch here three positions in regard to science that characterize some of the common attitudes toward this problem.

Position 1

Many branches of science have grown excessively during the recent decades; too large amounts of public support and too much scientific manpower are devoted to esoteric [=highly specialized] research in fields that have little to do with practical problems. Only such scientific research should be supported as that promising reasonable payoff in terms of practical applications for industry, public welfare, medicine, or national defense. Science as a study of nature for its own sake is appreciated by only a few people and has very limited public value. Its support should be reduced to a much more modest scale.

Position 2

Most of today's scientific research is detrimental to society because it is the source of industrial innovations, most of which have led and will lead to further deterioration of our environment, to an inhuman computerized way of life destroying the social fabric of our society, to more dangerous and destructive applications in weaponry leading to wars of annihilation, and to further development of our society toward [the kind of empty existence depicted in the novel *1984* by George Orwell (1903–1950)]. At best, science is a waste of resources that should be devoted to some immediate, socially useful purpose.

Position 3

The methods and approaches used in the natural sciences and in technology—the so-called scientific method—has proved overwhelmingly successful in resolving problems, in elucidating situations, in explaining phenomena of the natural world, and in attaining well-defined aims. It should be extended to all problems confronting humanity because it promises to be as successful in any area of human endeavor and human interest as it has been in the realm of natural science and technology. . . .

BASIC SCIENCE AND PRACTICAL APPLICATIONS

Let us [consider] position 1, the excessive cost of basic science. It is based on the supposition that most of research is unimportant and irrelevant if it is carried out without regard to practical applications. . . . The practical value of those parts of pure science which seemingly have no immediate connections with applications has been clearly brought out by H. B. G. Casimir [b. 1909], who collected a number of interesting examples of how decisive technical progress was made by scientists who did not work at all for a well-defined practical aim:

I have heard statements that the role of academic research in innovation is slight. It is about the most blatant piece of nonsense it has been my fortune to stumble upon.

Certainly, one might speculate idly whether transistors might have been discovered by people who had not been trained in and had not contributed to wave mechanics or the theory of electrons in solids. It so happened that inventors of transistors were versed in and contributed to the quantum theory of solids.

One might ask whether basic circuits in computers might have been found by people who wanted to build computers. As it happens, they were discovered in the thirties by physicists dealing with the counting of nuclear particles because they were interested in nuclear physics.

One might ask whether there would be nuclear power because people wanted new power sources or whether the urge to have new power would have led to the discovery of the nucleus. Perhaps—only it didn't happen that way, and there were the Curies [Marie Curie (1867–1934) and Pierre Curie (1859–1906)] and [Ernest] Rutherford [1871–1937] and [Enrico] Fermi [1901–1954] and a few others.

One might ask whether an electronic industry could exist without the previous discovery of electrons by people like [J. J.] Thomson [1856–1940] and H. A. Lorentz [1853–1928]. Again, it didn't happen that way.

One might ask even whether induction coils in motor cars might have been made by enterprises which wanted to make motor transport and whether then they would have stumbled on the laws of induction. But the laws of induction had been found by [Michael] Faraday [1791–1867] many decades before that.

Or whether, in an urge to provide better communication, one might have found electromagnetic waves. They weren't found that way. They were found by [Heinrich] Hertz [1857–1894], who emphasized the beauty of physics and who based his work on the theoretical considerations of [James Clerk] Maxwell [1831–1879]. I think there is hardly any example of twentieth century innovation which is not indebted in this way to basic scientific thought.

Some of these examples are evidences of the fact that experimentation and observation at the frontier of science require technical means beyond the capabilities of ordinary technology. Therefore, the scientist in his search for new insights is forced and often succeeds to extend the technological frontier. This is why a large number of technologically important inventions had their origin not in the desire to fulfill a certain practical aim but in the attempts to sharpen the tools for the penetration of the unknown.

The examples quoted are taken from past developments and it is frequently asserted that some branches of modern fundamental science are so far removed from the human environment that practical applications are most improbable. In particular, the physics of elementary particles and astronomy are considered to be in this category. These sciences deal with far-off objects; elementary particles in the modern sense are also "far off," because mesons and baryons appear only when matter is subject to extremely high energy which is commonly not available on Earth but probably occurs only at a few distant spots in the universe. The "far off" feature of these sciences is also what makes them expensive. It costs much money to create in our laboratory conditions that may be realized only in some exploding galaxy. It costs much to build instruments for the study of the limits of the universe. The argument against these sciences is that they are dealing with subjects far removed from our human environment and that therefore they are of minor relevance.

Let us consider the question of what constitutes the human environment. Ten thousand years ago there were no metals in the human environment. Metals rarely are found in pure form in nature. But after man had found out how to create them from ores, metals played an important role in our environment. The first piece of copper must have looked very esoteric and useless. In fact, man used it for a long time only for decorative purposes. Later, the introduction of this new material into man's ken gave rise to interesting possibilities that ultimately led to the dominant role of metals in his environment. In short, we have created a metallic environment. To choose another example, electricity appears rarely in nature in observable forms; for example, only in lightning discharges and in frictional electrostatics, which is not an important part of the human environment. After long years of research into minute effects, it was possible to recognize the nature of electric phenomena and then to find out what dominant role they play in the atom. The introduction of these new phenomena into the human world created a completely new electric environment in which we live today with 120-volt outlets in every wall. The most recent example is in nuclear physics. In the early days, prying into the problems of nuclear structure was considered a purely academic pursuit, directed only toward the advancement of knowledge concerning the innermost structure of matter. Rutherford said in 1933, "Anyone who expects a source of power from transformation of these atoms is talking moonshine." His conclusion was based on the same reasoning: The nuclear phenomena are too far removed from our human environment. True enough, apart from the rare cases of natural radioactivity, nuclear reactions must be artifically created at high cost with energetic particle beams. Most nuclear phenomena on Earth are man-made; they occur naturally only in the center of stars. Here again, the introduction of these man-made phenomena into our human world has led to a large number of interactions. Artificial radioactivity has revolutionized many branches of medicine, biology, chemistry, and metallurgy; the process of fission is an ever-increasing source of energy, for the better or the worse. Nuclear phenomena are now an important part of a new human environment.

These examples show the weakness of the argument that certain natural phenomena are too far removed to be relevant to the human environment. Natural laws are universal; in principle, any natural process can be generated on Earth under suitable conditions. Modern instruments did create a cosmic environment in our laboratories when they produced processes that do not ordinarily take place in a terrestrial environment. Astronomy and particle physics deal with previously unknown and mostly unexplained phenomena. There is every possibility that some of them one day could also be reproduced on Earth in some form or another and be applied in a reasonable way for some useful purpose. . . .

BASIC SCIENCE AND TODAY'S PROBLEMS

Position 2 is the expression of an attitude that makes science bear the brunt of public reaction against the mounting difficulties of modern life. . . .

Today it is fashionable to emphasize the negative aspects of technological progress and to take the positive aspects for granted. One should remember, however, that medical science has doubled the average life span of man, has eliminated many diseases, and has abolished pain in many forms. It has provided the means of effective birth control. The so-called "green revolution" created the potential to eliminate starvation among all presently living people. This is a scientific-technical achievement of momentous significance, even though the actual situation is a far cry from what could be achieved. One should also remember the developments in transportation, construction, and power supply provided by modern technology and their great potentialities for improving the quality of life.

The trouble comes from the fact that, in too many instances, technology has not achieved that purpose. On the contrary, it has contributed to a definite deterioration of life. Medicine may have abolished pain, but modern weapons are producing wholesale pain and suffering. Medical progress has achieved a great measure of death-control which has caused a population explosion; the available means of birth control are far from being effectively used. The blessings of modern medicine are unevenly distributed; lack of adequate medical care for the poor in some important countries causes mounting social tensions. The green revolution produces ten times more food than before, but the distribution is so uneven that starvation still prevails in many parts of the globe; further-

more, the massive use of fertilizers causes eutrophication [=a special kind of contamination] of many waters. Power production and
the internal combustion engine as a means of transportation have
polluted the atmosphere. Is it really impossible to avoid harmful effects when we apply our knowledge of natural processes for practical purposes? It should not be so.

There are two distinct sides to these problems: the social and
political aspect and the technical aspect. In some instances the
technical aspects do not pose any serious problems. The most important example is the use of technology for war or suppression.
The only way to prevent the application of scientific results to the
development of weapons is to reduce and prevent armed conflicts;
certainly, this is a sociopolitical problem in which scientists and
nonscientists should be equally interested, but it is not per se [=by
itself] a problem of natural science. Other more benign [=mild]
examples are the problems of congested transportation, of city construction, and of some, but not all, of the problems of pollution. In
these cases we know what causes the trouble and we know what
measures can be taken to avoid it. But we don't know how to convince people to accept these measures. The problems are political
and social. The natural scientists cannot help except by pointing
out as clearly as possible what the consequences of certain actions
or inactions will be. It is beyond the scope of this article to discuss
whether it is possible to resolve these political and social problems.
We take the only possible attitude in this dilemma: We assume that
there will be a solution at some time, in some form, to some of these
problems.

However, there are also many detrimental effects of technology
of which the physical causes or the remedies are not known to a
sufficient degree. Many detrimental effects of industrialization
upon the environment belong in this category; among these are
carbon dioxide production, long-range influences on atmospheric
currents and on climactic conditions, the influence of urbanization
on health, the problem of better means of birth control, and many
more. Here science has enormous tasks to do in discovering, observing, and explaining unexplored phenomena, relations, and effects. The problems deal with out natural environment and therefore necessarily pose prime questions pertaining to natural science.

What role does basic science play in these efforts? One could conclude that the tasks are for applied science only and that research
for its own sake, research that is not directed toward one of the
specific problems, is not necessary. It may even be harmful since it
takes away talented manpower and resources. This is not so. The
spirit of basic research is composed of the following elements: an
interest in understanding nature; an urge to observe, to classify
and to follow up observed phenomena for the sake of the
phenomena themselves; a drive to probe deeper into a subject by

experimenting with nature, by using ingenuity to study phenomena under special and unusual conditions—all in order to find connections and dependencies, causes and effects, laws and principles.

This attitude of basic research is necessary for the solution of today's pressing problems because it leads people to search for causes and effects in a systematic way, regardless of any ulterior aim. Many of today's troubles are caused by unforeseen consequences of human action on the environment, by interference with the natural cycle of events. The effects of accumulated technological developments are about to cover the entire surface of the earth. We face a complicated network of physical, chemical, and biological causes and effects, many of them only partially understood. Much painstaking basic research will be required before these problems can be tackled efficiently. If technical solutions are introduced before the conditions are thoroughly understood, one may well worsen the situation in the attempt to improve it. . . .

LIMITATIONS OF SCIENCE

Another motivation for the antiscience attitude expressed by position 2 is connected with a widespread critical view of science and the ways of thinking it fosters. In this view, science is considered as materialistic and inhuman, as an instrument of defining everything in terms of numbers and thus excluding and denying the irrational and emotive approach to human experience. Value judgments, the distinction between good and evil, and personal feelings supposedly have no place in science. Therefore, it is said, the one-sided development of the scientific approach has suppressed some most important and valuable parts of human experience in that it has produced an alienated individual in a world dominated by science and technology in which everthing is reduced to impersonal data.

The foregoing arguments are diametrically opposite to the views expressed in position 3, which contends that the supposedly rational, inemotive approach of science is the only successful way to deal with human problems of all sorts. Many of today's trends against science are based on the feeling that the scientific view neglects or is unable to take into account some of the most important experiences in human life.

This widely held belief seems to be in contradiction to the claim of "completeness" of science, which is the basis of position 3. It is the claim that every experience—whether caused by a natural phenomenon or by a social or psychic circumstance—is potentially amenable to scientific analysis and to scientific understanding. Of course, many experiences, in particular in the social and psychic realm, are far from being understood today by science, but it is claimed that there is no limit in principle to such scientific insights.

I believe that both the defenders and the attackers of this view could be correct, because we are facing here a typical "complementary" situation. A system of description can be complete in the sense that there is no experience that does not have a logical place in it, but it still could leave out important aspects which, in principle, have no place within the system. The most famous example in physics is the complementarity between the classical description and the quantum properties of a mechanical system. The classical view of an atom is a little planetary system of electrons running around the nucleus in well-defined orbits. This view cannot be disproved by experiment; any attempt to observe accurately the position of an electron in the atom with suitable light beams or other devices would find the electron there as a real particle, but the attempt to observe it would have destroyed the subtle individuality of the quantum state which is so essential for the atomic properties. Classical physics is "complete" in the sense that it never could be proven false within its own framework of concepts, but it does not encompass the all-important quantum effects. There is a difference between "complete" and something we may call "all-encompassing."

The well-known claim of science for universal validity of its insights may also have its complementary aspects. There is a scientific way to understand every phenomenon, but this does not exclude the existence of human experiences that remain outside science. Let us illustrate the situation by a simple example: How is a Beethoven sonata described in the realm of science? From the point of view of physics, it is a complicated quasi-periodic oscillation of air pressure; from the point of view of physiology it is a complicated sequence of nerve impulses. This is a complete description in scientific terms, but it does not contain the elements of the phenonenon that we consider most relevant. Even a psychological study in depth of what makes the listening to these tone-sequences so exciting cannot do justice to the immediate and direct experience of the ·music.

Such complementary aspects are found in every human situation. There exist human experiences in the realms of emotion, art, ethics, and personal relations that are as "real" as any measurable experience of our five senses; surely the impact of these experiences is amenable to scientific analysis, but their significance and immediate relevance may get lost in such analysis, just as the quantum nature of the atom is lost when it is subject to observation.

Today one is rather unaccustomed to think in those terms because of the rapid rise of science and the increasing success of the application of scientific ideas to the manipulation of our natural environment in order to make the process of living less strenuous. Whenever in the history of human thought one way of thinking has developed with force, other ways of thinking become unduly neglected and subjugated to an overriding philosophy claiming to encompass all human experience. The preponderance of religious thought in medieval Europe is an obvious example; the preponderance of scientific thought today is another. This situation has its root in a strong human desire for clear-cut, universally valid principles containing the answers to every question. However, the nature of most human problems is such that universally valid answers do not exist, because there is more than one aspect to each of these problems. In either of the two examples, great creative forces were released, and great human suffering resulted from abuses, exaggerations and from the neglect of complementary ways of thinking.

These complementary aspects of human experience play an important role when science is applied to practical aims. Science and technology can provide the means and methods to ease the strain of physical labor, to prolong life, to grow more food, to reach the moon, or to move with supersonic velocity from one place to another. Science and technology are needed to predict what would be the effects of such actions on the total environment. However, the decisions to act or not to act are based on judgments that are outside the realm of science. They are mainly derived from two strong human motives: the desire to improve the conditions of life, and the drive for power and influence over other people. These urges can perhaps be scientifically explained by the evolution of the human race, but they must be regarded as a reality of human experience outside the scientific realm. Science cannot tell us which of the urges is good or bad. Referring to the first rather than to the second urge, Archibald MacLeish has put this idea into verse: "No equation can divine the quality of life, no instrument record, no computer conceive it/only bit by bit can feeling man lovingly retrieve it."

The true significance of science would become clearer if scientists and nonscientists were more aware of the existence of these aspects that are outside the realm of science. If this situation were better appreciated, the prejudice against science would lose much of its basis and the intrinsic value of our growing knowledge of natural phenomena would be much better recognized. . . .

Science contains many activities of different aims and different character—the several basic sciences with all their variety of approach from cosmology to biology and the numerous applied sciences that are spreading and involving more and more aspects of human concerns. . . .

All parts and all aspects of science belong together. Science cannot develop unless it is pursued for the sake of pure knowledge and insight. But it will not survive unless it is used intensely and wisely for the betterment of humanity and not as an instrument of domination by one group over another. There are two powerful elements in human existence: compassion and curiosity. Curiosity without compassion is inhuman; compassion without curiosity is ineffectual.

Reading Questions

1. Would the funding for scientific research be increased or decreased by those advocating each of the three positions?
2. What is the point of the various examples given by Casimir?
3. Summarize all the arguments used by Weisskopf in his defense of the practicality of basic research.
4. What positive aspects of technological change are given and what is claimed to have prevented technology from ever reaching its goals?
5. What role can basic science play in conquering the bad side-effects of technology?
6. Explain Weisskopf's account of complementary aspects of the world—and how this conception is thought to reveal the true limitations and potential of science and technology.

Questions for Reflection and Research

1. Compare Weisskopf's view of the relations between science and technology with that of the McCain and Segal selection (#51).
2. Identify scientific findings that seem to have had very little practical value. Should the research on these topics have been done?
3. Can we control the evil potential of scientific and technological advances? (See selection #43 by Taylor for one opinion.)
4. Does Rescher in selection #42 agree with Position 3 that science is value-free? Does Weisskopf think science is value-free?
5. Should scientists be required to have training in ethics?
6. What is outside the realm of scientific study? (For ideas see selections in Section 1 and Section 3. Also see the Introduction to Section 6 and selections #36 by Hospers and #38 by Louch.)
7. Read Aldous Huxley's *Brave New World*, George Orwell's *1984*, and other works of fiction that attempt to portray a future world controlled by science. Are the authors' predictions coming true?

The Two Cultures: Science and the Humanities

The Author: Dietrich Shroeer. For biographical information see selection #20 on the implications of recent physics.

C. P. Snow (b. 1905) is the main focus of this selection. A native of England, he received a doctor's degree in physics from Cambridge University and became a government official dealing with scientific matters. At the same time he wrote an eleven-volume series of novels that studied English professional life. His published lecture *The Two Cultures and the Scientific Revloution* has become famous and is discussed below.

The Selection: The contents of and reactions to C. P. Snow's 1959 lecture are summarized. Snow's lecture asserts that there have developed among educated people two cultures: the culture of science and the culture of the humanities. Usually people trained in one culture have little understanding of and a dislike for the other. The humanistically oriented people tend to look to tradition, and the scientifically oriented to the future. Criticism of Snow's view is also given, including the very hostile response of the literary critic, F. R. Leavis.

INTRODUCTION

In 1959 Sir C. P. Snow's *The Two Cultures* was published. In this book he expressed his feeling that there is a definite polarization of society into two components: a scientific culture and an intellectual culture. In the scientific culture he included both scientists and technologists; in the intellectual culture he included the whole of

From Dietrich Schroeer, *Physics and Its Fifth Dimension: Society*, 1972, Addison-Wesley, Reading, Massachusetts, pp. 5–11. Reprinted by permission of Addison-Wesley Publishing Company, Inc.

the humanities, or those endeavors that aim to form a Complete Man. He then complained that these two cultures are too isolated from each other, and that this isolation is a threat to society.

The response to *The Two Cultures* was immense. There were innumerable book reviews and commentaries—some favorable, some not so favorable, and a few scathingly hostile. The main objections centered around taking this culture gap too seriously. These two cultures may be just the extremes of a very broad spectrum of intellectual attitudes. Indeed, the proper approach toward this problem may perhaps best be represented by the sign "Culture versus Agriculture" displayed during a basketball game between and A & T [=Agricultural and Technical] college and a school oriented toward the liberal arts. Yet the very magnitude of the reaction to this book suggest that it touched on a very raw nerve. And this concept of a cultural polarization does turn out to be a useful one insofar as it indicates a contrast in modes of thought which has characterized many trends in the development of the science-society interaction. . . .

THE TWO CULTURES OF C. P. SNOW

The use of the words scientists and nonscientists in the Introduction already hinted at a cultural dichotomy. Specifically, there appear to exist two intellectual subdivisions of people in the world, two distinct cultures. According to Snow, there is the scientific culture, with the physical scientist as an extreme, and there is the intellectual culture, with the literary figures as its aristocrats. This is a contrast with an honorable history, and some of our present conflicts plaguing our society . . . are in a broad sense derivatives of it. . . .

The effect of the scientific culture, through the technological and scientific developments of the industrial and scientific revolutions, is open, visible, and clear. Our whole way of life is permeated and controlled by the consumer plenty, the social mobility due to automobiles, and the communications possibilities of TV and telephone. The influence of the humanistic culture is somewhat more subtle; but through control of the contents of TV, newspapers, cinema, and books, it is equally pervasive.

There is a difference between these two cultures in outlook on life. Scientists tend to look at the present and to the future with confidence. Characteristic of this optimism is [the] comment [of Lord Rutherford (1871–1937)] about the 1930s, "This is the heroic age of science!" as well as the statement by physics Nobel prize winner Isodor I. Rabi [b. 1898] that

Science inspires us with a feeling of hopefulness and infinite possibility . . . the human spirit applied in the tradition of science will find a way toward the objective. Science shows that it is possible to foresee and to plan. . . .

While scientists can be religious, their future-oriented attitude makes them less able to accept an uncontrollable *fate*; they instinctively reject pessimism. In exchange for their precise ways of thinking, they become somewhat impatient and even to an extent shallow. And their concreteness is achieved at the expense of imagination.

The humanistic culture, on the other hand, has a great imagination but deals perhaps too much with the past. The humanists look at man; and since the human condition seems to have changed relatively little over the ages, they ask "Why look to the future?" In a way this looking toward the past tends to make the humanists too realistic, too ready to accept things as they are, too slow to change. Snow uses the word traditional in connection with the humanistic culture, implying thereby some of the stability of a status quo. A literary or art movement has arrived . . . when it has a name. But by that time it is already well-crystallized and stationary, ergo [=therefore] no longer a movement.

Basically, of course, it is not bad that there are two cultures in our society. Two points of view always contain richer possibilities than one; two cultures are always in a position to contribute to each other. Unfortunately, a breakdown in communications has led to a hostile polarization, which in turn has led to an impoverishment of both cultures due to a lack of crossfeeding. The lack of common images has oversharpened the contrast of scientific precision with humanistic imagination.

In the resultant hostility, the scientists see the humanists as being failures because they have not solved the world's basic problems, but rather appear to be always saying either "This is how it has always been" or "The way we used to do it was better." Of course, even the scientific culture sometimes has difficulty resisting the theme "Those were the good old days." But basically the scientific culture believes that there were no good old days, that only the rich or the humanists want to go back to them. So the scientific culture sees the humanists somewhat as wishful ostriches. On the other hand, the humanists see the losses due to the technological revolution, some of them very real. The population explosion leads to overcrowding so that there is no retreat from one's neighbor; the air stinks from technological pollution; the atom bomb is like the Sword of Damocles [= a sword suspended by a single hair]; the good things in life seem to be vanishing. The humanists see no sense of social responsibility in the scientists and consider them reprehensible for this lack.

At the risk of appearing presumptuous, let me summarize this split and its relevance by using myself as a microsample of the scientific culture. The key words are probably imagination-realism and past-future. I have not the touch, not the imagination. I see the consequences of real things, but not the multifaceted aspects of subtle things. My preference is history books over [the fiction of] D.

H. Lawrence [1885–1930]. Plays-within-plays, like *Kiss Me Kate* or Ingmar Bergman's movies, appeal to me, because there the basic plot is presented several times in slightly different guises. I found the lecturing in the course on which this book is based very hard. In a typical science lecture, the same theories are examined over and over, but always from a slightly different angle; many different problems are solved to illustrate a single principle. But in these lectures, as in much of literature, many relatively independent tales had to be told which only finally made up a whole. It is the creation of this impression, through all the right words, the ringing words, that is difficult for me.

CRITICISMS OF THE TWO CULTURES

We have presented the theory of two cultures which Snow readvanced in 1959. . . . But it might be worthwhile to . . . indicate the nature of the enormous reaction to the publication of *The Two Cultures*. Many valid questions were raised about Snow's theory. For example, are these social subsets homogeneous enough to be called cultures? There is, after all, some question as to how much the basic scientists and the applied engineers mix. But they do seem to make up one distinct culture; at least they can communicate since they speak the same language, and they certainly don't ignore each other. Another suggestion which has been made is that society is actually controlled by yet a third culture made up of sociologists, political scientists, economists, and politicians—all those people who are concerned with how human beings are living or have lived as a part of society. And furthermore, considering how technological our society has become, is not in fact the scientific culture right now totally dominant?

Since the reviews and commentaries frequently illustrated Snow's thesis in revealing the writer's prejudices, a few quotations will demonstrate that there is indeed a cultural gap. A. C. B. Lovell [b. 1913], the director of the Jodrell-Bank radiotelescope in England, reacted to Snow by stating that the free world was behind the Russians in science and needed more money to keep up with them (the necessity to keep up with the Russians was taken for granted). Lovell's version of a unified culture had a scientific tinge to it:

The restoration of a unified culture which might give us a basis from which to handle the problem is being hindered by the new crisis in the universities. . . . I am impatient with those who oppose from within the scientific revolution in the universities.

There seems to be an intrinsic lack of appreciation by scientists of the two sides of the problem; even C. P. Snow shows enough leaning toward the scientific culture so that he cannot be considered impartial. The scientific culture seems to be saying that it is the most important, since it is remaking the world.

The reactions of the other culture to Snow's book likewise illustrate this cultural split. The greatest modern British literary critic, F. R. Leavis [b. 1895], responded to *The Two Cultures* in such style that Leavis' publisher, prior to printing the criticisms, asked Snow whether he would respond by suing. Some quotations from Leavis' review indicate how difficult it would be to bring the two cultures together. [The following quotations are taken from *Two Cultures? The Significance of C. P. Snow* by F. R. Leavis (New York: Pantheon Books, 1963). Copyright, 1963, by Random House, Inc. Copyright, 1962, by Chatto and Windus Ltd.]

The Two Cultures exhibits an utter lack of intellectual distinction and an embarrassing vulgarity of style. . . . (p. 30.)

But the argument of Snow's . . . lecture is at an immensely *lower* conceptual level, and incomparably more loose and inconsequent, than any I myself, a literary person, should permit in a group discussion I was conducting, let alone a pupil's essay. . . . (p. 34.)

The judgement I have to come out with is that not only is he not a genius; he is intellectually as undistinguished as it is possible to be. . . . He is a portent [=a marvel] in that, being in himself negligible, he has become for a vast public on both sides of the Atlantic a master-mind and a sage. . . . He doesn't know what he means, and doesn't know he doesn't know. . . . (p. 28.)

But of history, of the nature of civilization and the history of its recent developments, of the human history of the Industrial Revolution, of the human significances entailed in that revolution, of literature, of the nature of that kind of collaborative human creativity of which literature is the type, it is hardly an exaggeration to say that Snow exposes complacently a complete ignorance. . . . (p. 28)

It is pleasant to think of Snow contemplating, daily perhaps, the intellectual depth, complexity and articulation (of the scientific edifice) in all their beauty. But there is a prior human achievement of collaborative creation, a more basic work of the mind of man (and more than the mind), one without which the triumphant erection of the scientific edifice would not have been possible: that is, the creation of the human world, including language. It is one we cannot rest on as something done in the past. It lives in the living creative response to change in the present. (pp. 47–48.)

It is as though the humanistic culture is saying that it is the most important since it understands people and human experience. . . .

Reading Questions

1. How are the two cultures supposed to differ?
2. In what ways is Schroeer himself typical of the scientific culture?
3. What criticisms have been leveled at Snow's views?

Questions for Reflection and Research

1. Do the characters in selection #53 by Pirsig exemplify the split of the two cultures?
2. Is there evidence that college teachers in the humanities tend to vote in elections more on the side of tradition than do scientists and engineers?
3. How have recent major writers of fiction portrayed science and technology? Do they show any understanding of science—or sympathy for its goals and practitioners?
4. How does Snow respond to his critics? Evaluate his replies.
5. Should a deep understanding of the humanities be required of science students? Should a deep understanding of science be required of students in the humanities?
6. What major figures in the humanities had a good understanding of science? Which historically important scientists have also been known for their understanding of the humanities?
7. Of what value are the humanities?
8. What is the standard portrayal of the scientist in the popular media? Is it fair? What are its bad consequences likely to be for science?

Individual Sciences and Philosophy: An Abbreviated Guide

The introduction to each section of this book includes a short guide to further reading in the various topic areas covered in the book. Besides the various philosophical problems relevant to most sciences that are discussed in this book, some philosophical problems are peculiar to individual sciences.

The literature concerned with philosophical problems within individual sciences varies considerably in amount and in complexity from one science to the next. One very good way to become acquainted with these philosophical problems is to read histories of the individual sciences. The history of a science often is filled with accounts of heated and long-lasting debates over methodology, goals, and implications. Below are listed some sources that are helpful as guides to philosophical issues in the individual sciences and/or as guides to further reading. Often references are given to *The Encyclopedia of Philosophy*, 8 vols., ed. Paul Edwards (New York: Macmillan Publishing Co., 1967).

Biology

1. *Man and Nature,* ed. RONALD MUNSON. New York: Dell Publishing Company, Inc., 1971.
2. *Philosophy of Biological Science* by DAVID HULL. Englewood Cliffs, N.J.: Prentice-Hall, Inc., 1974.
3. *Encyclopedia of Philosophy.* See "Biology" in the index for a list of entries on relevant topics and individuals.

Chemistry

1. *The Development of Modern Chemistry* by AARON J. IHDE. New York: Harper & Row, 1964.

428

2. *Encyclopedia of Philosophy*. See "Chemistry" in the index for a list of entries on relevant topics and individuals.

Engineering

1. *The Existential Pleasures of Engineering* by SAMUEL C. FLORMAN. New York: St. Martin's Press, 1976.
2. *Business & Professional Ethics: A Quarterly Newsletter/Report*, Troy, N.Y.: Center for the Study of the Human Dimensions of Science and Technology, Rensselaer Polytechnic Institute. This periodical often publishes information on issues in engineering ethics.

Mathematics

1. *Philosophy of Mathematics* by STEPHEN F. BARKER. Englewood Cliffs, N.J.: Prentice-Hall, Inc., 1964.
2. *Encyclopedia of Philosophy*. See "Mathematics" in the index for a list of entries on relevant topics and individuals.

Physics

1. *Philosophy of Science,* ed. ARTHUR DANTO and SIDNEY MORGENBESSER. Cleveland: World Publishing Company, 1960. See Part Three.
2. *Encyclopedia of Philosophy*. See "Physics" in the index for a list of entries on relevant topics and individuals.

Social and Behaviorial Sciences: General

1. *Knowledge and Society: An Introduction to the Philosophy of the Social Sciences* by ARNOLD LEVISON. Indianapolis: The Bobbs-Merrill Company, Inc., 1974.
2. *The Philosophy of the Social Sciences* by ALAN RYAN. New York: Random House, Inc., 1970.
3. *Readings in the Philosophy of the Social Sciences,* ed. MAY BRODBECK. New York: The Macmillan Company, 1968.
4. *Philosophy of Social Science* by RICHARD S. RUDNER. Englewood Cliffs, N.J.: Prentice-Hall, Inc., 1966.

Anthropology

1. *Rethinking Anthropology* by E. LEACH. London: Athlone Press, 1961.
2. *The Rise of Anthropological Theory* by MARVIN HARRIS. New York: Thomas Y. Crowell Company, 1968.

3. *Encyclopedia of Philosophy*. See "Anthropology" in the index for a list of entries on relevant topics and individuals.

Economics

1. *Encyclopedia of Philosophy*. See "Economics, Philosophy of" in the index for a list of entries on relevant topics and individuals. See also the entries "Economics and Ethical Neutrality" and "Economics and Rational Choice."

History

1. *Philosophy of History* by WILLIAM H. DRAY. Englewood Cliffs, N.J.: Prentice-Hall, Inc., 1964.
2. *Encyclopedia of Philosophy*. See "Philosophy of History" in the index for a list of entries on relevant topics and individuals.

Linguistics

1. *Introduction to Theoretical Linguistics* by JOHN LYONS. New York: Cambridge University Press, 1964.
2. *Encyclopedia of Philosophy*. See "Language, Philosophy of" in the index for a list of entries on relevant topics and individuals.

Political Science

1. *Contemporary Political Thought: A Critical Study* by EUGENE J. MEEHAN. Homewood, Ill.: The Dorsey Press, 1967.

Psychology

1. *Problems of Philosophy and Psychology* by JAY N. EACKER, Chicago: Nelson-Hall, 1975.
2. *Psychology's Scientific Endeavor* by CHRISTOPHER F. MONTE. New York: Praeger Publishers, Inc., 1975.
3. *Encyclopedia of Philosophy*. See "Psychology" in the index for a list of entries on relevant topics and individuals.

Sociology

1. *Scientific Sociology: Theory and Method* by DAVID WILLER. Englewood Cliffs, N.J.: Prentice-Hall, Inc., 1967.

2. *Sociology Tomorrow* by PETER PARK. New York: Pegasus Division of Western Publishing Co., 1969.
3. *Encyclopedia of Philosophy*. See "Sociology" in the index for a list of entries on relevant topics and individuals.

In the following areas I have been unable to locate helpful guides to philosophical issues: archaeology, geography, geology, meterorology, and oceanography. Readers are encouraged to forward suggestions.

Glossary

aesthethics:	the branch of philosophy concerned with art and beauty.
agnostic:	a person who suspends belief in something, especially in God. Contrasted with *atheist* and *theist*.
analytic:	having to do with the meanings of words; an analytic statement or analytic truth is one the truth of which is based on the meanings of words—as opposed to being based on observation. Contrasted with *empirical* or *synthetic*.
analytic philosophy:	a movement in twentieth-century philosophy that gives special attention to the role of language in philosophy.
anthropology:	a field of study devoted to the variety of human cultures.
a priori:	a Latin phrase meaning something known without the need for observation. Contrasted with *empirical*.
archaeology:	a field of study devoted to uncovering sites of past human life.
atheist:	a person who is confident that no supreme being exists. Contrasted with *agnostic* and *theist*.
behaviorism:	(1) a movement in twentieth-century psychology that advocates the study of human beings and animals by means of observations of behavior. (2) a doctrine

about the meaning of mental words (e.g., anger, pain, thought) that asserts that such words refer to behavioral patterns rather than to operations of the brain or the mind.

confirmation: a technical term in the philosophy of science used to refer to procedures involved in supporting hypotheses.

cosmology: the study of the origin and nature of the universe.

cybernetics: the study of automatic control systems.

deduction: reasoning in which the conclusion follows with certainty from the premises. Contrasted with *induction*.

deist: a person who believes God created the world but is no longer involved in it.

determinism: the view that all events are caused (including human behavior).

dualism: a theory that advocates the existence of two kinds of being; for example, the view that there exist in the universe two kinds of substances, material and mental.

empirical: based on observation. Contrasted with *a priori*.

empiricism: the view that knowledge is (or should be) based on observation.

epiphenomenalism: the doctrine that the brain controls the mind and the body, and that the mind controls nothing but is merely a strange by-product of brain activity.

epistemology: the field of philosophy concerned with the kinds, foundations, and possibility of knowledge.

existentialism: a twentieth-century philosophical movement that stresses the difficulty and importance of free decisions and the centrality of one's consciousness.

extension: the length, width, and breadth of an object.

factual science: empirical science; one based on observation. Contrasted with *formal science*.

falsify: term used in connection with hypotheses; to falsify a hypothesis is to exhibit evidence that is contrary to the hypothesis.

formal science: a field of study based solely on reason and not on observation, e.g., logic and mathematics. Contrasted with *empirical* or *factual science*.

humanities: classification of academic studies that usually includes literature, philosophy, and the study of religions and sometimes includes the fine arts and history.

hypothesis: a proposed solution to a scientific question.

idealism: the doctrine that all that exists is mental, nonphysical substance.

induction: reasoning in which the conclusion follows from the premises with some degree of probability and not with certainty. Often such reasoning proceeds from a set of sample cases to a generalization about a whole class. Contrasted with *deduction*.

introspection: observing one's own inner mental processes and sensations.

laws: generalizations describing regularities in nature.

libertarianism: the view that human beings can act freely; opposed to strict determinism.

logical positivism: a philosophical movement associated with a group of philosophers known as the Vienna Circle, asserting that the only real knowledge is that gained by observation or by means of logic or mathematics.

logical truth: a statement the truth of which is not based on observation but on the meanings of the words composing it; a tautology.

logically possible: not contradictory.

materialism: the view that only matter and physical energy exist; there is no mental or spiritual substance.

metaphysics: a branch of philosophy having to do with the basic kinds of things that exist, or with the basic concepts with which we grasp the world.

monism: the view that just one kind of substance exists. Idealism and materialism are monistic doctrines.

naturalism: the view that there is no reality that transcends nature (such as the transcendent God of Christianity).

neo-vitalism: a new version of vitalism. (See *vitalism*.)

nomological: lawlike; involving laws.

operational definition: explanation of a term by indicating the operations or procedures needed to produce an instance of it.

paradigm: a model; a set of beliefs and practices that define some field of study.

physicalism: the view that only a physical world exists; materialism.

physiology: the study of the functions of the parts of the body.

positivism: belief that science is the main road to truth. (See *logical positivism*.)

psychology: the study of human behavior and mental life.

quantum mechanics: division of contemporary physics dealing with the interactions of fundamental particles with each other and with radiation.

rationalism: belief in the power of reason; when contrasted with empiricism, it means the belief that certain truths determined by reason are innate.

reduction: showing that one set of statements is equivalent to (reduces to) some part of another set of statements.

scholastic: having to do with scholastic philosophy; Roman Catholic philosophy or medieval philosophy characterized by carefully drawn distinctions.

sense data: what is supplied to the mind by the senses.

social Darwinism: a nineteenth-century social and political doctrine that in society the fit prosper and the unfit do not; the poor should not be helped because this would interfere with the evolutionary mechanism.

sociology:	the study of society and social processes.
sophists:	ancient philosophers known for their ability to use clever and often tricky reasoning.
synthetic:	knowledge having to do with the world rather than with reason. Contrasted with *analytic*.
tautology:	a statement that is true by definition; analytic truth; logical truth.
technology:	aspect of culture having to do with factories, gadgetry, instruments, manufactured materials, and machinery.
teleological:	purposive; having or exhibiting a purpose.
theist:	one who believes in a supreme being. Contrasted with *agnostic* and *atheist*.
theology:	the study and clarification of religious doctrines.
vitalism:	the doctrine that organic life has in it some element or principle of organization that makes it fundamentally different from inorganic matter.
volition:	choice, decision, exercising one's will.